THE JOHNS HOPKINS UNIVERSITY STUDIES IN HISTORICAL AND POLITICAL SCIENCE

Under the Direction of the Departments of History,
Political Economy, and Political Science

SERIES LXVI   NUMBER 2

SCIENCE AND RATIONALISM IN THE
GOVERNMENT OF LOUIS XIV
1661-1683

By

JAMES E. KING

1972

OCTAGON BOOKS

New York

Reprinted 1972

by special arrangement with The Johns Hopkins Press

OCTAGON BOOKS

A DIVISION OF FARRAR, STRAUS & GIROUX, INC.

19 Union Square West

New York, N. Y. 10003

LIBRARY OF CONGRESS CATALOG NUMBER: 74-159202

ISBN 0-374-94585-3

Manufactured by Braun-Brumfield, Inc.
Ann Arbor, Michigan

Printed in the United States of America

To
MY MOTHER

PREFACE

It was with some sense of temerity that I first addressed myself to the task of writing a new study on the remarkable administration of Louis XIV and Colbert. The enormous amount of scholarly literature that has been produced, since the middle of the nineteenth century, on mercantilism in general, and on this administration in particular, seemed at first to prohibit any but the most specialized type of investigation. However, on further reading of the "authorities," I became more conscious of their various uses of the historian's prerogative of interpretation. Like that marvelous instrument the stereoscope, it transformed, in their hands, the plane surface of history by the addition of perspective. That there was one obvious vantage point which the historians had largely neglected, when viewing the structure of this administration, dawned slowly upon me. That it did so at all is due, I think, to my reading of the stimulating works of G. N. Clark on the seventeenth century.

When the government of Louis XIV, after 1661, is viewed from the vantage point of seventeenth-century science and rationalism, it undergoes a gradual series of alterations which results in a new and harmonious perspective. Policies and reforms, formerly associated in my mind with the struggle for power and glory, with nationalism, with the classical spirit, with art, or with the growth of commercial and industrial interests, became more meaningful when associated also with the spirit of the new science. Nearly every facet of this administration, when looked at in the new light, seemed to respond by a subtle change in appearance, and gradually all seemed to fit into one broad and consistent pattern. As a result, I am personally convinced that, whatever the importance of the other factors which influenced the policies and reforms of Louis XIV and Colbert, the spirit of science and rationalism was a powerful and ever-present determinant. To ignore it, or to under-emphasize it, is, I believe, to appreciate incompletely these policies and these reforms.

This study is essentially an interpretation. There is relatively little in the way of new materials offered. What is new, I think, is the orientation of the material. This orientation may some-

5

times persuade the reader that he is participating in an argument. From my point of view, nothing could be more desirable. Frequently, even as I wrote, I debated a conclusion by presenting to myself the other possible factors. However I must reiterate that I do not pretend that the spirit of science and rationalism was the exclusive influence on this government as administered by Louis XIV and Colbert. I see this spirit only as an ever important, often decisive, determinant.

My friends have repeatedly challenged me with the assertion that the administration of Louis XIV and Colbert was a failure, either as a whole, or in details. I am not able to deny or confirm most such opinions. If this study appears to be a defense of their administration, this probably arises from the generally favorable impression which one gets from the available sources, primary or secondary. Insofar as their government represents an attempt to reform the structure and relate policy in accordance with rational or scientific prescriptions, I assert that they were surprisingly successful. Whether their government, in the long or short run, improved the welfare of the people, increased the national wealth, or contributed towards the French Revolution are questions I leave, in the main, to others. All such points are, I feel, irrelevant to this work. If a merchant improves his conduct of business by the introduction of good bookkeeping techniques, it should follow that the books will balance but not necessarily that they will show a profit. Perhaps the new orderliness in the French governmental structure derived from the time of Colbert gave the later kings and ministers only the dubious advantage of estimating their misery better than did their forefathers.

I am tremendously indebted to the kind, if sometimes severe, criticism and guidance that I have received from others while writing this book. My gratitude is owed particularly to Dr. Frederic Chapin Lane and Dr. Sidney Painter of Johns Hopkins University and to Dr. Jerome Blum of Princeton University all of whom have read the work chapter by chapter and are responsible for many improvements. Dr. John R. Turner of the City College of New York, Dr. George Boas of Johns Hopkins, and Dr. Vladimir Gsovski of the Library of Congress have read and given me illuminating suggestions on chapters the subject of which belonged more to their fields than to mine.

Dr. Elio Gianturco of the Library of Congress has helped me in the translation of many difficult passages in the old French. The members of the Johns Hopkins Historical Seminar have also contributed to this study by their constructive inquiries. Though they have not read any of the manuscript, I am grateful to Dr. Robert Palmer of Princeton University for the encouragement he gave me to write on this subject, to Dr. John W. Olmstead of the University of California at Los Angeles for many hints and leads given me while the study was in the formative stage, and to Dr. Kent Roberts Greenfield, Historian of the War Department, under whose direction I first became interested in the field of history out of which this study grew. My task has been greatly lessened by the innumerable courtesies and aids extended me by the staff of the Library of Congress, especially by Col. Willard Webb, Chief of the Stack and Reader Division, by Mr. Chester Atkinson, Mr. Floyd E. MacPhearson and Mr. Bernard Goldberg. Finally I wish to acknowledge my debt to two ladies. To Mrs. Virginia T. Mankin who has generously subjected herself to a meticulous job of editing a work in which she has no reason to be interested, and to Miss Lilly Lavarello whose advice and labors on the technical side of this study have been indispensable.

JAMES E. KING.

Chapel Hill, N. C.
1949.

CONTENTS

CHAPTER I

INTRODUCTION

Voltaire saw the four most brilliant periods of man's estate as the ages of Pericles and Alexander, of Ceasar and Augustus, of the Renaissance Medici, and of Louis XIV. The reasons for his selections were intellectual and political and, in this regard, the approximate period of the reign of Louis seemed to him deserving of the highest place among the four:

> Enriched by the discoveries of the three others, it has done more in certain fields than the three others together. All the arts, in truth, have not been advanced more than under the Medicis, under the Augustans and Alexander; but human reason in general was perfected. True philosophy had been unknown until this time; and it may indeed be said that commencing with the last years of Cardinal Richelieu, up to those which have followed the death of Louis XIV, there has occurred in our arts, in our spirits, in our habits, as in our government, a general revolution which will remain as an eternal monument to the veritable glory of our country.[1]

Since the appearance, in 1752, of Voltaire's *Siècle de Louis XIV* many historians, guided by their prejudices or philosophy, or restrained by their research, have qualified or denied this opinion. This is particularly true in respect to the relation of the personality and government of Louis XIV to the age and, more particularly, to the age as it evidenced itself in France. Perhaps the most resounding dissent is the dictum of Buckle: "In 1661 Louis XIV assumed the government; and from that moment until his death, in 1715, the history of France, so far as great discoveries are concerned, is a blank in the annals of Europe." [2]

---

[1] Voltaire, *Histoire du siècle de Louis XIV,* edited by G. Masson and G. W. Prothero (3 vols., Cambridge, England, 1880), I, 11-12.

[2] Buckle does retreat a little from this position by specifying that no men of great ability "native" to France produced during this period. Huygens, Roemer, and Cassini, while working in France, were, he cites, foreigners in origin. He retreats again to admit that the fine arts flourished under Louis XIV but only, he says, in the early period of the personal reign. H. T. Buckle, *Introduction to the history of civilization in England* (2 vols., London, 1857-1861), I, 499, 501, 511-515.

It is not the intention in this study to render judgment, aside from the incidental evidence which the material will present, on whether the government of Louis XIV was a boon or a restriction to the development of the artistic, scientific, or rational spirit in France. The intention, rather, is to consider a reverse aspect, to suggest the influence of science and rationalism on that government. It is necessary, of course, when treating this subject, to deal frequently with the actual governmental sponsorship of scientific activities, but in these cases it will be clearly seen that such arrangements were by no means a mark of the unilateral beneficence of Louis XIV. Science received the protection of the King, but it in turn was required to produce at least an equal return in service.

Since the subject is " science " and " rationalism " and their effect on the government of Louis XIV, frequent use will be made of these terms to characterize some particular or general political or administrative policy. The fluctuations in meaning and the multiplicity of the connotations which these two words assume within different disciplines, at different times, when used by different authorities or applied to certain environments make some definition necessary. The limitations set by the time and area of the subject narrows such a definition to a purely historical one. The interest is in the meaning of science and what may be called "scientific" rationalism within the seventeenth century.

No historian of science or philosophy could fail to agree, in part, with the opinion of Voltaire that the period in question, though certainly too restricted by him in time, was one of a revolutionary change in the habits of man's thinking. The product of this change has been customarily called rationalism and it is usually agreed that the rational method was scientifically oriented. The distinction which is made today between science and philosophy was not clearly recognized in the seventeenth century, but the experimental stress of the non-mathematical scientists, particularly of such Englishmen as Gilbert, Bacon, Harvey, and Boyle, fortified by the emphasis on the inductive process by Newton, indicated the gradual generation of a distinction between theories derived from facts observed and the more tentative theories hypothesized remote from the facts.[3] But for the period under discussion, and the generalization applies even to those persons just cited, "science" was the real philosophy and any division would not only be considered arbitrary but unintelligible. In the years extending from Descartes to Newton, the term "science" might still be applied with validity, in the eyes of most people, as a descriptive of physics or morals. Part of this latitude in its application can be ascribed to etymological factors, but in many cases it appears equally appropriate to the metaphysical and universal nature of science itself as conceived by Descartes, his spiritual teachers, and his disciples. This universal quality of science would make extremely difficult, if not impossible, the isolation of a workable definition. For this reason it will be necessary to describe science and rationalism in a general fashion and then to attempt to educe those narrower attributes which are scientific or rational from the particular seventeenth-century viewpoint which is of interest.

The writer purposely refrains from a technical discussion of the progress of physical and mathematical sciences in the seventeenth century. This is a story which is generally known in broad outline, and is too complex a tale to tell in a reasonable space here.[4]

The history of rationalism has its roots well planted in the sixteenth century and is most conveniently associated with the development of the secular spirit. This is the point of view for which Lecky has given the classic exposition.[5] The sense of individuality and the feeling for the particular which had characterized the outlook of the humanist, or the artist, or the business man during the Renaissance had produced a widespread skepticism towards traditional forms of thinking which, in the name of the Church, confined imagination to the pat-

[3] A. Wolf, *A history of science, technology and philosophy in the 16th and 17th centuries* (London, 1935), pp. 629-630.

[4] Possibly the best treatment, in English, of this story is Wolf, *A history of science;* also useful are: F. Cajori, *A history of physics in its elementary branches, including the evolution of physical laboratories* (New York, 1899); F. Cajori, *A history of mathematics* (New York, 1894); W. T. Sedgwick and H. W. Tyler, *A short history of science* (New York, 1939).

[5] W. E. H. Lecky, *History of the rise and influence of the spirit of rationalism in Europe* (2 vols., New York, 1872). The first edition of Lecky's *History* appeared in 1865.

terns of God's limited universe and the Church's Aristotle. Skepticism which had represented a negative and pessimistic resort in a figure like Montaigne was created into a positive and optimistic instrument of reason by Descartes. Doubt was reduced to a formula in the *Discours de la méthode* and there, in its simplest expression, is to be found what can be termed the dominating criteria of the seventeenth-century reason. " The prince of mathematicians scarcely did anything but create philosophical romances," said Voltaire, but, nevertheless, he admitted that Descartes began the age of reason; for in his method was the " thread to the labyrinth." [6] At the center of this method was mathematics which became, for the period, the language par-excellence of reason.

From the standpoint of mathematics, the growth of the rational method shows certain of its more constructive and practical features. The rise of the merchant, with his economic dependence on calculations, was undoubtedly a factor of great, if non-measurable, importance in spreading exacting and matter-of-fact methods of thinking. As G. N. Clark has stated it: " Indeed, this spirit even helped science to hold fast that part of its method which seems at first sight most high and abstract—the mathematical part. It has long been recognized that the introduction of rational accounting in business in the later Middle Ages was another result of the habit of quantitative thinking which was married to experimentation in the work of Galileo and Newton. Science was applied in business; we must not forget that business was applied in science." [7]

The development of that mathematical quality at the heart of seventeenth-century science and reason carried also its metaphysical implications. E. A. Burtt, in his *Metaphysical foundations of modern science,* has presented a searching study of this aspect. A renewal of interest in Pythagorean and Platonic principles, particularly in the Italian universities, had led a number of humanists to foster doctrines suggesting a mystical relationship of numbers to the universal. Apparently influenced by his contact with this Italian humanist philosophy, Copernicus

[6] Voltaire, *Siècle de Louis XIV,* III, 100-101.
[7] G. N. Clark, *Science and social welfare in the age of Newton* (Oxford, 1937), pp. 78-79.

dared to reconstruct the universe, because, in so doing, he made it appear mathematically simpler. Kepler, attracted by the beauty and order of the Copernican system and fortified by his semi-worship of the sun, had tried to demonstrate a total mathematical harmony in the heavens. Galileo accepted the Copernican hypothesis because it was more plausible than the Ptolemaic and he outlined a new metaphysic with his universal mathematics. At the same time, by his emphasis on experimentation, he laid the groundwork of the "mathematical science of physical nature."[8] The natural world of Galileo was a mathematical extension operating mechanically and independently of man's purpose.[9] It was Descartes, however, who constructed the first modern mechanical and mathematical cosmology and it was through him that the implicit dichotomy of Galileo's infinite and finite physics assumed the form of a philosophy:

No mathematical object is a more cogent item of knowledge than the 'Cogito ergo sum'; we can turn our attention inward, and abstracting from the whole extended world, note with absolute assurance the existence of a totally different kind of entity, a thinking substance. Whatever may be the final truth about the realm of geometrical bodies, still we *know* that we doubt, we conceive, we affirm, we will, we imagine, we feel. Hence when Descartes directed his energies toward the construction of a complete metaphysic, this clean-cut dualism was inescapable. On the one hand there is the world of bodies, whose essence is extension, each body is a part of space, a limited spatial magnitude, different from other bodies only by the different modes of extension—a geometrical world—knowable only and knowable fully in terms of mathematics: . . . . This world has no dependence on thought whatever, its whole machinery would continue to exist and operate if there was no human being in existence at all. On the other hand there is the inner realm whose essence is thinking. . . .[10]

The scientific and rational significance of Descarte's dualism lies in the latitude it gives for personal investigation. In his vortex theory all the universe becomes natural phenomena calling for exploration. God is conveniently relegated to the office of first mover, man is tumbled from his high place and

[8] E. A. Burtt, *The metaphysical foundations of modern science* (New York, 1925), pp. 95, 197-201. See also Wolf, *A history of science,* on Copernicus, pp. 11-26; on Kepler, pp. 131-143; on Galileo, pp. 27-53.
[9] Burtt, p. 95.
[10] *Ibid.,* pp. 110-111.

2

the teleology of the scholastic is a thing of the past. Of this approach, Burtt says: "It was simply an incalculable change in the viewpoint of the world held by intelligent opinion in Europe."[11]

The general features of the scientific and rational attitude of the seventeenth century were clearly formulated after Descartes. The supernatural, otherworldliness of scholasticism, with its disregard or subordination of natural phenomena, was featured only in the universities. Though reason had become a source of knowledge to the scholastic it was always inferior to revelation and was bounded by the authorities and mysteries. Science is unlimited by dogmas; it is pervasive, secular and factual. Natural phenomena are important to it. If mysteries still exist; if Copernicus, Kepler, Descartes, Boyle, and Newton are strikingly religious they are, nevertheless, secondarily so and are primarily secular in their outlook. In the Middle Ages, Aristotle, a biologist, instructed his followers to classify, to enumerate, to distinguish. His teaching, as understood or interpreted by them, was qualitative. With Copernicus, Kepler, Descartes, and Newton the emphasis is more Pythagorean. They are more interested in the quantitative world of extension, mathematics, and measurement. The Middle Ages were intellectually habituated to a philosophy of ends; to the belief in the culmination in final good to which all tended. Science rejects this teleological doctrine for a mathematical doctrine of cause and effect.[12]

[11] *Ibid.,* pp. 115-116.
[12] Wolf, *A history of science,* pp. 1-6. Attempts have been made to picture the rise of the scientific spirit of the seventeenth century as the evidence of a revolt against an older tradition of "reason." Thus A. N. Whitehead, in his *Science and the modern world* (New York, 1925), maintains that the insistence by Galileo and his successors upon "irreducible and stubborn" facts was not an appeal to reason. Rather, he pictures it as an "anti-intellectualist movement" based on a "recoil from the inflexible rationality of medieval thought." (*Ibid.,* p. 12.) In reply Wolf asserts as follows: "Attempts have been made to claim rationalism for Scholasticism; Professor Whitehead has even gone so far as to describe modern science as 'a recoil from the inflexible rationality of medieval thought.' This is a somewhat misleading half-truth. No doubt the Scholastics were nimble intellectualists, and gave proof of great subtlety of thought. No doubt, also, they rendered valuable services in keeping the thought of Christendom alive during the lean Middle Ages. But their reasoning was always kept within the bounds of premises based on authority; they never attempted to exercise, nor permitted others to exercise, that wider rationality

Viewed in terms of " method " it becomes possible, working from the broad picture of seventeenth-century science and reason already presented, to distinguish certain of their more specific characteristics. In the beginning it seems necessary to note that the emphasis in the seventeenth century, as far as science and reason are concerned, was precisely on method. The most succinct definition of science by a seventeenth-century scientist is possibly that of Hobbes: " Science is the knowledge of consequences, and dependence of one fact upon another." This knowledge, according to him, is attained by " industry " and secondly " by getting a good and orderly method." [13] It was the method of science which was, consciously or unconsciously, a determining factor in leading lay governors to institute administrative changes, and it is this method, therefore, which is of greater interest to us in this study. Over long periods, metaphysical debates concerning the relationship of matter and the infinite, of man's place in relation to the Deity, may produce its effects in the constitutional structure of the government, but of more immediate significance is the method of science and rationalism. For this reason we may limit ourselves to specifying several of the characteristics or emphases which may be associated with this method.

The prime characteristic of science or reason, within the period, was its expression in terms of mathematics. Descartes was chiefly a mathematician; not because of any mystical regard for mathematics, but because it seemed to him to supply the simplest method for the conduct of reason.[14] The seventeenth century is a glorious period in the history of France, from the standpoint of pure mathematics, because of the work of Descartes, Roberval, Desargues, Fermat, and Pascal, respectively,

which seeks to embrace the whole of human experience without such arbitrary boundaries as dogmas prescribed by authority. Due regard to stubborn facts of observation is an essential part of any thoroughgoing rationality, not a recoil from it; and the kind of rationality that stops short of it is but imperfectly rational, however subtle and justifiable it may be in other respects." (*A history of science*, p. 2)

[13] Hobbes, *The leviathan, or the matter, forme and power of a commonwealth ecclesiastical and civil* (Oxford, 1881), p. 31. This edition is a reproduction of the original edition of 1651.

[14] Descartes, *Discours de la méthode,* edited with commentary by E. Gilson (Paris, 1930), pp. 7, 18-22, *passim;* see also Wolf, *A history of science,* pp. 644-650.

on analytical geometry, indivisibles, epicycles, the theory of numbers, and probability.[15] Collectively, they laid the groundwork for the formulation of the calculus of Leibnitz and Newton.[16] Fontenelle, the philosopher of the *Acadèmie des sciences,* thinking of the seventeenth century as the renaissance of science, noted: " It is scarcely than from this century that we can date the renewal of mathematics and physics. " Descartes and others had completely changed the face of things; ". . . the reign of words and terms is passed. . . . Finally, mathematics has not only provided, for some time, an infinite number of truths of the type which are peculiar to it; it has further, implanted generally in our minds a sense of exactitude more precious perhaps than all these truths." [17] It was this desire for certainty, exactitude, and precision which gave to mathematics its exalted place in the method of reason. The seventeenth-century scientist not only tried to reason mathematically and remolded pure mathematical philosophy as a means to penetrate old boundaries, he also significantly modified mechanics with new instruments of precision in order that this same exactitude and certainty might be utilized in experimental science. A distinction of modern science is the scientific instrument; for measurement is so important to it that it is difficult to imagine it without such instruments. The seventeenth century saw the introduction and improvement of a number of the essential instruments of our science: the celestial telescope, microscope, thermometer, barometer, pendulum clock, and micrometer being the more important ones.[18] These innova-

---

[15] Cajori, *History of mathematics,* pp. 157, 172-178, 183-189.

[16] *Ibid.,* p. 200.

[17] B. le B. de Fontenelle. " Preface de l'historie de l'acadèmie des sciences, depuis 1666 jusqu'a 1699," in *Oeuvres de Fontenelle, précedées d'une notice sur sa vie et ses ouvrages,* edited by J. B. J. Champagnac (5 vols., Paris, 1825), I, 1-2; Fontenelle's opinion on the importance of this century to the development of mathematics is still generally accepted. For instance Sedgwick and Tyler: " The invention of analytical geometry by Descartes in 1637 and the almost simultaneous introduction of integral calculus as the method of ' indivisibles ' may be regarded as the real beginning of modern mathematical science." *A short history of science,* p. 308.

[18] See Wolf, *A history of science:* on the telescope pp. 75-82; on the microscope pp. 71-73; on the thermometer pp. 82-92; on the barometer pp. 92-98; on the pendulum clock and marine clock, the forerunner of the chronometer pp. 109-120; on the micrometer pp. 168-174.

tions were but a further reflection of the mathematical tendency of the age.

Secondly, the method of seventeenth-century science was, generally speaking, sympathetic to experimentation. In this regard, historians, deluded by philosophers' distinctions, have persisted in over-emphasizing a struggle between the followers of Bacon, Descartes, or Newton.[19] Since the views given form by Newton are of perceptible importance in France only in the period following that of our interest, concern will be had only with the status of experimentation during a time in which Cartesian methodology was dominant there. Bacon, to the seventeenth-century intellectual, either in France or England, was likely to appear as the apostle of experimentation.[20] In a similar fashion, Descartes was the prophet of mathematics and mathematical, deductive reasoning. This does not mean, however, that Descartes was anti-Baconian. It is true that Descartes gave greater emphasis to his mathematical method. He believed it less subject to error and simpler than the inductive process beginning with observation, but, as the deductive process became more complicated, experiments were "the more necessary as one advances the more in knowledge."[21] Specifically referring to the work of Bacon, Descartes said of experimentation: "On that, I have nothing to say, after what Verulam[22] has written on it. . . ."[23] Furthermore, Descartes cited as one of the prime reasons for publishing his works his own inability to conduct the "infinity of experiments" which were necessary to advance his own self-instruction. Believing that he had discovered the best method and the central truths

[19] For instance, G. Lanson goes so far in regard to the status of experimental science in France in the seventeenth century as to declare: "Jusqu'à la fin du XVIIe siècle, la valeur des expériences, en dehors de quelque savants, n'etait pas appreciée"—see his "La réaction contre les géometres: l'abbé Dubos—Bayle—Fontenelle," in *Revue des cours et conférences* (1909-1910), I, 741, 734-743. The part of experimentation in seventeenth-century science is well presented in M. Ornstein *The role of scientific societies in the seventeenth century* (Chicago, 1938); H. Brown, *Scientific organizations in seventeenth century France (1620-1680)* (Baltimore, 1934), see particularly, pp. 262-265.

[20] Ornstein, pp. 39-44; see also Wolf, *A history of science,* pp. 632-640; Burtt, pp. 117-118.

[21] Descartes, *Discours de la méthode,* pp. 63-65.

[22] Bacon was Baron of Verulam.

[23] Gilson, "Appendice" to Descartes, *Discours de la méthode,* p. 276.

of nature, he gave his findings to others to extend by experimentation.[24] In addition, the Cartesian school aided the work of experimentation by its attitude of methodic doubt, a tradition of independence, free thinking, a mechanical explanation of natural phenomena and the insistence on mathematical certainty.[25] Finally one can cite the work of individuals like Roberval, Pascal, Picard and of the academies to illustrate the importance of the experimental spirit in seventeenth-century science in France.

Thirdly note should be made that the most widespread expression for the method associated with Cartesianism was the term "order." Descartes himself described his procedure of reasoning from simple to complex notions as the most valuable lesson he had to impart to his students so as to instill in them the "habit of order." [26] "Order," as generally used in the seventeenth century, was both a means and an end. It was a procedure but it also implied all the benefit of the rational approach when applied to any problem. "Order" meant, too, the new against the old; historically, it was the maxim of the present opposed to the confusion which was commonly associated with the "gothic" past. In all cases it meant the subjection of the irrational to formula whether in political, social, or intellectual fields and was, therefore, a corollary of the mathematical method considered so desirable.

Galileo's idea of a mathematical and orderly nature whose motions are regular and inexorable was, as we have noted, given philosophic and popular dimension in the work of Descartes. Largely by the vogue for Cartesian ideas, the notion of a material universe of extension, motion, and form, accessible

[24] Descartes, *Discours de la méthode*, pp. 74-75. Descartes described his method as, first, discovering "the principles, or first causes, of which all is, or can be, in the world, without considering anything, for this end, than God alone, who has created it, nor deriving them from any than certain seeds of truth which are naturally in our minds." Secondly, he deduces the stars, earth, air, water, fire, minerals and all the simplest things. Thirdly, as the process becomes very complex, he must use an inductive procedure which rises to "causes from effects." He envisaged an enormous amount of experimentation as necessary to give body to the skeletal truths already discovered by him. *Ibid.*, pp. 63-65.

[25] Ornstein, pp. 49-50.

[26] Descartes, *Discours de la méthode*, pp. 71-72.

to understanding through the medium of mathematics, became another of the postulates assumed in seventeenth-century science or rationalism.[27] Given such a notion and adding to it the prevailing dualistic picture of nature and the supernatural in which the areas of distinction were ill defined, the methods of natural philosophy could encroach in an asymptotic fashion on the metaphysical frontiers of knowledge. Nature and man became machines directed by set mechanical principles and therefore to be interpreted by mechanics which was but another expression of mathematics. "Mechanics," said a disciple of Descartes, "is only Geometry applied to local movement."[28]

A fourth general characteristic, then, of seventeenth-century science is the stress of mechanics as a governing principle. There were some who went further than Descartes in this direction. Hobbes, for instance, wished to subject the world of the mind as well as that of matter to terms of motion and sensation.[29] A representative scientist of the mid-seventeenth century commented on the wisdom of mechanical knowledge:

And as it is certain that nothing is done in the Arts, without the application of Mechanics; therefore it is necessary to recognize that nothing can be explained concerning the particular effects of Nature if the demonstrations of this science are not employed. Mechanics prescribes the rules of both types of Architecture, that is to say, Civil and Military. This it is which builds ships and pilots them. It constructs machines for lifting with ease the heaviest loads. It regulates the canals and directs their course and sluices into mills and into country seats. It plays the organ without bellows using but the fall of water alone. It gives tongue to the rocks in artificial grottoes where it makes them imitate the songs of birds and produces the sweetest concerts. That is a part of what it does when employed by the artifices of men. But what does it not do when employed by the industry of Nature itself? Is it not mechanics which fixes the Earth unshakably beneath our feet and which assigns all bodies the place which they must take in the Universe? Indeed, it is this which gives spherical form to the surface of the Sea and which filters its waters through subterranean conduits in order to give them egress in fountains and rivers: it is this which suspends the clouds in the midst of the air, which propels them from place to place by the wind and

[27] Burtt, pp. 204-211, 202-330.
[28] I. G. Pardies, "Preface," *Élémens de géométrie* (1671) published in *Oeuvres de mathématiques* (Amsterdam, 1725).
[29] Wolf, *A history of science*, pp. 640-641; Burtt, pp. 117-127.

squeezes the rain out of them in order to fertilize the fields: it is this which causes bodies to fall with that redoubling velocity and proportion which the Philosophers cannot sufficiently admire: this it is which gives the impulse to all the heavens and which maintains them in that movement so regular: it is this which gives the power of flight to birds and permits fish to swim in water and animals to walk on land: it is by its means that the heart is set to beating, the blood circulates, spirits are distributed and we breath: it is this which causes light and sound to travel with a circular motion, which causes them to reflect or be broken into echoes in mirrors and lenses. In short, nothing is done without it either in the Arts or in Nature: so that it is impossible to succeed in the consideration of one, or the practice of the other, without the knowledge and use of mechanics.[30]

A fifth general characteristic of science and rationalism, and this was a characteristic partly inherited from the period of the Renaissance, was its anti-authoritarian or, what was almost the same thing, secular emphasis. It is necessary at once, however, to qualify this statement by noting that the authorities which were, in effect, denied by the seventeenth-century rationalist were the traditional authority of the Church and the intellectual authority of scholasticism. In one sense, indeed, the new rationalist but reared new authorities. He substituted for the authority of the supernatural the authority of the natural. Above the authority of the society of the spirit he placed the demands of a lay society and the purely secular authority of the state. The rejection by Galileo or Descartes of the doctrine of final cause; the necessity, according to their teaching, for studying the essential connections between natural phenomena to deduce consequences; and their reliance on rigorously mathematical procedure to attain truth made them, whatever their disinclination to admit it, the advocates of a rational system which was inevitably antipathetical to tradition and, finally, to church doctrine. From this point of view the attack on Aristotle, the customary scapegoat of the rationalists, was perhaps less due to the errors of the great philosopher than to the fact that he had been raised by the Church to the status of an arbiter in fields not directly relegated to the direction of God.[31] Des-

[30] I. G. Pardies, " Preface " to his *Traité de la statique ou la science de forces mouvantes* (1673) in *Oeuvres de mathématiques,* pp. 107-110.
[31] Wolf, *A history of science,* p. 629; an interesting study on the effect of seventeenth century science on contemporary religious opinion, and on poetry form, is B. Willey's *The seventeenth century background* (London, 1934).

cartes, Bacon, and their disciples joined in expressing a wholesale disdain for those who limited their imagination by his
prescriptions. The dialectics of scholasticism were likewise a
matter for contempt. "And I have never remarked, further,"
wrote Descartes, "on any truths being discovered which were
unknown before by the methods of disputation which are practiced in the schools." [32] Neither Galileo nor Descartes, nor any
other Christian rationalist of the seventeenth century, acknowledged an attack on their faith, but the threat of their beliefs
to orthodoxy, a threat which they were loath to admit or failed
to recognize, was quickly detected by the Church itself. In the
case of Descartes it is difficult to believe that motives of convenience were not a major factor in his compromise version of
the relation of the physical and supernatural. As a case in
point we have his own description of his reaction to the news
of Galileo's condemnation, in 1633, by the holy office. In his
Discours de la méthode he tells us:

> Three years ago I finished the Treatise which contains all these
> reflections and I was commencing to revise it in order to place it in
> the hands of the printer when I learned that some persons [the holy
> office], to whom I defer and whose authority has scarcely less bearing
> on my actions than my own reason on my thoughts, had disapproved
> an opinion of physics [the revolution of the earth around the sun],
> published a short time before by another person [Galileo], which I
> do not wish to say I agreed with, but only that I had remarked noth-
> ing, previous to their censure, which I could imagine to be prejudicial
> either to religion or the State, nor, consequently, which would have
> prevented me from writing of it, if reason had persuaded me of its
> truth, and this made me fearful lest among my own opinions there
> might be some in which I was mistaken, notwithstanding the great care
> I have always had to refuse to receive any new point of which I had
> not some very certain demonstrations, and not to write anything which
> could harm anyone.[33]

At the time of Galileo's trial the French philosopher had
written his friend Mersenne noting that if Galileo's notions of
the heliocentric system were incorrect, then, "I confess . . . all
the foundations of my Philosophy are also . . . and it is so
allied with all the parts of my Treatise that I could not detach
it without rendering the remainder entirely defective." [34] But

[32] Descartes, *Discours de la méthode*, p. 69.
[33] *Ibid.*, p. 60 and notes on p. 440.
[34] Descartes to Mersenne, November 1633, quoted in notes, *ibid.*, p. 440.

he was, nevertheless, able to rationalize, in his vortex theory, a
kind of, as it appeared to him, orthodox Copernicanism which
left the world stationary in its vortex though circling the sun.
His difficulties were further eased, as he seemed to believe, by
a method in which he did not have to commit himself on such
problems as to whether " I believe it true or not." [35]

Whatever the compromises which necessity and comfort
might exact from seventeenth-century science the work of Descartes had effectively overturned the Platonic, Aristotelian,
Christian universe and paved the way for the mechanical, clock
world of Boyle, Locke, and Leibnitz.[36] Voltaire, the spokesman
for the Enlightenment, although finding much to criticize in his
work, saw Descartes as the destroyer of chimeras.[37] Fontenelle
saw the progress of the century as springing from a method in
which " Authority no longer carries more weight than reason;
what was received without contradiction, because it was traditional, is presently examined and often rejected." [38]

Another characteristic of seventeenth-century science or
reason, while not so pervasive as those already cited but so
widespread as to make it appear a dominant trait, was the
belief that they should serve practical ends. This was particularly true of the experimental tendency associated with Bacon
and given reality in the academies. A French scientist, Samuel
Sorbière, travelling in England in 1664, wrote:

. . . this country might dispute for Precedency with *France* and *Italy*
who glory in their *Galieus, Descartes,* and *Gassendus.* But to speak
the truth, the Lord Chancellor *Bacon* has surpassed all the rest in the
Vastness of his Designs, and that Learned and Judicious Tablature he
has left us, usefully to reduce the Knowledge we have in Natural
Things into Practice, without being incommoded with the Disputes
of the Schools, to the End we may apply them to Mechanism, and resolve the Difficulties that occur to us in our Lives.[39]

[35] Descartes to Mersenne, April 1634, *ibid.,* p. 441.
[36] Burtt, p. 105.
[37] Voltaire, *Siècle de Louis XIV,* pp. 100-101.
[38] Fontenelle, " Preface de l'histoire de l'acadèmie," *Oeuvres,* I, 2.
[39] S. Sorbière, *Voyage to England containing many things relating to the state
of learning, Religion and other couriosities of that Kingdom* (London, 1709),
p. 32. The first edition of this work appeared at Cologne in 1667. Sorbière
was made a member of the Royal Society during his visit. His book, because of
its frank portrayal of English character, aroused a storm of criticism and was
answered almost immediately by an ill-tempered book by Thomas Spratt the
author of the *History of the Royal Society.*

In France, Desargues, the geometrician, tells us:

> I freely confess that I never had taste for study or research either in physics or geometry except so far as they could serve as a means of arriving at some sort of knowledge of the proximate causes . . . for the good and convenience of life, in maintaining health, in the practice of some art . . . having observed that a good part of the arts is based on geometry, among others the cutting of stones in architecture, that of sun-dials, that of perspective in particular.[40]

The Jesuit Father Pardies also underlines the practical value of geometry: " I say only that if it has ever been of some utility in the study of natural sciences, and in the practice of the arts, it is now of the last necessity to both." [41] As a last example we may turn to Descartes. Of his new method he writes:

> I perceived that it is possible to acquire knowledges which may be highly useful in life and which instead of this speculative philosophy, which they teach in our schools, one can find a practical philosophy by which, knowing the force and actions of fire, water, air, stars, heavens and all the other bodies which surround us, as distinctly as we know the various crafts of our artisans, we may employ them to their proper use and thus make ourselves masters and possessors of nature. This is desirable, not only for the invention of innumerable artifices, by which we may provide ourselves, without any trouble, with the fruits of the earth and all the commodities to be found there, but principally also to conserve our health.[42]

Finally, a characteristic of science and rationalism during this period, in France, was its close alliance with the method and philosophy of Descartes. Cartesianism became something of a religion and the *Discours* of the philosopher provided the language of the salon and the discipline of the academicians. Though Cartesianism was officially condemned by the Church, the Sorbonne and the government, the followers were legion, and Descarte's physics, metaphysics and method were accepted on every hand, even by churchmen in the guise of Aristotelianism or by professed opponents.[43] The Jesuit Pardies is a case

---

[40] Quoted in Sedgwick and Tyler, p. 317.

[41] Pardies, " Preface," *Élémens de géométrie.*

[42] Descartes, *Discours de la méthode,* pp. 61-62. The reference to health reminds us of the fact that Descartes was much interested in medicine. He was quite influenced by the work of Harvey, frequently refers to him in his writings and buttressed his mechanical theories of physiology—expressed in *L'Homme*—with Harvey's discoveries relative to the circulation of the blood.

[43] F. C. Bouillier, *Histoire de la philosophie Cartésienne* (2 vols., Paris, 1868), I, 429-485.

in point. "Everyone has suspected him," said Bayle, "of wishing to establish by indirection the opinions of Descartes while seemingly refuting them, and in fact he answers so well his own objections that it is not difficult to divine what this signifies. . . ."[44] Malebranche is another example of a person who propagated the doctrines of Descartes although differing with him in particulars. Morris Ginsberg, speaking of their kinship, notes that where "he is not following Saint Augustine and the neo-Platonists, Malebranche's teachings may be regarded as following logically from the teaching of Descartes. The essential principles of method, the emphasis on the significance of clearness and distinctness, the mathematical or mechanical explanation of nature, are common to both philosophers. Malebranche retains too, the dualistic theory of mind and matter despite his doctrine of intelligible extension."[45] Among the elite of the intellectuals, Pascal, Arnould, Mersenne, the Duke of Luynes, Bossuet, Fenelon, and Fontenelle were but a few of those deeply influenced by him. In the language of the *précieux,* the daughter of Madame Sévigné called him "*mon Père*" and La Fontaine referred to "*Descartes, ci mortel dont on eût fait un dieu.*"[46] The theologians were not the only people who feared the effect of the intrusion of Cartesian principles into the metaphysical domain of the church. About 1670, the aging and exiled Saint-Evremond with gentle irony pointed out the lack of solace found in the prevailing substitution of Reason for the consolations of faith:

When a man has to reckon with his infirmities, even in matters of board and lodging, he is no longer of any account in this world. I only live now by reflecting upon life, which is hardly living, and without Monsieur *Descartes'* philosophy which says: *I think, therefore I am,* I would scarcely believe myself to be. That is all the benefit I have received from studying that famous man, whom they value so highly in France, but who was surely somewhat odd.[47]

[44] Quoted in "Pardies" in *Nouvelle biographie générale,* XXXIX (1862), 191. Even a most superficial reading of Pardies' *Elémens de géométrie* or his *Traité de la statique* and their prefatory remarks will affirm Bayle's opinion.

[45] M. Ginsberg, "Introduction" to Malebranche, *Dialogues on metaphysics and on religion,* translated and edited by M. Ginsberg (London, 1933), p. 61.

[46] E. Saisset, *Précurseurs et disciples de Descartes* (Paris, 1862), pp. 85, 83-184; Bouillier, I, 229-265.

[47] C. de Saint-Evremond, letter to the Marshal de Crequi (1671) in *Letters of Saint-Evremond,* translated and edited by J. Hayward (London, 1930), p. 129.

To retain perspective it is well to remind oneself that the age of reason arose in the midst of an age of credulity and faith. Although a Voltaire or Lecky may associate the rise of rationalism with the decline in the belief of miracles, this is a generalization which concerns only a small minority of the people; an intellectual aristocracy. The overwhelming masses of the people were undoubtedly ignorant and superstitious. When the notorious poisoner, the Marquise of Brinvilliers, was beheaded and burned at the Place de Greve, in 1676, her last-minute air of contrition and dignity led the people to fight over her ashes as the relics of a saint. A priest, Urbain Grandier, was burned alive, in 1634, for causing evil spirits to attack the nuns in an Ursuline convent.[48] The famous " affair of poisoners," involving some of the highest nobility of the land, was much confused by the added aspect of sorcerers, magicians, and diviners and led to a law in 1682 directed against these " imposters " who preyed on the " ignorant or credulous." [49] The practical conduct of the business of the state was not detached from the bizarre. At one time we find Colbert in receipt of a letter announcing the coming to Paris of one " Belbrune, surgeon . . . , who has told me that he has found a way to change tin into silver, and copper into gold. In truth," says the writer, " he has made the experiment before some of my friends. If he has the way to do it, it would enrich His Majesty," [50] In 1672, the Bishop of Fréjus sent the Minister an old horoscope which had predicted accurately the events of that year and which, since it was projected to the year 1680, might prove useful.[51]

[48] Isambert, Jourdan, Decrusy, Armet, and Gaillandier, Recueil général des anciennes lois françaises, . . . jusqu'à la révolution de 1789 (29 vols., Paris, 1821-1833), XVI, 413 note. It is said that Grandier had the added misfortune of being actively disliked by Richelieu.

[49] Ibid., XIX, 396-401.

[50] One Louvet to Colbert from Noyen, August 12, 1664, in G. B. Depping, Correspondence administrative sous le règne de Louis XIV, entre le cabinet du Roi, les secretaires d'État, le chancelier de France, et des intendants et gouverneurs des provinces, les présidents, procureurs et avocats généraux des parlements et autres cours de justice, le gouverneur de la Bastille, les evéques, les corps municipaux etc. (4 vols., Paris, 1850-1855), IV, 544-545.

[51] Ondedi, Bishop of Fréjus to Colbert, July 22, 1672, ibid., pp. 711-712. A letter of the Marquis of Castries to Colbert, December 29, 1664, was a little more critical, or, at least apologetic. " You are going to be surprised when you

Mystics, anchorites, saints, and Puritans adorned the " this worldly " society of Galileo, Descartes, and Newton, and it should not be forgotten that these men also had their religious and mystical attachments. Few persons achieved the eminence of Blaise Pascal in seventeenth-century science. Few, more than he, embodied the contradictory character of an age which bridged the old and the new. One of the truly creative geniuses of mathematics and experimental science, he came in his later life to perceive the limitations of natural reason and to find satisfaction in the mystical revelations arising from his conversion to Jansenism. " The heart has its reasons that reason itself does not know."

Just as science and rationalism intruded into a social and intellectual climate which yet remained predominantly uninformed or traditional in outlook, so the effect of the new currents of thought on political institutions was to revise or modify more frequently than to create anew. In one sense, indeed, the governmental reforms of Louis XIV perpetuated a time-honored tradition of French royal administration. If many new offices were invented, few among the multitude of old ones were destroyed. In fact, the tendency was to multiply non-essential positions and thus to provide a source of additional revenue by their sale. Superficially, then, the government of Louis XIV after 1661 must have appeared to be very much like the government of his predecessors. Certainly there were but a small number of new names in it; old titles, old jurisdictions and old dignities were largely retained but a closer inspection soon revealed that many of the earlier prerogatives were no longer retained with them. The conduct of the state was, for the most part, vested in a new and restricted bureau-

find this letter entirely filled with predictions and prophesies; speaking of stars and of the conjunction of planets. I do not doubt that at first you can only believe that I have lost my mind; but when you have attentively considered the book joined here, I am sure that you will lose the bad impressions the beginning of my letter has given you." The book, picked up in Paris, in 1660, predicted a sensational comet, now present, and also a change of the reigning house of the Empire and that Louis XIV would become the Emperor. This was foretold because Saturn which enters the house of Sagittarius every thirty years was now accompanied by Jupiter. This phenomenon occurs only every 800 years. The last time was in the period of Charlemagne. The Marquis desired Colbert's advice on whether the King should be informed of this curious circumstance. *Ibid.*, pp. 682-683.

cracy which centered in the King and permeated and absorbed the functions of the ancient structure of the monarchy. The minutes of the first state council called by Louis XIV after the death of Mazarin opened with the expression: *Annus novus a regimine novo.* This may have been only a formula but, if so, it was to prove a well chosen one. It could well be a translation into Latin of the phrase attributed by the secretary of the council to Louis on this occasion: *" La face du théatre change."* [52]

As will be seen, this change was to be associated with the creation of a more rational administration which, consciously and unconsciously, reflected the spirit of the seventeenth-century scientific method and emphases. In spite of institutional anomalies and anachronisms which would continue to encumber the mechanism of the state, and which finally brought it to ruin in the revolution of 1789, the actual improvements made by Louis XIV in the procedure of government gave him his true claim to the fame of which he was so jealous. This study has been limited to the years 1661 to 1683. This seemed justified by the fact that these were the years of innovation. In this period a regime designed to follow the " maxims of order " replaced a regime following the " maxims of confusion." During this period the main structural features of the *ancien régime* were created; features which were to persist, with minor alterations, until the eve of the revolution. This is the period, also, of the ministry of him who, with Louis XIV, deserves the title of " architect " of the new government: Jean Baptiste Colbert. Finally, the writer will admit a certain prejudice of sentiment in favor of the period. The correspondence of the men in the government reveals a general spirit of optimism, a sense of initiation and zest for experiment, a consciousness of achievement, an enthusiasm for work, and a confidence in order and system which cannot fail to be contagious for the reader. The administrators of France from 1661 to 1683 were convinced that they were the engineers of a successful revolution by bringing science into government.

[52] J. de Boislisle, *Mémoriaux du conseil de 1661* (3 vols., Paris, 1905-1907), I, 1, 3 notes.

CHAPTER II

THE IMPACT OF SCIENCE AND RATIONALISM ON POLITICAL PHILOSOPHY IN THE SEVENTEENTH CENTURY [1]

In the *De regimine principum*, attributed to Thomas Aquinas, monarchy is depicted as the most perfect form of government.[2] Four centuries later, in the Age of Descartes, few Frenchmen could have been found who would have justified any other view. Except for certain clerics, however, few of them would have justified it with the Thomistic argument that the best government is molded after the examples of God's heaven. They would, rather, have described it as fashioned after the prescriptions of Reason. Reason had become the guiding principle of the intelligentsia and there has been no influential political work which has not been, as Harold Laski has put it, " the autobiography of its time."

I

To be sure, in this Age of Reason, there were still those who turned reverently, so they would have us believe, towards the divine justification of authority or looked backwards to the practices of historic France for guidance. In political thought from the death of Henry II to the end of the reign of Louis XIV this traditional mode of thinking found expression even in the works of men who, in most respects, were thorough

---

[1] The following secondary works have proved of much value in writing this chapter: J. W. Allen, *A history of political thought in the 16th century* (New York, 1928); G. N. Clark, *The seventeenth century* (Oxford, 1929); G. N. Clark, *Science and social welfare in the age of Newton* (Oxford, 1937); G. P. Gooch, *Political thought in England from Bacon to Halifax* (London, 1937); J. N. Figgis, *Political thought from Gerson to Grotius, 1414-1625* (London, 1907); B. Hesson, " The social and economic roots of Newton's Principia," in *Science at the cross roads* (London, 1931); Frederick Pollock, *The history of the science of politics* (New York, 1883); Henri Sée, *Les idées politiques en France au XVIIe siècle* (Paris, 1923); K. B. Smellie, *Reason in politics* (London, 1939); Georges Weill, *Les théories sur le pouvoir royal en France pendant les guerres de religion* (Paris, 1892).

[2] Aquinas, *On the governance of rulers (De regimine principum)*, trans. from the Latin by Gerald B. Phelan (Toronto, 1935), pp. 38-39. On the authenticity of this work, which has often been questioned, see pp. 3-5.

disciples of the new thought. In general they belonged to the groups opposed to the absolute monarchy. It was to them that tradition gave the most support, and it was thus in their writings that it predominated. From Bodin to Locke, reason, generally, was most frequently pictured as in alliance with the interests of kings and, in France, the rational limitations to royal authority which Locke systematized were scarcely noticed at the time.

The Bourbon monarchy of Henry IV had inherited the troubles of the League, and the reign of Louis XIV was ushered in by the Fronde and ended under the cloud of the War of Spanish Succession. It was primarily in these periods, or in regard to those conditions which characterized them, that the opposition to absolutism expressed itself. The rebellious legists and political scientists of the times of the religious wars in France had turned automatically to tradition for buttress.[3] Among the Protestant Monarchomachs,[4] men like Du Plessis-Mornay, in his *Vindiciae contra tyrannos* (1576), and Francis Hotman, in his *La Franco-Gallia* (1574), placed the historical element at the basis of their opposition, and this was explicit in the work of the latter. Hotman's treatise is a long historical argument to prove that the French are a nation of free men.[5] The Monarchomachs, Protestant or Catholic, were alike in giving religion its traditional place above the level of temporal government and in their attempt to give ethical validity to their positions.[6]

In 1611, the Protestant Louis de Mayerne-Turquet, in his *Monarchie aristodémocratique*, attacked royal absolutism by referring to the feudal relationships and showing the reciprocal obligations of sovereign, vassals, and the people. The Estates-

---

[3] Weill, pp. 277-292.

[4] In France, the party of the radical resistance to the crown.

[5] Francois Hotman, *Franco-Gallia, or an account of the ancient free state of France and most other parts of Europe, before the loss of their liberties, written originally in Latin by the famous civilian Francis Hotman in the year 1574,* trans. by Robert Malesworth (London, 1711), copy used; see also Figgis, *Gerson to Grotius,* pp. 153-158; Weill, pp. 99-121; Allen, pp. 308-311; Beatrice Reynolds, *Proponents of limited monarchy in sixteenth century France: Francis Hotman and Jean Bodin* (New York, 1931), pp. 41-104; Du Plessis-Mornay, *A defense of liberty against tyrants, a translation of the Vindiciae contra tyrannos by Junius Brutus,* edited from the 1689 ed. by H. J. Laski (London, 1924).

[6] See " Introduction " of Laski, *ibid.*

3

General was presented by him as the traditional check on the power of kings and the conservator of sovereignty and the laws.[7] During the Fronde (1649-1653) the pamphleteers with their *Mazarinades* devoted most of their efforts to attacks against Cardinal Mazarin but the person of the King remained sacred. Limitations on the excessive prerogatives of the ministeriat and the defense of a more popular government were discovered by them through research into the historical constitution of the state.[8]

After the revocation of the Edict of Nantes (1685), there was a rebirth of criticism of the crown. The anonymous[9] author of the *Soupirs de la France esclave* (1689-1690) found the arguments against tyranny conveniently demonstrated in the record of the kingdom.[10] " It is necessary to remember," he wrote, " that we look into the ancient Government of our French Monarchy to create an opposition to the form of the present Government." With him it seemed a matter of returning to the traditional habits or seeing the destruction of the monarchy itself.[11] The economic decay, which contemporaries ordinarily associated with the revocation and with the ill effects of the disastrous wars at the end of the reign of Louis XIV, aroused the attacks of persons other than the Protestants. The Duke of Saint-Simon in comparing the reigns of Henry IV, Louis XIII, and Louis XIV awarded the laurels of superiority to that of Louis XIII.[12] In his " Mémoire sur la renonciation

[7] Louis de Mayerne-Turquet, *La monarchie aristodémocratique ou le gouvernement composé et meslé des trois formes de légitimes Républiques* (Paris, 1611), pp. 46-47, 52-54, 323-437.

[8] Of the Mazarinades see particularly " Lettre d'avis à Messieurs du Parlement de Paris, éscrite par un Provincial," March 4, 1649; " Le Raisonnable plaintif sur la dernière Déclaration du Roy," August 19, 1652, both in C. Moreau, *Choix de Mazarinades* (2 vols., Paris, 1853), I, 358-407; II, 452-465; see also on *Mazarinades,* Sée, pp. 88-108. A synthesis of the main currents of opposition thought of the Fronde was given by Claude Joly, *Recueil de maximes véritables et importantes pour l'institution de Roy* (Paris, 1652); on Joly see Sée, pp. 108-122; for a thorough treatment of the constitutional aspect of the Fronde see P. R. Doolin, *The Fronde* (Cambridge, 1935).

[9] Supposed to be Michel Levassor, a refugee priest turned Protestant.

[10] Michel Levassor, *Soupirs de la France esclave qui aspire aprés la liberté* (Amsterdam, 1689-1690), pp. 69-83, 85-100, 101-163.

[11] *Ibid.,* pp. 117, 165-179.

[12] Louis de Rouvroy, Duke of Saint-Simon, " Parallèle des trois premiers rois Bourbons " (May, 1746), *Ecrits inédits de Saint-Simon,* edited by M. P. Faugere (8 vols., Paris, 1880-1893), I, 384-390.

du Roy d'Espagne" (1712), he presumed to give historical proof that the King had no legal power to make fundamental changes in the law or guarantee great sanctions of the realm without the advice of his peers and the great officers of the crown.[13] Henri de Boulainvilliers, Count of Saint-Saire (1658-1722), in works published posthumously, although one of the more constructive political thinkers of his time, proposed no real reorganization of the state but simply advocated a renewal of traditional. restraints to autocratic rule.[14]

II

Thus opinions borrowed from the past were the customary weapons used by the opponents to absolutism. More expressive of the time was the reflection in the writings of the leading political philosophers of the attitudes associated with contemporary science and rationalism. They were strongly anti-traditional and scornful of older authority. They exhibited the same skepticism, employed the criterion of rational doubt and revealed the zeal for mathematical reasoning and the maxims of order which characterized the scientists and philosophers; and they attempted, in systematic treatises, to reduce the art of government to certain formulae. Thus politics, in their writings, became a scientific discipline.

In the preceding chapter we have emphasized the strong anti-traditional stress in seventeenth-century science and rationalism. Such notions were not, as seen, original with Descartes and it has been argued that Roger rather than Francis Bacon was the father of the seventeenth century in this regard.[15] Ancestors can also be found in the field of political thought. The sixteenth century presents the figure of Machiavelli who, in defiance of tradition, was most remarkable for his complete failure to attempt to found a philosophy of right. In

---

[13] Saint-Simon, "Mémoire sur la renonciation du Roy d'Espagne" (1712) *ibid.*, II, 202-286, 317-322; on the politics of Saint-Simon in general see Sée, pp. 235-270.

[14] Henri de Boulainvilliers, *Histoire de l'ancien gouvernement de la France avec XIV lettres historiques sur les parlemens ou États-Généraux* (3 vols., Amsterdam, 1727), particularly Vol. I; see Sée, pp. 270-285.

[15] This seems to be the position of E. E. Saisset, *Précurseurs et disciples de Descartes* (Paris, 1862), pp. 3-58, 85-86.

contrast to the political speculation of the past few centuries, which might be described as generally directed towards that end, Machiavelli subordinated right to the desirable: not to what ought to be desired but to what is desired.[16]

In France, we observe Jean Bodin, the spokesman of the *Politiques,* who, in his tremendous work the *Six livres de la république* (1576), attempted to construct a systematic treatise on political society and theory. He determined the best state to be a pure and absolute monarchy, the justification of which rested principally on the grounds that it represented man's creation to meet man's needs. "The originality of Bodin's theory of sovereignty consisted essentially, I think," writes J. W. Allen, "at least in relation to his own age, in the fact that he did not connect it specifically and directly with the will of God. It was the creation of man. . . ."[17] Bodin, himself, repeatedly asserted his independence of authority in supporting his arguments or censored the limitations and methods of lawyers and ancients when applied to current problems. He customarily wrote that not "one of the ancient Greeks or Latins, nor any other" had understood his major concepts.[18]

Early in the seventeenth century another Frenchman, Pierre d'Avity, published his *Les éstats, empires et principautéz du monde,* a comparative study of states. In his "Avant-propos," he criticized the reader of classics who shut himself off, consumed in the study of ancients, "without enquiring about the moderns, and apparently so admiring the dead that they have no care for the living." As he viewed it, the purpose of political discourse was to acquaint people with the world of reality.[19] In a political work, possibly the most clear-cut dec-

[16] Figgis, *Gerson to Grotius,* pp. 62-107, 84.

[17] Allen, p. 423.

[18] E.g., Jean Bodin, *Six livres de la République* (Lyons, 1579), p. 708. In general, in spite of his effort to systematize his subject, the *République* of Bodin is an extremely complex and incoherent work. It is for this reason that few political scientists seem entirely to agree on his meaning in even so fundamental a concept as that of sovereignty. See for example: Allen, "Jean Bodin," *Political thought in the 16th century,* pp. 394-444; M. A. Shepard, "Sovereignty at the crossroads—a study of Bodin," *Political science quarterly,* XLV (1930), 580-603; Figgis, *Gerson to Grotius,* pp. 126-130; Weill, "Bodin et Gregoire de Toulouse," *Les théories sur le pouvoir royal en France,* pp. 159-174; Reynolds, pp. 105-193.

[19] Pierre d'Avity, "Avant-propos," *Les éstats, empires et principautéz du*

laration, up to the time, of independence from older authority
is to be found in the *De jure belli ac pacis* (1625) of Hugo
Grotius.[20] Grotius explained in his "Prolegomena" that,
while he had consulted past authorities, he had used them
with caution and discrimination, realizing that each represented some particular interest. For instance, his distinction
between the law of nature and the law of nations was "not
to be drawn from the testimonies themselves (for writers
everywhere confuse the terms law of nature and law of
nations), but from the character of the matter."[21] With
reference to the most revered of ancient scholars, he wrote:
"Our purpose is to make much of Aristotle, but reserving in
regard to him the same liberty which he, in his devotion to
truth, allowed himself with respect to his teachers."[22]

Such examples make it clear that Descartes' *Discours de la
méthode* but translated into a positive discipline the doubt
already prevalent in regard to authority. Francis Bacon had
likewise stressed, before him, along with the need of learning
in governance, the danger of the dictatorship of "authors in
sciences."[23] The complaints of Descartes in regard to the
limited utility of pursuing the wisdom of the ancient philosophers, and his observations on the danger of attempting to
construct truth from a tradition based on fluctuating purposes
and produced by changing needs were ideas drawn from the
same cultural stream used by Grotius.[24] Thus the learned
Cardinal Richelieu might reflect the influence of Descartes,
or of Machiavelli, or simply of the mind of his time when
he voiced the opinion that in politics the "past cannot apply
to the present," and that there were none "more dangerous

*monde, représentez par la description des pays, meurs, des habitans, richesses des
provinces, les forces, le gouvernement, la religion, et les princes qui ont gou-
verné chacun Éstat* (1614).

[20] Though Dutch, Grotius spent most of the last twenty-five years of his life
in Paris as an exile and as ambassador representing Sweden. There he was
pensioned by Louis XIII and wrote the *Belli ac pacis*.

[21] Hugo Grotius, *De jure belli ac pacis, libri tres* (1625), trans. by F. W.
Kelsey with others (London, 1925), pp. 23-24.

[22] *Ibid.*, p. 26.

[23] Francis Bacon, "The advancement of learning" (1605), *The works of Francis Bacon* (3 vols., Philadelphia, 1853), I, 169-170, 172, 177-178.

[24] Renée Descartes, "Discours de la méthode et essais" (1636), *Oeuvres de
Descartes*, ed. by C. Adam and P. Tannery (10 vols., Paris, 1897-1910), VI,
4-16.

to the State than those who wish to govern Kingdoms by the maxims they take from their books." [25] Thomas Hobbes, thoroughly acquainted with the philosophical school of Descartes and intimately associated, in his youth, with Bacon, perhaps expressed the dictum of a disciple when he wrote in the *Leviathan* (1651) that " those men that take their instruction from the authority of books, and not from their own meditation . . . be as much below the condition of ignorant men, as men endued with true Science are above it." [26]

Broadly speaking the skepticism of seventeenth-century rationalism was inherited from the sixteenth century. Descartes was not an innovator in the field because he expressed doubt but because he projected an initial doubt into a constructive method. In this respect too, political science shared the principles of natural science and rationalism. The method of disciplined doubt which dominated the thinking of seventeenth century France, as we have seen, received its most popular expression through Descartes and under the name of " reason." As we have also observed, the heart and language of the method was arithmetical, or to be more precisely in key with the times, geometrical. The latter science was presented by the members of the school of Mersenne, Pascal, and their colleagues as the only means of conducting reason without error. [27] The measurement of mathematical terms was applied to the analysis of the most varied sides of society and its culture. Descartes wrote an *Abrégé de la musique* in which he used arithmetic proportions in the evaluation of the relative pleasure in listening to music, [28] while Hobbes found space sufficient in the *Leviathan* to discourse on the relationship of words to numbers. [29] With respect to the practice of accommodating the language of reason to other fields, related or distant, political

[25] Richelieu, *Maximes d'état, ou testament politique* (2 vols., Paris, 1764), I, 267.

[26] Thomas Hobbes, *The leviathan, or the matter, forme, and power of a commonwealth ecclesiastical and civil*, a reprint of the first edition of 1651 (Oxford, 1881), p. 22.

[27] See for instance, Blaise Pascal, *Pensées*, published posthumously *ca.* 1669 (ed. used, Paris, 1829), *passim*, but especially " Reflexions sur la géometrie en général," pp. 27-49, also p. 64.

[28] Descartes, " Abrégé de la musique," *Oeuvres de Descartes*, ed. by V. Cousin (11 vols., Paris, 1824-1826), V, 445-503.

[29] Hobbes, *Leviathan*, pp. 22-30, 23.

philosophy proved to be no exception. Grotius, Richelieu, Hobbes, and Spinoza, but to name a few, all took their turns in exposing and justifying the mechanics of politics by the mathematics of reason.[30]

Mathematical analysis had held a central position in the arguments of Jean Bodin in favor of " Royal Monarchy." He admittedly drew inspiration from Aristotle but he was certain that no one except himself had appreciated fully the value of " borrowing the principles of Mathematicians " and, therefore, his predecessors had neglected a conduct of the greatest consequence for " justice, as for the management of affairs of state and all the Republic." [31] It would be an error to conclude, because of the date, that Bodin's interest in this direction was but a reflection of the ordinary Renaissance admiration for the ancients. His own frequent assertions that he was improving on the ancients, his repeated claim to originality and the general atmosphere of rational doubt which runs through his work all argue that the practical aspect was, as he maintained, the primary virtue in measuring politics by mathematics.

The changes which marked the interval of time separating Bodin from Richelieu would justify the impression that, while the former may be called a precursor, the latter was perhaps but an enlightened member of his society. At least there seems to be no cause to believe that the Cardinal was using any unfamiliar symbols when he wrote of " reason " as dictating the maintenance of a " geometrical proportion " between the weight of government and the capacities of the masses to support it; between the size of the tax burden and the accumulative wealth of the taxpayers.[32] In 1632, for instance, Cardin

---

[30] For general discussions along this line see Smellie, pp. 43-56; Clark, *The seventeenth century,* pp. 209-232; Sée, *passim.*

[31] Greatly simplified, Bodin's analysis appears thus:

Arithmetical proportion—obtains in—equal government—or—democracy—with —equal law

Geometrical proportion—obtains in—class government—or—aristocracy—with— discretionary law

Harmonic proportion—obtains in—combination government—or—royal monarchy—with—equal law tempered by discretion

Six livres de la République, pp. 706-739, 708; compare with Aristotle, *Ethics,* Book V, chaps. 3-5; Louis de Mayerne-Turquet in his *La monarchie aristodémocratique,* as his title suggests, seems to show strongly the influence of Bodin.

[32] Richelieu, *Testament politique,* I, 226-227, II, 150.

Le Bret in his *De la souveraineté du Roy,* the writing of which had apparently been encouraged by Richelieu, had depicted a king whose sovereignty was no more " divisible, than the point in geometry." [33]

The *Leviathan,* produced by Hobbes near the end of eleven years of exile in Paris (1640-1651), is the creation of a complete rationalist.[34] Hobbes looked upon reason as the basis of political wisdom, and reason he defined as a process of arithmetic; of adding and subtracting notions. Bad reason was but bad arithmetic.[35] He accused past political philosophers of want of " Method "; a shortcoming which he claimed was responsible for many errors in their conclusions. In his own study he argued with the aid of the method of reason, as he saw it, beginning with clear definitions and proceeding in close pattern from one logical consequence to another.[36] This was the procedure ordinarily used " onely in Geometry " which was the " onely Science that it hath pleased God hitherto to bestow on mankind." Such a method, he asserted, was as essential to " Politics " as to " Geometry." [37]

In bringing to the support of their doctrines the mathematical method of reasoning and in accepting the premise of rational doubt, with the attendant skepticism of authority, the political scientist had assigned the problems of government to a realm which many then would term " science." [38] However, the actual use of the word " science " to describe government, or its philosophy, was rare in the first half of the cen-

[33] Cardin Le Bret, *De la souveraineté du Roy* (Paris, 1632), p. 71; on Le Bret see Sée, pp. 66-78.

[34] Gooch, pp. 35-57.

[35] Hobbes, *Leviathan,* pp. 26-27.

[36] *Ibid.* pp. 28-31.

[37] *Ibid.,* pp. 22, 29-30, 275.

[38] " All men are agreed that there is no higher science than that of government." So wrote Boulainvilliers near the end of the reign of Louis XIV. He continues: " As it is nearly impossible that the practice of the Government can succeed to one who exercises it without rules and without theory, it is necessary to conclude therefrom that there is no science which ought to be more assiduously and thoroughly cultivated . . . by the citizens." See his " Preface " to *Historie de l'ancien gouvernement,* I. The context of the passage containing the expression seems to justify the interpretation of Henri Sée that he was using the term " science " in its narrow sense. But Sée's further assumption, that Boulainvilliers was a precursor in this respect, is not borne out by the facts. See Sée, pp. 281-285.

tury; and, as it had not yet acquired its modern coloration, whenever used, it must be invariably scrutinized in the light of its context to ascertain its true application. Three examples, widely separated in time and by the training and character of the persons represented, will provide some idea of the change in the connotation of the word in its application to political theory. Pierre d'Avity (1614) applied a traditional sense when he wrote of the " science " of " politics " which he classified as a branch of morals, itself a part of *practical science* as distinguished from the *speculative sciences* of physics, mathematics, and metaphysics.[39] The priest, Jean Francois Senault (1661), appears to have gone a little beyond d'Avity in specializing the meaning of the word. He too dealt with the " science " of " politics " ; while he associated it on equal terms with morals, geography, and history, he was careful to separate these from the liberal arts of painting, music, and astrology.[40] Benedict Spinoza (*ca.* 1677), however, was using a much narrower interpretation when describing himself as treating the " science " of " politics " with the detachment of " mathematics." [41]

Much more common was the use of the word " art," or as Claude Joly (1652) in his enthusiasm termed it, the " art of arts," [42] in writing of the government of a state. Michel Levassor, in his *Soupirs de la France esclave* (*ca.* 1689), did not

[39] D'Avity, " Avant-propos," *Les estats du monde.* His scheme of the sciences appears graphically thus:

SCIENCE
I

SPECULATIVE	PRACTICAL
Physics—Medicine	Morals—Ethics, Economics, Politics
Math.—Arith., Geo., Music, Astrology	Dialectics
Metaphysics—Theology, Canon Law	Memory
	Grammar
	Rhetoric
	Poetry
	History
	Science of the World

[40] J. F. Senault, *Le monarque, ou les devoirs du souverain* (Paris, 1661), pp. 212-218, 219. This seems to be the approximate position of Saint-Evremond in his letter to Monsieur (1662), *Letters of Saint Evremond*, pp. 35-36.

[41] Benedict de Spinoza, " Tractatus politicus," in *The Chief works of Spinoza*, translated from the Latin by R. H. M. Elwes (2 vols., London, 1883-1884), I, 288.

[42] Joly, pp. 1-2.

apply the term "science" to the government in general but wrote, rather, of the "science" of taxation and finances in France which had become so complex that one must be very able to speak pertinently thereon.[43]

Whatever the terms used, among political thinkers, the tendency had long been evident by the time of Spinoza to treat of, or seek for, a science of government which would be useful in predicting or explaining the activity of the mechanism to which Hobbes applied the description: *Non est potestas super terram quae comparetur ei.*[44] The procedure of political reasoning to which Spinoza gave the name of "science" in 1677 had been described almost literally by Grotius, in 1625, as his own.[45] John Eon, in a passage of his remarkable treatise entitled *Le commerce honorable* (1646), pointed out clearly the presumed connection between the discipline of the political thinker and the science of mathematics:

It is with Political reasoning as with mathematical demonstrations. The latter emphasize the truth of their subject by the description of points, lines, angles, triangles and other figures circular or polygon, which they present to our eyes; and the former sets forth its truths all the more clearly, when they are founded on experience and on the most general induction from examples and specific circumstances of their subject.[46]

It would be useless to argue that the attempt, even by the most searching rationalists of political theory, to adapt the method of speculative mathematics to their field was anything but a brilliant failure. The attempt was made, however, and it reflected the conscious conviction in the science of that period that the answer of all problems lay somewhere revealed in the bosom of reason and numbers. In retrospective analysis, Fontenelle well observed that the sciences had become a "kind of theology" in the Age for which Descartes had set the tone.[47]

[43] Levassor, pp. 13-14.

[44] The motto taken from *Job* and placed above the head of the figure of the Leviathan in the frontispiece of the original edition.

[45] Grotius, *Belli ac pacis,* p. 30; Spinoza, "Tractatus politicus," *Works,* I, 288.

[46] Jean Eon, *Le commerce honorable ou considerations politiques sur l'estat du commerce de France* (Nantes, 1646), p. 28.

[47] B. le B. de Fontenelle, "Préface de l'histoire de l'acadèmie des sciences, depuis 1666 jusqu'en 1699," and "Préface sur l'utilité des mathématiques et de la physique et sur les travaux de l'académie des sciences," *Oeuvres de,* I, 1-18, 47-60, 54-56.

The sovereign authority engendered by this science of politics in the seventeenth century was both the product of reason and its instrument. It was true that laws of nature, of God, or of nations might be cited, and often were, as giving support to the sovereign, but, in general, no competing allegiance was permitted to stand above the rational will of the state. A person like Bossuet might technically subject his King to God but he, nevertheless, recognized no earthly limitation within the state to royal policy. In politics, as in contemporary science, the strength of tradition demanded the external recognition of the agency of God, but in politics, as in science, this agency was conveniently excluded from the physical aspects of society or nature. In effect, the justification of the state was divorced from a tradition which was fundamentally a limitation on its authority. Instead, a secular basis of its rights was discovered in expediency and explained as reason.

The King, in France, was elevated to the status of a living materialization of a sovereign reason, the symbol of the directive intelligence of politics. The relative wisdom of this sovereign would determine the relative fortune of the state. Seen in the light of the prevailing philosophical concept of his status in the rational state, the all-pervasive power of Louis XIV gave pointed cogency to the remark of a subject that " In effect the ignorance of a Prince is of so dangerous a consequence, that it is the source of most of the evils and disorders which occur in a state," or to the reciprocal remark that knowledge in a Prince was " the cause of its grandeur and its prosperity." [48] Antoine de Montchrétien, addressing himself to the young Louis XIII, in his *Traicté de l'oeconomie politique* (1615), praised the art of ruling well as " the most grand and glorious in the world. To be a King is to be all; to know well his craft, is to know all." [49]

Pascal's pronouncement that the " power of kings is founded on reason and on the folly of the people " [50] seems literally applicable to the political views of Richelieu. The Cardinal, in

[48] Joly, p. 3.
[49] Antoine de Montchrétien, *Traicté de l'oeconomie politique*, dedicated in 1615 to the King and Queen-Mother, edited by T. Funck-Brentano with an extensive " Introduction " (Paris, 1889), p. 337.
[50] Pascal, pp. 114-115.

his *Testament politique* (*ca.* 1642), created a grand argument for his ministry in which future plans and past deeds were explained or justified in the "light" of reason. The distinction which he claimed for the reign of Louis XIII, over others, was that great designs had been carried to the logical conclusions which reason dictated.[51] The policy and form of the state, according to him, were established as a consequence of man's natural reaction to practical considerations. "Natural intelligence informs everyone," he wrote, "that man having been created reasonable, ought to do nothing except by reason, since otherwise he would act against reason, and consequently against himself who is the author of it." Therefore, he concluded that man, being sovereignly reasonable, should subject himself to the reign of reason. A prince guided by reason would be loved and obeyed since "Authority constrains obedience but reason persuades one to it." The end of reason in the state was that subjection "so necessary" to its maintenance.[52]

Spinoza, frequently associated by seventeenth-century thinkers with Hobbes, was clearly influenced by him, but his most frequently tapped sources of inspiration were Descartes and the writings of the Hebrews. He was known to be a complete master of Cartesianism and was the author, in 1663, of the *Principles of Cartesianism geometrically demonstrated.*[53] His political treatises, the *Tractatus theologico-politicus* (1670), and the *Tractatus politicus* (left incomplete at his death in 1677), proposed reason as the foundation of the rights of supreme authority and the bulwark of the law. He made it the creator and limitation of sovereignty. The need for security led men to choose to live by reason and thus to form the state. Supreme authority represented the "mind of the dominion" and was incapable of wrong-doing except as it offended reason; an action which would tend to destroy it.[54] Bossuet, the primary apologist for the reign of Louis XIV, presumed to discover the justification for that government in the Scriptures.

[51] Richelieu, *Testament politique,* II, 9-10.
[52] *Ibid.,* pp. 6-8.
[53] Elwes, "Introduction" to Spinoza, *Works of Spinoza,* I.
[54] Spinoza, "Tractatus theologico-politicus," "Tractatus politicus," *ibid.,* pp. 200-206, 302-311.

The *Politique tirée des propres paroles de l'Escriture Sainte* (*ca.* 1670) is but another illustration of the adaptability of the word of God when conveyed through the medium of a dialectician of parts. In conformity with the practice of the day, he looked upon the royal authority and government as the product of reason and intelligence. In the prince resided the " reason which directs the State " [55] which, if he used it as he should, would render his dominion stable and his subjects fortunate. Princes, therefore, must particularly study to develop the wisdom which God bestowed only on those seeking it. Such studies should be directed towards affairs useful to life without attention to idle curiosa.[56]

III

Political thought in the seventeenth century had not only borrowed the instruments and attitudes of contemporary science and rationalism and affected some of the properties of an exact discipline; it was united to them by its utilitarian purpose. Indeed it was the stress on utility which marked more clearly than any other aspect of political science the union of science, rationalism, and politics in the nascent discipline of political economy. Science and politics ordinarily reflected the needs of two forces—the state and enterprise—married in the system called mercantilism.

An extreme view along such lines is taken by B. Hessen in his " Social and economic roots of Newton's Principia." However, his interest is directed specifically towards research into causation in natural science. In this regard he writes: " The new method of research which in the persons of Bacon, Descartes and Newton, gained the victory over scholastics and led

[55] Bossuet, *Politique tirée des propres paroles de l'Ecriture Sainte a Monseigneur le Dauphin* (3 vols., Turin, 1824-1825), II, p. 3; see Sée, pp. 145-181.

[56] Bossuet, I, 217-239. The Dauphin under his preceptor Bossuet and, later, the Duke of Burgundy, under Fenelon, were submitted to a rigorous educational program including mathematics, physics, astronomy, mechanics, philosophy, comparative history and politics, military art and science. The Dauphin appears to have derived little profit from the experience but Burgundy was the eventual delight of his teacher and the hope of reform elements. See Bossuet's letter to Innocent XI (1679), *Correspondance de Bossuet,* ed. C. Urbain and E. Levesque (15 vols., Paris, 1909-1925), II, 135-161; H. Druon, *Histoire de l'éducation des princes dans la maison des Bourbons de France* (2 vols., Paris, 1897), I, 217-357, II, 3-147.

to the creation of a new science, was the result of the victory of the new methods of production over feudalism."[57] In explanation and support, he presents a careful analysis of most of the problems which occupied the attention of that science and establishes, in this writer's opinion, a definite relationship between these problems and the requirements of the economic system. "If we compare this basic series of themes with the physical problems which we found when analyzing the technical demands of transport, means of communication, industry and war, it becomes quite clear," he concludes, "that these problems of physics were fundamentally determined by these demands."[58] G. N. Clark, in his *Science and social welfare in the age of Newton,* offers an extensive rebuttal to Hessen's thesis. This consists, primarily, in a determined denial of the justice of the emphasis that Hessen places on the economic aspect and in indicating additional influences.[59] These additions are properly advanced but the central assumptions of Hessen remain of paramount importance.

Political economy, as a discipline, unquestionably had its beginnings in a response to the technical requirements of a state allied with business interests. It was the spirit of mercantilism that gave to political economy its name. In the seventeenth century the term "political economy" was significantly appropriate. Before Locke, the political notion of the natural rights of men had not developed to the point where the interests of the individual were recognized as distinct from the state, and hence the economic problems and capacities of the people were intimately related by political scientists to those of the Leviathan.[60] It was certainly no accident that Montchré-

[57] Hessen, "The social and economic roots of Newton's Principia," *Science at the cross roads,* p. 62. In this article Hessen, a Soviet scholar, applies the method of dialectical materialism to the interpretation of Newton's theories. A more specific indication of his thesis is contained in the following quotation: "The brilliant successes of natural science during the sixteenth and seventeenth centuries were conditioned by the disintegration of the feudal economy, the development of merchant capital, of international relationships and of heavy (mining) industry," (p. 5).

[58] *Ibid.,* p. 16, *passim.*

[59] Clark, pp. 60-91. These other influences are: medicine (as in optics), the arts (as illustrated by music), religion (associated with the search for the key to the universe), beauty (the detached association of truth or knowing with beauty).

[60] The frontispiece of the original edition of Hobbes *Leviathan* is a striking, if

tien used the phrase " political economy " in the title of his *Traicté* of 1615 and it seems, besides, to have been in current usage to designate the relationship of the state with the livelihood of men.[61] If the economic concepts of Bodin, Bacon, Hobbes, Bossuet, or Boulainvilliers are divorced from their political works, these are incomplete. Reciprocally, the economics of Montchrétien, John Eon or Vauban are meaningless when separated from politics. The influence of business and national needs made the prejudices of mercantilism a pervasive atmosphere in nearly all political treatises of importance.

The *De rege et regis institutione* of the Spaniard Mariana is the work of an ardent advocate of a policy of economic paternalism for governments. In his writings the state was encouraged to do all in its power to foster the national prosperity.[62]. In England, Francis Bacon, in his " Essay on seditions and troubles," saw the best security of governments as derived from an attack on poverty. This could be directed by striving for a " well-balancing " of trade, by encouraging manufactures, by the banishment of idleness, the repression of waste through sumptuary legislation, the maintenance of a proper proportion between the productive and non-productive members of the commonwealth (that is, nobles and non-nobles), and the capturing of foreign profits.[63] Later, Hobbes invented his sovereign, not as an intellectual exercise but from utilitarian motives. He tells us that protection or safety is the purpose of the Leviathan. But to what end? By " safety here, is not meant a bare Preservation, but also all other Contentments of life, which every man by lawful Industry, without danger, or hurt to the Commonwealth, shall acquire to himself." [64] The very obedience which he pictures as the first requisite for the

not conclusive, demonstration of this idea. The state is pictured as an artificial colossus in the form of a king, his body composed of the innumerable figures of his subjects.

[61] It is a widespread custom among economists and historical economists to attribute the invention of the phrase to Montchrétien but it appears also in the work of Louis de Mayerne-Turquet, *La monarchie aristodémocratique* (1611), p. 558.

[62] John Laures, *The political economy of Juan de Mariana* (New York, 1928), particularly pp. 83-118.

[63] Bacon, " Essay on seditions and troubles," *Works*, I, 23.

[64] Hobbes, *Leviathan*, p. 261.

maintenance of the sovereign is likewise the key to the prosperity of subjects.[65] Like all mercantilists, he believed that the
riches, power, and honor of the state arose from the riches,
strength and reputation of the subjects. The sovereign could
not be strong if his dependents were poor and weak.[66] Gold
and silver were presented as the measures of wealth and the
blood which circulates through the body of the commonwealth
contributing nourishment to it.[67]

In France, the *République* of Jean Bodin was colored by the
ideas of a young mercantilism. A notable economic section of
his work is that in which is set forth what some have seen as
the original expression of the quantity theory of money.[68]
Montchrétien's *Traicté de l'oeconomie politique* of 1615 was
the most comprehensive exposition of economic doctrines to
have appeared in France up to its time, and it is almost equally
a book dedicated to giving instructions in the art of good government.[69] The airing of economic conceits occupies a substantial portion of the *Testament politique* of Cardinal Richelieu. As Henri Hauser has put it, the popular but " ridiculous
and trivial " formula that " Richelieu had three ends," the
ruin of the Huguenot party, the subjection of the nobles and
the humiliation of the Hapsburgs, ignores a fourth which the
Cardinal himself declares as " to put the State in opulence."
In his ideas he appeared to be a follower, though not a consistent one, of the school of Montchrétien. His own works,
and those inspired by him, frequently reproduce the theories
of the latter, or of others of similar persuasion.[70] During the

---

[65] *Ibid.,* pp. 264-265.

[66] *Ibid.,* pp. 143-144.

[67] *Ibid.,* pp. 194-195.

[68] C. W. Cole, *French mercantilist doctrines before Colbert* (New York, 1931),
pp. 47-57; Bodin, pp. 614-615.

[69] Montchrétien, *Traicté, passim;* see C. W. Cole, *Colbert and a century of
French mercantilism* (2 vols., New York, 1939), I, 83-100; Funck-Brentano's
" Introduction " to the *Traicté,* pp. i-cxvii.

[70] H. Hauser, *La pensée et l'action économiques du Cardinal de Richelieu*
(Paris, 1944), pp. 20-21, 185-187, *passim.* Also on the economics of Richelieu
see Cole, *Colbert,* I, 137-146; Funck-Brentano, in his 1889 edition of the
Traicté of Montchretien, wrote that Richelieu was one of the few contemporaries
who comprehended Montchrétien, " not only the industrial and commercial
measures of the Cardinal, but further the maxims on commerce, the navy,
manufactures which we find in his *Testament* reflect the thought of Montchrétien . . . ," in " Introduction," pp. xx-xxi; G. Viscount D'Avenel has ex-

reign of Louis XIV, Bishop Bossuet pretended no difficulty in extracting from the Bible, in his *Politique tirée des propres paroles de l'Escriture Sainte,* a number of the notions then common to mercantilist thought. Thus he discovered justification for the idea that gold and silver make a state flourishing; that its first source of wealth is trade and navigation; the second, natural resources and production; a third, the spoils from other nations; and, a fourth, from imposts judiciously levied. True wealth was seen to lie in the productivity of the land [71] and large populations. The greatest burden to a state was indolence and indigence.[72] The economic insecurity and decay which characterized France in the last years of the reign of Louis XIV was reflected in the dominant position given to such problems in the political treatises of Boulainvilliers. Near the core of his solutions was the repeated advocacy of a more assiduous shepherding by the state of its economic potentials. " The wealth of the merchants," he wrote, " is the soul of the Monarchy." He was particularly impressed by the importance of national resources, population and productive capacity to the strength and glory of the nation, and, in his work, the state often seems to assume the character of a directive agent in a vast corporate enterprise of member merchants, manufacturers, and farmers.[73]

The absorption by political science of current economic doc-

plained Richelieu's knowledge of taxes by pointing out his considerable experience with the Estates, see *Richelieu et la Monarchie absolue* (4 vols., Paris, 1895), II, 180; Richelieu, *Testament politique,* II, 126-176.

[71] A point suggestive of the physiocratic doctrine of the eighteenth century.

[72] Bossuet, *Politique tirée de l'Ecriture Sainte,* III, 110-132.

[73] Sée, " Boulainvilliers," *Idées politiques,* pp. 271-285; Henri de Boulainvilliers, *Mémoires présentez a monseigneur le duc d'Orleans, Regent de France. Contenant les moyens de rendre ce royaume tréspuissant et d'augmenter considérablement les revenus du Roi et du Peuple* (posthumous) (2 vols., Amsterdam, 1727), I, 16, 19-73; Boulainvilliers, *État de France, dans lequel on voit tout ce qui regardé le gouvernement ecclésiastique, le militaire, la justice, les finances, le commerce, les manufactures, le nombre des habitans, & en général tout ce qui peut faire connoitre à fond cette monarchie* (posthumous) (London, 1737), I, 30-78.

C. J. Friedrich has justly pointed out that the tendency in the twentieth century to advocate a politics of government control and planning for industry on a national scale is not a new philosophy but rather a return to an ideal dominant among the mercantilists. Sully, in France, and Burghley, in England, were, he suggests, the spiritual forefathers of Stalin. " Some thoughts on the politics of government control," *Journal of social philosophy,* I (1936), 122-133.

4

trines and its integration with political economy was an evident response to the pressure of requirements born of the practical relationship of the state and economic activity. Such an aspect was a direct reaction to the stimulus of national business. Another reaction to such conditions is undoubtedly manifest in a generally amoral justification of political institutions and procedures which is inevitably suggestive of the utilitarian attitude of the entrepreneur as expressed in the classic dictum that " business is business." This separation of ethics from the practical was likewise a common trait of current political science and natural science.

In the sixteenth century Machiavelli had implied, in the *Prince,* the existence of a sharp distinction between morals and the conduct of a state. It has been common among his disciples to erect the " Reason of State " into an ideal although it is possible that he himself did not so regard it.[74] J. N. Figgis has said of him, " it was not monarchy but efficiency " for which he cared.[75] In France, the victory of the ideas of the *Politiques* had marked the triumph in political reasoning of this secular attitude. Bodin's great treatise elevated into the rank of theory the division between ethics and politics which Machiavelli had apparently taken for granted. A similarly materialistic and amoral approach distinguished the political theory of the seventeenth century. The state was pictured as a rational and secular creation designed to meet men's economic needs and to control his irrational, individually confused and destructive nature. Utility and the practical dominated everything and man's personal rights, the moral prescriptions of religion and social ethics were usually ignored or else subordinated to the overpowering and impersonal order derived from the governance of the reason of the state.

Richelieu, for instance, in treating of the position of the people in the state, in a famous analogy, placed them in the situation of a mule which being relieved for a time of its customary burdens resists when needed. Order was essential to the state but impossible to maintain without obedience. The people would not be obedient unless constantly reminded that

---

[74] Figgis, " Luther and Machiavelli," *Gerson to Grotius,* pp. 81-95.
[75] *Ibid.,* p. 82.

they must be. A tax was, therefore, a necessary badge of sub-servience.[76] At about the same time, the Duke of Rohan, in his *Maximes des princes* (1638), gave an entirely pragmatical exposition of the methods useful to the princes of Europe in conducting their politics of survival. To him the international policy of states appeared a matter of arithmetic and, as such, should be divorced from morals. Religions or religious differences, to illustrate, should be given no account in determining alliances or selecting foes but only the hidden designs which religion frequently served to obscure.[77] In England, Hobbes reduced justice to the equation of power in a theory in which neither justice nor injustice existed before the creation of law.[78] In Holland, Spinoza denied the sanctity of treaties between nations. Treaties were but contracts representing an exchange of utility and when a condition proposed became harmful to either of the parties the contract was void.[79]

The characteristics of the seventeenth-century state ideal thus far listed—its rational origins, its useful purpose, its impersonal spirit—suggest the elements of a machine and, indeed, the state which generally emerged in the political treatises was, above all else, an orderly machine. The mechanical universe of science was reflected in the mechanical state. As nature could be controlled and understood by the knowledge of the mechanical principles which governed it, so the state would be understood and efficiently conducted by the knowledge of the mechanical principles which governed society. In the state,

[76] Richelieu, *Testament politique*, I, 225-227. He believed that common sense would set limits.

[77] Henri, Duke of Rohan, *Traitté de l'intérêt des princes. Intérêts et maximes des princes & des éstats souverains* (Cologne, 1666) 2d part, pp. 27, 58, 78-79. The editor of this edition, the original having been in 1638, is anonymous. He claims that the work of Rohan was much less extensive and that he, the editor, has added to it but proceeding along the lines and thoughts of the originator.

[78] The only natural rights left to man under the Leviathan consisted in not being bound to destroy himself, accuse himself, or abstain from self preservation. (*Leviathan,* pp. 91-121.) Sir William Petty probably represents an extreme in the expression of an amoral discipline. Any means employed by government to increase national wealth was justified. For instance, in regard to a forced transportation of the Irish population, the question to be considered was not comfort or humanity but "whether the benefit expected from this transplantation, will exceed Seventeen Millions?" Sir William Petty, *Political arithmetic* (1690), in C. H. Hull, *The economic writings of Sir William Petty* (2 vols., Cambridge, Eng., 1899), I, lxii, 285-288.

[79] Spinoza, "Tractatus politicus," *Works,* I, 306-308.

as in science, therefore, there was an emphasis on order and on system. The attempt of the scientist to reduce the principles of mechanical nature to workable formulae or laws for the improvement of man's fortune was paralleled by the attempt of statesmen to reduce the principles of political wisdom to codes and *règlements* which imposed order on every possible social activity considered relevant to the general good of the state.

An ancient tradition was the depiction of the state as a body,[80] and the image of the Leviathan might seem literally to be derived therefrom. But the Colossus of Hobbes, with its blood of metal, conceived by reason and preserved by power, seems endowed with no human quality except form. It is a machine in the mold of man. A mechanistic concept of the state was implicit in the *Politica methodica digesta* of Johannes Althusius as is suggested by his often quoted statement: *Quod Deus est in mundo, lex est in societate.*[81] Even the company of the *précieux* included Georges de Scudéry (1601-1667) who wrote of the government as "this great machine."[82] In 1667, a defender of Spain against France pictured the Hapsburg kingdom as too great a "machine" to be easily shaken and hence well designed for defense but too vast and complicated to operate effectively in offense.[83] Another foreigner, looking at the government of France during the ministry of its finances by the mediocre Le Pelletier (1683-1688), concluded that the

[80] Guillaume de la Perrière in his *Le miroir politique contenant divers manières de gouverner et policer les républiques* (Paris, 1567) wrote in one place of a machine administered by God, but his usual metaphor was the body.

[81] Johannes Althusius, *Politica methodica digesta,* ed. by C. J. Friedrich from the 3d edition of 1614 (Cambridge, 1932), "Introduction" by Friedrich, p. lxviii; the most comprehensive work on Althusius is probably that of O. F. Gierke, *The development of political theory,* trans. by B. Freyd (New York, 1939).

[82] Scudéry was one of the better known literary figures of his day in France. *Discours politiques des rois* (Paris, 1663), p. 5. The first edition appeared in 1648. The anonymous writer of the "Lettre d'avis a Messieurs du Parlement de Paris, escrite par un Provincial" (March 4, 1649) saw the members of the Parlement of Paris as the "first springs" which given motion to all the Province by the balance of your judgments," in Moreau, *Mazarinades,* I, 362.

[83] F. P., Baron de Lisola, *Bouclier d'état et de justice contre le desseing manifestement decouvert de la monarchie universelle* (2d ed., 1667), p. 323. He was attacking the *Maximes des princes* (1638) of the Duke of Rohan who had similarly described Spain (pp. 83-84).

department of the minister was " such a great machine composed of so many wheels which for the most part are unknown
to him " that he was incapable of properly administering it.[84]

Reliance on the ethics of utility and the adoption of the
mechanical concept of the state were but two aspects of political expression which suggest the outlook of the enterpriser and
the scientist. To these might be added the idea of a *balance,*
either in power, trade, or property as a determinant of state
structure or policy. The balance is a quality of mechanics or
mathematics most clearly applicable to the quantitative evaluation of a commodity in trade or to the casting of accounts. Just
as the balance of a scale denotes the exchange of equivalents
in value in commerce, so a balance of power was seen by some
to indicate the existence of a beneficial relationship among nations which might exclude the operation of jealousy.[85]

Machiavelli implied the idea of a balance of power as the
goal of international efforts [86] and a century later, in France,
the Duke of Sully disclosed his Great Design which would
establish such equality among the nations of Europe in territory, religion, commerce and political weight that peace would
be assured.[87] Probably the most careful demonstrations made
in the seventeenth century of the functioning of the mechanical
principle of a balance among states were those of the Duke of
Rohan and his pen opponent, the Baron of Lisola. The
Maximes des princes (1638), of the former, argued that the
power of Spain created a disequilibrium in the system of
Europe in answer to which France must play the part of a
counterweight. The *Bouclier d'état* (1667) of the latter agreed
with the doctrine of Rohan but asserted that the apparent preponderance of Spain was a fiction created by the clever propa-

[84] Girolamo Venier, Venetian Ambassador to Louis XIV (1682-1688),
" Relazioni," *Le relazioni dagli Etati Europei lette al Senato dagli ambasciatori
Veneti,* ed. by N. Barozzi and G. Berchet (10 vols., Venice, 1856-1878), seria
II—Francia, III, 450.

[85] Louis XIV, for one, was quite aware of this " natural principle " which
determined foreign policy.

[86] Figgis, *Gerson to Grotius,* p. 85.

[87] M. de B., Duke of Sully, *Mémoires des sages et royales, oeconomies d'estat,
domestiques, politiques et militaires de Henry le Grand,* Vols. II-III, 2d series
of *Nouvelle collections des mémoires pour servir à l'histoire de France, dépuis
le XIIIe siécle jusqu'à fin du XVIII,* ed. by MM. Michaud and Poujoulat (32
vols., Paris, 1835-1839), III, 323-354, 329-330.

ganda of the French. In conclusion he reiterated the proposition of Rohan, and anticipated that of Fenelon at the end of the century, by stating that " their principal interest is to maintain the Balance so equally between these two great Monarchies, that one, whether by Arms or by Negotiation, can never be preponderant, and that in this equilibrium only consists repose and the security of all the rest." [88]

Related to the theory of power balance was another mechanical idea, that of balance of wealth. The wealth of the world was a fairly inflexible quantity some of which was apportioned by trade among the various nations. Such a view led Francis Bacon to observe that among nations " whatsoever is somewhere gotten, is somewhere lost." However, the idea of balance of trade, unlike that of balance of power, was ordinarily urged not as a method of equilibrium but disequilibrium with eventual economic or power balance perhaps implied as a goal. Thus the term of Bacon, the " well " balance of trade becomes in economic parlance the " favorable " balance [89] and the thorn of international relations. John Eon, in his *Le commerce honorable* saw commerce as the universal principle which gave motion to the state and as an example of " political reasoning " gave a statistical exposition of the unfavorable position of France in the trade balance of Europe. By a proper encouragement of foreign trade the state would open up the gates through which had traditionally come the wealth which carried peoples to the " apogee " of power.[90]

A third idea of balance is met with in the *Oceana* (*ca.* 1656) of James Harrington wherein he explained the phenomenon of political revolution as a reaction to a change in the distribution of property. Change in government was a necessary adjustment to an unbalance in property. The first step in establishing

---

[88] Lisola, pp. 320-321, and *passim;* Rohan, *Maximes des princes,* 2d part, pp. 3-27, *passim;* Fenelon, " Examen de conscience sur les devoirs de la royauté," *Écrits et lettres politiques,* ed. by C. Urbain (Paris, 1920), p. 83. Another work showing the influence of Rohan was G. de Courtilz de Sandras, *Nouvelle intérêts des princes l'Europe où l'on traité des Maximes qu'ils doivent observer pour se maintenie dans leurs états . . .* (Cologne, 1685).

[89] For the implicit relationship of balance of trade with balance of power as seen by Bacon, see his " Essay on seditions and troubles " and " Essay on empire " in *Works,* I, 22-24, 26-28.

[90] Jean Eon, *Le commerce honorable,* pp. 28-43; Cole, *Colbert,* I, 209-226.

a firm empire must be, therefore, the creation of a balanced distribution of property defined by law.[91]

There was yet another opinion admired by the seventeenth-century political scientist which acquires additional interest when viewed in the light of its environment. The Aristotelian [92] thesis that climate is the essential determinant of character was revived and elaborated. In the late sixteenth century Jean Bodin gave an extensive treatment of the idea in the *Six livres de la république* and it has been described as the basic consideration of his whole philosophy of government.[93] Constitutions reflect the character of the citizens who make them, but that character, in turn, is created by climate. This was his reasoning, and Bodin, as usual, claimed it to be original with him.[94] Johannes Althusius, strongly influenced by Bodin in general, repeated the doctrine in his *Politica methodica digesta*.[95] A well-known reiteration occurs in the " Essay upon the original and nature of government " (1672) of Sir William Temple:

> The Nature of Man seems to be the same in all Times and Places, but varied like their Statures, Complexions, and Features, by the Force and Influence of the several Climates where they are born and bred. . . .
> This may be the Cause that some Countries have generally in all Times been used to Forms of Government much of a Sort; the same Nature ever continuing under the same Climate, and making Returns into its old Channels, though sometimes led out of it by Persuasions, and sometimes beaten out by Force.[96]

[91] James Harrington, " Oceana " in *Ideal commonwealths,* ed. by H. Morley, pp. 186-187, 189, 204-205, 261.

[92] Aristotle, *Politics,* Book VII, chap. 7. It also appears in Thomas Aquinas, *On the governance of rulers,* pp. 113-120, and in Pierre Dubois, *De recuperatione terre sancte* (*ca.* 1307), ed. by C. Langlois from MSS in the Vatican (Paris, 1891), pp. 67, 139.

[93] This is the opinion of Allen, *Political thought in the 16th century,* pp. 431-434.

[94] Bodin, *République,* pp. 461-488. Comparison with Aristotle, Aquinas, or Dubois seems to justify the claim, in the main.

[95] Althusius, *Politica methodica digesta,* pp. lxx, 212-213.

[96] Continuing: " Thus the more Northern and Southern Nations (Extremes, as they say, still agreeing) have ever lived under single and arbitrary Dominions; as all the Regions of *Tartary* and *Muscovy* on the one Side, and of *Africa* and *India* on the other: While those under the more temperate Climates, especially in Europe, have ever been used to more moderate Governments, running anciently much into Commonwealths, and of later Ages into Principalities

The reappearance and extension of this ancient idea was scarcely fortuitous. As an expression of a mechanical operation of naturalistic determinism it was appropriate to the rationalistic spirit of the age. The causes of national character were determined by a formula permitting some degree of certainty and predictability. The theory is also applicable to nationalism. Thus, in all cases, the area with the most propitious climate is discovered by the user to be coincident with his own residence. Finally, it is suggestive of certain principles of mercantilism. While useful in glorifying national primacy, it emphasizes international differences. The recognition of such natural distinctions implies the need for trade and the ability of the favored nations to dominate it. John Eon argued, in the *Commerce honorable,* that France was naturally endowed with the essentials of leadership in commerce but Frenchmen were not sufficiently aware of the need to pursue it. A proof of the need lay in the doctrine of climatic determinism:

Commerce is no less necessary and favorable to the diffusion of arts and sciences. Each climate receives its particular influences; these influences communicate divers qualities, and the qualities create divers talents of the mind, and by consequence divers kinds of sciences and industries among men. Some are suited for Philosophy, others for mechanics, others to some arts and particular exercises: the Author of nature distributing thus unequally his gifts and his talents to men, in order to render them reliant on one another, and to oblige them to share what they have in particular.[97]

Reflection in political science of the impact of science and the economic system such as its fusion with political economy, its utilitarian approach to ethics, the popularity of ideas like the balance of property, power and trade and the theory of climate represented more than an incidental borrowing of a language. Political science was designed as a positive method to instruct in the duties and purposes of government, and, in a mercantilistic society, this meant also to reply to the economic needs.

Economists, political scientists or scientists, had such distinctions been justified, would have agreed in seventeenth-

bounded by Laws, which differ less in Nature than in Name." Sir William Temple, "Essay upon the Original and Nature of Government" (1672), in *The Works of Sir William Temple, Bart* (2 vols., London, 1750), I, 95-108.

[97] Eon, p. 135.

century France or England that the state and Enterprise were united by interest. Without commerce, said John Eon, the state is inert.[98] Another writer urged the encouragement of mechanical arts as necessary to a healthy state: " the arts are undoubtedly the lime and cement which join and tie to the edifice of the Republic the portions which are scattered by nature." [99] Richelieu observed that reason prevents a Prince from taxing excessively, or having a disproportionate treasure of gold or silver, as " the wealth of the Prince would in this case be his poverty, since his subjects would have funds neither to undertake commerce nor to pay the taxes which they legitimately owe their Sovereign." [100]

Along with the recognition of the aid of enterprise to the state went the admission of the benefit of the state to enterprise. The minimum return to the taxpayers for his investment was public works, peace, and the protection of property [101] but governments were urged and agreed to positive programs to increase wealth. Bacon advocated the sponsorship of production of raw materials, manufactures and transport of commerce as means of increasing the strength of the state. Of these the last two were the superior methods as the people of the Low Countries had proved having " the best mines above ground in the world." [102] Hobbes desired laws to encourage arts, navigation, agriculture, fishing and all manner of manufactures.[103] Merchants and merchant interest would have an important part in the government visualized by Louis de Mayerne-Turquet.[104] Fenelon, investigating the duties of rulers, believed that the king should know thoroughly the details of commercial, manufacturing and agricultural problems and conduct in order to provide improvements.[105]

The standardization of weights and measures to facilitate long-range commercial transactions, desired by mercantilist writers like the Laffemas,[106] had been previously advanced by

[98] *Ibid.*, pp. 5-6.
[99] Montchretien, *Traicté*, p. 123.
[100] Richelieu, *Testament politique*, II, 151, 126-141.
[101] *Ibid.*, I, 226.
[102] Bacon, " Essay on seditions and troubles," *Works*, I, 23.
[103] Hobbes, *Leviathan*, p. 271.
[104] Mayerne-Turquet, *La monarchie aristodémocratique*, pp. 25, 18, 210-211.
[105] Fenelon, " Examen de conscience," *Écrits*, pp. 35-37, 47-48.
[106] B. de Laffemas, "Le commission, édit et partie des mémoires de l'ordre et

Bodin in the *République*.[107] Vagabondage and idleness, deplored by all mercantilists, were likewise decried by such political philosophers as Montchrétien, Richelieu, Bossuet, Bacon, and Hobbes.[108] The fostering of inventions as one of the main sources of increasing wealth in a state occupied the interest of statesmen,[109] mercantilists [110] and political theorists. In the *New Atlantis* of Bacon, the Hall of Fame housed the statues of great inventors, and the marvel of the land was the museum displaying models of the products of their imagination.[111]

Bossuet relates how Solomon by establishing peace, reducing taxes and making an alliance with Tyre, then the most experienced merchant nation of the world, had enabled his own people to instruct themselves in the " secrets " of commerce and thus prepare to assume an important role in the economic sphere.[112] In his usual tortuous way the renowned churchman was using the Bible to demonstrate the ethics of a political response to business need. That technical education is necessary to enterprise, and that the state should encourage it, was a platitude of mercantilism. Other political writers were more explicit. In the Utopias of More, Campanella, and Harrington, the provision of practical education for the multitude in agricultural, mechanical or commercial sciences was among the paramount duties of the government.[113] Louis de Mayerne-

establissement du commerce général des manufactures en ce royaume " (Paris, 1601) in *Documents historiques inédits tirés des collections manuscrites de la bibliothèque nationale*, ed. by M. Champollion-Figeac (4 vols., Paris, 1848) (in Collection des documents inédits de l'histoire de France), IV, xxvii.

[107] Bodin, *République*, p. 170.

[108] Montchrétien called indolence the " fatal scourge of rich and flourishing states," *Traicté*, p. 101; Richelieu, *Testament politique*, II, 149, I, 225-227; Bossuet, *Politique tirée de l'Écriture Sainte*, III, 130-132; Bacon, " Essay on seditions and troubles," *Works*, I, 23; Hobbes, *Leviathan*, p. 271.

[109] See Sully's " Cabinet of affairs of State," *Oeconomies*, III, 290-296.

[110] See I. de Laffemas, " L'histoire du commerce de France " (Paris, 1606) in *Archives curieuses de l'histoire de France depuis Louis XI jusqu'à Louis XVIII*, ed. by L. Cimber, F. Danjou and others (27 vols. Paris, 1834-1840), 1st series, XIV, 414-415; B. de Laffemas, " Recueil présenté au Roy de ce qui se passe en l'assemblée du commerce au palais à Paris " in *Documents historiques inédits*, IV, 285-289, 296, 298-299, 301.

[111] Bacon, " New Atlantis," *Works*, I, 269-270.

[112] Bossuet, *Politique tirée de l'Écriture Sainte*, III, 116-117.

[113] More, " Utopia "; Campanella, " City of the Sun "; Harrington, " Oceana "; in *Ideal commonwealths*, ed. by Morley, pp. 40, 54-55, 144-149, 352-357.

Turquet asserted that the education of the youth of all classes was the first obligation of kingship.[114] He proposed that all peoples in the monarchy be divided into five strata by occupation: the rich, men of letters, business men and merchants, artisans and, finally, laborers. A fundamental law of the realm would require fathers to register their children in these groups and all children should then be commonly schooled for a few years. Gradually they would be segregated in their training to prepare them for the exercise of their special callings.[115] Antoine de Montchrétien projected, in his *Traicté*, the creation of " divers ateliers " scattered through the provinces to nourish an " exact knowledge and the excellent practice of the arts " and to serve as " cradles of artisans." [116] The problem of technical training for the aid of business had become a question of state and was, in consequence, a proper subject to exercise the mind of political scientists. A widening realization of the importance of technical craft in a world of mechanics probably was responsible for a rise in the respectability of its discipline. Bacon urged men of learning to erase their disdain of business and apply their skill to writing books thereon, since only " some few scattered advertisements " existed on its " wisdom." [117]

The idea, common in the seventeenth century, that the state as an entity, was endowed with a kind of synthetic intelligence far superior to the feeble capacities of individuals, has been suggested as the justification of the thorough-going intervention of the government in the concerns of industry. It was partly a reflection of the belief of persons, like Colbert, that the state alone had sufficient perception and power to surmount the difficulties of a naturally irrational enterprise.[118] Such notions did not, however, prevent the advocacy by numbers of persons that the state should adopt more rational methods in the direction of its own affairs.

Criticism was particularly levelled at the notorious mis-

---

[114] Mayerne-Turquet, *La monarchie aristodémocratique*, p. 170.
[115] *Ibid.*, pp. 99-104.
[116] Montchrétien, pp. 27, 38, 101-105.
[117] Bacon, " Advancement of learning," *Works*, I, 229.
[118] P. Boissonade, *Colbert; le triomphe de l'étatisme, la fondation de la suprématie industrielle de la France, la dictature du travail* (1661-1683) (Paris, 1932), p. 3.

management of its finances. The discreet author of the *Secret des finances de France* (1581), masquerading under the name of Froumenteau, presented, in his huge work, what purported to be absolute proof of the most shocking malversation in the handling of national revenues. The financiers were pictured as lock-pickers who had cleaned the treasury and deprived France of its natural fruits.[119] In order to remedy a similar situation in Spain, Juan de Mariana, in 1609, saw as necessary the institution of a strict system of accounting applicable to all royal officials.[120] Simon Stevin (1548-1620), the Dutch mathematician, in his work on "bookkeeping for merchants and for princely governments," published in Amsterdam in 1604, pictured himself as convincing Prince Maurice, in debate, of the merits of applying double-entry bookkeeping to governmental departments. The book was rewritten in 1607 in the form of a letter addressed to the Duke of Sully to acquaint him with the methods successfully practiced by the Hollander.[121] Barthélemy de Laffemas had previously proposed to Henry IV the use of a design requiring the standardization of tax rates and the maintenance of permanent record of tax payments by individuals to assure better accountability.[122]

In the centralized administration of the *Monarchie aristo-démocratique* of Louis de Mayerne-Turquet, finances were to be managed by the smallest number of persons possible, with the officials directly accountable to the crown. Standardized and invariable tax levies were considered desirable, and these were to be collected by royal officers. Accounts of all the revenues would be kept at the capital city.[123] The *Traicté de l'oeconomie*

---

[119] Froumenteau, *Le secret des finances de France* (1581), pp. ii-iii.

[120] In his *De monetae mutatione*, see Laures, *Juan de Mariana*, pp. 219-227.

[121] Sections of this work are reproduced and translated with notes in J. B. Geijbeek, *Ancient double-entry bookkeeping, Lucas Pacioli's Treatise (A.D. 1494—the earliest known writer on bookkeeping) reproduced and translated with reproductions, notes and abstracts from Manzoni, Pietra, Mainardi, Ympyn, Stevin and Dafforne* (Denver, 1914), pp. 11-13, 114-136; see Clark, *Science and social welfare in the age of Newton*, p. 79, note.

[122] He proposed regulating taxes in the elections by a standard of 1 *sol* per *livre* so that the ignorant poor would know their duty and thus avoid litigation due to misunderstanding. The records of all litigation should be preserved for future reference. Tax rolls should be carefully kept in order to check against the assessments of the next year and thus prevent persons from escaping payment. B. de Laffemas, " Recueil présenté au Roy," pp. 294-295.

[123] The administration should center in four departments: justice, arms, finances,

politique of Montchrétien was likewise a plea for more efficient government. The king was urged to keep himself exactly informed by means of accounts of receipts in all generalities of the wealth and revenue of his realm. When he recognized the malpractices of finance he could correct them. By simplifying the accounting system, reducing the number of financiers and liquidating debts, he would transform the science of finances from its status as a conspiracy to defraud the king and people into a serviceable arm of administration.[124] During the Fronde, the obvious flaws in the direction of finances under Mazarin's ministry provided an open sesame for the critics [125] and, near the end of the reign of Louis XIV, the desperate revenue measures countenanced to support the War of Spanish Succession provided new grounds of censorship. In his " *Plans de gouvernement concertés avec le Duc de Chevreuse* " (1711), Fénelon presented a list of reforms which included a request for the application of more thorough accounting to determine the exact relationship between expenditures and revenues.[126]

From a quantitative point of view the ability to make a true assessment of its revenues was, in a sense, to be able to calculate the potential power of the state. Competitive nations,

and domain, police. In each much attention must be given to accounts, registers, and rolls to provide for accountability of ships, officers, fortresses, armies, arsenals, etc. Mayerne-Turquet, *La monarchie aristodémocratique*, pp. 28, 183-188, 197-200.

[124] Montchrétien, pp. 357-359.

[125] See for instance " Catéchisme des partisans, ou resolutions theologiques touchant l'imposition, levée et emploi des finances, dressé par demandes et par réponses, pour plus grande facilité, par le R.P.D.P.D.S.J." (February 14, 1649), in Moreau, *Mazarinades*, I, 277-289; a most curious and contrasting attitude was presented by Fortin de la Hoguette in his *Testament ou conseils fideles d'un bon pere à ses enfans ou sont contenus plusiers raisonnemens Christiens, moraux, & politiques* (Paris, 1661). Therein he included what was represented as being a royal catechism conducted between the young King and his Governor. The King enquired if he should not give attention to the details of his finances where he was certain great abuses existed. The Governor admitted his ignorance in this direction and his dismay over the idea of treating such a complex and intricate problem. The King then admitted the intricacy but noted that the wealth of the financiers indicated their dishonesty. The Governor replied that as a perfumer smells of perfume, so His Majesty should not deem it strange if, money being more viscous still and more adhering than musk, the financiers should have some (pp. 34-36, last section).

[126] Fénelon, " Plans de gouvernement concertés avec le duc de Chevreuse pour etre proposés au duc le Bourgogne " (Nov. 1711), *Écrits et lettres politiques*, pp. 101-102.

like competitive businesses, counted their money assets as their primary armor in rivalry. Probably one of the most overworked aphorisms in political writings was that which declared that "finances are the sinews of war," and Richelieu, for instance, pronounced finances to be the "Nerves of the State" and gold and silver the "Tyrants of the world." [127] It is easy, therefore, to understand the emphasis placed by political theorists on the need of the adoption by governments of accounting techniques to assure the best possible receipt from tax levies. Excessive costs for administration and collection were a substraction from the surplus of power and a dangerous strain on the main sources of wealth—the merchants and common people.

Another suggestion of such a quantitative spirit was displayed in the popular interest in comparative studies of nations. *Les estats, empires, et principautéz du monde* (1614) of Pierre d'Avity had as an object the "pleasant" but "profitable" presentation to the reader of comparative facts and statistics on the habits, housing, sciences, crafts, resources, agriculture, geography, manufactures, produce, religions, and revenues of the countries of the world.[128] A series of such writings followed, one press alone publishing ten editions between 1626 and 1642 including works on Hungary, Italy, the Holy Roman Empire, France, Poland, Scotland, and England.[129] Richelieu and Bossuet wrote of the pertinence to sound government of a knowledge of other nations,[130] and critics of the monarchy as Levassor and, later, Boulainvilliers found justification for their complaints in comparative figures on the revenues of France and other lands.[131] Such comparative enquiries represented, on the whole, a serious attempt to assess the position of the state in relation to other states, and to discover means of improving that position.

---

[127] Richelieu, *Testament politique*, II, 141-142.

[128] D'Avity, "Avant-propos," *Les estats du monde*, also see sections on England, France, the Americas: pp. 2-24, 41-103, 197-251.

[129] The Elzevier Press in the Republica series. H. B. Copinger, *The Elzevier Press, a handlist of the productions of the Elzevier presses at Leyden, Amsterdam, The Hague and Utrecht, with references to Willems, Berghman, Rahr and other bibliographers* (London, 1927); see Clark, *The seventeenth century*, pp. 214-215.

[130] Richelieu, *Testament politique*, I, 267; Bossuet, *Politique tirée de l'Écriture Sainte*, I, 256-259.

[131] Levassor, *Soupirs de la France esclave*, pp. 14-15; Boulainvilliers, *Mémoires presentez a monseigneur le duc d'Orleans*, II, 85-92, 67-72.

In a period of struggle for power the husbanding of resources and the ability to properly evaluate the potentials of a rival were matters of grave concern to the contenders. As the most certain means of indicating distinctions and rendering judgment the value of statistics was increasingly recognized. It is possible that the growing importance of bourgeois elements in the state, both as contributors to its wealth and as administrators of its affairs, suggested the advisability of a more rational and businesslike conduct of politics. The reliance which the merchant had long placed on numbers was reflected in the heightened attention given by political scientists to the use of accounting methods and statistics in the conduct of efficient government. Foreign competition suggested the need for comparative statistics on nations; an intensified interest in commerce for figures on interregional and international flow of commodities; the increasing demand for taxes for a more thorough evaluation of the wealth of the taxpayers and their numbers.

Several political writers advocated the conduct of a census of total population or property. Perhaps the first to do so was Jean Bodin. A census or "estimate of the goods of everyone," he argued, would be a first step towards understanding the problems of finances in a Republic. It seemed difficult to imagine why nations had abandoned a practice which had proved so useful to the Greeks and Romans and other ancients. Among the benefits to be expected of such a census, he listed the reduction of lawsuits by indicating the estate of individuals, the detection and riddance of vagabonds and "vermin," the detection and cure of unjust taxation, the suppression thereby of tax discontent, the discovery of the quality, number and property of persons, of the number of arms bearers and of the subsistence needs of the state.[132] Montchrétien also proposed a state census and reproduced and amplified the arguments of Bodin in its favor. The census would enable the sovereign to have such an exact knowledge of the resources of his realm that he would be able to regulate production, export, import, taxes, labor, colonization, and warfare, and generally operate his kingdom as "a perfect instrument of power and glory."[133]

---

[132] Bodin, *République,* pp. 581-586.
[133] Montchrétien, pp. 344-353.

Fénelon expressed the opinion, in his " Examen de conscience," that a king to know the number of his people need only wish to do so; and though not quite so optimistic, Boulainvilliers thought that a thorough evaluation of the resources of the kingdom would not be difficult.[134] By the time these men wrote, much effort had already been expended by the state towards such ends. The Duke of Saint-Simon clearly thought too much had been done. In an anonymous letter to the King in 1712 he complained that while he recognized that the progressive increase in the tax needs required some investigation of the property and numbers of people, he felt it had been carried to extremes by forcing the revelation of the most " important secrets of families," and he cited the displeasure of God over David's taking a census of Israel.[135]

The census desired by the political scientists did not consist of a simple enumeration of population. It called, instead, for a searching statistical presentation of the wealth and potentialities of a mechanical state. Such demands embodied an implicit tribute to the directive force of a sovereign power operated by reason. The political thought which contained such notions had itself reacted to the materialistic rationalism of the time by presenting aspects of a scientific discipline. The mechanical and geometric spirit glorified by Descartes as " Reason " seemed to supply the needs of the most various studies and crafts. As Fontenelle remarked: " The geometric spirit is not so attached to geometry that it cannot be withdrawn and transported to other knowledges. A work of morals, of politics, of criticism, perhaps even of eloquence, will be improved, all things being equal, if guided by geometry." [136]   The foremost political thinkers of the period, men such as Bodin, Althusius, Grotius, and Hobbes, consciously strove to apply the rational control of this geometric spirit to the formulation of a systematic science of politics. Not only did the work of political theorists ordinarily share the prejudices of seventeenth-century science in regard to tradition, method and language but also in its purpose. The principle of utility which dominated and united

---

[134] Fenelon, " Examen de conscience," *Écrits*, pp. 35-37; Boulainvilliers, *Mémoires presentez a monseigneur le duc d'Orleans*, I, 103-104.

[135] Saint-Simon, " Lettre anonyme au Roi," pp. 50-51.

[136] Fontenelle, " Preface sur l'utilité des mathématiques," *Oeuvres*, I, 54.

mathematics, mechanics, philosophy, or physics was mirrored in a political science which was usually political economy as well. As such, it defended current economic dogma and conceived of a rational state which was regularly endowed with the impersonal qualities of an efficient machine ready to service the wants of enterprise joined to those of the nation. Divorced from sentiments of divinity, it provided the formula for national wealth and its reciprocal, power; for the state of reason and order which answered the tastes of a Colbert or Louis XIV. Such was the climate of political opinion when Louis XIV brought about his political reforms. Had he desired to rule after the examples of his forefathers, he would have defied the political and intellectual currents of his time.

CHAPTER III

THE PRECURSORS

Political circumstances, combined with the personalities of men of vast initiative, effected in France, in a brief space of about twenty years, fundamental changes in the constitutional structure[1] and in the methods of conducting the state. Inseparable from these changes, symptomatic of them, was the emergence into distinguishable focus of the spirit of scientific and rational government. Certainly, as we have seen, the spirit was not new. Theorists and statesmen had applauded it in their writings, but only after 1661 was the cooperation with government of science and the methods of science, that is to say of mechanical and technical procedures associated with science such as statistics, surveys and administrative archives, a clearly defined and patently indispensable part of efficient administration. Even so, in practical politics, as in theory, to picture the first twenty years of Louis XIV's personal reign as a period of pure innovation in the processes of political management would be to create a conception divorced from reality. In his completed structure there were many new elements but there were, as has been remarked, more old ones, and perhaps very little indeed that had not been hoped for in the past and less that had not been thought of.

In writing of the development of the scientific and political attitudes characterizing seventeenth-century thought, we have, up to this point, considered, along with the works of Frenchmen, the works of foreigners. This is justified by the fact that most of the intellectual leaders were associated by their membership in an invisible college which transcended national boundaries. Therefore, while the sum of their thought, at any particular time, might have a peculiarly Italian, French, or English orientation, it represented, broadly viewed, a pervasive

[1] For a discussion of whether France had a constitution under the *ancien régime,* see J. B. Brissaud, *A history of French public law,* translated from the French by J. W. Garner (Boston, 1915), pp. 330-345. On this subject also see P. R. Doolin, *The Fronde,* pp. 58-164.

intellectual atmosphere simultaneously shared and contributed to by the thinkers of Western Europe generally.

Turning to the consideration of the more practical political or administrative antecedents of the rational government of Louis XIV, it is clear that developments in the administrative practices of foreign governments had also their influence. The relative importance of such contributions would be impossible to assess, but it is significant that there were other governments which employed, at a much earlier date, and in varying degrees, many of the procedures characteristic of the rational administration of Louis XIV. In particular one can cite the development in Renaissance Italy of what Burckhardt has termed " the state as a work of art." In Italy there originated, for modern times, according to Burckhardt, a state which was the outcome of reflection and calculation; a rational state in which prince or oligarchy pursued a deliberate policy of the adaptation of means to an end. There despots and sovereign cliques, within the city states, constructed more centralized and rational judicial, political, and financial systems and, for the first time recognized and utilized the science of statistics in government.[2]

In France itself, the first half of the seventeenth century prepared for the development of the government in the second in at least three respects. In the first place, the pragmatical philosophy, associated with Descartes, had achieved the dominion of the mind or excused the inclinations of men bent on change. Traditions and even God were submitted to the measurements of reason. The penetrating influence of rational doubt was leading the followers of all professions, that of government not excluded, to re-examine and re-evaluate the supposed facts of their craft. Under such conditions Louis XIV would probably have considered it a derogation of his glory to have retained intact the " gothic " and irrational structure of the old state. Secondly, and against such an environment, one must place the rather startling fact that, after the reign of Henry IV, there was an apparently progressive deterioration in the financial administration of the state which widely advertised the need for more efficient techniques of control; for the introduction of rational methods of business into the direction

[2] Jacob Burckhardt, *The civilization of the Renaissance in Italy*, translated by S. G. C. Middlemore (Vienna, 1937), pp. 1-69.

of fiscal affairs. Finally, the first half of the century witnessed the solidification of the institution of the intendants which, whatever its original purpose, was to be the foundation of a regime of inquiry.

I

To select this half century in which to discover, in France, the practical anticipations and demands for the kind of government given by Louis XIV, after 1661, is, of course, to do arbitrary violence to history. From one point of view it appears to be, in fact, an inadmissible procedure. It would be necessary to go far behind the seventeenth century to find a time, if indeed such a time existed, when some element of the quantitative rationalism, commonly associated with business and science, was not an essential emphasis in the working government.

This is most strikingly true in the administration of finances. As one statistician has said: " The domain of finances is essentially the domain of figures and, consequently, that of statistics." He continues to point out that " in every organized society . . . there is . . . a subject which it is impossible to avoid measuring numerically, that is, financial facts, the total of receipts and expenses which are inseparable from the very existence of the state, however modest their character." [3] He is, however, in agreement with the historian of the ancient French finances, Vuitry, that the old monarchy never employed true budgets and that neither receipts nor expenditures " were yet of such a nature that they could be seriously assessed in order to be as a consequence checked by the government." [4]

From the reign of Charles VII the *taille* was a permanently established royal impost levied without the renewed consent of the Estates-General.[5] An examination of the royal tax

[3] F. Faure, " The development and progress of statistics in France," in J. Koren, ed., *The history of statistics* (New York, 1918), p. 224.

[4] *Ibid.*, p. 225, citing and quoting from A. Vuitry, *Études sur le régime financier de la France avant 1789* (3 vols., Paris, 1878-1883), II, part i, 303.

[5] For the history of taxation under the monarchy before 1789 see the following: Vuitry in his three volumes of the *Études sur le régime financier* traces the financial history only to 1380. There is an interesting summary account however in the " Introduction " to volume I, i-x; for a general guide to the study of French finances see R. Stourm, *Bibliographie historique des finances de*

ordonnances from this time reveals an ever more exacting specification of procedures in the maintenance of accounts and records of the tax receipt and expenditure of the income therefrom. As early ·as 1444, the purpose of these specifications is clearly set forth in the *Lettres sur le governement des finances* issued five years after the definite establishment of the permanent *taille*. The King therein prescribed rules for his treasury and the accountability of his revenues, in order to provide a " more clear notion than we have had formerly of all the expenditures " from the treasury.[6] An *édit* of Francis I, in the year 1523, provided for the use of two registers, each page being signed by a treasury secretary. The first register was designated for receipts to be signed by the receiver and the payor; the second was to note restitutions. Whatever the utility of the device, the declared intention was that " we can see or have seen in our council the funds and state of our finances, whenever it may please us." [7] The need for efficient accounting was more emphatically expressed in an *édit* of a few years later. There is a strong note of urgency in the expressed desire " to bring to light all our ordinary and extraordinary revenues . . . to have prompt and certain knowledge of receipts and expenditures: to eliminate the means of receivers general and particular, accountants and clerks to avail themselves of deceits, procrastinations, delays. . . ." [8]

Ordonnances, édits, règlements and *lettres* governing the collection and administration of royal revenues, succeeding each other, showed an increasing complexity in the decreed machinery of finances and a continuous effort to improve the position of the central authority in the control of its monies:

---

la France au XVIII'eme siècle (Paris, 1895). While this deals primarily with the eighteenth century a number of works cited therein extend into periods before and after. On the *taille*, specifically, see M. Marion, *Histoire financière de la France depuis 1715* (5 vols., Paris, 1914-1931), I, 1-10; A. Esmein, *Cours élémentaire d'histoire du droit française a l'usage des étudiants de première année* (Paris, 1930), pp. 528-567; Brissaud, *A history of French public law*, pp. 445-448; J. J. Clamageran, *Histoire de l'impôt en France* (3 vols., Paris, 1867-1876), II.

[6] Isambert, IX, 120-123.

[7] " Édit portant réglement sur l'administration des finances," December 1523, *ibid.,* XII, part i, 222-228.

[8] " Édit portant réglement sur les finances," December 1542, *ibid.,* part ii, 796-805.

Nearly all decrees lamented the ineffectual application of past regulations, provided additions or improvements and reiterated the frustrated desire of the kings to keep track of the state of their finances. From these decrees, during more than two hundred years, gradually emerged the essential structure and processes of the revenue system of the *ancien régime*—the parishes, elections, generalities, courts of accountability, *élus*, receivers, farmers-general, intendants, *maîtres de requêtes*, and the numerous other officials and agencies created and fitted into the sprawling organism of state finance. From the top to the bottom, from the royal *conseil des finances* to the village curé, ledgers, roles, balance sheets, inspections and reinspections were provided to assure proper and honest administration.[9]

To one who assigns himself the tedious, if enlightening, task of perusing these *ordonnances,* the first reaction will probably be to admire the apparent thoroughness of the machinery created for obtaining strict accountability in the collection and handling of tax funds. It is, therefore, proportionately surprising to note the recurrent admission, in the laws themselves, that the system functioned inefficiently. In the seventeenth century, Henry IV and Sully, Richelieu, Mazarin, Louis XIV and Colbert unanimously deplored the corruptions which they considered practically inherent to financial administration. Only Sully and Henry and Louis XIV and Colbert succeeded in applying any remedies beyond the complaining and planning stages.

II

Sully's solution to the administration of royal finances, was, from one point of view, simplicity itself. He, in effect, proposed to handle them personally as far as that was humanly possible. He made no major innovations; rather, he contented himself with utilizing to the best possible advantage the system he had found in operation, with making the best of a bad fiscal system " by force of order and energy." [10] Precisely because of the personal character of his government of the

[9] The above is based on a perusal of finance *Ordonnances* found in Isambert, IX-XVIII, covering the reign of Charles VII and extending into the early years of the reign of Louis XIV.

[10] G. Pagès, *La monarchie d'ancien régime* (Paris, 1928), pp. 42-43.

finances, historians have had to rely heavily on the memoirs of Sully to study that administration. C. W. Cole very justly, and anyone who has read them must agree, classifies them as " among the most curious and aggravatingly informative books ever written."[11] But whatever the obvious exaggeration of his role in this work, as Hauser and others have suggested, it is necessary to admit that that role was very large in truth;[12] that Sully actually enjoyed a great share of the confidence of Henry IV and that his " clearest title to glory " belongs to his functions as " financier, *grand-voyer*, restorer of agriculture." It is in these fields, indeed, that his critics have found that he has written " generally the truth."[13]

Sully, in his memoirs, drew a clear portrait of himself as a completely unpleasant individual who scarcely trusted the capacities or the intentions of anyone—with the notable exception of Henry IV—and consequently saw himself forced to

[11] Cole, *Colbert*, I, 41.

[12] The official titles of Sully are listed in P. Viollet, *Le roi et ses ministres pendant les trois derniers siècles de la Monarchie* (Paris, 1912), p. 168 as follows: " conseiller d'État, surintendant des finances, grand-voyer, grand maître de l'artillerie, surintendant des bâtiments et des fortifications, grand maître des ports et hâvres, captaine héréditaire des eaux et rivières, était une manière de vice-roi: il présidait les Conseils en l'absence de Henri IV." See also p. 219. For a detailed discussion of his offices and their functions see F. de Mallevoue, *Les actes de Sully passés au nom du roi de 1600 à 1610 par devant Me Simon Fournier* (Paris, 1911), pp. xxviii-lix.

[13] H. Hauser, *Henri IV (1589-1610)*, Vol. IV of *Les sources de l'histoire de France XVIe siècle (1496-1610)* (4 vols., Paris, 1906-1915), pp. 24-30. For further observations on the reliability of the *Oeconomies* in the same work, see pp. 8-9, 18-20, 76; de Mallevoue, *Les actes de Sully* provides substantiation for much of the *Oeconomies* by comparison of assertions made there with acts. See especially his " Introduction," pp. lv-lxxi. He concludes that " they remain, in their original form the best source to consult for the history of the reign of Henry IV," p. lxxi, see also p. xvi; a voluminous and controversial literature exists on this subject, see: H. Carré, " Sully historien, Les economies royales," *Sully sa vie et son oeuvre (1559-1641)* (Paris, 1932), pp. 375-387; C. Pfister, "Les economies Royales de Sully et le grand dessein de Henry IV," *Revue historique*, LIV (1894) 300 ff.; LV (1894), 67 ff.; LVI (1894), 33 ff.; 304 ff. deals more extensively with this problem. Other studies mentioned by Pfister include: M. Perrens "Mémoire critique sur l'auteur et la composition des Oeconomies royales," *Séances et travaux de l'académie des sciences morales et politiques* (1871), pp. 119-156, 546-570; M. Ritter, " Die memoiren Sully's und der grosse Plan Heindrichs IV," *Aus den Abhandlungen der k. bayer. Akademie der Wissenschaften* (III Classe, XI, part iii); Desclozeaux, " Étude critique sur les Économies royales: Gabrielle d'Estrées et Sully," *Revue Historique*, XXXIII (1887), 239-295; M. Philippson, " Appendice," *Heinrich IV und Philipp III* (Berlin, 1876), pp. 495-500.

rely upon his own work and perspicuity. It was in harmony with his personality, therefore, that he relates that when the King assigned him, in 1596, the task of unravelling the current financial difficulties he proposed and executed a scheme of visiting personally the administrative districts where he himself inspected the accounts and records of receivers general and particular, treasurers of France, comptrollers and clerks, and the lowliest officers. He pictures himself as returning triumphant from this tour, to the complete discomfiture of a hostile cabal of financiers and ministers, to receive the congratulations of the King. With him came a train of seventy carts loaded with money.[14]

Sully, while admitting the need of curbing Henry's unusual extravagance in respect to his mistresses, spoke also of the King's close attention to the details of finance and his frequent requests for accounts and summaries of the money received into, and expended by, the royal treasury.[15] When the Minister required, as he noted he customarily did, the rechecking of accounts, or the inclusion of better or more exact entries, he usually reminded the treasurers that the King himself would inspect them.[16]

A *conseil des finances,* as a distinct body, did not definitely emerge until the reign of Louis XIV; and the reign of Henry IV, in spite of Sully, witnessed no marked change in this regard. So technical and specialized a task as the annual casting of accounts of the treasury and the issuing of the *brevet* for the allotment of the *taille* for the coming year, was still performed by the King in full council with the advice of his ministers, the dukes and peers of the realm, and councillors.[17] But the

[14] Maximilian de Bethune, Duke of Sully, *Mémoires des sages et royales oeconomies d'éstat, domestiques, politiques et militaires de Henry le Grand,* Vols. II-III, 2d series, of *Nouvelle collections des mémoires pour servir a l'histoire de France, depuis le XIIIe siècle jusqu'à fin du XVIIIe,* edited by M. Michaud and Poujoulat (32 vols., Paris 1935-1839), II, 224-236 (referred to hereafter as *Oeconomies* followed by volume number); Viollet, *Le rois et ses ministres,* p. 219, disagrees on date; for full account of this tour see A. Chamberland, *La tournée de Sully et de Rybault dans les généralitiés en 1596* (Chartres, 1909).

[15] *Oeconomies,* II, 170-171, 260-267, 286-290.

[16] *Ibid.,* III, 260-261, 257-258. This last practice was also a favorite policy of Colbert to inspire thoroughness in reports from his subordinates.

[17] *Ibid.,* pp. 268-269; A. de Boislisle, "Les conseils sous Louis XIV," in A.

control of finances was acknowledged by the other councillors as the special province of Sully. He had the number of assisting intendants reduced from eight to two, and financial direction subordinated to the *conseil des parties* where he was sure of meeting little or no opposition.[18] At that time, the department of finances was a distant and esoteric branch of the government functioning in mysterious fashion beyond the comprehension of most of the highest officers of the state. One could not fail to detect a note of awe in Henry's request for his confidant to continue his attention to the business of finances as his " principal work " in order to " try to penetrate into the most profound secrets of them." [19]

Sully's method of penetrating the hidden recesses of these mysteries was described by him as the function of vigilance and doubt, as the strenuous work of checking and rechecking of accounts and ledgers, of visitations announced and unannounced to the various generalities, and of the centralization of accounts and administration in the Louvre or at the Arsenal.[20] He pictured himself and his master as keeping themselves carefully informed of the current status of the receipts and expenditures by the use of ledgers and statements, by clearly noting and separating levies, wage discounts, receipts and expenditures. He saw such practices as something in the nature of innovations and certainly necessary for enforcing efficiency and honesty.[21] By such means, and, if we are to believe the complaints of discontented parties of the time, by pure niggardliness, the coffers of the Bastile gave up to Marie de Medici, in 1610, the unprecedented reserve for the state of forty-three million livres.[22] Sully himself explained his success as arising from an administration " so well regulated, that a single *denier* could not be diverted by any person accountable, even by the Treasurers of France, nor even by the Chamber of accounts." [23]

From the standpoint of applying rational methods in gov-

de Boislisle, *et al.*, eds., *Mémoires de Saint Simon* (28 vols., Paris, 1879-1919), V, 380-381; VI, 477-487.

[18] Pagès, *La monarchie de l'ancien régime*, pp. 149-150.

[19] Letter of Henry to Sully, 1601, *Oeconomies*, II, 362.

[20] *Ibid.*, pp. 267, 359; III, 177-178, 230-231, 257-258, 280-281, 269-271.

[21] *Ibid.*, II, 170-171, 260-267, 286-290, 359, 534; III, 268-275.

[22] De Mallevoue, p. lxii.

[23] *Oeconomies*, III, 269.

ernment, the most interesting section of the *Oeconomies* is that in which the Minister described the project of the "Cabinet of Affairs of State and War." The idea of such a cabinet was attributed by him to Henry IV, who, in 1609, proposed to him the construction of a cabinet of drawers lined with crimson velvet, and very rich, which would be housed in the Louvre. It was to be sufficiently commodious and complex to hold an amazing variety of papers, books, *règlements,* records, orders, instructions, and inventories. All these items were to be segregated according to nature and filed in separate drawers so that the King would have immediately available accurate and detailed information on all manner of affairs useful to the conduct of the business of state, military, police, and finances. The Cabinet represented a remarkable anticipation of the need of a centralized authority for formulating policy from and operating a state through, the accumulation, assimilation and classification of social and statistical data.[24]

The financial administration of Sully and Henry IV was a certainty which made a deep impression on those who followed them, and it served as an ever useful example of the unlimited resources of integrity, application, and system when directed to the interests of the state. It was not surprising that Colbert dated the history of the decay of the financial conduct of the government from the death of Henry IV.[25] A surplus in the treasury was the unanswerable buttress to Sully's argument, in his memoirs, for the efficacy of introducing method into the direction of finances. In contrast, the " Cabinet of Affairs of State and War," unlike Sully's picture of his financial activities, had perhaps no reality apart from the description in the *Oeconomies*. That work is generally believed to have been written between 1617 and 1638. At the latter date it was finally published following last-minute additions and revisions. It is an apology, as well as a memoir, and many advanced ideas of the period probably found expression in the production of an ex-minister whose imagination and sense for originality per-

---

[24] *Ibid.,* pp. 268-275, 290-296.
[25] Colbert, " Mèmories sur les affaires de finances de France," in P. Clement, *Lettres instructions et mémoires de Colbert* (7 vols., Paris, 1861-1882), II, part i, 18-19. (This series will hereafter be referred to as: Colbert, *Lettres,* followed by the volume number.)

sisted into the years of his retirement.[26] The " Cabinet " cannot fail, for instance, to suggest Bacon's institution of the " Solomon's House " in the *New Atlantis*. The emphasis in the reign of Louis XIV on the utility of creating repositories for the social and political statistics of the kingdom might well have a common source with the musings of men who, in their minds, had reared such institutions and foundations to the end of acquiring " the knowledge of causes, and secret motions of things and the enlarging of the bounds of human empire, to the effecting of all things possible." [27] One wonders how much of the glory of Louis XIV was assured by the knife of Ravaillac.

III

During the troubled regency of Marie de Medici (1610-1617) few constructive changes in the field of government might have been expected and few were made. Where the central authority could not maintain the *status quo* it was threatened with rebellion, paralysis, or anarchy. The necessary policy of the Queen and her ministry was one of retrenchment and concessions while trying to maintain most of the authority of the governor intact until France should again have a major King. Perhaps the most important event, from the standpoint of the development of the government, was the Estates-General of 1614. The last of assemblies of the Estates before the Revolution was notable, aside from its chaotic wranglings, for the formulation of numerous *plaintes* to the crown which were the basis of the famous *Code Michaud*.[28]

The *Code Michaud* of 1629 terminated a series of varied and, one might say, often encyclopaedic *ordonnances* of reform, the beginning of which Esmein traces to the fourteenth century.[29] Its 461 articles constituted the most elaborate and extensive of all the royal decrees up to that time. Those sections which specified the procedure in the collection and account-

[26] Pfister, " Les économies royales de Sully," *Revue historique, passim*.

[27] Bacon, " New Atlantis," *Works*, I, 266.

[28] Isambert, XVI, 223-344; G. Picot, *Histoire des États Généreux . . . de 1355 à 1614* (4 vols., Paris, 1872), III, 327-410, 449-450; Esmein, p. 739.

[29] Esmein, pp. 738-739. The greatest activity in creating such *ordonnances* came in the last half of the sixteenth century and in the early seventeenth. Particularly noteworthy were the *Ordonnances* of Orleans (1560), Moulins (1566), Blois (1579). These are in Isambert, XIV.

ability of state revenues were framed with the closest attention
to detail. Seemingly every move through the complex structure
of the tax revenues was so minutely set forth that peculation
appears to the reader, unfamiliar with the then notorious
capacities of the financiers for such things, to be thoroughly provided against.[30] The *Code* was associated by contemporaries
with the Chancellor de Marillac and its name "Michaud" is
a pejorative corruption of his first name applied, after his disgrace, by the parlementarians hostile to its enforcement. It
is frequently stated that it was little observed by the parlements, but it should be noted that, with less detail, most of
the financial provisions are to be found reiterated in the *Édit
sur les tailles* of January 1634.[31]

Richelieu's occupation with foreign wars and the suppression of the Huguenots and nobles seems to offer a plausible
explanation of why this Minister, so aware in his writings of
the need of reform in the realm of finances, did so little to
effectuate any. At least, it would be unwise to accept so harsh
and unreasonable a judgment as that of one critic that in regard
to this field of administration "his incompetence prohibits
him from all personal action."[32] For in his written works
Richelieu revealed a clear interest in and some familiarity with
the difficulties of finance and the ideas of economic administration. The character of this interest has led some scholars to
suppose the influence of Montchrétien. Whether this be true
or not, it is certain, as Cole has pointed out, that, at the time
of Richelieu's writing, "the ideas and concepts summed up
by Montchrétien in 1615 were steadily gaining ground. They
were not only dominant; they were becoming universally
accepted."[33]

In his *Testament Politique,* the Cardinal devoted considerable space and effort to stating the problem of the department
of the state income. He drew up an itemized account of the

---

[30] "Ordonnance sur les plaintes des états assemblées à Paris en 1614; et de
l'assemblée des notables réunis à Rouen et à Paris, en 1617 et 1626" (January,
1629), *ibid.,* XVI 223-344, for finance sections see Articles 344-349, 363-370.

[31] For conflicting opinions on the matter of its observation see Esmein, p. 739;
Picot, III, 450; this *Édit* is printed in Isambert, XVI, 389-406, see, particularly,
Articles 37-65.

[32] Pagès, pp. 85-86.

[33] Cole, *Colbert,* I, 137, 146; see note 70, Chapter II, above.

revenues showing that part contributed by each of the various sources: *tailles, gabelles, aides, rentes reduction,* farms, and numerous other imposts and rights. To the total of 35,000,000 *livres* he proposed adding another 15,000,000 by the process of abolishing or relaxing the direct tax of the *taille* and relying instead on a greatly increased rate in certain indirect taxes. Thus the salt revenues, for instance, could be increased from 5,250,000 to 25,000,000 *livres.*[34]

These proposed tax reforms of Richelieu, whether feasible, or not, deserve attention only as representing an aspiration. What he considered as a more practical solution, again a solution not applied, would have been more simple. He described the total royal levy in the kingdom as amounting to something better than 80,000,000 *livres* from which more than 45,000,000 had to be deducted under the euphemism of *charges.* It was in this difference that he estimated sizable economies could be exercised,[35] but the method he suggested was indeed a poor substitute for the application of a Sully and a confession of the limitations of the rational administration which he professed. The machinery of financiers appeared to him as a necessary evil in the state. After weighing various means of reducing the proportions of this evil, of depriving the financiers of the ability to practice their incorrigible malversations, he concluded with the observation: " I dare say that there is no better way than to reduce them to the least possible number." This was the only remedy, for without it, " whatever regulation one might make it will be totally impossible to conserve the money of the King, not having any instrument of torture efficient enough to prevent that many officials of this kind would not appropriate a part of that which will pass through their hands." [36]

In spite of the example of Sully before him—and there is a suspicion that the Minister of Henry IV published his *Oecono-*

[34] Richelieu, *Testament politique,* II, 153-156; on the authenticity of the Testament see G. Hanotaux, " Études sur des maximes d'état," *Journal des savants* (1879), pp. 429-436, 561-570, 502-513. Colbert who apparently liked to think of himself as an executor of Richelieu's policies, significantly adopted this method for a part of his financial program.

[35] *Testament politique,* II, 159-162. Such also was to be a major premise in the financial system of Colbert.

[36] *Ibid.,* I, 221, 223-224.

mies as an oblique lesson to the Minister of Louis XIII—
Richelieu never chose, personally, to uncover the *delapidations*
which seemed to him inherent to finances. Unlike Sully, he
was the Prime Minister, and in the department of revenues, as
in the provinces of war, marine, and foreign affairs, he was in
a position to impose his authority and direction. He did not
do so, and the *surintendants* operated as in an almost independent division of the government. Perhaps partly due to
this lack of supervision from above, the misconduct of business
in the upper councils of finance during the ministry of Richelieu taxes credulity. When a *surintendant* came to him for instructions, Richelieu replied: " I confess my ignorance is so
great in affairs of finance, that the only advice that I can give
you is to avail yourself of those whom you will find most
useful." [37] His biographer, in the thorough account which he
gives of his administration, concludes that the Cardinal de
Richelieu " was an admirable minister of foreign affairs, an
able minister of war, and a nullity as a minister of finances." [38]

Richelieu's failure to supervise the central financial administration of the state was a fault perpetuated by his successor.
Confusion in such affairs during the period of the Fronde is
understandable, but the succeeding period of consolidated
royal power, at least during the lifetime of Mazarin, brought
no improvements.[39] Lavisse has stamped the financial regime

---

[37] D'Avenel, *Richelieu*, II, 181, note. The larger part of this volume is devoted
to a description of the financial administration of Richelieu and Louis XIII.

[38] *Ibid.*, p. 181.

[39] The study of Mazarin's administration of finances has been seriously limited
by a dearth of records thereon. Fouquet's documents were mostly dispersed
during the Revolution, and the two finance historians, Mallet and Forbonnais,
who probably had access to such records, give little information on the period.
See J. de Boislisle, ed., *Mémoriaux du conseil de 1661*, I, lxxxiii-lxxxiv; F. V.
D. de Forbonnais, *Recherches et considérations sur les finances de France depuis
1595 jusqu'à 1721* (6 vols., Liege, 1758), I, II; J. R. Mallet, *Comptes rendus
de l'administration des finances du royaume de France, pendant les onze dernières
années du régne de Henri IV, le régne de Louis XIII & soixante-cinq de celui
de Louis XIV* . . . (Paris, 1789), this is the posthumous work of M. Mallet
who was *commis des finances* under Desmaretz, *Contrôleur Général des Finances*
during the years 1708 to 1715. This work was actually written about 1720.
The author claimed that nothing had happened in the administration of finances
for the " past thirty years" of which he had not had an " exact knowledge"
(p. vii); other general accounts will be found in Clamageran, *Histoire de
l'impôt en France*, II, 533-598; A. Cheruel, *Histoire de la France pendant la
minorité de Louis XIV et sous le ministère de Mazarin* (7 vols., Paris, 1879-

of these years—(1653-1661)—as *Le desordre parfait.*[40] and, in this, the other historians of the age have concurred. The Cardinal delegated the administration of finances, after 1653, to Nicholas Fouquet [41] with the title of *surintendant des finances* and associated with him, probably as a check, Abel Servien, Marquis of Sablé. The perpetual conflict which arose between these two men resulted in a division of their authority. Servien was charged with the expenditure and Fouquet with the procurement of funds for the state. The influence of the latter continually increased at the expense of the former and was effectively unchallenged after the death of Servien in 1659. Fouquet pursued a day-by-day policy in his department: borrowed for the state at usurious rates from wealthy bourgeois and succeeded in so completely confusing his own finances with those of the King that even he was unable to define the separation. The revenues for several years in advance were

1883), VI, VII, *passim;* E. Lavissee, *Louis XIV. La Fronde. Le Roi, Colbert (1643-1685),* Vol. VII, part i of *Histoire de France depuis les origines jusqu'à la Révolution* (9 vols., Paris, 1903-1911), pp. 78-87; Lavisse cites: A. Cheruel, *Mémoires sur la vie publique et privée de Fouquet . . . d'après les lettres et des pièces inédites* (2 vols., Paris, 1864); J. Lair, *Nicolas Fouquet, procureur géneral, surintendant des finances, ministre d'état de Louis XIV* (2 vols., Paris, 1890).

[40] Lavisse, *Louis XIV,* p. 81. As in the regency of Marie de Medici, great personal pressure was brought to bear on the Queen-Mother, Anne of Austria, to distribute the royal revenues freely among a nobility which had too long submitted to the hard mastery of Richelieu and Louis XIII. As in the previous regency, also, the Regent found herself incapable, or unwilling, to resist the role of a bountiful princess. To attain the rewarding graces of the Queen there were, according to Cardinal Retz, but these few words in the French language: " La Reine est si bonne!" In the streets the new financial administration was memorialized with the refrain:

> La reine donne tout
> Monsieur joue tout
> M. le prince prend tout
> Le cardinal fait tout
> Le chancelier scelle tout.

Quoted in G. Martin and M. Bezancon, *L'histoire du credit en France sous le règne de Louis XIV* (Paris, 1913), p. 3. For a general resumé of the financial disorder of this period, see *ibid.,* pp. 1-73.

[41] The Abbé de Choisy describes Fouquet: " Nicolas Fouquet avait beaucoup de facilité aux affaires, et encore plus négligence; savant dans le droit, et mêmes dans les belles-lettres; la conversation légère, les manières aisées et nobles," *Mémoires pour servir a l'histoire de Louis XIV,* edited by MM. Champollion-Figiac and Aimé Champollion Fils (Paris, 1839), p. 573. On his death bed Mazarin seems to have given the *Surintendant* a recommendation to Louis XIV as having " very great intelligence and resources for finances." Colbert, *Lettres,* I, 534.

expended in anticipation of their receipt. He recognized the need for reform but was continuously putting it off to times of peace.[42]

At one time Mazarin had attempted to introduce some surveillance into the division by assigning the banker Hervart, as clerk of the treasury, to keep an account of all sums deposited by Fouquet and withdrawn by Servien from the public treasury. But the opposition of the *surintendants* and their submission of falsified accounts made the effort ineffective.[43]

The Cardinal was well advised on the shortcomings of Fouquet by Colbert, then *intendant* of Mazarin's personal finances. Colbert was continually urging his master to apply himself, individually, to these affairs. As early as 1652, he had warned him that " I believe certainly that lack of funds will ruin the State, if Your Eminence does not strive to learn the basic cause and correct it so far as that is possible." [44] In October 1659 he addressed to the Minister a long memoir suggesting changes in the administration of finances. It was, in effect, a frontal attack on the policies of Fouquet and set forth the reforms which Colbert himself was to attempt later. The mission of the reform was to substitute the *" maxime d'ordre "* for the then prevailing, *" maxime de confusion."* The first condition of the new order was to be the institution of a complete system of strict accountability. Fouquet was advised of the plans by his agents, who intercepted and copied them enroute to the Cardinal, and through his influence, or perhaps partly due to the enforced attention of Mazarin to foreign affairs at the time, or his personal obligations to the *surintendant,* or even to his dislike of all violent actions, nothing was done to alter the prevailing system.[45] The progressive disintegration in the fiscal administration from the time of Sully to the eve of Louis XIV's assumption of personal rule had become the most notorious scandal in France. It is little wonder that it was precisely in this area that Louis was to initiate his program of rational reform.

[42] Cheruel, VI, 116, 250-251; Lavisse, pp. 79-82, 85-86; Clamageran, II, 585-598.

[43] Cheruel, VI, 270-271; VII, 276.

[44] Quoted in Cole, *Colbert,* I, 282, from letter of Colbert to Mazarin, February 22, 1652, in Colbert, *Lettres,* I, 192.

[45] Colbert to Mazarin, October 1, 1659, *ibid.,* VII, 164-183; Clamageran, II, 606-609; Cheruel, VII, 277-282; Lavisse, pp. 182-183.

IV

In administration, possibly the most significant development in the first half of the seventeenth century was the solidification of the institution of the intendant. The establishment of this office is rather popularly assigned to Richelieu and specifically to his *Édit de creation des intendants* of May 1635. An examination of the meaning of the *Édit* reveals that the functionaries termed therein " intendants general " were " presidents in the bureaus of our finances." The new title was given to sanction the separation of their office from that of the treasurers of France, and they had little in common with the intendants of justice, police, and finance so well known to history.[46] D'Avenel, while maintaining, with some justice, that Richelieu deserves the title of creator which history has been accustomed to grant him, admits that, taken as a whole, " the intendants had no act of birth. No royal declaration, no edict had created them. It seems that these newcomers being gradually introduced into the administrative organism, had prospered there, as true parasites, at the expense of all the others." [47] The same author, after searching the *Mémoires,* the personal papers kept at the bureau of foreign affairs, and the *Testament politique* of Richelieu, could discover little, if any, evidence that the Cardinal placed any marked dependence on these officials.[48] In fact, the *Testament* alone offers something substantial concerning the Minister's attitude towards their functions. Oddly enough, this statement is expressed in terms which would suggest that, under Richelieu, intendants never existed at all:

I believe that it will be very useful to send frequently into the Provinces some of the Councillors of State, or well chosen *Maitres des Requêtes,* not only in order to carry out the function of an Intendant

---

[46] Isambert, XVI, 441-450; particularly Articles (1-4); d'Avenel, *Richelieu,* IV, 199-200; Esmein, *Histoire du droit,* p. 573. For the origin of the system and the role of Richelieu see Chapter V in d'Avenel's *Richelieu,* IV, 193-215; G. Hanotaux, " Les premiers intendants de justice," *Revue historique,* XIX (1882), 1-20, 308-330; XX (1882), 73-87; XXI (1883), 59-90; Esmein, pp. 573-574; Isambert, XII-XVI, *passim.* The following account of the development of the system will be based on these works unless otherwise indicated.

[47] D'Avenel, IV, 199, 202.

[48] *Ibid.,* pp. 202-204.

of Justice in the Capital Cities, which can be of better service to their vanity than of utility to the public; but in order to go into all the districts of the Provinces, to enquire of the customs of the Officers of Justice and of the Financiers; to see if the taxes are levied in conformance with the Ordonnances, and that the Receivers commit no injustices there vexing to the people; to discover the fashion in which they exercise their offices; to learn how the Nobility governs itself, and to arrest the course of all types of disorders, and especially of the violences of those who are powerful and rich, oppressing the weak and the poor subjects of the King.[49]

In the sixteenth century the policy of fiscality which resulted from the pressing financial needs of the Valois had led to the multiplication of hereditary offices. The gentlemen of the *Robe* were subtly undermining the royal authority which had been recaptured after so many centuries of struggle with the nobility.[50] The religious conflicts of the last half of the century had further endangered the monarchy with its concomitant resurgence of the power of the great lords. Finding that the regular administrative hierarchy, represented by the parlements and governorships, either was incapable or uncooperative in effectuating their desires in the provinces, the kings had recourse to a sure and devoted emissary. This agent, armed with a specific mandate, and called a *commissaire,* was assigned to carry out some particular policy. From the middle of the century, these *commissaires* were in constant use. They went throughout the kingdom carrying the will of the King, supervising the collection of a special impost, providing for the publication and execution of an onerous *édit,* repressing the signs of rebellion, regulating a private matter of the royal house, and always reporting back with what they had seen, or heard, or done.

Paralleling, for a time, and perhaps antedating the function of the *commissaire* was the practice of the *chevauchée,* or official inspection, or visitation. The *édit* on finances of 1523 prescribed *chevauchées* to the treasurers of France and generals of finances of at least twice a year in their district in order to " augment our revenue." [51] A declaration of 1547 mentions the *chevauchée* as part of the regular duties of the *senechaux.*[52] An

[49] *Testament politique,* I, 217; d'Avenel, IV, 203-204.
[50] Pagès, pp. 16-17.
[51] Isambert, XII, part i, 228.
[52] *Ibid.,* XIII, 18.

édit of 1551 created administrative districts, 17 in number, called receiverships-general, and defined the authority of the treasurers-general. An annual *chevauchée*, with attendant reports to the royal council, on the value of the generality, constituted one of the main duties of this official.[53]

At times, the area of enquiry of the *commissaire* became extensive, and the ambulatory nature of the office in this case was designated by the term *chevaucheur*. Usually, the *commissaire* was chosen from among the *maîtres de requêtes* of the Hotel de Ville of Paris and was thus strictly beholden to the King. The general *chevauchée* had become annual by the middle of the sixteenth century and by the early seventeenth century the investigatory prerogatives of these *maîtres de requêtes departis,* as they were now called, had extended to most important administrative matters.

In the sixteenth century one meets also with the *intendant de justice*, a true precursor of the administrative intendant of the seventeenth and eighteenth centuries. This official was a *commissaire* whose powers were not limited to a single thing but rather concerned with a collection of functions connected with the pacification of a determined region. At the same time, intendants were to be found in the armies, officials responsible for providing rations and pay and regulating the discipline of the corps, and, incidentally, performing the police power through a sort of martial law in those districts occupied by the armies. Placed by the king in his army to curb the excesses of the soldiery, he remained in the district, after the army had departed, ready to exercise over the community the same authority.

Whatever the attitude of the regularly constituted provincial agents towards this interloper, during the period when the royal armies occupied the territory, there was no effective opposition. But what was necessary in war became intolerable to them in peace. Resistance was practically universal, extending to all levels: governors, parlements, municipalities, and, because they followed their leaders or because the intendants were frequently the executors of unpopular decrees, even the people were frequently allied against them. The entrenchment

---

[53] " Édit de creation de dix-sept recettes générales," January 1551, *ibid.,* pp. 236-247.

of the intendant was a slow and bitterly contested progress. When Henry IV assumed the effective management of the state, a large number of these *missi dominici* were spread through the provinces, but the succeeding years of peace witnessed a gradual retreat from this royal policy before the consolidating forces in the country. During the first half of the regency of Marie de Medici only a very small number were sent out, and these, usually, carried commissions limiting their office to a year.

If the principle was submerged during this period, it was not abandoned, and, where intendants were present, their duties were more clearly defined and their powers made more effective. During the last years of the regency of Marie de Medici and with the increasing influence of Richelieu, there was a resurgence, and by 1627 it was possible to speak of intendants and governors in the same breath.[54] Under his administration these heirs of the *commissaire* and *maître de requêtes* regularly joined to their prerogatives of justice and police those of army and finances, in short, all the necessary attributes of executive power.[55] However, the area in which they were to exercise these rights was still a fluctuating quantity, sometimes limited to a special district, sometimes to a generality, sometimes to both.[56]

Whether the honor of creating the intendancy historically belongs to Richelieu or not, in the Frondeur reaction, which followed on his death and that of Louis XIII, the literate element attributed it to him. Among the remonstrances of the Parlement of Paris to the crown, no demand was more emphatic than that calling for the abolition of this hateful instrument of the tyranny of the late Prime Minister. A declaration of the King (1648) revoked all extraordinary commissions, even those of the intendants of justice, in the provinces of the realm.[57]

[54] D'Avenel, IV, 201-202.

[55] *Ibid.*, p. 205; Hanotaux fails to find any clear innovations under the regime of Richelieu. "Les premiers intendants," *Revue historique*, XX, 79-87, XXI, 63-70.

[56] D'Avenel, IV, 214.

[57] Omer Talon, *Mémoires de Omer Talon, avocat général en la cour de parlement de Paris,* edited by MM. Champollion-Figeac and Aimé Champollion, Fils, Vol. VI, 3rd series of *Nouvelle collections des mémoires pour servir à l'histoire*

The succeeding defeat and humiliation of the parlements and the discrediting of the princes were attended by a bursting revival of the royal power which shivered into fragments all hopes of the proponents of a monarchy limited by any constitutional restraint. The intendancy, like other contested instruments of the central control, was re-established and placed beyond challenge.

Louis XIV inherited from his predecessors, in the intendancy, an efficient machinery for giving meaning to his projects. But the intendant was more than an expression of power. From another point of view, the governmental evolution of the office may be considered as a political complement of a growing dependence by the royal authority on reliable administrative data. The reportorial function had always been, if not emphasized, at least explicit in their commissions. Under Louis XIV and Colbert it was to become capitally important.

During the first half of the seventeenth century political interests had dominated and directed the course of the state. For the most part, the economy seemed " struck with inertia," [58] and reform in administration seemed, with the exception of the short reign of Henry IV, confined to the literature, but there was no dearth in the production of ideas and projects. Barthélemy and Isaac de Laffemas, Montchrétien, Sully and Richelieu had felt and expressed the need for change. The accomplishments of Sully and the aspirations of others were only accentuated by the conspicuous failure in the direction of internal affairs. The " distractions of the times " was the only impediment to the application of the solutions of sovereign reason. By 1661 such " distractions " were generally at an end.

de France, depuis le XIIIe siècle jusqu'à fin du XVIIIe, edited by MM. Michaud and Poujoulat (32 vols., Paris, 1835-1839), pp. 250-252, 247; Doolin, The Fronde, pp. 11-13; d'Avenel, IV, 206; Pagès, pp. 130-131, the gentlemen of the "Robe" complained in a cahier of 1648: " Si ces dangereuses nouveautés continuent et son autorisées, il ne nous reste plus nos offices qu'un vain nom de magistrat " (p. 122).

[58] The expression belongs to Moreau de Jonnès, and is applied by him to the reign of Louis XIII. A. Moreau de Jonnès, État économique et social de la France depuis Henri IV jusqu'a Louis XIV (1589-1715) (Paris, 1867), p. 138.

CHAPTER IV

LOUIS XIV AND COLBERT IN THE REGIME OF ORDER

An inquiry into the nature of the administrative reforms carried forward in the central government during the period 1661 to 1683 logically begins with a consideration of the attitudes and political habits of the two men most responsible for those reforms. As we have seen, the climate of opinion, cultural and political, was favorable, when Louis XIV assumed power in 1661, to the institution of a more rational government. However, in a strong monarchy like that of France, it was necessary that the king himself be, as it were, a " convert to the times " before such a regime could be created. Louis XIV was such a king.

I

Louis XIV and his collaborator, Colbert, whatever might have been their official attitude towards Cartesian principles, as a philosophy *per se,* committed themselves by their written opinions and by their actions to the application of such principles to government. If these opinions had been restricted to their *mémoires,* we might dismiss them after a bow to antiquarian interest. Indeed, Richelieu, whom one historian has called " entirely Cartesian before Descartes," [1] had offered, in his *Testament politique,* a more striking verbal tribute to the ideal of government by "Reason" than was ever to be made by Louis XIV or Colbert. But whatever the declarations of the great Cardinal the *Testament* remains as a monument to aspirations and a sort of apology for government by expedient. It has been recently said of it, referring specifically to its economic formulae, that it was " almost as if he wished to have posterity know that his heart had been in the right place, even if fate had driven him to devote his major efforts to diplomacy and war." [2] If Colbert and his master were less literate than their illustrious predecessor, they at least were

[1] Pagès, p. 88.
[2] Cole, *Colbert,* I, 208.

enabled to fortify their professions with accomplishments in internal affairs.

Possibly no government of modern times has been more closely fashioned after ideas of an individual than was that of France under Louis XIV. Certainly, there was little distinction, in his own mind, between the glory of the nation and the glory of the King, between the purposes of the master and the functions of the state. His individual success provided the greatest distinction of the realm, but this success, to be assured, must come from the exercise of a reasonable policy, on his part, in response to conditions observed or reliably reported.

In the royal state, as he envisaged it, the King ruled by reason; the reason turning on the sifting and judgment of information and counsel and on personal observation. His boast to his son that he had governed himself " by reason " [3] may be attributed to the vanity of the *roi soleil,* but even he never judged his wisdom as superior to the facts. The " function of kings " consisted " primarily in allowing good sense to work." That it did " naturally and without effort." Thus, as he told his son, the " epitome " of the art of politics consisted essentially in " common sense " and the " use of it." [4]   But this reason, this superior wisdom, was to be employed by him as the final arbiter between the contending interests of the state. He did not create a condition. Rather, his role appeared to him to be that of making a decision only, of selecting the best among situations as a policy. The King, he wrote, must hear all sides, looking towards the past and on the present, then make the choice which " if we lack neither sense nor courage, no other can do it better than we; for decision requires the spirit of a master and it is without comparison easier to do what one is, than to imitate that which one is not." [5]   Whatever the limitless capacities of kingship, kings were but men and it was impossible " that a single man know and do everything." The very boundaries of their position as men would render more glorious their actions as kings.[6]

[3] J. Longnon, ed., *Louis XIV, mémoires pour les années 1661 et 1666 suivis de morceaux divers* (Paris, 1923), p. 63.

[4] *Ibid.,* p. 66; P. A. Grouvelle, ed., *Oeuvres de Louis XIV* (6 vols., Paris, 1806), I, 185.

[5] Longnon, *Louis XIV, mémoires,* pp. 82, 225.

[6] *Ibid.,* pp. 70, 59-60.

Following the death of Mazarin, the first public action of Louis had been to call into being the new council of ministers, the *conseil de trois*. This act on the part of a king who publicly declared his intention to rule alone seemed paradoxical to some contemporaries.[7] It is clear that to Louis no other action was possible. " In proportion as I had the ardor for distinguishing myself," wrote Louis to his son, " so had I the the fear of failing; and, regarding as a great misfortune the discredit which pursues the least faults, I desired to show in my conduct the greatest precautions. . . . I did not believe in treating details of affairs until account had been given me by those who were the best informed."[8] Commenting on his early political decisions, the King declared to his son: " Two things were absolutely essential to me: a great deal of work on my own part and a wise choice of persons who could second it."[9] The King was supreme, but " it was necessary to divide my confidence and the execution of my orders, without giving it entirely to any one, assigning these various persons to various affairs according to their various talents, which is perhaps the first and greatest gift of princes."[10] He was resolved to hold personal conferences with his new ministers " when they least expected it " that they might remain fully aware of his capacity to discourse seriously on any subject at any time. This ability to render intelligent opinion and response to all affairs was based on the assimilation of a multitude of small details acquired " piece by piece " in a " thousand things which are not without usefulness in general resolutions, and which we ought to know and do ourselves if it was possible."[11]

To provide these details, the opinions and advice of a council were essential. He was, by his own account, even willing to overlook the obvious faults of a councillor in order to avail himself of his seasoned knowledge of the affairs within the kingdom.[12] As to delegating the legally inalienable authority of kings by reliance on ministers, probably no king was ever

[7] J. de Boislisle, ed., *Mémoriaux du conseil de 1661*, I, viii-x; see E. Spanheim, *Relation de la cour de France en 1690*, edited by C. Schefer (Paris, 1882), p. 7.
[8] J. de Boislisle, *Conseil de 1661*, I, viii.
[9] Longnon, *Louis XIV, mémoires*, p. 64.
[10] *Ibid.*, p. 70.
[11] *Ibid.*
[12] *Ibid.*, p. 74.

more constantly aware of the least appearance of such a danger. The son of Louis XIII and Anne of Austria had every reason to remember Richelieu and Mazarin. But, as grave as the sacrifice of power would be, " to govern oneself, and to hear no counsel . . . would be another extreme as dangerous as being governed. The most able individuals take advice from other persons able in their little interests." In short, the decisions of kings were of such importance that they should not be made without the aid of " the most reasonable and wisest among our subjects." [13]

If the desire for information was important enough to Louis to lead him to risk the use of a *conseil de trois*, it is also fair to note his insistence, up to the point of decision, on complete liberty of opinion among his advisors. Thus, to his valued Vauban, he wrote in 1693: " Continue to write me whatever comes into your mind and be not discouraged, although I don't always do what you suggest," for, as he pointed out, " I am satisfied to profit from what good things they contain according to my designs which do not accord entirely with your thoughts." [14] In his *conseils,* the King habitually insisted on full and free discussions, and on extensive study of all issues by his ministers, the secretaries of state, councillors and *maîtres de requêtes.* He ordinarily aligned himself with the majority opinion, and was even known to have decided affairs in a manner contrary to his own feeling. [15]

The concerns of Louis with matters of state showed a nearly limitless variety extending from broad policy to the individual problems of the most humble subjects. To make the weight of kingship apparent in all the corners of the realm was one of the ends of his craft. This could be done by the knowledge of every possible detail of his state. His memoirs display an emphasis on information which, perhaps, extends beyond the merely reasonable requirements of royalty; to know was akin to a passion. [16]

[13] *Ibid.,* p. 81.

[14] P. Gaxotte, ed., *Lettres de Louis XIV* (Paris, 1930), p. 93.

[15] A number of writers have referred to this characteristic of Louis XIV's conduct in his councils. See particularly, the essay of A. de Boislisle, " Les conseils sous Louis XIV," *Mémoires,* V, 461, 472, 474, 476-477; VI, 232, 503-505; VII, 175, 436.

[16] Longnon, *Louis XIV, mémoires,* p. 67.

In the eyes of the King, the first function of ministers was to keep him well informed. Colbert, for one, was prudently aware of his responsibilities in this respect and slavishly and efficiently performed the duties of reporter. To implement his cherished reforms in commerce, for instance, he exposed his programs to Louis in clear, precise memoirs containing the digested facts, showing the changes deemed necessary, and stating the expected results.[17]

This reporting function of his ministers was reiterated continuously in the official correspondence. When his secretary of state for war, Louvois, was away with the armies, as was frequently the case, Louis required a constant interchange of letters of advice and information. "Continue to send me," he wrote the Minister from Versailles during the campaign of 1676, "and send me from all sides, as you have done, the copies of the letters [speaking specifically of Louvois' letters to various marshals and generals] in order that I may be very well informed of everything, so that I do not give orders that can leave those to whom they are addressed uncertain." [18]

The reporting function of the ministers was reciprocated by the King who was careful to keep them advised of his own attitudes or of important developments concerning their departments which might arise in their absence. Writing to Louvois, on another occasion of separation, he noted that " I have ordered Pomponne [19] to make some abstracts of all the news which I will receive, and of the resolutions which I will take, so that you may be informed . . . and that you may always have the position of affairs in your head." [20] Apparently the ministers did not hesitate to request such information of the King if it was not provided unasked.[21]

As far as he was personally concerned, Louis, in his direction of affairs, gloried in his capacity for work, in his personal supremacy, in his complete knowledge of the facts of the realm, in his role of royal accountant and in his rescue of the

[17] P. Boissonade, *Colbert,* p. 8 and *passim.*
[18] Louis to Louvois, July 26, 1676, Grouvelle, IV, 91.
[19] Simon Arnauld, Marquis of Pomponne, Secretary of State for Foreign Affairs (1671-1679). Born 1618, died 1699.
[20] Louis to Louvois, December 23 and December 26, 1672, Grouvelle, III, 276, 290.
[21] Colbert to the King, with his responses, May 1672, *ibid.,* V, 497.

state from the throes of disorder. In all these ways he saw himself as an innovator, and undoubtedly this sense of the new was largely responsible for the energy and optimism which seemed to permeate his government in the early years. His contemporaries viewed with various degrees of awe, pleasure, or censure the changed complexion of affairs. In later years the central theme of the resisting elements, under various disguises, was to be the return to the good old days before 1661.

A casual survey of the collections of official correspondence for the period from 1661 to 1683 is likely to leave the reader with an exaggerated estimate of the influence of Colbert on the institution of the new regime. It is this sort of obvious prominence which led Saint-Simon to brand the government of Louis XIV as an association of clerks. A closer inspection always reveals the unmistakable preponderance of Louis in the councils and even in the effecting of the minor details of the business of the state. He perhaps did not consider it commensurate with royal dignity meticulously to delineate the mechanics of his rule, but he was never above pointing out the most insignificant error in the exercise of his craft by his ministers. It may be necessary to agree with Saint-Simon that his reign was the tyranny of the *roturier,* but it is also true that the King bore many of the marks of a *roturier* in himself.

The evaluation by Voltaire of the weight of Louis XIV in his government is still valid and, perhaps, conservative:

We see, from this view-point, what changes Louis XIV made in the State; useful changes, also, since they still remain. His ministers enviously competed in seconding his motions. We doubtless owe to them all the detail, the execution; but to him the general plan. It is certain that the magistrates would not have reformed the laws, that order would not have been introduced into finances, discipline into the military, general police into the kingdom; that there would have been no fleet, that arts would have lacked encouragement . . . if a master had not been found who had in general all these grand views, with a strong will to fulfill them.[22]

All important decisions of state had to be made by the King; the minister could use his powers of persuasion to influence this decision, but Louis XIV jealously reserved to himself the final word. When he received an important communication

---

[22] Voltaire, *Histoire du siècle de Louis XIV,* III, 79.

from his kinsman, Colbert de Terron, intendant at Rochefort, Colbert, as secretary of state, was not empowered to answer the problems set forth. The King was off to the wars. Instead, he replied, " I have sent your letter to my son in order to render account to the King, and that in a few days you will receive the letters of His Majesty on this subject. . . ." [23] In a dispatch to the engineer de Clerville, the Minister explained that he had " rendered account to the King of the contents of your three letters of the 26th of August and the 1st and 8th of this month." He continued to outline the King's responses, point by point, on details extending from the mechanics of supply to the choice of building materials and problems of cartography. [24] In order to goad the intendent at Dijon into rendering certain military accounts with a show of greater exactitude and application, Colbert warned him that " the King continues always to examine carefully and exactly things which must be done to place the frontiers of his realm in good state. . . ." [25]

The requirement of transmitting important reports to the King for his individual inspection could prove particularly embarrassing to the nepotistic ambitions which Colbert shared with most officials of his day. "You will see by the marginal notes to the report you have sent me," he wrote to his relative, the intendant of Alsace, " that it is so badly done that I have not dared to show it to the King." [26] His hopes for his son, Seignelay, made him peculiarly emphatic in this direction. He was continually urging him to diligence and to write more frequent and better reports. He warned him that this was particularly important since " I cannot prevent that a prince as penetrating as he is, that he may not see well that there is much negligence on your part." [27]

If the majority of the reports on his state were relayed to the King by his councillors, there still remained a number of facts which both he and his ministers wished to be delivered to him directly or conjointly. Louis, rather indignantly, com-

---

[23] Colbert to de Terron, April 25, 1674, Colbert, *Lettres,* V, 106.
[24] Colbert to de Clerville, September 23, 1671, *ibid.,* pp. 58-59.
[25] Colbert to M. Bouchu, October 25, 1670, *ibid.,* p. 39.
[26] Colbert to de Terron, November 15, 1670, *ibid.,* p. 40.
[27] Colbert to Seignelay, April 12, 1672, *ibid.,* III, part ii, 76.

plained to M. de Baas, Governor and Lieutenant Governor of the Isles of America, that the reports he received from this department were not so full as those from others:

> I have been surprised at receiving a letter of only a few lines from you, undated, and even that which you write to Colbert ought not to be more ample, seeing that you are sufficiently informed of the consideration I have for the Isles of America to be persuaded that I will be well pleased to know in detail the state in which you have found them since your arrival.[28]

Several years later, it was still necessary for Colbert to order M. de Baas to give an exact account " directly to the King and not to me " as he had been doing.[29]

The personal application of kings to the business of foreign affairs was a tradition. Perhaps in no field of state interest would Louis XIV have been less likely to surrender his ideas of individual supervision and correlatively more insistent on receiving direct reports. In the first days of his full power, his foreign minister,[30] Huges de Lionne, had written to the French Ambassador in Poland:

> The King has ordered me to tell you on his behalf that, when there may be in negotiations some very important details and circumstances which you judge requires a greater secrecy than others, you should include them in a letter which you will write directly to the King himself, and that you will address it to me in order to be presented to H. M., who will instruct me afterwards in what he wishes to do.[31]

[28] Louis XIV to M. de Baas, June 12, 1669, *ibid.*, p. 453.

[29] Colbert to M. de Baas, May 17, 1675, *ibid.*, pp. 590-591.

[30] Actually the title is a courtesy since the de Briennes were technically in possession of the office of secretary of state for foreign affairs until 1663, but de Lionne was universally recognized as being the true foreign minister.

[31] Hugues de Lionne to M. de Lumbres, May 6, 1661, quoted in part in J. de Boislisle, *Conseil de 1661*, I, 278-279. In his council of May 9, 1661, the King ordered that all foreign ministers who wrote him in the future on their business were to accompany the dispatch with " a letter to the secretary of State in which they put those particular things which, through respect, they will not believe they ought to write to the King, and will send the whole in an envelope to the secretary of State." (Minutes of the seance in *ibid.*, p. 276.) The care of Louis to attend personally to such matters was carried to the point of jealousy. De Lionne wrote to the Ambassador, de Cominges in London: " Though I always show the King the private letters with which you honour me, and that it might appear that it comes to the same, as his Majesty is equally well-informed, be the letter for him or for me, you must always, if you please write direct to his Majesty, even when you have nothing else to say than that you have nothing to say. Write me only three lines for the forwarding of the

The pride of Louis XIV in his abilities in the science of fortification has been frequently referred to by historians. It was reflected in the unusual favors showered on Vauban, the first engineer to become a Marshal of France, in the constitution of the engineering corps as a distinct division of the army, and in his own close attention to the affairs of the science. He personally investigated the minute details of proposed fortifications, consulting with Louvois and such generals as Condé and Turenne on plans submitted by engineers as Vauban or Clerville. He frequently made alterations, sometimes to the poorly concealed displeasure of the technicians on the spot.[32] When some particular work was underway the King required progress reports every few days.[33] At one time, Colbert described the King poring over plans of fortifications brought to him by Vauban and " approving everything with praises."[34] At another time an engineer submitted plans and memoirs which were too complicated or of too great magnitude for the King to make decisions from them only; then it was suggested that he appear and make his explanations to the King personally.[35] When the King was in the field and available to him, Colbert advised the engineer, D'Aspremont, in response to his report on the works at Auxonne that " I will only say to you that being at present near the King, you can take the orders of His Majesty on this subject."[36]   Louis

packet. I clearly saw the advantage of this plan when I read to his Majesty the last letter with which you favoured me; for he then inquired why you did not write rather to himself. I answered that the cause was probably the want of any matter of sufficient importance. . . . But I think his Majesty did not hold the reason a sufficient one, and that he prefers you to do otherwise. You will also please him very much in continuing what you so handsomely began, and forwarding in a separate sheet the most curious of the Court news." Letter of August 5, 1663, quoted and translated in J. J. Jusserand, *French ambassador at the court of Charles the second* (London, 1892), p. 43.

[32] Colbert to de Clerville, December 8, 1671, Colbert, *Lettres,* V, 61-62 and notes on both pages; Colbert letters to intendants, *ibid.,* pp. 72-75; Colbert to M. de Aspremont, engineer, May 8, 1673, *ibid.,* p. 77. H. Guerlac, " Vauban, the impact of science on war," in E. M. Earle, ed., *Makers of Modern Strategy* (Princeton, 1943), p. 48.

[33] Colbert, *Lettres,* V, 72-75.

[34] Colbert to de Terron, intendant at Rochefort, March 5, 1674, *ibid.,* p. 100.

[35] Colbert to d'Aspremont, March 10, 1677, *ibid.,* pp. 182-183.

[36] Colbert to d'Aspremont, June 16, 1674, *ibid.,* p. 114 n. In a letter of August 1, 1673, Colbert wrote to the King describing the progress on various fortifications and citing cost figures. The Minister had requested authorization

himself conducted surveys of the fortresses. Thus, in 1676, he wrote to his Secretary of State from the provinces that the fortifications of Picardy were not all they should be and ordered immediate action to repair the defects he had noted.[37]

If in this government, as seen by Louis XIV, the importance of information in shaping policy was a fundamental tenet, the vastness of the task of reviewing the data on a kingdom like France, no matter how efficient or wise the directors, required a prodigious application to business. In this regard, at least in the early years of his personal reign, the King was relentlessly demanding on his ministers; but, reciprocally, his ministers could have no legitimate complaint that he was not cooperative to the full limits of his ability and the allowances of protocol.

His delay in assuming direction of affairs might be attributed to his respect for Mazarin, his reluctance to quit the kingly delights of his youth, the Valois tradition of pleasures, or, as he himself admitted, a dread of the burdens of state. At any rate, though he lamented to his son his earlier laxness, he was certain that his efforts afterwards to repair it could not have failed as a result of " negligence or of indolence." [38] He himself described the beginning of his personal rule: "I commenced by casting my eyes on all the various affairs of the State, and not with indifferent eyes, but with the eyes of a master, sensibly touched at seeing nothing which did not invite and press me to bear a hand at it; but observing carefully that which time and circumstances would permit. Disorder reigned throughout." [39] As to work, he warned his son that " it is by that that one reigns, for that that one reigns." But these labors, he emphasized, would never prove burdensome if one were in a position of losing them.[40]

The first act of Louis XIV in the new council which he called together, after the death of Cardinal Mazarin, had declared his intention to rule alone. The Chancellor of France

for outlays in excess of the original budget. The King, in the field at the time, in his marginal responses promised to give a decision after a personal interview with the engineer concerned. *Ibid.*, pp. 89-90.

[37] Louis XIV to Colbert, June 5, 1676, *ibid.*, p. 170.

[38] Longnon, *Louis XIV, mémoires*, p. 54.

[39] *Ibid.*, p. 56.

[40] *Ibid.*, p. 64.

was ordered to seal nothing without the King's express permission and, similarly, the secretaries of state were to carry
out no acts without his knowledge.[41]   The day following, the
grands and peers of France received from the King the official
declaration of the policy which announced the end of their
importance in his councils.   The younger Brienne, in the
minutes of the *conseil de trois*, told how:

> The King had assembled . . . in the chamber of the Queen-Mother
> where the councils were held formerly, all those whom he had cus-
> tomarily called, composed of the princes, the dukes and ministers of
> State only, in order to have them hear from his own mouth that he
> had taken the resolve to govern his State personally without relying
> on anything than his own efforts (these were his own words), and
> dismissed them most civilly in telling them that, when he had need
> of their good advice, he would call them.[42]

It became the custom of the King to spend every morning
from mass to the hour of dinner in the council; the afternoons
also were allotted to further councils or affairs of state.   Almost
nothing could alter this "order of things," not even the most
demanding business of the family.   When he was away in
the field, the same assiduous attention was given to duties.
At the celebrated operation for the fistula, in 1686, almost
his first move after coming from the hands of the surgeon
was to summon the council of ministers.   When he had a
severe relapse, the morning meeting of the council was delayed
till the evening.   There were practically no " infractions to
the rule." [43]   As he instructed his son:

> I imposed on myself as a law to work regularly twice a day, and
> two or three hours each time with various people, not counting the
> hours which I passed privately, nor the time which I could give beyond
> this to extraordinary affairs if they arose. . . .

---

[41] Minutes of the seance of March 9, 1661, in J. de Boislisle, *Conseil de
1661,* I, 1.

[42] Minutes of March 11, 1661, *ibid.,* p. 18. The Prince of Condé, first prince
of the blood and present at the historic meeting, wrote a letter a few days later
to the Court of Poland. He described the King's reliance on Le Tellier, Fouquet
and de Lionne for all " ordinary " matters and of the honor of being himself,
with other princes, dukes and grandees, consulted on " extraordinary " matters.
He cited the King's esteem of the Queen-Mother, but " the King takes personal
cognizance of everything and rules on it as he pleases." Quoted in *ibid.,* p. 67,
note.

[34] A. de Boislisle, " Les conseils sous Louis XIV," *Mémoires*, VII, 436-439,
E. Spanheim, *Relation de la cour de France,* pp. 1-2.

He continued by asserting that " there was not a moment when it was not permissible to speak to me, provided that the affairs were pressing. . . ." [44]

The first appearances of the new aspect of things after the death of Mazarin evoked no little astonishment and much admiration on the part of subjects and a world used to the regime of the Cardinals. The Dutch Ambassador wrote the Grand Pensioner from Paris on the eighteenth of March 1661:

They speak, since the death of the cardinal, with praise, and even with affection, of the resolutions the King has taken to assume himself the government. It is said that the King does not employ the three ministers . . . except to take lessons from them, from the first [Fouquet] on finances, from the second [Le Tellier] on the business of war, and from the third [De Lionne] on foreign affairs. . . . Everyone says unanimously that it is unbelievable with what promptness, what clarity, what judgment, and what intelligence this young prince treats and expedites business, this which he accompanies with a great agreeableness towards those with whom he deals, and with a great patience in listening to that which one has to say to him: which wins all hearts. [45]

There had been not a few skeptics who had anticipated or hoped that this unexpected diligence of a French king was but a passing enthusiasm. They were disappointed however. De Lionne in August of that year wrote to the French Ambassador in Germany:

Those who have believed that our master would soon relieve himself of affairs are indeed deceived, since, the more we move forward, the more pleasure he takes in applying himself thereto and in giving himself entirely to it. You will find very convincing proof in this dispatch . . . when you will see the resolve which H.M. has taken to answer personally all the letters of his ambassadors on the most important affairs, and to write them even directly when it will deal with occasions of this nature, as he commences to do this day with you. [46]

As for Louis XIV, he received too much pleasure in his

[44] Longnon, *Louis XIV, mémoires*, p. 65. He made an exception to foreign ministers since their opinions he considered too weighted to listen to directly.

[45] J. de Boislisle, *Conseil de 1661*, I, 363-364; for similar letters in the same volume, Le Tellier to M. de Bezons, intendant in Languedoc, April 1, 1661, pp. 364-365; le Brienne, fils, to M. Chassan, April 1, 1661, p. 365.

[46] *Ibid.*, p. 279.

new mode of conduct ever to think of quitting it. " I cannot tell you," he informed the Dauphin, " what benefit I received immediately from this resolve. I felt myself as elevated in mind and courage, I was another person, I discovered in myself unknown things, and reproached myself with joy for having so long been in ignorance of it." [47]   After a decade of what was one of the most successful administrations of French history, the King could well afford to exult in the evident fruits of his decision:

> Time has made apparent that which it is necessary to believe, and it is thus the tenth year that I have proceeded, as it seems to me, quite constantly along the same route, never relaxing in my application; informed of everything; listening to my least subjects; always cognizant of the number and quality of my troops, and the state of my places; incessantly giving my orders towards all their necessaries; treating immediately with the foreign ministers; receiving and reading dispatches; giving myself a portion of the replies, and giving to my secretaries the substance of others; regulating the receipts and expenditures of my State; having directly submitted to me an account by those whom I place in important positions; dealing in my affairs as secretly as any other has done before me; distributing gifts by my own choice, and retaining, if I am not mistaken, those who served me, although loaded with benefits for themselves and theirs, in a modesty quite distant from the height and power of prime ministers.[48]

In the same year, Sir William Temple, writing on the greatness of France, which appeared to him " designed for greater Achievements and Empires, than have been seen in *Christendom* since that of Charlemaign," saw the first asset of that nation as arising from the " Genius of their present King ":

> . . . a Prince of great aspiring Thoughts, unwearied Application to whatever is in pursuit, severe in the Institution and Preservation of Order and Discipline: In the main a Manager of his Treasure; and yet bountiful from his own Motions . . . To this in the Flower of his Age at the Head of his Armies, and hitherto unfailed in any of his attempts at home or abroad.[49]

There had been hints of the future assiduity of Louis XIV

[47] Longnon, *Louis XIV, mémoires,* p. 65.
[48] *Ibid.,* p. 77.
[49] Sir William Temple, *"A Survey of the Constitutions and Interests* of the Empire, Sweden; Denmark, Spain, Holland, France, *and* Flanders; *with their Relation to* England, *in the year 1671," Works,* I, 91.

in the life time of Mazarin,[50] but his actual labors in government from 1661 to 1715 were nothing short of astonishing. It was to be perhaps the highest glory of this monarch, whatever his other errors, that he maintained, until death, an unflagging devotion to the duties of the state.   Arthur de Boislisle, in his *Conseils sous Louis XIV,* makes the statement that in his fifty-four years of personal rule Louis XIV never for a " single day " dispensed with the practice of consulting his councillors.[51]

The variety of the King's interest extended from the most elevated problems of state to the trivial needs of personal and selfish whim, and imposed on such a faithful minister as Colbert multiple tasks which must have been truly galling to him, burdened as he was with so many real responsibilities. It might, for instance, be necessary to take time off from his other duties to purchase bracelets and other costly gifts for the ladies of the Court and carefully arrange the details for a pleasant lottery.[52]   At another time, the King expressed his satisfaction to the minister with the painter Le Brun sent by him to the armies to render permanent the glory of the King's presence at the siege of Cambrai.[53]   The royal Palaces, parks, and hunting lodges were closely supervised by Louis XIV who carried a knowledge and application to them which suggest the enthusiasm of a French peasant for the administration of his lands.   As superintendent of buildings, Colbert had an official interest in furthering the King's plans in that direction. When it was a matter of the Louvre, this interest was real, but, unfortunately, as the first supervisor of the construction of Versailles, he performed tasks the end of which was an extravagance he consistently deplored.[54]   Nevertheless, the correspondence exchanged between the Minister and his master shows them both carefully inspecting and providing for work on its canals, lakes, reservoirs, aqueducts and fountains, speculating on the desirable dimensions and depths of them;

[50] J. de Boislisle, *Conseil de 1661,* I, i-v.

[51] A. de Boislisle, " Les conseils sous Louis XIV," *Mémoires,* VII, 433.

[52] Louis XIV to Colbert, May 2, 1664, Gaxotte, *Lettres de Louis XIV,* pp. 22-23.

[53] Louis XIV to Colbert from Cambrai, April 17, 1677, Grouvelle, *Oeuvres de Louis XIV,* V, 564.

[54] Colbert, *Lettres,* V, xxxi-xlii.

projecting, rejecting and altering buildings, and stairways;
dealing with architects, gardeners and workmen; arranging the
finances and touching the thousand intricacies which confront
any housebuilder.[55]   But the building of Versailles was not
the only such job which possibly proved disagreeable to Colbert.
The King also requested plans, suggestions and progress
reports on such chateaux as that of his mistress, which he
built at Clagny, his own at Chambord, and that of the Duke
of Maine.[56]   In his position, the most menial duties could
fall to the lot of Colbert; as when he was forced to play the
role of the royal pimp, negotiating the differences between
Louis XIV and the Uriah of his Bath-sheba, Montespan.[57]

The seemingly limitless concern of the King with the details
of his realm was reflected in the diversity of subjects treated
in his letters.   To his cousin, the Admiral Duke of Beaufort,
he wrote, in 1666, explaining the sending of one d'Eslivalle
to have his inventions tested in the navy; [58] to the *intendant
des meubles,* Du Met, requiring an account of the furniture
of Fouquet which might be suitable for " my use "; [59] to Colbert
to act as his intercessor in obtaining a greater modesty in the
demands of the Grand Mademoiselle,[60] to the famous Chevalier
Bernini requesting him to bring his art to France.[61]   In return,
unsolicited, the ministers brought to his attention, for his
settlement, such minor particulars as the giving to the Queen,
in his absence, of 2,000 *pistoles* for alms; of the death of a
foreign worker and the desire to recompense the widow with

[55] *Ibid., passim*; Colbert to the King, March 1, 1678, Gaxotte, *Lettres de Louis
XIV,* pp. 68-71.

[56] Louis XIV to Colbert, June 12, 1674, and May 18, 1674, *ibid.,* pp. 49-51;
Colbert to the architect Le Vau, July 12, 1669, Colbert, *Lettres,* V, 288 and
note 3; Colbert to M. de La Saussaye, July 30, 1670, *ibid.,* p. 303; " Introduction," *ibid.,* pp. xxx-xlii; " Appendices," *ibid.,* pp. 569-584.

[57] Louis XIV to Colbert, June 15, 1678, Gaxotte, *Lettres de Louis XIV,* pp.
71-72; Colbert to the King, June 17, 1674, Colbert, *Lettres,* VI, 325; Colbert
to the King, May 24, 1678, *ibid.,* pp. 346-348 and notes, p. 347.

[58] Louis XIV to the Duke of Beaufort, March 30, 1666, Grouvelle, *Oeuvres
de Louis XIV,* V, 373.

[59] Louis XIV to M. Du Met, August 7, 1668, *ibid.,* p. 437.

[60] Louis XIV to Colbert, October 5, 1681, P. Gaxotte, *Lettres de Louis XIV,*
pp. 74-75. This was the Duchess of Montpensier, cousin of Louis and greatest
heiress in France; she tirelessly begged the conferring of honors on her dashing
but worthless husband, Lauzun.

[61] Louis XIV to the chevalier Bernini, April 11, 1665, *ibid.,* pp. 24-25.

the right of *aubaine;* [62] to whom to assign the lodgings in the Louvre occupied by the late M. La Bas "most clever man in Europe for telescopes and mathematical instruments." To all the King would respond in the margins created for that purpose.[63]

When in the field, Louis gave careful consideration to the smallest military details, and drew up full and itemized schedules daily of projected movements and dispositions. At the front and at home, his closest collaborator and agent was Louvois, with the exception of the earlier years when Le Tellier still directed these affairs and Turenne was at the height of his influence. If the King was not with the army, he dictated programs and generally made his influence felt by working through Louvois who sent reports. Following the campaigns and the movements through such reports, and on maps, he directed his responses to his war minister to be effectuated.[64]

But Louis XIV did not limit his labors to personal items, or to those areas, historically the most ready instruments for magnifying the glory of Kings, such as foreign affairs and war. It was probably true that the goal of his policy was renown, but he fully realized the necessity for the economic health of the nation to sustain his glory. In the accomplishment of Colbert's program for industry, for example, his application and his direct encouragement of manufactures by subsidies and by receiving personally and soliciting the advice of merchants, by presiding over councils of commerce, by his presence in the councils of finances, by his personal visitations and inspections of establishments such as that at Abbeville, or of the other ateliers and factories as the Gobelins, Beauvais, and Dunkerque, and by the simple part of acquiescence to the implementation of the grandiose schemes of the Minister, made him the indispensable and senior partner in the plans for an industrial state.[65]

---

[62] Right of the foreigner to inherit.

[63] Colbert to the King, March 21, 1677, Gaxotte, *Lettres de Louis XIV,* pp. 66-67; for similar letters and responses see those of August 14 and 18, 1673, *ibid.,* pp. 44-47.

[64] "Mémoires militaires," Vols. III and IV of P. A. Grouvelle, *Oeuvres de Louis XIV, passim,* especially Vol. III, see "Ordres et dispositions de Louis XIV pour la campagne de 1672," pp. 133-301. In the same volume also see letters exchanged between Louvois and Louis XIV, May 24, 1672, pp. 154-169; Guerlac, "Vauban," p. 28.

[65] This subject is thoroughly treated in Boissonade, *Colbert,* and in Cole, *Colbert.*

II

The Venetian Ambassador, Francois Michiel, admitted in 1674 that the " King alone governs," but he recognized that his aides, Colbert, Louvois, and Pomponne were, nevertheless, essential to him in a " governmental machine . . . too vast " not to provide much work for all.[66]   And, indeed, however diligent Louis XIV might have been, some of his ministers, particularly Colbert and Louvois, were more so.   The King, after all, customarily resolved problems which were presented to him in council or in predigested memoirs representing, frequently, long periods of tedious preparation.   The earlier ministers were chosen and retained favor because of their proven or credited abilities to perform such editing functions with exactitude, sense, and honesty.   In some later cases, as with Le Pelletier and Chamillard, the multifarious demands of their tasks were either too heavy or too discouraging and led to their disgrace or retreat.

The Marquis of Saint-Maurice, writing to his master, the Duke of Savoy, in September 1669, described the departure of the Court to Chambord, and the retirement of the ministers to their country houses: " it seems that everyone thinks only of taking an airing or of amusing himself except M. de Colbert who must go to visit Le Havre de Grace and M. de Louvois the new fortification which are built in Flanders." [67] The Ambassador had pictured Louvois, a couple of years earlier, as the hardest worker he had ever seen.   At another time these labors were " inconceivable," and he excused his inability to see him by relating how, for months, every time he had gone to his apartments he had found the antechamber filled with a hundred and fifty officers.[68]

However, of all the ministers it was Colbert who best symbolized the new order of things.   Though, in his last years, the influence of this Minister with the King was contested by Louvois, historians and contemporaries have generally agreed

[66] A. de Boislisle, " Les conseils sous Louis XIV," *Mémoires*, VII, 434-435.

[67] Marquis of Saint-Maurice to the Duke of Savoy, September 17, 1669, in T. F. C., Marquis of Saint-Maurice, *Lettres sur la cour de Louis XIV*, edited by J. Lemoine (Paris, 1910), pp. 338-339.

[68] Marquis of Saint Maurice to the Duke of Savoy, June 13 and September 23, 1667, *ibid.*, pp. 66, 137; also pp. 151-152; Spanheim, *Relation*, pp. 192-194.

535*51*

with the sentiment of Pagès that: "*La Monarchie Louisqua-torzienne est l'oeuvre personnelle, et commune, de Louis XIV et de Colbert.*" [69]

The Savoyard Ambassador was so impressed, in 1670, with the preponderant position of the financier in the councils that he wrote his master that Colbert could assume at will the ministry and govern with more authority than had even Mazarin.[70] Perhaps no better evidence of his prestige could be found than the suppliant letter of Monsieur, the King's brother, written in the same year to this bourgeois Secretary of State. He pleaded with him, as the only practicable inter-cessor, to obtain from Louis some relaxation of the harsh treatment accorded to his favorite, the Chevalier de Lorraine.[71] The King himself gave frequent evidence, publicly and privately, of his esteem for the man who was so often doing, as he put it, "more of the impossible." [72]

The Abbé de Choisy, opinionated but penetrating in his characterizations, wrote of Colbert as an "*Esprit solide, mais pesant, né principalement pour les calculs . . .*" in whom, "*Une application infinie et un désir insatiable d'apprendre lui tenoient lieu de science. . . .*" [73]

From the very inception of his personal reign, this Minister appears to have been the intimate and active colleague of Louis XIV. The direction taken in the management of an absolute

---

[69] Pagès, *La monarchie d'ancien régime*, p. 135; Alvise Sagredo, Venetian Ambassador to Louis XIV (1663-1665), in his "Relazioni" noted that: "to him alone the internal management of any business and affair of the King is given," *Le relazioni*, seria II—Francia, III, 153.

[70] Marquis of Saint-Maurice to the Duke of Savoy, May 2, 1670, *Lettres sur la cour de Louis XIV*, p. 429. A similar opinion was given by a Bolognese traveller to France in the years 1664-1665. S. Locatelli, *Voyage de France, moeurs et coutumes Françaises*, edited by A. Vautier (Paris, 1905), p. 207.

[71] Monsieur to Colbert, February 2, 1670, Grouvelle, *Oeuvres de Louis XIV*, V, 461-463.

[72] Louis to Colbert, February 24, 1678, *ibid.*, pp. 572-573; other instances are related in letters of the Marquis of Saint-Maurice to the Duke of Savoy. In one, he describes the ostentatious visit of the King to see Colbert in Paris. Louis remained closeted with him for two hours, apparently to dispel the rumors, then current, of the imminent disgrace of the Minister. *Lettres*, pp. 159, 240-242.

[73] F. T. l'Abbé de Choisy, *Mémoires*, p. 575; on Choisy's *Mémoires* see E. Bourgeois and L. André, *Les sources de l'histoire de France: XVIIe siècle (1610-1795)*, (8 vols., Paris, 1913-1935), II, 136-138.

monarchy, such as that of Louis, was perforce a reaction to the inclinations and desires of the King. It was primarily Colbert, however, who was the architect of the new government. It was he who gave concrete expression to the aspirations of the King, and, probably, suggested almost all of the forms which these expressions should take. It was he who most frequently drew up the specifications, regulated the proportions of the structure, suggested the issues of policy and generally performed the heavy tasks of advisor, secretary, planner, and activator. It would be impossible to segregate those portions of their system of government which stemmed from the interests of the King or the desires of Colbert. In most cases, it is clear, the interests of one complemented the purposes of the other. It is certain that, in administration, Colbert steered his course and determined his position with reference to the Glory of his Master, as a navigator places his ship with reference to the polar star. In any case, as all matters of importance had eventually to pass the inspection of the King, it would have been impossible for Colbert long to foster any policy inconsistent with that of Louis. In general, then, one may conclude that the attitudes of the Minister reflected the policies of the King and his actions were a mirror of the royal will. The offices of Colbert permitted him to exercise only a limited influence in the departments of war, justice, and foreign affairs. There Louvois, Le Tellier, and De Lionne, respectively, were, for almost all of his administration, the directors. Louvois and, to a lesser extent perhaps, Le Tellier were men of the stamp of Colbert, and in their areas of competence emulated or paralleled his example with numerous reforms directed towards the creation of a systematic administration.

Colbert seems to have regulated his entire life by work. It is no less striking that he guided his efforts by method.[74] Louis XIV believed he must know the realm to rule it well, and there can be no doubt that Colbert shared this opinion.

[74] Pagès on this score writes, half quoting Lavissee: "Il . . . regla sa vie entière en vue du travail et ne se lassa jamais du plaisir qu'il prenait a démêler, à débrouiller les affairs difficiles. Une méthode précise, le pure méthode cartésienne, lui fournissait des principes certains et fixes, et lui inspirait, son enquête terminée cette certitude qui rend l'esprit lucide et joyeux." La monarchie d'ancien régime, p. 138.

Physical limitations forbade the literal deed of personal discovery. The use of reports and statistics was the necessary solution of reason. As far as possible they would thus avoid the folly which Descartes ascribed to the art of Lulle, " to speak without judgment of these things one is ignorant of." [75] But work, and information on which to render judgment, were not enough. The information had to be accurate, in orderly form, tested and checked, and no pertinent details could be omitted. To obtain such information was the constant task of Colbert and the perpetual expectation of Louis XIV.

The essential doubt which appears always to dominate the correspondence of Colbert and to guide his administration of affairs, marks him as a man of the age. It was reflected in his highly critical attitude towards broad reports, in his repeated demands for proof or the fortification of generalizations with numbers, in his insistence on frequent personal inspections, and his tenacity in pursuing affairs " to the bottom." Incidentally it was probably the chief basis of his personal unpopularity. He was seldom content to issue orders without following them with inquests and his own investigations to see that they were carried out. For this purpose, he required reports from technicians and agents scattered everywhere.[76]

When his own kinsman was suspected by him of inefficiently, or, perhaps, dishonestly, administering the program of the Minister for the construction of the fortress of Brisach, he sent the capable engineer De Clerville to review and to untangle the difficulties. It proved to be an extremely embarrassing assignment to the Chevalier who soon found himself torn between the natural disinclination to find fault with the practices of the relative of his superior, and the pressing demands of Colbert for accuracy. The latter instructed him to examine the affair to the depths by comparing registers and by investigations on the spot. " I do not know if I am mistaken, but it seems to me," he was informed, " that having these registers in your

[75] René Descartes, " Discours de la méthode et essais," Oeuvres, VI, 17-18.
[76] This is also the observation of Boissonade, Colbert, p. 14.

hands and being on the spot, you have too much penetration not to discover the bottom of all that has happened." [77]

From the beginning of his influence in affairs, Colbert showed his tendency to place research before policy. The result was frequently a complete alteration in the nature of projects conceived. In 1663 he had assigned De Clerville to conduct a general survey among the merchants and shippers of the coast towns of Artois and Normandy with a view, primarily, of discovering their ideas towards the reduction of certain imposts, particularly on sugar and tobacco. The investigator found the problem assumed much larger proportions: the disparate interests of the merchants, the difference in the routes of trade of their ships, and other factors, demonstrated the necessity for a more general revision of imposts, also for changes in local duties and more extensive remedies touching piracy, foreign relations, and the unequal needs of Dieppe, Havre, Rouen, Dunkerque, Calais and Boulogne.[78]

The methodical approach of Colbert and the King to the use of administrative data was also indicated by the emphasis placed on their presentation and preservation in orderly and standardized tables, memoirs, registers and periodic accounts. Further, they insisted on the perfection of certain techniques and mechanical methods of presentation.

While Colbert was training his son, Seignelay, to prepare him for the responsibilities of directing the navy department, he drew up for him numerous rules as guides to efficiency. He presented to him as a maxim, for instance, that " It is necessary always to keep a memoir, in table form, of all the places where the King's ships may be found, and to send me a copy each month." It would likewise be necessary to " send me an exact extract of all entries which are made monthly in the agenda of funds, divided by chapter, to the end that I can know if the entries are well made." A packet of information should be accompanied always with an inventory, written in his own hand, of its contents because " only thus will he learn to make a perfect dispatch so that nothing is lacking." [79]

[77] See the letter of Colbert to the intendant, December 27, 1670, and to De Clerville, the same date, Colbert, *Lettres*, V, 42-45 and notes.

[78] De Clerville to Colbert, May 1663, Depping, *Correspondance*, III, 335-337.

[79] " Maximes pour mon fils," Colbert *Lettres*, III, part ii, 69.

Whatever the regulations and instructions, it is clear that they did not meet with complete compliance. The intendant at Metz, de Choisy, was apparently incapable or unwilling to send information, in acceptable form, on provisioning in his generality. Colbert complained his memoirs showed neither understanding nor relationship and that they were incomplete. The intendant was finally discharged.[80] On at least one occasion, the Minister felt called upon to censure his ordinarily very capable cousin, Colbert de Terron, intendant at Rochefort. It " is nearly impossible to discover the payments which have been made to these squadrons by the accounts which you sent, as a result it is necessary to do much calculation to clarify it." He grumbled: " This affair will give me much worry until we have remedied it." [81]

Colbert did not hesitate to criticize the technicians on the performance of their craft when it came within his sphere. After the astronomer-mathematician Richer had returned from his scientific expedition to Cayenne,[82] he was employed as an engineer in the construction of several fortifications. The plans of such places which he sent to the Secretary of State occasionally drew forth expressions of dissatisfaction. Colbert reproached him for failing to use three different tints to distinguish the progress of the works. One day he claimed his plan was particularly bad. " It will be quite necessary that you apply yourself to drawing a little better than you do, there being nothing more necessary to an engineer than to know how to draw well." [83] The plans of Metz sent by the academician, Niquet, occasioned the comment, " if you don't know how to draw better, it would be better that you not bother with it, all the more as such plans cannot be shown to the King." [84]

No criteria received greater stress in the correspondence of Colbert than clarity. In a tone of high indignation, he expressed his exasperation with the habitual vagueness of the memoirs of one intendant: " as if I were a man to be content with these general terms, which mean nothing. . . . If you . . . examine

[80] Colbert to de Choisy, October 28, 1672 and October 4, 1673, *ibid.*, IV, 77-78, 98.
[81] Colbert to de Terron, December 26, 1671, *ibid.*, III, part i, 409.
[82] See Chapter VIII on the *Académie des sciences.*
[83] Quoted in note, Colbert, *Lettres*, V, 155.
[84] Colbert to the sieur Niquet, September 27, 1675, *ibid.*, p. 155.

your letters . . . you will see that neither I nor anyone else could comprehend anything there. . . ." [85] We can hardly escape the impression that he was grinding his teeth as he rather patiently explained to a *commissaire de marine*, " I have already told you, that when you request something, you must explain yourself in a manner that I may not be obliged to guess, as is necessary that I do so often." As an example, he pointed out that " you include in your estimate: some anchors without giving the number; some cannon . . . without mentioning the calibre, nor the quantity. . . ." These things, he expounded, with modest resignation, were necessary to know if the request was to be fulfilled.[86] He wrote to another official acknowledging the receipt of a report on fortifications, but expressed the grievance which he was so often wont to use in reference to their accounts: " Your letter tells me nothing of all the other works as masonry, carpentry, and palisades, nor anything of all that which ought to be done to the fort of la Prée." [87]

The importance to the King and Colbert of having creditable sources for information and faithful and efficient personnel to carry out their policies led them to set great store by proven colleagues. The dependability, technical aptitude, and unequalled devotion for work which characterized Vauban, coupled with the recognition by the King of his sterling worth, made him one of the commanding figures of the age. But it was easy to favor the benign engineer. It was proportionately difficult to work with the dour, uncompromising Huguenot admiral Du Quesne. Nevertheless, for years, Colbert, and even the King, wrote letters to him pleading, half-threatening, mollifying, insisting, and compromising. However disagreeable he might be, they knew him as a first-class seaman and commander, and as an indispensable prop in the navy; and they almost invariably supported him against his enemies, even the most powerful. In January 1671, Colbert wrote to the Count of Estreés, Vice-Admiral of the Atlantic, requesting him to overlook the recognized deficiencies of Du Quesne as he was known to be a very able navigator and capable in everything naval. He

[85] Colbert to M. Arnoul, fils, intendant de marine at Toulon, May 8, 1677, *ibid.*, III, part i (addition), 52-53.

[86] Colbert to the sieur Dumas, July 21, 1669, *ibid.*, III, part i, 149.

[87] Colbert to M. de Dumuin, March 23, 1674, *ibid.*, V, 103.

explained that " in the lack we have of able men in his science, so long unknown in France, I believe it conducive to your and the King's good service, and even to your particular glory " to work with him and overlook his personality.[88]

The advisability of comparing accounts to provide against the compromising of funds was often stressed in the maxims for the government of the navy which Colbert drew up for his son:

It is necessary to send carefully to the intendants and *commissaires généraux de marine* copies of the orders given to the treasurer to remit funds, each in their department; to order them at the same time to send, every six months, a statement of all the funds which will have been remitted by the treasurer to the steward serving near them; and to take care that they execute this order, to the end of verifying if the treasurer has remitted all the funds which he has been ordered to do, and if his steward serving in each department has made the disbursement by the orders of the intendant or *commissaire général* who has the authority to so order.[89]

The ultimate measure of the efficacy of surveys was the personal inspection. The memoir of an intendant being so general in nature as to be unsatisfactory to the King, or Colbert, the intendant was ordered to reinvestigate the conditions of his generality, visiting carefully each election by turn.[90] When the sieur Pène, one of the King's cartographers, was sent on a mission to draw up some exact maps of a region, he was instructed that the information for them should be " taken on the spot, without reliance on the reports of anyone." [91]

[88] Colbert to the Count of Estrées, January 18, 1671, *ibid.*, III, part i, 333.
[89] " Maxims pour mon fils," *ibid.*, III, part ii, 66; a further example on the same page: " Comme il se peut faire que, nonobstant la précaution que l'on prend pour les dépenses de marine, les commis des trésoriers qui sont dans les ports pourroient faire quelque omission de recette que les intendans et conseillers généraux de marine, qui font rendre compte par estat auxdits commis, fin de chacune année, pourroient laisser passer, soit pour n'avoir point conservé les copies desdits ordres qui leur sont envoyés, soit par oubly ou négligence, il faut, tous les trois mois, ou au mois tous les six mois, expédier un extrait en forme de tous les ordres qui auront esté donnés, tiré sur l'agenda des fonds, collationné et signé par mons fils, et l'envoyer aux intendans. Et, en fin de chacune année, il faut vérifies si toutes les sommes qui ont esté envoyées seront employées dans l'estat de recettes et dépenses, qui est arresté en chacun port."
[90] Colbert to M. Foucault, intendant at Montauban, July 14, 1682, *ibid.*, II, part i, 199.
[91] Instruction to the sieur Pène, February 5, 1678, *ibid.*, III, part i (addition), 78.

The Secretary of State reflected his desire for accuracy in the stress often placed in converting general statements to numerical expressions. Writing to the intendant Foucault, he indicated, with reference to his last report, that " His Majesty not being content with what you say in general that the animals are much multiplied in the area of your generality, it is necessary that, in the report which is made thereon to him, His Majesty may see the account of the number of animals in each election." [92]

" Exactitude " as a descriptive imperative was perhaps employed more frequently than any other in the correspondence of Colbert. It expressed the end standard of all reporting, and, as a personal attribute, it provided a most emphatic recommendation for employment in public service. A certain sieur Andréossy was guilty of the " insolent " crime of drawing up an unauthorized chart of specific works of the engineer Riquet which were state secrets, but Colbert felt his chart all the more censurable as it was " not exact." [93] When it was necessary to carry out a task which required a particularly reliable man, Colbert chose M. Perrin whom he had tested and found to be " of a great fidelity and of a singular exactitude." [94]

In particulars, Colbert or Louis XIV were advocates of clarity, exactitude, personal inspection, accounting techniques, orderliness, experimentation, application and thoroughness in the formulation and presentation of information. In general it can be said that the suspicion of tradition and traditional practices and the premise of doubt required the setting of such criteria. But all administration would be ineffective and pitiful without the guiding principle of reason. Louis XIV believed that the exercise of it was the greatest glory of kings. Colbert in large and small matters demanded of his subordinates the use of what one might call the rational approach or arithmetic reasoning.

The Minister repeatedly accentuated the utility of common sense in naval administration in the maxims for his son. By taking the most simple examples imaginable, he drew up a kind of primer of business sense to instruct young Seignelay.

[92] Colbert to M. Foucault, July 14, 1682, ibid., II, part i, 199.
[93] Colbert to the sieur Riquet, February 15, 1670, ibid., IV, 344.
[94] Colbert to M. de La Guette, intendant de marine at Toulon, September 8, 1662, ibid., III, part i, 13.

He should never, he told him, "send any new order to the chandler without sending him at the same time a draft on the treasurer of the navy." So elementary a lesson must have been needed for he wrote:

Only three days have passed since I wrote you this maxim; however, as if you have not read it or that you have forgotten it in three days time, you send an order to a chandler to furnish 450,000 rations amounting to 123,750 livres, without sending him the order to receive the money.

You can see very clearly that he will write you that he cannot execute your order without money, and that he cannot even have a good opinion of you for giving an order which cannot be carried out.[95]

He never tired of stressing to him the use of judgment in even the least details. Thus, he sent him congratulations on his progress in mastering the techniques of sound reporting, but he pointed out that he had been wrong in sending his last memoir by courier: "that is not a great error, but it is necessary to accustom your judgment to distinguish when it is necessary to send a courier express and when it is not necessary." [96] Again, he advised him: "Never give an order to send any sum to the ports until after having verified on the agenda of funds that he [the treasurer of the navy] has had the sums on hand." [97] At another time he presented him with a current sample of bad management to add to his wisdom:

In the list of the squadron of M. le Vice-Admiral, the ship *le Vigilant* is marked for repairs and ought to be boarded by Belile-Erard. This captain is at Rochefort. The ship ought to arrive the 20th of April at Havre, and there is no news that it has already arrived. Captain Méricourt, who commands it, ought to serve as second on the ship *l'Hercule,* which is at Brest. It is up to my son to judge if the navy can be conducted with mischances and contradications of this nature.[98]

An interesting and amusing example of Colbert's rationalistic approach to reports, and its effect, is illustrated in two letters exchanged between the Minister and M. Morant, intendant at Aix. In the first, the Minister wrote to acknowledge

[95] Colbert to Seignelay, September 24, 1673, *ibid.,* III, part ii, 131.
[96] Colbert to Seignelay, August 24, 1673, *ibid.,* p. 127.
[97] " Maxims pour mon fils," *ibid.,* p. 64.
[98] *Ibid.,* pp. 69-70.

the receipt of the news that the ordinarily recalcitrant Estates of Provence had passed a grant of 600,000 *livres* for the King, which was done with " all the obedience and the submission that His Majesty can desire." However, referring to reports on the province and the enlargements on its misery customarily found in them, Colbert added:

> But I am constrained to say to you for you alone that His Majesty has not been persuaded of the great misery of this province and that all great terms of exaggeration which are met with in all the letters which are received have not found much credence, His Majesty knowing well how much money he sends every year into this province and the little he gets in return.
>
> I tell you this only to warn you that you ought to avoid using these terms of exaggeration which are of the ordinary style and which the King sees every year.
>
> I will say further, that if you wish individually to judge well and reasonably if there is misery in the province, consider whether the cities depopulate, if commerce, if marriages diminish, if offices, lands and houses decrease in prices or not. These are the sure means of judging the state of the province; and certainly you will find by this examination that the province is not as miserable as some would have you believe.[99]

Two years afterwards, in a letter to Colbert, the intendant referred to this advice. "Applying myself the methods which you have had the goodness to demonstrate to me as the most certain to recognize the true state of the cities and the strength or weaknesses of provinces, I have remarked . . . ," and he proceeded to use the method to prove the contrary of what Colbert had said he would find. The province, he wrote, actually was in the worst condition it had been in for many years. As proof he cited that the money crops of grains, olives, and almonds had been very small that year. But rather than speak " as formerly, of considerable losses " he would specify by marks almost certainly indicative of the dearth of money. The practice of holding feasts, and all other such extravagances, had almost entirely ceased. Burials, the last place to expect economy, were simple, even for the great. The same simplicity distinguished the celebration of marriage. In Aix and the other important cities he had not observed any recent expenditures on fine furniture or superb buildings. A certain sign of

[99] Colbert to M. Morant, December 18, 1680, *ibid.*, IV, 141-142.

the lack of money was the fact that creditors, generally, were being forced to abandoned seized properties for the want of purchasers. In the last session of Parlement only five cases had been handled. This could hardly be called an evil, in an area famous for the number of its ligitations, but it was, he averred, a sure indication of the lack of money.[100]

The role of teacher appeared to be a natural one for Colbert, whether as a father instructing his son or as a paternalistic minister initiating his subordinates in the rational procedures of a new system. When he wrote to the intendant at Roche-fort announcing that the King wanted to know " exactly and in detail how much a ship of each size cost him," he outlined the method by which this data was to be obtained:

In order to give, him this information, it is necessary to examine how much wood enters into the construction of the ships of each class, formulate .the price according to that of the ordinary cost; do the same with iron and all the materials which go into the said construction; examine finally the number of days of all the workers and their price; and finally make the calculation from all this to what comes the cost of the construction of the hull of the ship.

Then do the same with all the rigging, apparatus, masting, orna-ments, artillery and generally of all that which makes up a ship and places it in a state of readiness for sea.[101]

This request ended as such requests usually did, with an admonition for urgency. " It is necessary to have this memoir as soon as possible in order to give this satisfaction to his majesty." [102]

The ministry was always impatient with delay; the ancient custom of procrastination and leisurely procedure which had seemed practically wedded to French administration could only exasperate a person of the stamp of Colbert, perpetually in a hurry. Typical was a circular letter to the intendants in 1670 in which he called for them to " lose not a moment " in veri-fying the debts of the towns and hastening their liquidation and to " let me know every week in what state is this work." [103]

[100] M. Morant to Colbert, November 7, 1682, *ibid.*, pp. xxii-xxiii.
[101] Colbert to de Terron, June 7, 1671, *ibid.*, III, part i, 372-373, and notes. The same letter was addressed to the intendants at Toulon and Brest. Two days later, he wrote his brother in London to send the same information on the British navy for a comparative study.
[102] *Ibid.*, p. 373.
[103] Circular letter to intendants, December 12, 1670, Depping, *Correspondance*, III, 36-37.

8

If the insistence of the most important lay official of the land was not enough to produce speed, the name of the King could be used to advantage, and frequently was. " He [the King] orders me, further, to say to you that he will see by the place whence your letters will be dated, if you have promptly executed the orders which he gives you." [104]

The case of Colbert versus Pierre Arnoul *fils, intendant de marine* at Toulon, provides a pertinent and curious example of an unsuccessful attempt of the Minister to indoctrinate a subordinate with sound principles, and, in an individual record, touches on his various doctrines and standards of administration. For four years, Colbert showed an unadmirable self-control as in repeated letters he bewailed Arnoul's confusion, and the consequent cost to the state, and tediously instructed the intendant in the proper methods. It is difficult not to censure the immoderate patience which the Secretary of State extended towards the son of an old friend and childhood companion of Seignelay.

In December of 1675 Colbert severely reprimanded the intendant for the vagueness and inaccuracy of his memoirs, which in a particular case had embarrassed the King and his Minister, when on the basis of it, the King had " delivered a reprimand to a major officer " who did not merit it. But he was to have another chance:

> It is time that you seek means of profiting by my instructions, and finish once for all the trouble you give me . . . because it is impossible that the service of the king be advanced if you do not correct these very great faults which you commit in nearly all relations.[105]

The dispatches of the young man appear to indicate a real attempt to comply with Colbert's wishes, but one suspects him of suffering from a massive stupidity. In September 1676 the Minister again complained:

> I always find, whenever I have time to examine what you have done with a little attention, that your little exactitude pitches us into the greatest confusion.[106]

---

[104] Circular letter to intendants, June 1680, *ibid.,* p. 41.
[105] Colbert to Arnoul, December 28, 1675, Colbert, *Lettres,* III, part i, 574-575, xxxvi-xxxviii.
[106] Colbert to Arnoul, September 18, 1676, *ibid.,* III, part i (addition), 37.

The inclination of Arnoul to excuse his own incapacity by reference to the shortcomings of others, a habit which may have been principally responsible for Colbert's grievance in 1675, was unwisely applied by the intendant in 1677 in a complaint against some advice of Du Quesne. Colbert's response was sharp and insulting: " be assured that, when you will have studied yet twenty years under the said sieur du Quesne, you will not be as able as you now think yourself." In a letter of a few days later, the Minister, on longer reflection, found cause to revise his estimate to " forty years." [107] The cost to the administration of Arnoul's incompetence was the point, the following month, of another censure from Colbert:

I vow that I comprehend nothing in all that which you write me concerning the departure of the convoy. You wrote me the 6th of April, that you had no hemp and that when you would, the convoy could not leave than by the 20th of May. I have given on this ground very pressing orders to M. Rouillé for Provence and M. Daguesseau for Languedoc. In response, you have not written me a word in order to let me know if you have any hemp or not, but you tell me only that the convoy will not delay. . . .[108]

In January 1678 the Minister wrote him that his maintenance in an office, for which he was patently unsuited, was an occasion of constant " astonishment " to himself, and that the " friendship which I had for your late father must be very great " to continue that goodness.[109] So Arnoul was retained and Colbert continued to deplore his unfitness and particularly the unreliability and vagueness of his reports. " Then disentangle for me this chaos, and send me promptly a certain memoir on which I can give my orders," he wrote in June.[110] But the end was only reached in November 1679 after the loss of more than

[107] Colbert to Arnoul, April 10 and April 17, 1677, *ibid.,* pp. 45, 47.
[108] Colbert to Arnoul, May 8, 1677, *ibid.,* p. 52.
[109] Colbert to Arnoul, January 21, 1678, *ibid.,* p. 173. February 22 he wrote him complaining of his failure to get anything done at Toulon, " in the universal order of nature, weather ought to be there more fair than here [Paris], and I see nevertheless that, every time you have four ships to arm, it seems that God opens the cataracts of the skies in order to rain continuously and to make all the tempest fall on this little canton of land in order to retard the execution of the orders of the king, not seeing one of your letters, in these occasions, which do not inform me of continuous rains or of prodigious tempests which prevent all sorts of work." *Ibid.,* p. 83.
[110] Colbert to Arnoul, June 15, 1678, *ibid.,* p. 112.

eight hundred men by the breaking up of two ships, the *Sans Pareil* and *Conquérant,* loss of a third, the *Content,* run aground to save the crew, and the near loss of the *Arc-en-Ciel* which barely limped into port in time to escape a similar end. Colbert attributed the tragedy to the " horrible negligence " of the intendant in repairing them when they were in his yards. He admitted however, that he would have to reproach himself " all my life " for failing to discharge a person whose incompetence had been long known to him, and thus, in a way, making himself accessory to the commission of the loss. Finally Arnoul was advised that "the King can no longer use you." [111]

The Arnoul affair is a reminder of the possible conflict between custom and the attempt of Louis XIV and Colbert to institute a regime of method. Nepotism had perhaps no stauncher advocate at the time than Jean Baptiste Colbert. His cousins, brothers and descendants played as large a role in the government as he could well manage.[112] But the vested right of certain families of the *robe* and nobility of the sword to the highest offices in the bureaus representing the crown was a long established fact when Colbert rose to power and was to continue to be so afterward.

Whatever the accidents which might befall the efforts to create an administration of reason, in general, it appears that Colbert and Louis XIV visualized few limitations to the effectiveness of order, common sense, and application. It was this spirit which led Colbert to exclaim to a subordinate, in order to spur him on to the accomplishment of greater tasks: " We are not in a reign of little things, you will see that it is impossible to imagine anything too grand." [113] Granting the use of intelligence, work would answer all difficulties. " Above all," he declared, work " with great diligence, and be persuaded that in proportion to the enthusiasm you have in furthering them, if you apply yourself there, you will find the means." [114] To be always persuaded that one could

[111] Colbert to Arnoul, November 16, 1679, *ibid.,* p. 173.

[112] See Chapter XXXIII in P. Clement, *Historie de Colbert et de son administration* (2 vols., Paris, 1892), II, 447-481; Cole, *Colbert,* I, 296-299; Spanheim, *Relation,* pp. 177-178.

[113] Colbert to de Clerville, October 4, 1669, Colbert, *Lettres,* V, 17.

[114] Colbert to M. de Linières, intendant of fortifications, June 16, 1674, *ibid.,* p. 113.

do better was truly a maxim for all who wished to profit or advance themselves.[115]   This was the spirit of optimism which permeated the enterprising opinion of the age.   Bacon had heralded the century with his trust that it would produce greater glories than Greece or Rome.   In characteristic fashion, Descartes had created a constructive philosophy from a premise of despair.   In such an environment, those standing at the threshold of the personal reign of Louis XIV, who viewed their Sovereign, a man of ambition, diligence and reasonableness, and who saw him surrounded by a progressive ministry, might well declare, as Montchrétien had so inappropriately done long before: " The time is come."

---

[115] Colbert to M. de Seuil, intendant de Marine at Brest, *ca.* 1671, *ibid.,* III, part i, 342 note.

CHAPTER V

THE GOVERNMENT AND ITS SYSTEM OF INQUIRY

To Louis XIV, as we have seen, the throne was the embodiment of sovereign reason and directed the fortunes of the state by the exercise of that judgment which is reason. This judgment, in relation to the state, constituted the proper selection of policy from a mass of presented issues. In his view, the function of his government was to present exact information from which the common sense, natural to a king, should construct a rational conduct for the kingdom. To translate the aspirations of Louis XIV into a reality, a government by inquiry was a necessity. The spirit of the age was favorable and the accidents of politics had already created an institution tailored to supply the data needed by a ministry sensitive, and apparently agreeable, to the ideas of the King. The basic element in a regime which was to operate on statistics and reports was to be the intendancy.

I

In order to make plain the nature of the intendancy and its place in the scheme of political organization, and, also, to provide a point for reference in later considerations of the government, it seems well to present here a brief outline of the structure of the monarchy of Louis XIV as it emerged in the period 1661 to 1683.

At the top of the system was the King, the natural source of law, justice, and police. Below him was the office of minister. After 1661 no minister received a patent. Ministers received their office only by virtue of the verbal command of the King. This was usually signified by the simple method of their being invited to attend the *conseil d'en haut* or *d'État*. In our period, these ministers were Michel Le Tellier (minister from 1661 to 1685), who held also the offices of secretary of state for war and then chancellor of France; Hugues de Lionne (minister, 1661-1671), also, secretary of state for foreign affairs after 1663; Nicolas Fouquet (minister, March 1661-September 1661), also, *surintendant des finances;* J. B. Colbert (minister, 1661-1683), also secretary of state for marine, *contrôleur général des finances, surintendant des bâtiments;* the Marshal de Villeroy (1661-1685), a confidant of the King and perhaps deserving of the title of minister; Simon Arnauld, Marquis of Pomponne (minister, 1672-1679 and 1691-1699), also, secretary of state for foreign affairs; the Marquis of Louvois (minister, 1672-1691), son of Michel le Tellier, also secretary of state for war and *surintendant des bâtiments;* and Colbert de Croissy (minister, 1679-1696), and secretary of state for foreign affairs, also a brother of J. B. Colbert.[1] These ministers were the closest advisors of the King and were consulted by him daily. Their number at any one time never exceeded five, including the Marshal de Villeroy, and from 1661 to 1715 the total number was only seventeen.

Below the position of ministers, though frequently ministers themselves, were the four secretaries of state. The secretary of state for war, the post held successively by Le Tellier and Louvois, administered the army and artillery. The title of secretary of state for foreign affairs, held successively by the Counts of Brienne, Hugues de Lionne, Pomponne, and Colbert de Croissy, is self-explanatory. The secretary of state for marine, held successively by Henri de Guénégaud, Colbert and Seignelay, his son, directed the business of the *maison du roi,* the clergy and the marine. The other secretary of state concerned himself with the affairs of the " so-called " reformed religion and this post was held during all our period by Chateauneuf de la Vrillière. Aside from these special preroga-

---

[1] A. de Boislisle, " Les conseils sous Louis XIV," *Mémoires de Saint-Simon,* V, 453-454. This work and those listed following are the main sources for this description of the government: P. Clement, *Le gouvernement de Louis XIV, la cour, l'administration, les finances et le commerce de 1683 à 1689* (Paris, 1848) ; *L'État de la France* (2 vols., Paris, 1661) (1663) (1665) (1669) (1672) (1674) (1677) (1678) (1680) (1682) (1683), a semi-official publication giving the list of the peerage, great officers and offices; Pagès, *La monarchie d'ancien régime en France;* A. De Vidaillan, *Histoire des conseils du Roi depuis l'origine de la monarchie jusqu'a nos jours* (2 vols., Paris, 1856); L. Mirot, *Manuel de géographie historique de la France* (Paris, 1930); Esmein, *Histoire du droit francais;* Marion, *Histoire financiere de la France depuis 1715,* I; J. de Boislisle, *Mémoriaux du conseil de 1661.*

tives, which were frequently overlapping, the secretaries of state were the general administrators of the kingdom for the affairs of police and order, and through their agents in the provinces they supervised all the other necessary functions of the central government which were not specifically allocated to particular secretaries or other officials. For this purpose the provinces and generalities of the realm were divided among them in four, more or less equal, divisions.[2]

Three other great officials should be placed beside the secretaries of state. The highest lay office of the kingdom, aside from that of the king, was the chancellorship of France. This officer was the representative of the king in his councils and the chief of them in the king's absence, and, as chief magistrate of the kingdom, he was automatically the head of all courts and tribunals. All royal acts passed through his hands and he was traditionally the keeper of the seals. This privilege had been taken away, however, and vested in another officer, the *garde des sceaux*. But the three chancellors in our period, Pierre Séguier (1635-1672), Etienne d'Aligre (1674-1677), and Michel Le Tellier (1677-1685), except for a short period when Louis himself kept the seal, filled both offices.[3] In 1665 the office of *contrôleur général* was created for Colbert. However, most of the functions and privileges of the position had belonged to him since 1661 in his capacity as *intendant des finances* in the council of finances. This was to remain perhaps the most important single charge in the government of the *ancien régime*. The *contrôleur général* was, generally

---

[2] Clement, *Le gouvernement de Louis XIV*, pp. 29-31. In this arrangement conflicts of authority were bound to occur and general ordinances would be differently applied in each of the divisions. It seems odd that Louis did not eliminate this anomaly. However he had applied certain remedies. Thus the affairs of marine which had been divided between the secretaries of state for war and foreign affairs were transferred so that these affairs entire belonged to the secretary of state for marine. Certain provinces or generalities were reshuffled for greater convenience. Fortifications, formerly directed by each of the four secretaries, were divided between the secretaries for war and marine. Finally the activities of the secretaries were given greater coordination by the requirement of their carrying their problems to the *conseil des depeches*. Pagès, pp. 153-156; E. Lavisse, *Louis XIV*, Vol. VII, part i, 150-156.

[3] *Ibid.*, p. 150; Pagès, pp. 146-148. After Seguier's death, January 1672, the King kept the seals until April when he made d'Aligre *garde des sceaux* but d'Aligre was not made chancellor until January 1674. *Etat de la France* (1674), II, 61.

speaking, the economic and finance administrator of the kingdom. During the reign of Louis XIV his powers were never clearly defined; perhaps because of Louis' fear of even appearing to delegate any of his authority. Aside from finances, the *contrôleur* directed affairs of agriculture, general industry, domestic and foreign commerce, and colonies.[4] The other great office was that of *surintendant des bâtiments* which included the supervision of royal building and the royal arts and manufactures of France. This position, likewise, was held by Colbert and, after his death, by Louvois.

Except for tête-à-tête conduct of the business of the government by the king and his ministers, the routine method of coordinating the various departments under the great officers was by means of councils and their committees, subcommittees and bureaus. The government of Louis XIV, at the center, was essentially a government by councils consulted by the king. It was in Louis XIV's reign that this system became clearly defined and the councils assumed set prerogatives and distinctions. There were four great councils.

The oldest of these was the *conseil d'état et privé* or, more commonly known as *conseil des parties*. In the sixteenth and early seventeenth centuries this council had had ill defined authority over justice, finance, and general administration. Under Louis XIV a separation was produced and the *conseil* was left, in spite of the protest of parlements and estates, as the supreme regulator and interpreter of all laws, private or public, within the kingdom. It was capable of judging even in the first instance and of directing all courts or parlements as to their procedure and duties. Dukes and peers and a host of other personages who had enjoyed the privilege of entrance to this council were excluded by *règlement* in 1673 while retaining, in most cases, the empty title of " *conseillers du Roi en ses conseils.*" The personnel of the council was made up of the chancellor, as head, with twenty-four councillors of the *Robe*, three councillors representing the church and three the nobility—all called collectively the councillors of state—the

---

[4] See H. de Jouvencel, *Le contrôleur général des finances sous l'ancien régime* (Paris, 1901). Other outstanding *controleurs général*, after Colbert, were: Pontchartrain (1689-1699); Desmaretz (1708-1715); John Law (1720); Abbé Terray (1769-1774); Turgot (1774-1776); Necker (1777-1781) (1788-1789) (1789) (1790); and Calonne (1783-1787).

contrôleur général des finances and two *intendants des finances.* The ministers and secretaries of state had ex-officio rights of entrance.[5]   Besides the councillors of state, who regularly attended the council meetings, there was a group of *maîtres de requêtes,* from eighty to eighty-eight in number, alternating by quarters, who served as their aides. Their duty was to study, with the councillors, and report on all affairs introduced to the jurisdiction of the body. They also introduced certain cases on their own, served as delegate judges in the provinces or as special investigators and served other councils and ministers. In short, they were the reporters, clerks, and work-horses of the councils and from their number were usually derived the secretaries of state, ministers, and intendants.[6] Louis XIV was rarely present at this council which, as he told his son, " does not deal with anything than some private suits between individuals." In his absence decrees were terminated with the phrase *" Le Roi en son Conseil,"* or, if present, with the additional phrase *" Sa Majesté y étant."* [7]   As in our congress, the work of the *conseil des parties* was largely performed in *bureaux du conseil.*[8]   In summary, the *conseil des parties* was the supreme deliberative tribunal of the kingdom. Unlike the other great councils, it usually functioned in comparative independence of the King, issuing decrees, however, in his name.

" *M. le Cardinal ne fut pas plus tôt mort, qui le Roi fit appeler MM. Foucquet, Le Tellier et de Lionne, pour leur donner à eux seuls la plus secrète part dans sa confiance."* [9] This laconic statement marks the origin of the *conseil d'en haut* of Louis XIV. It was made in the minutes of the first meeting of March 9, 1661.[10]   The kings had always had some sort

---

[5] Rights which they seldom exercised, however, because of their failure to retain precedence in that *conseil.* Lists of *conseil* personnel may be found in the *État de la France,* see for instance (1674), pp. 91-92.

[6] A. de Boislisle, " Conseils sous Louis XIV," *Mémoires de Saint-Simon,* IV, 379-434.

[7] *Ibid.,* p. 416-418.

[8] *Ibid.,* pp. 423-434.

[9] J. de Boislisle, *Conseil de 1661,* I, 1.

[10] The younger Count of Brienne shared with his father the post of secretary of state for foreign affairs. He was chosen as recorder of the new *conseil* and the minutes were his. Jean de Boislisle and his father, A. de Boislisle seem to be somewhat in disagreement as to this *conseil de trois* being the original

of private council in which they conferred on important matters, but, like the other councils considered here, the *conseil d'en haut* or, to give it its other name, *conseil d'État*, was not definitively constituted until the reign of Louis XIV.[11]   The Venetian Ambassador describing the *conseil d'en haut*, in 1653, noted it as including the King, the Queen-mother, the ministers of state, the Duke of Orleans, the Princes of Conde and Conti, Mazarin, the Duke of Longueville, the *Garde des sceaux*, the *surintendant des finances*, the Duke of Vendome, the Marshals du Plessis-Praslin and de Villeroy, and the secretaries of state.[12]   After the death of Mazarin, the multitude in this council was dismissed and, until Louis' death, there were never more than four or five members.   Membership was the automatic mark of a ministry.   The Dauphin was not admitted to its meetings until he was about thirty years old, and neither Phillipe, the King's brother, nor the Princes of the Blood were ever invited.   Secretaries of state did not enjoy entry unless specifically called, and even the chancellor of France, the representative of the King in his other councils, was not necessarily included in its membership.[13]   The *conseil d'en haut* was uniquely the King's council at which he always presided.   Spanheim, the Ambassador from Brandenburg described its powers in 1690:

It is in this Council of Ministers that all the great affairs of the State, either concerning war or peace, are dealt with; where the ministers come and report on whatever concerns their particular departments; where the dispatches of the representatives of the King in foreign courts are read, responses are made and instructions sent out to them: where deliberations are made on treaties, alliances and the interests of the Crown with foreign countries; finally there is proposed and resolved all which concerns the government and which can be of some importance for the King, the Court, the State, in short, for whatever concerns the interior and exterior affairs of the Kingdom.[14]

Besides political considerations, the *conseil d'état* was fre-

---

of the *conseil d'en haut* but their difference is probably only due to a distinction in terms. See J. de Boislisle, *ibid.,* p. vii; A. de Boislisle, " Conseils sous Louis XIV," *Mémoires de Saint-Simon*, V, 442.

[11] *Ibid.,* pp. 437-439.
[12] *Ibid.,* p. 440.
[13] *Ibid.,* pp. 443-448.
[14] Spanheim, *Relation de la cour de France en 1690*, p. 159.

quently the authority of last resort in judicial cases of a civil or administrative nature. These cases were prepared by committees of councillors of state and reported from the *conseil des parties* by *maîtres de requêtes* for the final decision of the King in his highest council.[15]

"The domain of politics is reserved to the *conseil d'État d'en haut,* that of the judicial to the *conseil privé;* the administrative domain is divided between the *conseil des dépêches* and that of finances."[16] The *conseil des dépêches* had existed with distinguishable functions since the regency of Anne of Austria.[17] Under Louis XIV it served as the chief administrative body of the realm and provided the principal means of coordinating the functions and policies of the ministers and secretaries of state relative to affairs within the state. It was presided over by the King and attended by the ministers and the secretaries of state. All business concerning the provinces was introduced to it by the four secretaries of state. They could, however, withhold, for private consultation with the King, affairs which they deemed unimportant or of no particular interest to others. The council ordinarily met every two weeks. Its competence was complex and extensive: the administration of the temporal affairs of the church, discipline of the clergy and holy orders, affairs of hospitals and charities, communities and municipal corporations, relation of the central government with provincial estates, administration and discipline of the judiciary, affairs of the nobility and seigneuries, naturalizations, pardons, public works, agriculture, commissions and contracts, brevets for governors, commandants and other officers representing the King in the provinces and, sometimes, even the settling of cases of judicial contention.[18] For matters of current administration the secretaries of state executed, in their own departments, the decisions taken by the King in the *Conseil*. This they did by letters, *dépêches,* declarations, *lettres de cachet,* brevets, letters-patent, *ordonnances,* or *règlements,* a clerk placing the signature of the King above that of the secretary. Declarations, ordinances or *règlements,* the general laws of the realm, were issued from

[15] A. de Boislisle, "Conseils sous Louis XIV," *Mémoires,* V, 461.
[16] *Ibid.,* p. 464.
[17] *Ibid.,* pp. 464-468.   [18] *Ibid.,* p. 468-469.

this council with the traditional heading "*De l'avis de notre Conseil, et de notre certaine science, pleine puissance et autorité royale. . . .*"[19] At each meeting of the council each secretary of state submitted to the King, for his inspection, a list of all the executions signed and issued in his department in the fortnight since the last session.[20]

The other great council was the *conseil des finances,* or, as it was frequently called, the *conseil royale* and it too was presided over by the King. It, more than any other *conseil,* was an original institution. The distinct creation of Louis XIV and of Colbert, it lay at the heart of their reformed financial structure and will be dealt with later.

Aside from these four councils, there were others which, often of great weight in their particular areas of action, were, nevertheless, so indistinctly constituted or else so specialized as to deserve but little notice here. Perhaps first among these should be named the *conseil de guerre.* It appears that there was, during the reign of Louis XIV, no permanent council for war or, at least, any which had defined membership or functions.[21] The *État de la France,* a semi-official government list of high nobility, royal officers, courts, councils etc., ordinarily speaks of such a council attended by the King with " the Princes, the Marshals of France, and other Seigneurs who have served as Lieutenant Generals in the Armies."[22] A most important council was that called the *conseil de conscience.* This met regularly and was usually made up of two persons, the King and his confessor. The distribution of bishoprics, abbeys, and benefices was the primary function of this council.[23] Perhaps the most interesting of these 'other' councils was the *bureau* or *conseil de commerce.* A similar assembly, headed by Barthèlemy de Laffemas and including councillors of state and members of parlement, had functioned for a while under Henry IV. Richelieu re-created such a body, but it disappeared again during the administration of Mazarin. In 1664, the

[19] *Ibid.,* pp. 477-478.
[20] *Ibid.,* p. 479.
[21] *Ibid.,* VII, 405-407.
[22] See for instance, *État de la France* (1665), II, 66-67; (1672), II, 66; (1674), II, 65.
[23] Clement, *Le gouvernement de Louis XIV,* p. 36; A. de Boislisle, " Conseils sous Louis XIV," *Mémoires de Saint-Simon,* VII, 407-410.

idea was revived and a *conseil* was officially constituted by an edict of that year. In it the King, his ministers, the chancellor and two councillors of state, with two *maîtres de requêtes*, consulted with representatives of the merchants of the realm and considered ways of improving commerce and manufactures. These councils met every two weeks, until 1667, and a number of commerce edicts marked their work. After that, its function seems to have been absorbed into the new departments of Colbert as *contrôleur général* and secretary of state for marine. Colbert maintained a small advisory committee, meeting weekly, and made up of three farmers-general and three representatives of commercial interests, but appears to have put greater reliance on information supplied by his own bureaus.[24]

Such was the central government of France in the period 1661 to 1683. It is necessary to remind oneself that most of its actual work was performed in committees, subcommittees of the councils, and in the bureaus functioning under the various ministers and secretaries of state. In the provinces the will of this organization was exercised, in the main, through four distinct structures: that of justice, finances, the military, and the church. The last of these we can omit from our considerations as it has no direct bearing on our story.

The justice of the King was carried to the kingdom by the "sovereign" parlements. These were, for all but extraordinary cases, the supreme courts of the realm. To them came appeals from all the lower courts, as the *presidiaux, bailliages,* or *senechaussées,* in their particular jurisdictions. The chief of these parlements in prestige and real authority was that at Paris. This might be called the king's parlement. Other parlements were situated at Toulouse, Rouen, Grenoble, Bordeaux, Dijon, Aix, Rennes, Pau, Metz, and Besançon, and several sovereign courts functioned elsewhere. The natural head, excluding the king, of all these courts was the chancellor of France, and it was through his department that appointments to them were made. The *conseil du Roi,* as represented in any of its four divisions, might override the decisions or opinions of the parlements.[25]

---

[24] *Ibid.,* pp. 415-421; see also Boissonade, *Colbert,* pp. 15-16.
[25] Acquisitions in territory made the number of parlements vary in our period,

The financial administration of the kingdom, and this must be extended to include economic as well as tax administration, was carried on, primarily, by the intendants with their subordinates. In our period, France was divided into twenty-six large tax districts, for administrative purposes, called generalities.[26] There were headed by twenty-five intendants.[27] The generalities, in turn, were subdivided into smaller districts called elections and the elections into parishes. A regular hierarchy of officials, within these areas, supervised the levying and collection of taxes, judged cases involving taxation, performed accounting, kept tax rolls, and allocated sums for local costs of government.[28] Under the intendants operated a separate group of officials, with undefined powers, who supervised or interfered in these functions.

The so-called military government of the king was exercised by royal governors in thirty-seven governments.[29] These men

therefore, few of the secondary works agree on this point. See, for instance, Clement, Le gouvernement de Louis XIV, pp. 42-43; Lavisse, Louis XIV, VII, part i, 164; I have used Mirot, Manuel de géographie historique, pp. 222-223, also see pp. 173-178 and the various État de la France for the period.

[26] They were Alencon, Amiens, Pau, Bayonne, Bordeaux, Bourges, Caen, Chalons, Grenoble, Limoges, Lyon, Montauban, Moulins, Orleans, Paris, Poitiers, Riom, La Rochelle, Rouen, Soissons, Tours, Provence (at Aix), Burgundy (at Dijon), Montpellier, Toulouse, Brittany, (at Nantes or Rennes), and to these might be added: (Metz, Toul, Verdun), Besancon (1676), Valenciennes (1678), Perpignan (1660) and Strasbourg (1682). Mirot, pp. 219-221.

[27] Montpellier and Toulouse were administered together as the intendancy of Languedoc. Ibid., p. 221.

[28] The chief place in each generality possessed a tribunal of finances. The main officers here were called the treasurers of France. The intendants had, however, assumed much of their power and carefully checked their activities. In each election was another tribunal, the members of which were called élus. These officers judged all affairs connected with the tailles and aides. The élus selected, from among the taxpayers in each parish, certain collectors who had the miserable duty of distributing and collecting taxes. The sums collected were turned over to receivers in each election, who, after subtracting authorized sums for local charges, paid the remainder into the treasury of the receiver-general of the generality. This receiver made his authorized deductions and turned the rest into the royal treasury. (Clement, Le gouvernement de Louis XIV, pp. 39-40.) This description cannot begin to indicate the complexity of the French tax structure. See Marion, Histoire financière de la France, particularly vol., I, pp. 1-40.

[29] The governments were: Picardy, Normandy, Ile-de-France, Champagne, Brittany, Orleannais, Maine, Anjou, Touraine, Poitou, Aunis, Berry, Nivernais, Burgundy, Lyonnais, Bourbonnais, Auvergne, Marche, Saintogne, Limousin, Guyenne, Bearn, Languedoc, Foix, Dauphine, Provence, Roussillon, Franche-

were ordinarily the peers of the realm or princes of the blood. Many of the ancient prerogatives of these gentlemen, as governors, had been drained off by the agents of the secretary of state for war and the intendants, but their prestige was still very considerable and if the governor was a man of capacity, cooperated with the intendants, was friendly to and trusted by the king and ministers, he could still wield considerable influence. Below the governor were usually four or five lieutenant-generals and, beneath them, governors of local places, cities or royal chateaux. Lieutenant-generals and these local governors were often almost independent of the provincial governor and were also usually chosen from the higher nobility. The primary duties of the governors were to maintain order and obedience to the crown in the provinces and to give armed support, if necessary, to the executions and functions of the other administrations.[30]

II

The administrative prerogatives of the intendant as supervisor of the royal services of justice, police, and finances in the provinces had been rather clearly defined by the time that Colbert assumed his full role in the government.[31] During the personal reign of Louis XIV, these powers were even more definitely organized and solidified and the monarchy assumed the form which it was to retain almost to the end of the *ancien régime*. At the center of this monarchy was the officer called the *contrôleur général*,[32] and, intimately allied to his functions

Comte, Alsace, French Flanders, Paris, Boulogne, Dunkerque, Le Havre, Saumur, Toul, and (Metz-Verdun). Mirot, pp. 214-217.

[30] Clement, *Le gouvernement de Louis XIV*, pp. 37-38.

[31] The duties and powers of intendants are set forth in most secondary histories of the period of Louis XIV. Recommended are Esmein, *Histoire du droit francaise*, pp. 576-578; H. de Jouvencel, " Le contrôleur général et les intendants des généralities," *Le contrôleur général des finances sous l'ancien régime*, pp. 88-95. Their role in specilaized fields as finances, commerce, agriculture and manufactures can be studied in Cole, *Colbert;* Boissonade, *Colbert;* A. P. Usher, *History of the grain trade in France (1400-1710)* (Cambridge, 1913); but to fully perceive the multiplicity and extent of their powers see A. de Boislisle, ed., *Correspondance des contrôleurs généraux des finances avec les intendants des provinces (1683-1715)* (3 vols., Paris, 1874-1897); Clement, *Lettres instructions et mémoires de Colbert;* and Depping, *Correspondance administrative sous le règne de Louis XIV.*

[32] As seen above (p. 118), while exercising most of the authority of the office for some years preceding, Colbert did not receive the title of *Contrôleur général* until 1665.

and carrying his authority throughout the realm were the intendants of the provinces. This close relationship, or interdependence, was largely the creation of Colbert. The expression of it was the development of the practice of regular correspondence between the intendants and the *contrôleur général*. From the very beginning of his administration, Colbert maintained a prodigious [33] correspondence with his subordinates and, particularly, with the intendants. The reciprocal necessity of submitting reports, surveys and memoirs to the *contrôleur général* became a regular duty of these officials. This was the most striking innovation of the minister in the government. As Usher writes in his *History of the grain trade in France,* " The development of the informing function of the intendants was thus one of the most direct results of the personal influence of Colbert. Nor was any function of the 'new administration more important or more literally unique." [34]

Under the regime of Colbert and Louis XIV, the intendant assumed the part of delegate administrator in the most obscure sections that the royal power penetrated. Boissonade, for instance, sees Colbert as the initiator of the policy of using the intendants for the new mission of economic government; an integral segment of their prerogatives for nearly a hundred and fifty years.[35] A literal reading of the instructions and circular letters sent to the intendants or *commissaires departis* into the generalities and *pays d'elections* from 1663 through 1683 would probably leave the researcher at a loss to imagine any possible field of government which was not committed to their inspection. But every inspection required the return of a report or written survey to the King, the secretaries of state, or the *contrôleur général*, and it was on such reports that *ordonnances* were formed, policies decreed, and projects drawn up by the ministry for presentation to the councils and the King.

It was the desire of the King, according to his Minister,

[33] The nine large volumes of Colbert's letters, edited by P. Clement, represent but a small fraction of those letters still to be found in various archives. See " Avertissement," to first volume.

[34] Usher, *Grain trade,* p. 270; see also de Jouvencel, p. 92; the same idea is often put forth by A. de Boislisle, Clement, and Depping.

[35] Boissonade, *Colbert,* pp. 16-18.

9

that the intendants should come to know " perfectly all abuses "
in the area of their responsibility, and to know them appears
to have been considered as equal to remedying them.[36]   The
insistence on thorough penetration into the most obscure
corners of provincial affairs was the theme dominating instructions.   The King recognized the physical limitations of his
own personal desire to learn of the details of his realm " piece
by piece," details which he would acquire himself if it were
possible; therefore, trusted emissaries must perform the
vicarious functions of a protean crown.   At the top, the King
observed all that a mortal man of royal capacities might of
the conditions of his realm; his ministers added their lesser
powers to his, and the intendants informed the ministers of
affairs escaping their notice, and, below the intendants, *subdélégués, échevins* and *curés* extended the threads of the
royal sense into the remotest parish.   The doubt which ruled
the intelligence of the age was reflected in a king who, had
it been possible, would have personally discovered and administered every need of his kingdom.   The same spirit directed
the actions of Colbert, and, if his admonitions were as seriously
accepted as rendered, guided his subordinates.   From the King
downward, the best test in all matters was personal inspection.

The intendants were, then, the legal eyes of the Monarchy.
Colbert wrote his intendants and ordered them carefully, and
personally, to investigate the levying of all taxes in all the
elections of their generality " in a way that nothing escapes
you." [37]   He spurred them on to greater thoroughness by
representing these requests as being relayed from " His
Majesty " who urged them to make " a serious reflection on
all that which happens in the area of the Generality in which
you serve . . . that you enter into the detail of the conduct of
all those who are employed thereto."   He acknowledged the
difficulty of knowing all the various matters to " the depth,"
but this difficulty only emphasized the need of more continuous
application to the task, in order that he might give to " His
Majesty all your advice on all that which can apply in the
future to the end which he sets for himself." [38]

[36] Circular letter to intendants, May 18, 1683, Depping, *Correspondance,*
pp. 46-47.
[37] Circular letter to intendants, August 7, 1681, *ibid.,* pp. 42-43.
[38] Circular letter to intendants, January 2, 1682, *ibid.,* p. 44.

As had been customary with the *commissaires*, the intendants were usually chosen from a panel of the *maîtres de requêtes* of the Hôtel de Ville of Paris; nominated by the *contrôleur général*, the secretary of state for war, or perhaps noticed by the King in his councils; they were dependent on the royal favor for past benefits and for all future preferments.[39]   A high degree of loyalty could be expected, and was reflected in the reliance which the central ministry placed in them to the detriment of older or more traditional officers. As early as April 1661, we find Louis XIV clearly expressing his preference for these direct agents of the crown as more satisfactorily fulfilling the needs of royalty. When the Estates of Artois sent emissaries to complain directly to the Royal Council of the excessive *don gratuit* required, the King ordered his Minister, Le Tellier, to write them a rebuke manifesting the royal displeasure. He was angry because they had appealed directly rather than through the *commissaires* who were " well informed of his intentions." [40]

The multifarious functions of the intendants and the essentially informative character of these functions are progressively evident in early correspondence of Colbert with them.[41] Usher asserts that technical and statistical information was less frequently required of the intendant than a statement of the general impression of conditions in his generality; however, as time passed the Minister became ever more exacting in his demands and increasingly discriminating in the segregation of fact from rumor. His persistency in insisting on adequate and valid information had the end result of developing an administrative standard of expectation and compliance which accounts for the fullness of the reports of the intendants

[39] de Jouvencel, pp. 89-91; Clement, *Le governement de Louis XIV*, p. 31 note; Esmein, p. 572.

[40] Minutes for the seance of [the 4th] April 4, 1661, in J. de Boislisle, *Memoriaux du conseil de 1661*, I, 142. This preference for information supplied by these agents of the crown is emphasized twenty years later in Colbert's letter to M. Morant, intendant at Aix, November 6, 1682, in which he discourages the sending of useless delegations from the city to a King who is much better informed by his intendants. Colbert, *Lettres*, IV, 164-165.

[41] The letter of April 5, 1663 to his kinsman, Charles Colbert, intendant of Alsace, is an interesting sample; much boiled down, the instructions therein contain many of the points soon to be dealt with in the great inquest. Colbert, *Lettres*, IV, 11-12.

after Colbert's death. The requirement of continuous reporting, the necessity for presenting, to the ministry, digested summary statements of the most diverse facts in his generality, placed the intendant, perforce, as another writer has observed, in the midst of numbers. By the very nature of his functions, he became a statistical agent of the central government.[42]

The general pattern of government by inquiry was precisely laid down in the *Instruction pour les maîtres des requêtes, commissaires departis dans les provinces* of September 1663. This circular letter significantly and, in a sense, officially underlined the henceforth consistent policy of Colbert and Louis XIV in regard to the duties of the intendants. It initiated a vast inquest into the state of the realm with the intendants as the royal investigators; an inquest which was never completed in the life of its originator. The correspondence of Colbert reveals that most of the information requested at this time was still being sought by him twenty years later. Twenty years after that the Duke of Beauvillier made almost the same inquiries when forming his famous memoirs for the instruction of Louis XIV's grandson, the Duke of Burgundy. However imperfectly the designs of the inquest might be carried out, the instruction of 1663 was an unqualified endorsement by Louis XIV and his Minister of the ideal of administration based on the accumulation of political and social statistics. The purpose of the inquiry was declared in the preamble:

The King desiring to be clearly informed of the state of the provinces within his kingdom, His Majesty has willed that this memoir be sent in his name to the various *maîtres des requêtes,* so that each can work in the area of his employ and inform himself carefully and exactly of all the articles contained herein.

First on the list was the order to seek all maps of the generality or province that could be obtained. These were to be personally verified by the *maître.* If they were deficient, capable persons must be sought to correct them. If such persons could not be found, it would be necessary to draw up memoirs on the old ones which could be submitted to the royal

---

[42] Usher, p. 270; F. Faure, "The development and progress of statistics in France," p. 253; see also J. de Boislisle, "Introduction" to *Conseil de 1661,* I.

geographer [43] as a guide to drawing up new ones. The administrative character of the maps was emphasized by the order
to show in them the divisions of the four governments:
ecclesiastical, military, justice, and finances. These must be
outlined in general and include as well the subdivisions of
each. For example, under the heading of ecclesiastical, the
maps should show the bishoprics, each distinguished from the
other; each bishopric should show the archdeaconries, the arch-
presbyteries, the names of all parishes in each division so that
the total number in each bishopric would be readily available;
the abbeys and other benefices were to be distinguished as
subject to the bishop or exempt, and further abbeys or other
benefices having exempt privileges elsewhere. Similar break-
downs were specified to be applied to the military, judicial,
and financial districts.

Aside from this, the *sieurs commissaires* would be required
to familiarize themselves with all these divisions and draw
up "true" memoirs on that which they were required to learn.
Thus in regard to the ecclesiastical: the number of bishops,
their jurisdiction; their temporal seigneury and the cities,
parishes, etc. making them up; whether the bishop was a temporal lord of a cathedral city; the age, name, estate, and disposition of the bishop, whether native to the area of his
bishopric, if ordinarily resident, if he made his proper visits,
his credit in the bishopric, his authority in trying times, his
reputation among the people; whether he conferred the benefices of his chapter, the value of the benefices conferred, etc.

Further the memoirs should answer queries relative to abbeys
and all ecclesiastical houses, lay and regular: the number of
brothers, their qualifications, customs, conduct, and reputation.
They should produce numerous other facts concerning convents,
religious reform, the relationship of family to offices, qualifications for entrance and for orders.

As to the military government, the *maîtres* were not to be
prevented by the fact that the King knew " all the talents of
the governors and lieutenant generals of his provinces " from
investigating the alliances of their houses with the provincial
nobility; whether they were in actual residence, if their conduct

[43] Nicolas Sanson of Abbeville (1600-1667) from 1665, historian and
geographer ordinary of the King.

was good or bad, whether accused of malversations, whether
these accusations appeared well founded, whether they protected the weak, their credit among the people, etc. In short,
the King desired to be carefully informed of the past conduct
of his governors that he might be well advised where to place
his confidence in the future.

Next the upper nobility were to be investigated and their
family alliances indicated along with the extent of their property, their habits, their violences, details of their wrong doings,
whether they hindered royal justice, and an estimate of their
credit in the country. For the lesser nobility, it would be
well to know the number and the names of the most reputable,
whether they were warriors and if they cultivated their own
lands or farmed them out. For the nobility in general, the
King would like to know the true number of them divided by
bailliages and *séneschausées;* the number of nobles distinguished by connections of family, by virtue of personal merit
or services, the number and revenues of their lands and
properties.

When inquiring into the administration of justice, the
maîtres des requêtes were to examine carefully " in general
and in particular " the personnel of the parlements and other
sovereign courts in those provinces possessing them. They
should particularly investigate their conduct during the minority of the King. If their conduct had been unsatisfactory, the
maîtres should attempt to estimate if the causes of their return
to the fold appeared sufficiently strong to justify a confidence
in their future loyalty under similarly unfavorable conditions.
The King should know in detail the interest and qualities of
the principal officer of these companies, the number of officers
in each, the names, alliances, good and bad qualities, and credit
of the principal officers.

Further the commissaires should disclose the facts pertinent
to the kind of justice given or withheld, the causes, and the
persons associated with corruption or oppression. They must
investigate suspicions and detect reasons for delays or excessive
costs in court processes and supply many other details related
to justice and injustice in the generalities. Like investigations
were to be made in the lower branches of justice in the
bailliages, séneschausées and *presidiaux.*

Turning to finances, the *maîtres* should know, in the provinces where there were *cours des aydes,* the names of the officers, their merit, alliances, reputation for justice; if there was manifest corruption among them and details of such. They should inquire what vexations the people might suffer, of the length of court suits, and remedies proposed for the evils. They should seek out those who escaped taxation by falsely posing as nobles, and suggest remedies for this evil also.

It would be well to mention the number of elections under the jurisdiction of the *cours des aydes,* the number of officers in each; the towns, cities, and parishes in each election or salt farm and, from this, the number and quantity of all the parishes under the jurisdiction of the *cours des aydes,* at least to the limits of the province assigned to the *maître des requêtes.* The same type of research should be conducted in relation to the offices of the treasurers of France.

They should examine carefully the annual amounts, and the means of collection in each province pertaining to the sources of royal revenues, such as: *droits d'entrée et de sortie, aydes, gabelles* and *tailles.* This inquiry should be pushed further to discover any imperfections in the systems, to hear and report on complaints of merchants, the contrary reasoning of farmers, and the relationship between taxes and commerce. They were to seek out injustices or undue hardships which such imposts produced among the people and suggest remedies. In short, they were urged to pursue the intricacies and malpractices of the tax systems to the bottom.

Similar inquiries were to be made on the grants and tariffs of cities, their authorization, effect, use, and misuse. While considering local tariffs, they would be required to report on the status of community indebtedness and investigate the means of reducing or liquidating it.

The quantitative study of social and economic facts was to engage the attention of the *maîtres* in formulating memoirs on the general situation in the provinces. They were to examine the humor and temper of the people in each province and city; whether they were inclined to be warlike or pacific, whether they were by nature directed towards agriculture, commerce, manufacturing or the life of the sea. If, perchance, the province was maritime, was there a supply of good sailors and what was their reputation as seamen? Was the land rich or poor, cultivated or fallow? Where did any of these conditions obtain? If fertile, what was the produce? They were to estimate the diligence of the farmer and whether they applied themselves to raising crops most suitable to the lands, and if they knew good management. They were to observe the state of the forests and consult the instruction already issued on the reformation of them. They were to note what type of trade and commerce was carried on in each province and what kind of manufactures.

Specifically, on business and manufactures, they were to inform the King of what changes had taken place, in that regard, during the past forty or fifty years. If any foreign trade had died out, they should seek to discover the causes of the decay and the means of re-establishing it. They were to seek out cities where an inclination was evident to establish, or re-establish, manufactures, projects which the King was anxious to aid. For such affairs they were to seek the advice of the most intelligent persons of the province. With reference to the navy, the *commissaires* were to inform themselves of the number of ships belonging to the subjects of the King. The principal merchants and business men were to be urged to purchase new ones to augment the number, and to form overseas companies with the assurance of royal protection.

By visitations, surveys, and consultations with local inhabitants and technicians, the *maîtres* were to discover and inform the King of all the needs and recommendations pertinent to the improvement of transportation by the building or repair of canals, dikes, roads, bridges, and by the dredging of river channels.

Like researches were to be conducted by them to the end of establishing or re-establishing the industry of horse breeding. Finally, they were to investigate the sources of the continual complaints regarding the issuance of debased money. All the points touched in this memoir, and we have given an abridged account, were presented to the *maîtres* as simply a beginning to which they would find " an infinity of things to add " which would be suggested to them by their own prudence.

The initial plan was to assign the *maîtres des requêtes* to a province for four or five months in order to carry out this investigation. At the end of this period they were to be transferred to new provinces leaving their memoirs and instructions to be extended by their successors and receiving those of their predecessors in the new area. The King hoped that " by an assiduous labor and an extraordinary application, the said *maîtres des requêtes* " would have visited all the provinces of the realm in seven or eight years and thus prepare themselves for the greatest offices, " His Majesty reserving to himself to recognize those who will be the best acquitted, by the account which they will have the honor to render him in his council." [44]

The final provision of the scheme was not realized but the general memoir remained as a kind of permanent instruction for the intendants in their provinces and generalities. In their letters, Louis XIV and Colbert continued to reiterate, elaborate, extend and regularize the demands for information which it contained. It is, therefore, misleading to accept the statement of the historian Levasseur that the inquest remained " unachieved." The more important point is that a system was officially initiated which committed the government to the continuing task of collecting valid social data and statistics. In a real sense, as is true today, this task cannot be completed in a dynamic society. If the results were not assembled into compact volumes, as were the memoirs of the intendants of 1700, one need seek no further for the explanation than to recall that these later memoirs were specifically formulated for the instruction of the heir apparent. Memoirs and reports were submitted, nevertheless, in response to the inquest of 1663 and deposited in the official archives which were formed for administrative use and where several have been found. From the archives of Colbert, his colleagues, and successors was derived much of the material for the work of the intendants of 1700. [45]

[44] Colbert, " Instruction . . . ," September 1663, *Lettres*, IV, 27-43, ii-vii.
[45] A. de Boislisle, ed., " Introduction " to *Mémoire sur la généralité de Paris*, Vol. I of *Mémoires des intendants sur l'état des généralitiés, dressés par l'instruction du Duc de Bourgogne* (Paris, 1881) in (Collection des documents inédits de l'histoire de France); see also E. Levasseur, *La population francaise, histoire de la population avant 1789* (2 vols., Paris, 1889-1891), I, 55-56 and notes; Pagès, *La monarchie d'ancien régime*, pp. 160-61; Colbert, *Lettres*, IV, ii-vii, 1-180.

Among the memoirs resulting from the inquest of 1663 those of Charles Colbert de Croissy, a brother of the Minister, are singled out by Clement as of superior quality, displaying, besides a diversity of information, an unusual frankness. His reports on Poitou, Touraine, Anjou, Alsace and the three bishoprics of Metz, Toul and Verdun were notably detailed and revealed the sad plight of their peoples. Other such memoirs have been discovered on Brittany, Rouen, Champagne, Burgundy, Bourges, Berry, and Moulins dating from the early years of Colbert's administration.[46]

The utility of a summary account of the personal qualities of the members of the parlements, and other superior courts, probably seemed particularly pointed to Louis XIV and Colbert, both of whom always kept the lessons of the Fronde carefully nurtured in their memories. We have seen the attention given to this detail in the third section of the memoir. All the intendants of the provinces were requested to submit careful notes on the morals, capacities, influence, property, connections, and functions of the personnel of these courts. The resulting reports were in many cases partial and in most cases must have appeared inadequate. But this might be expected at a time when the intendants were but beginning to assume the new role assigned to them by an exacting Minister. At any rate, the " Notes secrètes " sent to Colbert in response to this request form an extensive and entertaining part of the administrative correspondence edited by Depping.

M. Lamoignon of the Parlement of Paris was a pompous person with an " affectation of great probity and of a great integrity hiding a great ambition." [47]   M. Bailleul had a " gentle and easy disposition, acquiring through his civility many friends in the Palais [of the Parlement] and at the court." One de Nesmond " married to the sister of Mr the first president, is governed by her." M. Menardeau-Sampré was " very capable, firm, obstinate . . . governed by a damlle of the rue Saint-Martin." As for M. Fayet, he was "less than nothing." In the Chambre des Enquestes, M. Faure was

---

[46] Ibid., pp. iii-vii, and note p. vii; A. de Boislisle, Mémoire sur la généralité de Paris, I, ix; Levasseur, La population, I, 55-56 and notes.

[47] Guillaume de Lamoignon, First President of the Parlement of Paris. One of the most able men of the law of his century in France, and one of the strongest opponents of Colbert and Pussort in their program of legal revision.

" stupid, ignorant, brutal, fearing extraordinarily M. Hervé; he is a man of letters, but loves extraordinarily his own interests." But this was a report on all the major courts of the kingdom; in the Parlement of Brittany, the sieur De Brequingy had good intention " but he is weak and of a very mediocre mind." Jacquelot, sieur de la Motte was " without capacity, and addicted to debauches with women and wine," but M. Montigny had " many of all kinds of good qualities and no bad ones." The reporter on the councillors of the *cours des Aydes* at Rouen contented himself almost entirely with variations on the two words: " *probité* " and " *capacité.*" If his subject was very commendable he had both " *probité* " and " *capacité.*" [48]

However deficient some of the first reports of the intendants might be, it would appear that, with practice, the technique could be too well mastered. In July 1676, Colbert wrote in perplexity to M. Le Blanc at Rouen, " I have received the account of the provender which has been consumed in your generality during the winter quarter; but you fail to explain for what reason you send it to me, and I cannot supply it." [49]

III

Although the intendants were the peculiar and central figures around whom was constructed the reportorial bureaucracy in the reign of Louis XIV, these agents by no means enjoyed the exclusive privilege of writing to the ministry. If they were the first sources to whom the King or Colbert might turn for facts on the provinces, they did not monopolize that reliance. An active and informative correspondent with Colbert was the Duke of Chaulnes, Governor of Brittany. [50] Georges de Guiscard, Count of La Bourlie, Lieutenant General then Governor of Sedan, wrote him letters describing the manufacture of cloth, and reporting, as a result of personal investigation, his findings on the numbers and condition of workers therein, the quality of the goods produced, estimates of future prospects, and the possibility of importing workers from

[48] Depping, *Correspondance*, II, iii-iv, 33-132.
[49] Colbert, *Lettres*, IV, 121.
[50] Examples of letters in Depping, *Correspondance*, III, 254-262, 608-611; see Boissonade, *Colbert*, pp. 14, 22-23.

abroad.[51] Colbert, himself, wrote to the consul of France in Cyprus ordering him to continue " always to inform me of all that happens in the area of your consulate concerning commerce and navigation." [52] The Minister, and to a lesser extent the King, maintained a continuous and personal exchange of reports and advice with technicians like the engineer De Clerville, ambassadors, provincial officials and scientists.

Colbert established, besides, the corps of *commis ou inspecteurs regionaux des manufactures.* These ubiquitous functionaries carried the economic instructions and *réglements* of the *contrôleur général* into the most distant areas of industrial France.[53] The instructions to a *commissaire général de la marine* outlined the duties of another inspecting official. Travelling with the fleets, he was to consider the making of surveys on them as his main responsibility. These surveys were to be conducted monthly, time and seas permitting, and a report of them forwarded to the King. They should include various items: rolls of crews and stowaways, materiel accounts and suggestions for general improvements in the navy. From him Colbert was to receive such data as records of the supplies and the consumption of them aboard ships. He was to observe if the victuals were of " good quality and if they are delivered in the required quantity to nourish each man." He was to inspect to see if the *écrivain,* a kind of purser, aboard the ships performed " well the duties of his office, taking a good inventory of the entire armament of war, rigging, . . . and generally of all that which should be in his inventory to the end of being able to render an exact and faithful account." When ships arrived in port for disarmament, the *commissaire général* was to make " an exact survey of all the crews, before any sailor or soldier can go ashore, and, on these surveys, His Majesty desires that payments be made, and the discounts regulated." [54] Ashore, these officials were sometimes delegated to

[51] See letters of September 4, 1664; August 13, 1665; December 10, 1665, Depping, *Correspondance,* III, 696-699.
[52] Colbert to M. Sauvan, November 6, 1671, *ibid.,* IV, 580.
[53] Boissonade, *Colbert,* pp. 20-22; Colbert was the creator, according to Boissonade of the official service of the inspection of manufactures, the inspectors general and special. See pp. 18-20; also Cole, *Colbert,* II, 416-427, 573-588; also Chapter VII of this study.
[54] Instruction to the sieur Brodart, *commissaire général de la marine,* April

carry out similar surveys, relative to the navy, working with the intendants, general and particular, lieutenant governors and others.[55]

The intendants, in turn, because of the extraordinary demands made on their capacities, found the delegation of their duties imperative. They created their own informing agents, the *subdélégués*. Although the charge was not officially existent until 1704, Colbert himself had recognized their usefulness, but only within limitations and surrounded by restrictions. Gradually they came to exercise, in the elections, the functions which the intendants enjoyed in the generality; this in spite of the pronounced policy of Colbert, after 1674, to curb their prerogatives. Apparently the Minister feared, even then, the potential threat to the centralized authority which these officers were to translate into reality in the eighteenth century.[56]

IV

The inquest of 1663 had only suggested the multiplicity and variety of reports, surveys, and isolated data that would be demanded and accumulated by the central authority during the ministry of Colbert. The sense of urgency and innovation which pervades the official correspondence in this regard suggests the naive interest of a child first grasping the abilities of his senses. Information was required on ships on the oceans and on swans on the Seine. A request for a memoir, or an investigation on which to base one, seems to be the subject of the majority of the letters from the *contrôleur général*. By thousands of demands for specific reports the inquest of 1663 was converted into a continuous system. Ordinarily, the surveys projected were restricted to some particular interest, but cumulatively they expressed the desire to discover the smallest causes of the motions of the state. In the time of Colbert no further investigations of the scope of that of 1663 seems to have been required, yet this was only apparent, since, as

15, 1669, Colbert, *Lettres,* III, part i, 117-119; similar instructions, pp. 193-195.

[55] *Ibid.,* pp. 159, 166-167, 219.

[56] J. Riccomard, ." Les subdélégués des intendants jusqu'à leur érection en titre d'office," *Revue d'histoire moderne,* XII (1937), 339-368.

already indicated, this inquest served practically as a permanent commission to the intendants. The circular letters sent to these officials sometimes approached the breadth of the original inquest in the extent of their requirements. In June of 1680, for instance, Colbert ordered them " to examine with the greatest care the state of the wealth of the land, the nature of the animals, manufactures, and all that which contributes in each election to attract money there." They were also to seek the means of forwarding such a desirable end. They were to examine, " to the bottom," the system of the division and collection of *tailles*. By personal visitations to the elections, they were to discover the costs, malpractices and obstacles present in the collection of taxes and report thereon to the King. They were to consult the local inhabitants on these problems, listen to all complaints and send " an exact memoir of all that which you will have observed, with your ideas of the remedies which you believe can be applied there." [57]

In certain respects, some colonies provided an area where the standards for surveys could be set higher than in France. The paucity of the population, the relative unimportance, or absence, of traditional political structures and social prejudices to impede the agents, the simplicity of the government and the economy, the comparatively small area of actual settlement, the newness of its history; all these factors came to the aid of a Frontenac, or of any special commissioner, sent to obtain exact information on the country. Thus the ministry desired to know the situation of the country, its latitude, the length of its days and nights, of the good or bad qualities of the air, of the regularity and irregularity of the seasons and how much the country was exposed.

After these first researches, it will be a-propos to distinguish carefully the fertility of the land, for what it is suitable; what grains, seeds or vegetables grow there most easily; the quantity of workable lands there, those that can be cleared in a certain time, and to what culture one could put them . . . to what particularly the inhabitants apply themselves; in what consists their trade, the means they have of subsisting and of rearing their children.

. . . .

He will inform himself carefully of the total extent of land which is occupied by the French, by each inhabitant in particular, of the

[57] Depping, *Correspondance,* III, 38-40.

number of families and of persons of which they are composed, and of the sites of their locations, from which it will be necessary to draw up a form of map as exact as possible.

He will make mention of the number of *arpents* of land which will be worked and enclosed in each habitation, and of what quality are those not cleared which are found between the said habitations.

He will inform himself also of the quantity of grain which the land can produce, ordinary year, if it produces a greater quantity than is necessary to subsist the inhabitants, and if there is some sort of hope that it will increase or not. . . .

The sieur Gaudois will observe if there is a deficit in the said country of wives and girls, to the end that the number necessary for the next year be sent.[58]

In the administration of the navy, the reports demanded of the aides were often highly technical or statistical in nature. An intendant of marine in an arsenal port was required to submit an annual account of all the merchandise, munitions, or arms that he would need for the coming year for all purposes: for ship construction, repairs, rigging, armaments, or for placing in reserve in the warehouses, in order that the Minister might give the orders necessary to procure such provisions from various sections of the kingdom. Further, he was required to send at the end of each year a general account of everything stored in the warehouses in order that " His Majesty may be informed of the state in which they are." At the beginning of each year the Minister must receive a complete account of all expenses of the year preceding. This, likewise, was to be presented to the King.[59]

The pretentions of France to assume in the seventeenth century the political preponderance which the Hapsburgs had held in the sixteenth was indissolubly allied with the hope of grasping the greater share of the commercial and industrial advantages which other nations were felt to enjoy. The business of running the foreign policy of the government was more

[58] Instructions for the sieur Gaudois on being sent to Canada, May 1, 1669. Colbert, *Lettres,* III, part ii, 444-446.

[59] Instruction to the sieur Matharel when being sent to Toulon as intendant, April, 1670, *ibid.,* part i, 224-233; a letter to the sieur Leger, *contrôleur général* of the arsenal at Toulon, January 16, 1670, shows the requirement carried to a lower level. He was to work " without loss of time " to make an inventory of equipment in the warehouses and on all armed ships in the port of Toulon and an account of the last year's expenses as he [Colbert] had already received them from other ports. P. 208.

than an affair of politics, it was also a matter of economics. It is not surprising, therefore, to discover that Colbert played an important role in a department which would ordinarily be the province of Hugues de Lionne, the secretary of state for foreign affairs.

The reports of ambassadors frequently resembled the reports of intendants by the technical character of the information provided. In his correspondence with the representatives of France abroad, Colbert revealed a constant care to be posted on the status of commerce in all parts of Europe, Asia, and Africa where there were agents. He even requested statistical accounts of trade exchange in foreign ports.[60] To be sure, the intendant system could not be extended beyond the boundaries of the French state, but the functions of foreign representatives could be somewhat modified to give them some of the duties of the regularly constituted reporting agents within the kingdom. " He made of political and consular agents," writes Segur-Dupeyron, " veritable . . . commercial agents, placing them in a way, at the disposition of the merchants." When a certain sieur Catelan of Rouen was proposed for the consular post at Cadiz, the Minister wrote the intendant at Rouen to inquire carefully among the merchants of that city if he was " capable of fulfilling exactly all the functions " of such a responsible place.[61]

In his estimation, the first rival of France, in a mercantile sense, was Holland and he was proportionately anxious to discover commercial facts which might prove of advantage in combatting her. His letters on this matter are filled with demands for detailed accounts on her commerce, manufactures, tariffs, and trading companies.[62] Sweden, Denmark, Spain, England, Venice, and all states, where there appeared to exist the possibility of making a commercial treaty, or the need of protection against their manufactures or natural produce, elicited from him a multitude of requests for surveys, memoirs, and statistical reports.[63]

[60] Depping, Correspondance, III, xxxix; P. de Segur-Dupeyron, Histoire des négociations commerciales et maritimes du règne de Louis XIV, considérées dans leurs rapports avec la politique générale (3 vols., Paris, 1863-1872), I, 173-174.
[61] Quotation without source cited. Ibid.
[62] See letters in Depping, Correspondance, III, 438-461.
[63] On Spain for example see: Colbert to Archbishop of Embrun, Ambassador

He desired to make the French navy superior to that of any other nation. In this work he started from practically nothing. It was necessary to imitate or surpass the methods and experiences of the Dutch, English, and, to a lesser extent, the Venetians,[64] in shipbuilding, in naval administration and discipline, in nautical arts and in equipment. Therefore, the gathering of such technical data from these countries was an integral part of the navy program. In 1670 Colbert wrote to the French Ambassador in England:

As there is nothing so important for the perfection of the works which are underway in our ports as to profit from the knowledge which the English have acquired in the navy, I have instructed the sieur de Monceaux, who will bring you this letter, to examine carefully all that is done in England, whether in the construction of ships and docks, or for 'the purification of water, and even the order which is observed in the arsenals for the conservation of the merchandise serving for the armaments. . . .

The Ambassador was ordered to give him all possible assistance " in order that he may draw some utility for the service of the king from this voyage." [65] In 1672 he was still writing the Ambassador requesting such things as any books printed on the subject of policing the arsenals or on the duties of the naval officers, on ship maneuvering, naval law, tactical practice

to Madrid, 1663, *ibid.*, p. 338; Marquis of Villars, Ambassador to Madrid, to Colbert, 1669, *ibid.*, pp. 435-438; on England, letters to Colbert de Croissy, Ambassador to England, March, September, October 1669, *ibid.*, pp. 424-428; on Denmark, Colbert to the chevalier de Terlon, Ambassador to Denmark, October 1662, *ibid.*, IV, 667-668; on Sweden, Arnoul de Pomponne, Ambassador to Sweden, to Colbert, September 17, September 24, March 3, 1668, *ibid.*, III, 407-408, 408-409, 410-411; on Venice, Colbert to the Count of Avaux, Ambassador to Venice, September 1672, Colbert, *Lettres,* V, 335.

[64] For the general history of the development of the navy under the leadership of Colbert and his son Seignelay, see C. de la Roncière, *Histoire de la marine française* (6 vols., Paris, 1899-1932), V, VI.

[65] Colbert to Colbert de Croissy in London, September 2, 1670, Depping, *Correspondance,* III, 431. In a letter to the same, March 20, 1669, Colbert had written: "I will be well pleased to see the memoir which you have drawn up on the English navy, which I request that you penetrate well, so that we may profit from their great experience in this type of warfare." And further: " Above all I will be well pleased to know, if possible, how they measure the capacity of the ships, and on what basis they regulate the number of the crews; if you can get the orders of their battle-array when they are put to sea, you will oblige me by sending them to me; but I know that this is a delicate matter." *Ibid.,* p. 425.

or laws "and generally of all that may concern the navy."
In short, he was desirous of obtaining a " profound knowledge
of all the English navy." [66]

De Pomponne, the Ambassador to Holland, received similar
instructions. Someone had discovered a new secret in cannon
loading. The Ambassador was to discover his terms and start
negotiations. Meanwhile Colbert would consult the King for
his thoughts on the matter.[67] At another time, he was to try
to obtain all the orders of battle which the Dutch had observed
" with the figures and names of the vessels." This was to be
gotten from de Ruyter, or some of the principal officers, in a
manner disguised as "simple curiosity on your part." [68] Later,
he was to send a secret for the preservation of water on long
voyages which Colbert would have tested at the arsenal of
Rochefort.[69]

Aside from the ambassadors, Colbert received data from
specially designated agents sent to carry out researches, often
secretly. The carpenter Hubac studied shipbuilding methods
in Venice, Holland, and Britain. The manufacturer Noisette
was sent abroad to discover methods of fabricating *bas de soie*
and London serges; the engineers La Feuille and Chenier to
enquire after improvements in milling, public works, and mining. His own son Seignelay was given most meticulous instructions and submitted elaborate reports on naval activities in
Venice, Holland, and England when making the tour of these
places which Colbert designed for his instruction preparatory
to taking over the administration of the navy.[70]

[66] Colbert to de Croissy, January 16, 1672, *ibid.*, IV, 706-707.

[67] Colbert to de Pomponne, June 21, 1669, *ibid.*, III, 439-440.

[68] Colbert to de Pomponne, December 19, 1669, *ibid.*, p. 444.

[69] Colbert to de Pomponne, February 13, 1671, *ibid.*, p. 457.

[70] Boissonade, *Colbert*, pp. 33-34; Colbert to de Pomponne in Holland,
October 4, 1669, Depping, *Correspondance*, III, 441; Colbert to M. Arnoul,
intendant des galères at Marseille, ordering his son P. Arnoul to Venice to
observe their knowledge of galley construction and navigation, May 31, 1669,
Colbert, *Lettres*, III, part i, 131; Colbert to Hubac, January 28, 1670: " Surtout
informez-vous adroitment de l'usage des chevilles de chesne vert dont les
Anglais se servent dans leurs constructions; s'ils en employent pas tout le
vaisseau, ou seulement depuis la première préceinte en haut; de quelle grosseur
elles sont à proportion de la grandeur des vaisseaux . . . Faites des dessins tant
de leurs différentes sortes de bastimens que des engins et machines dont ils se
servent dans leur marine, pour me les envoyer," *ibid.*, p. 211; concerning
Seignelay see " Instructions a Seignelay," *ibid.*, III, part ii, *passim*, but par-

Other affairs abroad were of interest to Louis XIV and his ministers in guiding the competitive policy of the state. The administrative and financial practices of other nations provided a natural realm of inquiry to a government which was much occupied with changing its own. Louis was quite curious, for instance, concerning the operation of the parliamentary system of England and requested enlightenment thereon from his Ambassador, the Count of Cominges.[71] Observations from M. De Bonzi, the Ambassador at Venice, on the revenues of the Republic and the management of them were examined by the King " with much care and exactitude." [72] The secret minting methods of England were considered probably uneconomical for France, but, nevertheless, Colbert promised to examine them carefully.[73] The fascination with Spanish treasure was also a very important matter of practical politics in an age when " gold equals power " was a platitude of politics. The Ambassador at Madrid was asked for details on the treasure fleet arriving from the Indies and " above all with how much silver it will be loaded, as much for the catholic king as for the merchants." Colbert further informed the Envoy:

> I have read the king the dispatch . . . with the reports concerning the administration of finances and to what the revenues consist in the realms of Castile and Leon . . . with which H.M. has been quite satisfied, having even testified to an impatience to see the other pieces which you promise me on the same. . . .[74]

It is a working principle of science that correct opinion can only arise from a critical examination of relevant data. Reason, in this sense, as Descartes so often defined it, is a process of selection. In the rational state, the product of reason is state

ticularly in " Instruction pour mon Fils, pour bien faire la première commission de ma charge,"—1671—, pp. 55-56, and " Instruction pour le voyage de mon Fils à Rochefort,"—April 2, 1673—pp. 91-95. For Seignelay's reports on Italy, Holland, England, Rochefort, Toulon, Marseille, and Calais, see pp. 222-384; for similar instructions on projected trips to Rochefort, England and Holland, see F. V. D. de Forbonnais, *Recherches et considérations sur les finances de France*, III, 58-78.

[71] Jusserand, " The liberties of England," *A French ambassador at the court of Charles II*, pp. 98-109.

[72] Colbert to M. de Bonzi, June 15, 1663, Colbert, *Lettres*, V, 237.

[73] Colbert to the Count of Barillon, Ambassador at London, February 20, 1679, Depping, *Correspondance*, IV, 598.

[74] Colbert to the Archbishop of Embrun. July 1663, *ibid.*, III, 338.

policy, and if this policy is to be wisely conceived, it must be reasonably arrived at by the process of selection. The source of good policy, then, depends on full information, and the statistical bureau becomes the most rational instrument for the guidance of statecraft. The first twenty years of the personal reign of Louis XIV witnessed the definite, and initial, establishment in France of an integral relationship between the art of government and the practice of deriving data from social and statistical surveys conducted among the governed. It was a development which reflected the emphases of contemporary science and rationalism.

This chapter has concerned the building up, under Louis XIV, of a machinery of statistical and social survey as a necessary part of his government. It was in the period of Colbert's ministry, and primarily through the agency of the intendants, that such a system was created. These officials saw their administrative prerogatives extended and had added to them the important duty of serving as reporters. The nature of the demands made upon the intendants by the central government gradually transformed them into the main statistical agents as well as the political representatives of the royal power. The structure of the system of inquiry, as well as the general nature of the surveys made, having been discussed, the relationship of this new science to the government will be considered in greater detail further on in this work.

CHAPTER VI

THE MECHANICS OF THE REGIME OF ORDER:

RECORDS, FINANCES, STATISTICS AND REPORTS

I

The accumulation of administrative data was but one phase of the rational government of Louis XIV. It was equally necessary to apply the discipline of order both to the gathering of information and to the distribution of the services to be based on the information. In the interest of orderly rule, it was not sufficient that the King and his colleagues rely only on work, reporting, and common sense. Any long-term policy must of necessity, in this kind of regime, arise from a considered examination of a mass of data derived from sources scattered geographically and in time, and requiring, therefore, collation and classification. It is difficult to imagine such a system without the provision of administrative archives.

" To the government of Louis XIV belongs the merit, not only of having improved and, in certain branches, organized the public administration in France, but further of having done everything for the conservation of the acts of his administration." This opinion is shared by Arthur de Boislisle who asserts, in his *Correspondance des contrôleurs généraux des finances,* that when Louis XIV assumed the active direction of his kingdom not a single department had what could be called archives. At the end of the reign, not a single department of administrative importance had failed to take measures to preserve its papers.[1] The archivist Depping observed, near

---

[1] Depping, *Correspondance*, I, i; A. de Boislisle, *Correspondance des contrôleurs généraux des finances,* I, iii. Depping and Boislisle, together with Pierre Clement, have been the most assiduous workers in the archives of the seventeenth and early eighteenth centuries in France. The " Avant-Propos " of Boislisle's *Correspondance,* I, i-lix, is entirely concerned with presenting a historical essay on the foundation and development of archives under Louis XIV and through the efforts of Colbert, Louvois, and their successors. The following account, unless otherwise specified, is derived from this essay and from Depping, *Correspondance*, I, i-viii and selected letters, *passim;* and from Clement, *Lettres instructions et mémoirs de Colbert,* II, part i and V, selected letters *passim;* and from the articles: " Archives " and " Bibliotheque " in Maurice Block's *Dictionnaire de l'administration française* (2 vols., Paris, 1905).

the middle of the last century, that if posterity had been as careful in preserving archives as the government of Louis XIV was in collecting and classifying them, he would have on this reign a mass of data " more complete than that of any reign either before or since." [2]

The institution of administrative archives by which data, derived through the machinery of inquiry, could be made available for present or future reference was an analogous expression in government of the urge of contemporary science to tabulate, arrange, and classify for use, pertinent facts concerning nature. Almost a century before the *Encyclopédistes* the state recognized the practical value, in administration, of the lessons of Bacon and the academicians.

As it was, the large-scale preservation of records by the central power was delayed in France more than in most other European countries of importance. The archives of the reign of Louis XIV were not the first in the kingdom however. It is believed that during the Merovingian and Carolingian periods administrative archives were kept, perhaps in imitation of the Romans. Under the early Capetians all trace of such a collection seems to have been lost until the creation of the *Tresor des Chartes* by Philippe Augustus. This did not prevent high functionaries from forming their own archives to the detriment of the monarchy. Religious houses, cities, corporations, and seigneurs retained charters which forced the kings frequently to turn to the registers of the scattered parlements and chambers of accounts for whatever information they could get.

The indifference of the government seemed to sanction the departure of the records with the departure of the minister or secretary. The most valuable documents of the kingdom formed parts of private legacies or were lost through neglect. In the sixteenth and early seventeenth centuries, many persons were interested in the collection of political records, doubtless a reflection of that delight in the curious which characterized the Renaissance. Some of these collections were famous in their day.[3] Mathieu Mole and Michel de Marillac, in the reign of Louis XIII, made efforts to give new life to the *Tresor*

---

[2] Depping, *Correspondance*, I, i.

[3] Boislisle mentions those of Pierre Pithou, Jacques-Auguste de Thou, Ambassador de Brienne and the Count of Bethune.

des Chartes, and Cardinal Richelieu did much towards building up useful archives. When he had assumed the secretaryship of state for war, he had been embarrassed by finding neither administrative dossier or archives to guide him, his predecessors having carried them off. Similarly, when taking over the running of the navy from the Duke of Montmorency, the records had been so abandoned that although the Duke had promised to render them to him he was unable to do so.[4] But Richelieu, at his death, willed his own papers to his niece, the Duchess of Aiguillon. Mazarin defied custom by leaving his own records to Colbert to be of use to the King if required. His colleague, Michel Le Tellier, was to leave three hundred volumes of dispatches to his son the Archbishop of Reims.

The Duke of Saint-Simon correctly attributed the creation of permanent governmental archives to the reign of Louis XIV, but, as in many things connected with the reign, he was convinced that it was the working of a dark policy. He believed that Louvois had originated these record stores in order to conceal the secrets of the state. Louvois, although he founded the depôt of the archives of war in 1688, placed them in the *Hôtel de Louvois.* It is clear, therefore, that he still thought of himself as master of his own papers. Only in 1701, after the death of his son Barbezieux, and, on the order of the new secretary of state for war, Chamillard, did these archives actually become the property of the state. They had been, however, much neglected since the death of Louvois in 1691.

Saint-Simon ignored the previous role of Colbert in this field, a role which by its precedence and magnitude probably assigns to him the honor of being the real founder of the administrative archives of France. From 1662, through archival agents as Carcavy, Godefroy, Clément, du Fourny, d'Hérouval, Ondedei, Baluze, and Clairambault, through intendants searching in generalities and through consuls and ambassadors spread over Europe and the Orient, the Minister pursued with a keen intensity the task of collecting rarities and administrative data. Some collections were made at his own cost, others at the expense of the King; some, apparently, with the notion of private

[4] La Roncière, *Histoire de la marine française,* IV, 582.

ownership, others for the King, and others for purely administrative purposes. The administrative importance of these collections was clearly recognized and is distinctive.

The King's agents were instructed to search through old churches, monasteries, and court depositories to find records valuable to the state. Where these records could not be taken away, they were to be classified for ready reference and inventoried so that the contents might be known to the government. For example, Colbert wrote to the First President of the Chamber of Accounts in 1680:

The King having learned that many of the documents and papers in the *Chambre des Comptes* are thrown indiscriminately into the chambers, without inventories and without being put in order, and since they can be of consequence, both for his domains and for history, His Majesty orders me to make known that he desires that you order, in his name, M. d'Herouval to apply himself with care to survey all these documents, to place them in order, and to make some inventories of them.[5]

If possible, the collections to be found scattered through the kingdom, if interesting or useful, were to be acquired and transported to the capital. The intendants were usually instructed, when handling such cases, to desist from using force but rather to employ the arts of reason, persuading colleges and other religious bodies to surrender their records in the interest of better preservation and greater usefulness or in order to make them available to the public.[6]

The utility of such old records was illustrated in even the small matter of protocol. Having recently assumed the position of secretary of state, Colbert was grateful to the sieur Godefroy for documents which he had uncovered purportedly showing the manner in which these officers had written to princes and people of quality for the past hundred and fifty years.[7] But perhaps the most apparent need for them was

[5] Colbert to F. Nicolay, December 19, 1680, Colbert, *Lettres,* V, 416-417; Colbert maintained a frequent correspondence with the sieur Godefroy who spent most of his time digging into the old archives and drawing up inventories thereof. See letters in same volume dated November 12, 30, 1668, January 11, 1669, pp. 274-276.

[6] Colbert to M. Daguesseau, intendant at Toulouse, August 11, 1680, January 16, 1680, *ibid.,* pp. 414-415 and note p. 415; Colbert to M. Boudon, tresorier de France at Montpellier, March 12, 1681 and February 19, 1682, *ibid.,* pp. 417, 422-423.

[7] Colbert to the sieur Godefroy, March 5, 1669, *ibid.,* p. 278.

found in supplying evidence to buttress Louis XIV's foreign policy, particularly in substantiating royal claims against the Austrian and Spanish Hapsburgs in the ancient territories of Burgundy and Lorraine.

In August of 1663 Colbert wrote the King, concerning his rights in the three bishoprics of Metz, Toul, and Verdun ceded to France by the treaty of Munster. He observed that:

After having carefully examined this affair, I have seen that there was nothing more important for the establishment and conservation of the privileges ceded to Your Majesty by the said treaty, than to make an exact research of all the documents, papers and information which are deposited in the cathedral churches, abbeys, towns and communities, and to make some good and faithful inventories thereof, being certain that in all these documents will be found much which will be very advantageous to Your Majesty for the clarification of his rights. . . .[8]

Following the signing of the Treaty of Aix-La-Chapelle with Spain, in May 1668, the archivist Godefroy was employed, to the entire satisfaction of Colbert, in discovering titles and documents to be used in " justifying the demands . . . made in the name of the King, by *Messieurs* his commissioners . . . in the execution of the treaty." [9] In the time that the French were occupying Ghent during the war with Holland (1672-1678), the same sieur Godefroy and several colleagues were employed to examine the records of the Citadel. The King did not wish that these be removed " publicly " as it would violate the conditions of the capitulation. Nevertheless, the archivist was secretly instructed to " adroitly " steal as many as possible. In August 1678, Colbert wrote to congratulate him on a job well done and requested him to send the chest of documents accompanied by an exact inventory of the contents.[10]

[8] Colbert to the King, August 23, 1663, *ibid.*, II, part i, 11. The letter continued by emphasizing the possibility that the counts of Furstemberg, who had conflicting interests in the territory, and to whom the repositories were accessible, might find it convenient to purloin certain documents.

[9] Colbert to Godefroy, January 11, 1669, *ibid.*, V, 276 note. Colbert congratulates him on his perfect exactitude in the matter.

[10] Colbert to Godefroy, June 23, 1678, August 5, 1678, *ibid.*, pp. 383, 385 and note. The character of these documents is suggested by the divisions of the inventory. I, documents regarding France and her sovereignty over Flanders and Artois; II, regarding the kings of France and their families; III, on bulls and briefs of Popes; IV, on the Christian emperors of Constantinople and Germany, the kings of Hungary, Bohemia, Sweden and some kings of Sicily, Castile,

The practical information to be derived from collected records, to be easily applied, required the creation of some implementing machinery of reference. The solution reached by Colbert, and eventually imitated by the other secretaries of state, was to have written, in bound registers, all the acts of his department. He also collected thus all the reports, memoirs, and letters addressed to him, classified by date. The registers of ministerial acts were the work of copyists and included tables of names and contents to facilitate their use. Depping writes that the idea of like registers never appears to have come to any minister of preceding reigns,[11] that it was Colbert who conceived the plan and executed it. Afterwards nothing was found more feasible than to continue the project, and the various departments followed the system closely until about 1784. For the reign of Louis XIV, the registers of the secretariat of the *maison du roi,* which was perhaps the least affected by subsequent losses, alone comprises fifty-six volumes *in-folio.* The correspondence of Louvois with his administrators is preserved in volumes more orderly "if possible" than Colbert's. Voluminous records exist in the archives of the navy dating from this period. In chronological order are to be found the dispatches of Colbert and his successors on the navy, foreign commerce, the Levant, consulates and other related topics. The Chancellory of France began to keep a register of its orders and decisions under Michel le Tellier to some extent, and under Boucherat less so, but the records of the chancellorship of Pontchartrain are preserved in many volumes.[12]

Navarre, and Portugal; V, on the kings of England, Scotland, Denmark, princes of the house of Austria, the cities of Besancon, Tournai, Cambrai; VI, on the bishops, the chapter and city of Liege. May 22, 1681, Colbert wrote to Godefroy at Lille: "Le plus important travail que voys ayez à présent à faire dans la Chambre des comptes de Lille, est celuy qui regarde la recherche des titres des engagemens que les roys catholiques ont faits de leurs domaines. Ainsy, appliquez-vous particulièrement à rechercher tous ces titres et à en faire des extraits bien justes et bien certains. Prenez garde de n'entreprendre point ce travail généralement dans toute l'estendue des pays conquis, mais appliquez-vous à le faire par chastellenies et par prévostes; et prenez bien garde de n'ommetre aucun des engagemens que les roys catholiques ou leur prédécesseurs ont faits. Surtout que ce travail soit secret et que personne n'ayt connoissance de l'ordre que je vous donne sur cela." *Ibid.,* II, part i, 153.

[11] It is however strongly suggestive of the Cabinet of Sully .

[12] Depping, *Correspondance,* I, i-viii. It was probably such registers that Colbert had in mind when he wrote to the First President of the Chamber of

Immediately following the death of Colbert, large segments of his records were withdrawn, particularly by the archivists Baluze and Clairambault. The remainder formed, with other series, the *Mélanges Colbert,* the principal source of Clement for his *Correspondance,* and represent the first archives, properly speaking, of the *contrôle général des finances.* Boislisle concludes, with reference to the Minister's work, that, whereas is seems clear that Colbert, like le Tellier and Louvois, cannot be rigorously considered as the founder of the archives, since he amassed as much for his own satisfaction as for the administration, still, the example set meant that in the future the preservation of state papers was considered essential to the government.[13]

Paralleling the development of archives in the reign of Louis XIV was the new impetus given to the enlargement of the royal library. The origins of this institution have been traced to Charles V who is said to have placed 900 volumes in the *Tour de la Libraire* at the Louvre.[14] During the English occupation, these works were apparently completely dispersed and it was not until the reign of Louis XI that a serious attempt was made to reassemble a royal library. From this time through the reign of Henry II dynastic accidents and foreign expedi-

---

Accounts at Dijon on July 17, 1663 and, referring to some pieces preserved at that place, requested copies to be made: "and you will find appended here a sheet of paper the size of the manuscripts that I keep in my books." (*Ibid.,* IV, 532-533.) The correspondence of Louvois fills nearly 900 volumes. C. Rousset, *Histoire de Louvois et de son administration politique et militaire* (4 vols., Paris, 1862-1864), I, v.

[13] After the death of Seignelay, large sections of the archives passed to his family and although almost all were returned to the state as a gift in 1732, yet a very important part, including the collection of official letters addressed to Colbert in his administration, was not reunited until the Revolution. The depot of the papers of the Contrôle Générale was definitely organized from the ministry of Desmaretz. The latter firmly established this archival deposit and made it useful for future administrators by having it completely catalogued, classified and inventoried before leaving his office. From 1703 to 1708, in all the departments under Desmaretz, the habit developed of conserving scrupulously all papers, "even the least notes," which dealt with his affairs. From this time this preservation was almost perfect. A de Boislisle, *Correspondance des Contrôleurs généraux,* I, viii, xvii-xxi.

[14] The following summary of the history of the royal library from Charles V to 1683, unless otherwise indicated, is drawn from Isambert, XV, 106-107 and note; Depping, *Correspondance,* IV, xxx and letters passim; Colbert, *Lettres,* V, lxxvii-lxxxi and letters *passim.* P. Clement, *Histoire de Colbert et de son administration,* II, 453-459.

tions gradually added such collections as those of the house of Orleans and of the Sforza and Visconti of Milan. One historian of the library stated that an *ordonnance* of Henry II, in 1556, required printers to furnish the library with a sample of all books printed by privilege. The editors of the *Recueil général des anciennes lois françaises*, however, admitted themselves unable to find a trace of such a law. Francis II and Charles IX added little and under Henry III a large proportion of the volumes were carried off or stolen. Henry IV, in 1695, reunited a collection and placed it in the College of Clermont in Paris, and, when the college was turned over to the Jesuits, in a building on the rue de La Harpe. At the suggestion of the parlementarian bibliophile, de Thou, he united with the royal library the valuable one of Catherine de Medici.

The first *ordonnance* to be found in *Isambert* in connection with the library is that of 1617 providing: " in order that the best editions which by the passage of time and divers accidents may become rare can be promptly found and serve the public," and in order to render the Kingdom " flourishing in all kinds of science and belle-lettres," no one was to " print or put up for sale any book but at the charge of placing gratuitously two examples in our public library." [15] This *ordonnance* was only occasionally enforced until the reign of Louis XIV.

Mazarin demonstrated his predilection for literature and the arts by collecting a cabinet of curiosities and the finest privately owned library in France up to his time. It was Colbert, however, who expended the greatest efforts yet made on furthering the growth of the royal library. While still the *intendant* of Mazarin's fortune, he succeeded in placing his brother Nicolas in charge of the King's collection. At that time it contained 16,746 printed works or manuscripts. At his death, this number had quadrupled, and the whole had been reorganized and moved from its obscure housing in the rue de la Harpe to magnificent galleries constructed by Mazarin.

Several considerable gifts and purchases added to its richness around this period. In 1656, Jacques Dupuy had offered Louis XIV his library of 9,000 volumes and 200 manuscripts.

---

[15] "Declaration portant qu'il sera remis à la bibliothèque du roi deux exemplaires de tous les ouvrages qui seront imprimés," Isambert, XV, 106.

Shortly thereafter the death of Gaston of Orleans provided a new and valuable legacy which, Colbert wrote the Cardinal, should be rightly assigned to the royal collection. In 1663, the count of Bethune gave his famous collection of letters and documents to the King. Notably, the manuscripts of Brienne, and the libraries of the savant Carcavi, and that of Fouquet were acquired through purchase.

Beyond this, Colbert and his son Seignelay, and after them Louvois, worked assiduously through their agents gathering manuscripts and rare books throughout much of the world. For instance, we find Colbert sending instructions to the *intendant des galères* at Marseille, in 1671, to provide all the necessaries for one Vanslèbe who the King was sending to the Levant " and particularly into Ethiopia, in order to seek some rare books and other curiosities which can serve to embellish the library of His Majesty." [16] From later trips, Vanslèbe sent back 334 Arabic, Turkish and Persian manuscripts.[17] In a circular letter to all the consuls of France in the Levant, Colbert urged them to seek diligently for manuscripts and unusual books. Nothing should escape their search and those found should be well attested for genuineness. The captains of returning vessels were to be warned to transport such works with great care.[18]

The parallel treatment given to the growth of the royal library under the auspices of Louis XIV and his ministers, and to their creation of administrative archives, implies a certain common purpose which, though sometimes vaguely felt or expressed, was certainly present. It is true that Colbert was constantly searching for the " curious " and " rare " with which to "; embellish " the library, but it is no less certain that such curiosities were used to justify the acts of reunion. After examining an inventory of certain " curious pieces " found by one of his agents, Colbert requested that he be sent copies because, " I have not found any there which have not appeared very important to me, and of which I can have need on occa-

---

[16] Colbert to M. Arnoul, April 1, 1671, Colbert, *Lettres,* V, 307-308.
[17] *Ibid.,* p. 307 note.
[18] Circular to consuls of France in the Levant, November 29, 1672, Depping, *Correspondance,* IV, 594; see also letter of Colbert to M. Sauvan, consul in Cyprus, November 6, 1671, *ibid.,* p. 580.

sion."[19] After a visit to his library, in 1667, the Savoyard Ambassador wrote his Master describing the two hundred volumes of Mazarin's negotiations which he had seen there and expressed the desire to return to discover among them some matters "concerning the interests of your Royal Highness."[20] To the Grand Monarch, jealous of his glory, and surrounded as he was by a servile coterie, books had a special meaning. In them his own acts would be preserved for the judgment of all the centuries, and they offered to princes "a thousand truths without any mixture of flattery."[21]

II

"If Mazarin left at death forty millions to his heirs, and some empty coffers to France," wrote the literary historian Lemontey, "it should occasion no surprise; for this miserly foreigner had released the finances of the kingdom to Fouquet, and confided his own to Colbert."[22] An anecdote relates how the dying statesman excused his own wealth to the young Louis: "I owe you everything, Sire; but I believe I acquit myself in some manner in giving you Colbert."[23] Whatever the truth of the story, almost from that date it became increasingly clear that the cooperation of the King and the former steward of the Cardinal was the dominant fact in the financial administration of the realm. Forbonnais in his *Recherches . . . sur les finances* saw two great advantages arising from the demise of Mazarin; first, the determination of the King to conduct his own affairs; and, secondly, the choice of Colbert as his prime colleague.[24]

[19] Colbert to M. Duguay, July 17, 1663, *ibid.,* pp. 532-533.

[20] Marquis of Saint-Maurice to the Duke of Savoy, May 27, 1667, Saint-Maurice, *Lettres sur la cour de Louis XIV,* pp. 47-48.

[21] J. de Boislisle quoting Louis XIV from his memoires: "Les Rois doivent pour ainsi dire, une compte public de leurs actions à tout l'univers et à tous les siècles . . . le commerce des livres et des historiens est le seule où les jeunes princes trouvent mille vérités sans nul mélange de flatteries." *Mémoriaux de conseil de 1661,* I, xxviii.

[22] P. E. Lemontey, "Jean-Baptiste Colbert," *Essai sur l'établissement monarchique de Louis XIV,* Vol. V, of *Oeuvres de P. E. Lemontey* (7 vols., 1829-1832), p. 236; see also Clamageran, *Histoire de l'impôt en France,* II, 598.

[23] Abbé de Choisy, *Mémoires pour servir a l'histoire de Louis XIV,* p. 579.

[24] Forbonnais, *Recherches et considérations sur les finances de France,* II, 122-123.

In March of 1661 Fouquet had entertained some expectations of succeeding to the role of Prime Minister. Hence the decision of Louis to assume that position himself was a disappointment to the financier, but he had the consolation of seeing himself selected as one of the triumvirate of the *conseil de trois*. He had confessed his errors of management to the King and was retained. The Abbé de Choisy tells that he misinterpreted the King's early zeal as an enthusiasm which would soon disappear before the renewal of longing for old pleasures. Consequently he presumed to submit a report in which expenditures were padded and revenues diminished. The King gave the account to Colbert who quickly pierced the deception. Pressed by the King, Fouquet persisted in his obstinate deception and was soon disgraced.[25] The Abbé, with an eye to art, had reduced the details of the truth to an interesting narrative which preserved the sense if it ignored the complexities.[26]

From the fall of Fouquet, Colbert was publicly acknowledged as the guiding hand in finances; but, if the King owed his ideas in this field to Colbert, Colbert owed whatever success he had in carrying them out to the support of the King. Louis XIV solemnly pledged himself by decree personally to supervise the finances of the state knowing that he could not give " any greater demonstration of his love for his peoples."[27] It was a resolve from which he never departed.

A few hours after D'Artagnan had arrested Fouquet at Nantes, Louis wrote to his mother:

I have discussed afterwards on this accident with the Messieurs who are here with me; I have told them that I no longer wish a *surinten-*

---

[25] Abbé de Choisy, *Mémoires*, p. 581.

[26] It seems likely that the retaining of Fouquet was a temporary expedient from the beginning. Certainly Colbert had long been working towards discrediting him and the Cardinal was fully aware of his failings. An unjustified fear of his wealth and the influence it gave him was apparently the main factor in deterring Louis and Colbert from acting against him sooner than they did. See Colbert, *Lettres*, II, part i, i-xlvi; in the same volume, Colbert's " Mémoires sur les finances," pp. 24-39; E. Lavisse, *Louis XIV*, VII, part i, 142-146, 178. In his defense at this trial, Fouquet disclaimed responsibility for any faults committed in his department after March 9, 1661 because he asserted that actually finances had been assigned to Colbert from that date as if he had been the superior. J. de Boislisle, *Conseil de 1661*, I, xci.

[27] " Réglement pour l'établissement du conseil royal des finances, dont les décisions seront rédigées en forme d'ordonnance et signées par le roi," Isambert, XVIII, 9.

dant, but to work personally on finances with some faithful persons who will act under me . . . I have already commenced to enjoy the pleasure which there is in working oneself in finances, having, in the little application I have given to it this afternoon, remarked some important things which I am not pleased with, and which I doubtless will not continue.[28]

The King dutifully read the financial and economic reports of Colbert and always gave his responses to them. There were undoubtedly times when the intricacies of the system made it difficult to follow, but this never deterred him from making the attempt. In such cases he usually deferred to the judgment of his *Contrôleur Général* but, sometimes, with reservations. Thus, when the pressures of the Dutch war forced Colbert to recommend certain extraordinary measures, he answered:

I have carefully read the letter which you have written me. . . . I find some inconveniences to whatever steps that may be taken there; but as I trust entirely in you and since you know better than anyone else that which will be most proper, I defer to you and order you to do what you believe will be most advantageous to me.

But further along, he expressed doubt as to the desirability of such measures at " this time " which might be interpreted abroad as a show of the " least weakness." [29]

If attention to the details of finance was seen by Louis XIV as a duty, it does not appear to have been an unwelcome one. But the pleasure which he derived from it was undoubtedly enhanced in the early years by the pecuniary rewards which he frequently received due to the orderly management of his Finance Minister. Thus, for instance, he wrote in response to the favorable annual report of Colbert on January 1, 1673:

I have been agreeably surprised by the letter which you have written me, where you inform me that my revenue has increased. I vow to you that I had not expected it. But with your industry and zeal, I ought to promise myself everything.

I assure you that you have made me begin the year gaily. . . . To-morrow you may render me an account in greater detail of everything.[30]

---

[28] Louis XIV to Anne of Austria from Nantes, September 5, 1661. Grouvelle, *Oeuvres de Louis XIV*, V, 53-54.

[29] Louis XIV to Colbert, May 18, 1674, Gaxotte, *Lettres de Louis XIV*, pp. 49-50.

[30] Louis XIV to Colbert, January 1, 1673, *ibid.*, p. 44.

Ten days after the arrest of Fouquet, the King issued from Fontainebleau the famous *Règlement pour l'établissement du conseil royal des finances. . . .*[31] This *ordonnance*, in the succinct, orderly style which distinguishes the laws of Louis XIV from those of the sixteenth and early seventeenth centuries, created a highly effective and centralized organization for the control of state finances. The history of former councils is a dismal record of division and irresponsibility. Following the reign of Henry IV, the number of persons at such meetings had progressively increased until as many as 120 of various capacities, powers and designs fished in the troubled waters of high finance.[32]

Louis described this act to his son as the product of the need which he saw for reform. In order to better perform his new functions he had decided

to establish a new council, which I called the royal council. I composed it of the marechal de Villeroi, of two Councillors of State, d'Aligre and de Sève, and of an intendant of finances, who was Colbert; it is in this council that I have worked continuously since, to unravel the terrible confusion which obtained in my affairs.

He observed that the people were surprised at his accomplishments in this direction but this could only arise from their incomprehension of the true motives of a prince as distinguished from the implied motives of financiers. As a king, he saw only "loss in confusion" and desired "order and clarity in all things."[33]

As would be expected, Colbert, aside from the King, was the dominating figure in the new council. The *Chief de Conseil*, the Marshal de Villeroi, had the first honors after Louis, but was without real authority.[34] The two Councillors of State,

[31] Isambert, XVIII, 9-12.

[32] A. de Boislisle, "Les conseils sous Louis XIV," *Mémoires de Saint-Simon*, VI, 477-487.

[33] Louis XIV in Memoirs written about 1671, Grouvelle, *Oeuvres de Louis XIV*, I, 108-109. See E. Spanheim, *Relation de la cour de France*, p. 233.

[34] Madam de Motteville (1615?-1689) wrote of Villèroy: "his destiny was to be all his life proposed for the first places without having them, and of having the most honorable titles that a man could have in the kingdom without the functions belonging to them; although he was very able and very capable of performing them. As he had been the governor of the King while Cardinal Mazarin was superintendent of his education, and marshal of France

11

d'Aligre and de Sève, were actually the assistants of the third, Colbert, in his capacity as *intendant des finances*. After 1666, when the King bestowed on him the title of *contrôleur général,* the distinction became formal and perpetual. In the absence of the King, the chancellor of France presided over the meetings and was present at other times on royal invitation.[35]

The functions of the new body were to fix annually the total sum of direct taxes to be levied on the kingdom, the respective share to be borne by the generalities and the share of each election therein.[36] With the *conseil des dépêches,*[37] it drew up the terms of tax contracts between the King and the various provincial Estates. It formulated and granted leases for indirect levies to the tax farmers and supervised their execution. It had cognizance of accounts and administration of all farms, domains, and forests. It examined and kept the accounts of the treasury. It provided for industrial concessions and grants. To it belonged the right of surveying, creating, and suppressing royal offices and the incomes pertaining thereto. Although only the King authorized *ordonnances comptables,*[38] the council examined all projects for the distribution of funds and made recommendations. It verified the annual true accounts and the accounts of receivers and treasurers.[39]

Colbert, as intendant of finances, had the treasury in his department. He received the registers of receipts and expenditures and all finance *ordonnances* passed into his hands to be carried to the King for approval and signature. All accounts

without commanding any armies, he was also declared *chief du conseil des finances* without any authority." Motteville, *Mémoires,* Vol. X, 2nd series, in *Nouvelle collection des mémoires pour servir a l'histoire de France,* edited by MM. Michaud and Poujoulat (32 vols., Paris, 1835-1839), p. 525.

[35] See for more adequate description of this council. A. de Boislisle, " Conseils sous Louis XIV," VI, 477-512; A. de Boislisle, *Correspondance des contrôleurs généraux,* I, 578-581; Isambert, XVIII, 9-12; Clamageran, II, 604. For a nearly contemporary account see " Relazioni " of Alvise Grimani, Venetian Ambassador to Louis XIV (1660-1664) in *Le relazioni,* seria II—Francia, III, 85.

[36] See *Brevet* for the *Taille* of 1682 reprinted in Colbert, *Lettres,* II, 783-784.
[37] See Chapter V, above.
[38] Drafts payable by the treasury. For the unusual side of the story of this particular aspect of royal expenditures see F. Weiss, *Histoire des fonds secrets sous l'ancien regime* (Paris, 1939).
[39] A. de Boislisle, " Conseils sous Louis XIV," VI, 487-488; Isambert, XVIII, 9-12.

of farms, forests, domains, extraordinary taxes, receipts general, and others of all types were sent to him to be reported to the council. In practice, Colbert—and his successors as *contrôleur général* preserved the same policy—rarely allowed anything to appear before the council until the two councillors of state had been previously informed of his opinion. No business went directly before the council but rather through the *contrôleur général* to be dealt with *tête à tête* with the King, or allocated to other committees from whence it sometimes found its way back to the council of finances or might be resolved in other councils as in the *conseil des parties*. After the death of Colbert and Louvois, the councils generally became less important as the conduct of business became more and more a personal affair between the King and his ministers.[40]

As observed by Colbert to Mazarin in his memoir of 1659, the first requirement in making a reality out of the "*maxime d'ordre*" was to be the establishment of an effective system of accounting. The centralization of affairs in the council of finances was a function of the constant desire for simplicity. The task of the King and his council was to be further eased by the institution of an exact and full set of accounts, simple in form and rigidly checked.[41]

At the beginning, three registers were maintained: first, the *journal* in which was entered, day by day, notation of authorized *ordonnances* of expenditure, and, in the margins, the funds on which they were assigned and the receipts in the treasury. Secondly, a *registre des funds* contained extracts, or summary statements, of sums due the treasury from farms, general receipts, forests and other sources with note of sums actually received and the deduction which should be made thereby. A third, the *registre des d'epenses* noted the *ordonnances* of expenditures arranged by the nature of expenditures authorized. All three registers contained separately what they contained

[40] A. de Boislisle, *Correspondance des contrôleurs généraux,* I, 578-579; A. de Boislisle, "Conseils sous Louis XIV," VI, 496-499.

[41] See Colbert's "Mémoires sur les finances de France pour servir à l'histoire," Colbert, *Lettres,* II, part i, 17-68. Clement describes this as the longest writing of Colbert. It was illegibly written and almost defied his editing in some places. See particularly pp. 20, 40-41, 44-45; also VII, 164-405; Mallet, *Comptes rendus de l'administration des finances du royaume de France,* pp. 404-405; Clamageran, II, 606, 608-609.

together and could thus be used to check each other. In 1667, the last two registers were combined into one.[42]

At the end of each month these registers were totaled and checked by the *contrôleur général* and carried by him to the council. Each article was called aloud by *contrôleur,* using the *journal,* and checked by the King, using the *registre des fonds,* with the word *" Bon."* After this verification was made the King noted his initials in his own hand in the *journal.* At the end of receipts he would write:

Somme totale de la recette faite en mon Trésor royale pendant le mois de . . ., six millions. . . .
Fait et arresté en mon Conseil royal des finances, tenu à . . ., le. . . .

At the end of expenditures he wrote:

Somme totale de la dépense faite en mon Trésor royale pendant le mois de . . ., dix millions. . . . .
Savoir: en assignations et en deniers comptans. . . .
Et la recette faite comptant en mon Trésor royale monte à. . . .
Partant elle excede la dépense de. . . .
Plus, il restoit . . . ès mains de . . ., par l'arresté du mois dernier, cy-devant fol. . . .
Partant, restera en ses mains la somme de . . ., qu'il employera à la dépense du mois suivant.
Fait et arresté en mon Conseil royale des finances, tenu á . . ., le. . . .

The King signed first, followed by the council. The *contrôleur général* then noted at the top of the margin of each page of the *journal* where the receipts were registered, these words: *" Vu et apostille de la main du Roy sur le registre des fonds."*

At the end of each year similar calculations were made for the totals. The King would write:

Vu et vérifié
Bon   A . . ., le. . . .

Or, if there remained an unexpended sum:

Vu et vérifié
Bon pour . . ., partés en l'année . . .
                A . . ., le. . . .[43]

---

[42] Colbert's " Mémoires sur les finances," Colbert, *Lettres,* II, part i, 44-45; A. de Boislisle, *Correspondance des contrôleurs généraux,* I, 578; Lavisse, *Louis XIV,* VII, part i, 183-184; Clamageran, II, 608-609; Cole, *Colbert,* I, 303.
[43] A. de Boislisle, *Correspondance des contrôleurs généraux,* I, 580-581.

Louis XIV was, further, kept currently informed of the status of his finances by statistical extracts or " projects " giving summary accounts of receipts and expenditures accompanied by explanatory notes. These were prepared by Colbert with great care.[44] The King explained to the Dauphin that signing all *ordonnances* for expenditures was not sufficient means of keeping track of one's finances. He had likewise taken the trouble to

note by my own hand, in a little book which I could see at any time, on one side, the funds that were due to me each month, and on the other, all the sums paid by my *ordonnances* in that month; setting aside for this task, always one of the first days of the following month, to the end of having in it the most current memoir.[45]

The accounting reforms of Colbert were extended far beyond the royal council. Financial officials in the generalities and elections and in the scattered courts of accounts were forced to keep regular and detailed records, and the intendants with their agents were commissioned to maintain a close surveillance over them.[46] In the departments under his direction, the *contrôleur général* formulated systems of bookkeeping to keep himself exactly informed of the conditions of the finances and the progress of his works. For example, in his bureau of buildings, the size of sheets, segregation of entries by types, the bindings of the registers, the forms of calculations, and the procedures in checking were carefully specified. All expenditures in these divisions had to be authorized by registration in his books and by his own initialling. Abridgements of the records were made quarterly and annually. Accounts were periodically checked against the receipts by the courts of

[44] Several of these projects on finances are reprinted in Forbonnais, III, 104-105 and *passim*. The King was provided with similar memoranda on many phases of the administration. See, for instance, those on the forests reproduced in A. de Boislisle, " Introduction " to *Mémoire sur la généralité de Paris*, I, 578-585; 588-589 and notes; for further projects on finances see Colbert, *Lettres*, II, 121-127, 140-141, 771-782.

[45] Louis XIV, "Mémoire 1662," in Grouvelle, *Oeuvres de Louis XIV*, I, 146-147; Lavisse, VII, part i, 184.

[46] Cole, *Colbert*, I, 303; Mallet, *Comptes rendus des finances*, pp. 101-102; Jouvencel, *Le contrôleur général des finances sous l'ancien régime*, pp. 88-95, 183-196; " Edit portant réglement pour les chambres des comptes," August, 1669, Isambert, XVIII, 311-319.

accounts and the treasury, and multiple verifications were required.[47]

[47] The system maintained in his department of buildings will serve as an example of his methods. Colbert was appointed to the office of Superintendent of Buildings January 1, 1664. It carried with it, besides the direction of buildings, the control of arts, tapestries, manufactures, the artisans employed under the great gallery of the Louvre, and the supervision of the maintenance of the royal chateaux and parks. (The ordonnance of grant is reprinted in Colbert, *Lettres,* V, 449-450.) In a set of " Observations and indications " which Colbert drew up soon after receiving the appointment, he provided for a register which was to keep him closely informed of the status of the buildings and which was always to be kept near at hand for ready reference. As usual, in affairs of this nature, he drew up meticulous specifications. Having performed the same functions for Mazarin he carried into the royal program the system he had used under the Cardinal. The register was to be of the same size as his registers of funds and expenditures and was to be bound in morocco leather to preserve it " as the others." It was to be numbered from beginning to end with a blank section provided at the beginning for the entry of a table. It was to be titled " Bâtimens du Roy (année, 1664)."

" It is necessary to keep this register in the same form as was formerly kept those of His Eminence; that is, a first chapter of receipts for which 25 pages will be left blank, in which, day by day, the orders on funds which will be dispatched are to be registered, in order to deliver them thereafter to the treasurer.

" Following these 25 pages will commence the expenditures, which will be divided by chapters, and these chapters subdivided into various others; of each nature of works, for example:

Louvre	*sheets*
Masonry of the new building	6
Carpentry	4
Roofing	3
Plumbing	3

And so forth for a total of 213 pages. The divisions or chapters within the the pages, " Louvre," " Palais-Royal," " Versailles," etc. were to be intersticed with series of blank pages making the whole total 245 sheets.

" In each chapter, after having put the title, it will be necessary to put in the margin the price of the works, when it will be regulated by the *ordonnances.* For example, for the Chateau of the Louvre:

Masonry of the new building

Great facade, per fathom (*toise*)	210 livres
Partition walls	90 livres
etc.	

" It is not necessary to deliver any *ordonnance,* either of funds or expenditure, unless it be registered and initialed by my hand.

" For this effect, it is necessary to place the register on my table every time that there will be something to register.

" Every three months, regularly, it will be necessary to stop each chapter of the register and to place in it an abridgement of receipts and expenditures, as was done in the registers of His Eminence.

" It is necessary that the registration be brief, and contain only that which will be important in the *ordonnance.*

A multitude of reports were required of his *intendants de marine* touching all angles of naval finances. As Clement observed in this regard: " Exact in sending to the intendants of the ports the sums which he had allocated to them, Colbert

" *Ordonnances* of which the sense is entirely set down in the registration, it will be unnecessary to keep a copy of.

" For those which are longer and more difficult, it will be necessary to retain a copy and make mention of it in the margin of the registration."

The archives have revealed such registers and resumés for the years 1664 to 1673 which followed this plan. From 1673 a more complicated form was developed including numbers of items not in the earlier volumes; the expenditures were more completely indicated and detailed but resumés and tables were missing.

The following are some instructions given by Colbert on the subject of accounts of buildings: (no date)

" It is necessary to see the duplicate of the statements balanced by me and the accounts tendered to the Chamber [of accounts] the three past years by the treasurer of the buildings, to examine in detail, to see the notations I have put on the said statements and those which the Chamber has put on the said accounts, to note and examine the differences, to make a report thereon and let me see it.

" The duplicates of the accounts are in the hands of the said treasurers, and they ought to submit me a copy of them.

" In regard to the receipt which is made at the royal treasury, it is always necessary to compare it with my register of the finances and discover if there is any article omitted, and finally it ought to be verified by the duplicates of receipts given to the royal treasury and signed by the first clerk of the said treasury.

" In case there is there another receipt, it ought to be verified by my orders and the duplicates of receipts.

" As for expenditures, my ordonnance and a quittance passed before a notary will be necessary in each article. . . .

"When there are roles of workers, it is necessary that they be certified by the contrôleur and noted by me without quittance.

" In regard to wages, it will be necessary to report the statement and the receipts in good form.

" The maintenance of the royal houses, *idem.*

" It is necessary to make a memorandum on each statement and verify the calculation four times, and that it appear on the memorandum that it has been verified.

" On this memorandum, it is necessary to put the notations in order to make me see them, and finally I will write them in my own hand."

For the above see " Appendice," *ibid.*, pp. 451-455: Year by year accounts of royal building expenditures exist for France only from the administration of Colbert. Scattered registers for specific palaces or works, all of partial character and fragmentary, with little application of method, have been found. However, the innovation of Colbert did not eliminate inexactitudes and irregularities. Inefficiency did not disappear over night, but much greater order existed than formerly. The accounts for royal building from 1664 through 1715 have been edited by J. Guiffrey; see his " Introduction," *Comptes des bâtiments du Roi sous le règne de Louis XIV* (5 vols., Paris, 1881-1901), I, i-lxxiv.

was no less so in controlling expenditures, and the aridity of this task was never for him a reason to dispense with it." [48] For instance we find one of these officials at Toulon being required to send him " an exact memoir of all the reductions of expenses which you have made since you went to Provence, and all those you expect to make next year." [49] M. Demuin, the intendant at Rochefort was reminded that, " I request every year, about this time, a plan of all expenses to be made in the next year in the navy in the port and arsenal of Rochefort "; therefore, he added, " you ought to work on it incessantly." [50] The intendant des Galères at Marseille was inaccurate in his accounts and was informed that, " if I find again any faults in your accounts . . . you may rest assured that I will hold you responsible." [51] The sieur de Clairembault, *contrôleur de Marine* at Brest, had neglected his records. " I have been extremely surprised," complained Colbert to learn of the quantities of wood, iron, and muskets placed in deposit in the warehouses without registration or receipts. He was warned that such practices had to cease as nothing could cause more " disorder and confusion." [52] Nor were the agents in the most distant areas of French control free from similar requirements. The intendant in Canada, M. Duchesneau, was advised that the King had inspected " the inventories and accounts which you have sent; but he desires that you make them more exact, that you sign them and send them by the first ships." [53]

The Finance Minister could not limit his interests to his own departments. The letters of the Marquis of Saint-Maurice provide a glimpse of Colbert participating in war council of Louvois in order to discover the financial needs of the armies and provide for them in the coming year. [54] It was stated as a maxim by him that " finance is the nerve of war," [55] and Louis

[48] Colbert, *Lettres,* III, part i, xxxii.
[49] Colbert to M. Matharel, February 20, 1671, *ibid.,* p. 338.
[50] Colbert to M. Demuin, August 13, 1674, *ibid.,* p. 523.
[51] Colbert to the sieur Brodart, August 10, 1682, *ibid.* (addition), p. 239.
[52] Colbert to the sieur de Clairembault, December 13, 1681, *ibid.,* p. 216. Literally hundreds of letters similar in nature to the above fragments can be found in the *Lettres,* Vols. III, part i, and III, part ii.
[53] Colbert to M. Duchesneau, April 15, 1676, *ibid.,* III, part ii, 608.
[54] Marquis of Saint-Maurice to the Duke of Savoy, November 11, 1667, Saint-Maurice, *Lettres sur la cour de Louis XIV,* pp. 153-154.
[55] Colbert, *Lettres,* III, part i, lxvi.

XIV himself recognized that it was "Finances" which contributed "motion and action to all this great body of the monarchy."[56]

To properly appreciate the order introduced into the financial administration by Colbert and Louis XIV, it is necessary to remind oneself just how new and unprecedented this order was. Today it is superfluous to insist on the need of maintaining a well-ordered accountability of public finances. In the seventeenth century, on the contrary, the practice of good bookkeeping in that field was exceptional.[57] In theory, to be sure, the treasurers, down the line, were supposed to render true accounts of receipts and authorized expenditures to the established chambers of accounts. But at the end of the reign of Louis XIII, ten treasurers of the royal treasury, more than a hundred receivers general, and more than a hundred farmers had failed to do so for some five years. The *prôcureur-général* of the chamber of accounts admitted it was impossible to discern true receipts and expenditures.[58] During the administration of Sully, it is true, the *surintendant des finances* had been required to submit annually to the king an *état au vrai*, or an account of the year's receipts and a computation of probable expenditures for the coming year. Since the reign of Marie de Medici, however, the rendering of such an account had become impossible.[59] J. R. Mallet, for many years of the reign of Louis XIV an accountant and then chief clerk of the office of the *contrôleur général*, was the author, in 1720, of the most informative single work on the finances of the *ancien régime*. Therein he admitted his inability, though all the preserved records were available to him, to compile any tables on royal revenues before 1661 except on those revenues which were actually received into the royal treasury. Even this was impossible for the years 1657 through 1660.

In contrast, from 1661, he was able to present complete tables for the total amounts of revenues collected, the deductions for expenses and the net receipts into the treasury. It

[56] Longnon, *Louis XIV,* mémoires, p. 57.
[57] G. Martin and M. Bezancon, *L'histoire du credit en France sous le régne de Louis XIV* (Paris, 1913), pp. 42-43.
[58] *Ibid.,* pp. 11-13.
[59] *Ibid.,* pp. 5-6.

had been impossible to make such distinctions before, because it was only with Colbert that exact registers began to be maintained on the revenues of the King.[60]   From 1661 on, Mallet tells us, the data provided by the office of the *contrôleur général* were sufficient to enable him to draw up "all the tables one could wish!"[61]   It was Colbert's ideal that all essential operations in finance should be traceable in the records.   This was the explanation for the maintenance of the registers and for the work of the *conseil des finances*.   To this end, he, with the cooperation of Louis, followed a rigorous program of forcing accountability by the treasurers and other officials and canalized these activities into the office of the *contrôleur général*.   In so doing he laid the bases for the organization for the control of public accountability in France.[62]   The most spectacular evidence of the new order of things, under the regime of Colbert, was the great drop in the so-called *charges annuelles* assigned on the revenues of the King.   These were what might be designated the operating cost of the tax system, and, naturally, it rose and fell with relation to the efficiency of surveillance and the enforcing of accounting.   Whereas the gross revenues increased, in the period 1661-1683, from 84,000,000 livres to 116,000,000, these *charges* declined from 52,000,000 to 27,000,000.[63]   This, then, was the final realization of the aspirations of Richelieu.   These brilliant results of the strict order imposed on those who handled the royal revenues justified the plaudits which historians have, almost without exception, given to the financial work of Colbert.

The advice of Simon Stevin to the Duke of Sully urging the adoption by the government of a merchant's methods of bookkeeping, and Montchrétien's emphasis on the virtues of governmental accounting were lessons in a special branch of statecraft which would have been fully appreciated by Louis XIV.   As for Colbert, with his merchant-banker background and relationships and his long apprenticeship in the tradition of economic stateism, the use of business methods was a *sine*

[60] Mallet, p. 182.
[61] *Ibid.*
[62] Martin and Bezancon, p. 78.
[63] Mallet, pp. 287, 315. The actual sums listed by Mallet were: 84,222,096; 116,053,374; 52,377,172; 27,376,752.

qua non of rational administration. This quantitative emphasis which produced the reforms in the financial structure of the state also dominated, as we have noted, the rational and scientific movement in the seventeenth century. In science and government there was a new consciousness of the veracity of mathematics and its utility as a guide to reason, and as a certain measure in calculation. The financial reforms on the part of Louis XIV and Colbert survived all the misfortunes of the reign to form a permanent contribution to the science of government in France.

III

In Chapter V it was shown how the intendants flourished under the regime of Louis XIV and Colbert and how, along with other duties and privileges, they assumed the role of the primary statistical agents of the central power. As we have seen, the technical, social, or economic data collected by them and by other agents were of utmost utility to a King who wished to measure the springs of his power and to a Minister who conceived of the state as an economic unit. It might be said that Louis XIV was interested in power and Colbert in wealth, but, in the eyes of either there was little if any distinction between these interests. Statistics from abroad, or from the provinces, on the flow of trade, on production, tariffs, or agriculture were of equal import to Colbert or his master. For example, in a circular instruction to the intendants in 1679 Colbert expressed the wish of the King that they investigate the status of commerce and manufactures and the number of animals in their generalities. They should consider " these three points as the fecund sources from which the people draw money, not only for their subsistence, but further in order to pay taxes." [64] Thus in practical administration was met the same declaration of the reciprocal interest of enterprise and the state which was so often cited by economists or political scientists in the seventeenth century. In an age witnessing the dominance in philosophy of the mathematical spirit of Descartes, and in productive politics of the tenets of mercantilism, statistics was a reasonable instrument of order and

[64] Colbert, " Circular instruction to the intendants," April 28, 1679, Colbert *Lettres,* II, part i, 97.

evaluation. Because of its importance in their government and its future importance in the operation of all efficient government, it will be our purpose to enlarge here on the development of the science of statistics in the century and its application to the problems of the state, particularly in France.

As has been observed before, statistics was not the creation of the seventeenth century. Bodin, we noted, in his *République,* praised the use of population enumerations by the Ancients and recommended the revival of the practice by the modern state.[65] Montchrétien, in 1615, largely reiterated these views in his *Traicté de l'oeconomie politique.*[66] The value of such enumerations which Bodin and Montchrétien set forth, namely, to ascertain the wealth and manpower of the kingdom, to facilitate tax collection and the just distribution of the tax burden, to detect and eliminate vagabondage, and to determine the proper regulations necessary to the maintenance of production, export, import, colonies, and warfare was the general estimate of their value given by the ministry of Louis XIV. As early as 1570 Charles IX, with the idea of establishing more productive imposts, had commissioned a certain Louis Boulenger, a geometrician and financier, to draw up a *cadastre* on the dimensions and capacities of the kingdom. The resulting work, *Calculation et description de la France* (1575) was a bizarre exaggeration, but some of its errors persisted in other books well into the next century.[67] The *Secret des finances* (1581) and the *Cabinet du Roy de France* (1581) of Froumenteau[68] purported to give statistical evidence of the financial and moral bankruptcy of the kingdom. Along with fabulous figures on revenues and expenditures, the author did not hesitate to include those on the number of girls violated, bastards, and the carnal exploits of churchmen.[69] Over a hundred years later a hostile English traveller took his proof of the depravity of the French clergy and nobility from Froumenteau.[70] As a statistical source Froumenteau scarcely

---

[65] See Chapter II, above.
[66] *Ibid.*
[67] Jonnès, *État économique et social de la France,* pp. 11-15.
[68] See Chapter II, above.
[69] Froumenteau, *Le cabinet du Roy de France* (1581), pp. 18-279, *passim; Secret des finances* (1581), *passim.*
[70] *Six weeks observations on the present state of the court and country of*

deserves notice but he was widely used afterwards and his work certainly evidences an increasing interest in such evaluations.[71]

The *États, empires, royaumes et principautéz du monde* (1614) of Pierre d'Avity initiated a series of works giving comparative statistics on the various countries of Europe and the world.[72] Again the figures appear unreliable [73] but they reflect an interesting intent, namely, to calculate the power potentials of one state in relation to another. The statistical analysis of Jean Eon in his *Commerce honorable* (1646), while subject to the usual criticism in this regard, represents another attempt to show the validity of applying the science of numbers to the measurement of national wealth and promise.[74] In the course of the century there were published a number of unofficial histories, inventories of benefice returns or properties, general surveys of districts, cities, chateaux or provinces, which contained statistics and were sometimes used by the intendants in their own reports.[75] The *Paris ancien et nouveau* (1685) of one Le Maire, for instance, gave a census of that city, by quarters, basing the totals on an arbitrary estimate of four heads of families to each house.[76]

France (London, 1691), pp. 22-23, 58-59. For differing views on the value of Froumenteau, see F. Faure, "The development and progress of statistics in France," in J. Koren, ed., *The history of statistics,* pp. 236-237, notes; E. Levasseur, *La population française,* I, 190-192, notes.

[71] For example, around 1600, an anonymous author wrote of his disgust with the general claim that there were too many clergymen and, therefore, a need for a change in religion. For his own satisfaction, he claimed, he made a statistical study, which he admitted was not exact, to determine the number. He arrived at an estimate of 80,000. This he agreed was too many. The solution was not to turn Calvinist, however, but to work against such excesses within the church itself. " Le nombre des ecclesiastiques de France celuy des religieux et des religieuses le temps de leurs etablissement, ce dont ils subsistent et quoy ils servent" (Paris, c. 1600) in *Archives curieuses de l'histoire de France depuis Louis XI jusqu'à Louis XVIII,* edited by L. Cimber and others (27 vols., Paris, 1834-1840), 1st series, XIV, 431-467.

[72] See Chapter II, above.

[73] For instance, on the revenues of France (1547-1580), he draws from Froumenteau. *États, empires,* pp. 80-82; see Levasseur's opinion in the *La population française,* I, 49-50, notes.

[74] See Chapter II, above; Cole, *Colbert,* I, 212-215.

[75] See the bibliography in A. de Boislisle, *Mémoire sur la généralite de Paris,* I, viii-ix and notes.

[76] Thus: " The quarter of the Hôtel-de-Ville . . . contains fifty-three streets, eighteen churches and convents, seven hotels, a hospital, two public fountains, nineteen hundred and fifteen houses, seven thousand six hundred and sixty

The main work in statistics was not, however, the result of such private investigations. Publicized surveys usually displayed but fragmentary knowledge and an inferior quality of understanding or even arithmetic. The more extensive statistical estimates were conducted by the state and, for the most part, these remained secrets of the state. In France, the government undertook three great inquests of its resources or capacities during the seventeenth century. The first was that initiated by the Duke of Sully soon after assuming the direction of the finances. The results are, except for the vague references of Sully himself in his *Oeconomies,* generally unknown. An elaborate, if not too successful, statistical inquiry seems to have been made by him and his colleagues, and it is possible that the construction of a " Cabinet of Affairs of State and War," pictured by him as an administrative archival deposit for such data, was actually begun before the death of Henry IV. At any rate, Sully's methods were abandoned and his cabinet, if it existed, disappeared after his retirement.[77]

As we have seen Colbert likewise began his regime with an inquest. The great survey of 1663 evolved into the continuing policy of internal administration. The statistical function of the intendants, which grew out of the survey, remained one of their salient duties under all successive *controleurs-général.*[78] The departmental archives which Colbert, Louvois, and their colleagues started likewise persisted as essential agencies of government.

The *Mémoires des intendants* of 1697-1700, in one sense, scarcely deserve to be called the result of a third inquest since they were the product of the agents and a system long functioning and relied heavily on reports and surveys previously made. As a combined work, however, they represent the most complete description of the economic and administrative condition of the France of the *ancien régime.* These memoirs, like the greater amount of the other statistical data assembled by the government in the period, were kept in manuscript form

inhabitants, on the basis of four heads of a family only for each house, and is superintended by nineteen police officers." Extract quoted in " Appendice " of *ibid.,* pp. 422-423.

[77] See Chapter III, above, for a more detailed description; Faure, " The development of statistics in France," pp. 243-247.

[78] See Chapter V, above.

and supposedly were only available to administrative officials. Such secrets, particularly a census, were difficult to keep, however, and fragmentary data were reproduced in published works like Vaubans' *Le dîme royale* (1707), Saugrain's *Le dénombrement de la France par généralities, élections, paroisses, et feux* (1709) and Boulainvilliers' posthumous *l'État de la France* (1727).[79]

Perhaps the first important use of the financial statistics collected in the archives of the *contrôleur général,* in a published work, were those released to Forbonnais for his *Recherches et considerations sur les finances de France depuis 1595 jusqu'en 1721* (1758). The earlier work, that of J. R. Mallet, also contained such official statistical data. Although written about 1720 it was not published until 1789.[80]

Several developments of major importance to the progress of statistical science occurred during the seventeenth century. The study of the theory of probability begins then which, in turn, provides the background for the derivation of the normal curve of distribution. In 1654 Blaise Pascal and Pierre de Fermat exchanged their celebrated letters on the subject of the division of stakes between two gamblers who separate without finishing their game.[81] Three years later appeared Christian Huygens' *De ratiociniis in ludo aleae* which dealt with the same subject.[82] On April 25, 1671, Jan De Wit, to support the issue of a state annuity, presented the members of the States General of Holland with the first known formal work

[79] *Ibid.;* also, Faure, " The development of statistics in France," pp. 249-256. A. de Boislisle, " Introduction," *Mémoire sur la généralite de Paris, passim* and notes; Levasseur, I, 55-56, notes, 201-203, notes; Jonnès, pp. 260-263.

[80] Full title: J. R. Mallet, *Comptes rendus de l'administration des finances du royaume de France, pendant les onze dernières années du régne de Henri IV, le régne de Louis XIII, et soixante-cinq années de celui de Louis XIV; avec recherches sur l'origine des impôts, sur les revenus et depenses de nos rois, depuis Philippe-Le-Bel jusqu'a Louis XIV; et différents mémoires sur le numeraire et sa valeur sous les trois régnes ci-dessus;* (*ouvrage posthume de M. Mallet, premier commis des Finances sous M. Desmaretz, Contrôleur-Général des Finances, pendant les années 1707 a 1715* (London and Paris, 1789); F. V. D. Forbonnais, *Recherches et considérations sur les finances de France depuis 1595 jusqu'a 1721* (6 vols., Liege, 1758).

[81] H. M. Walker, *Studies in the history of statistical method* (Baltimore, 1929), pp. 4-6.

[82] *Ibid.,* p. 6 and note; see also A. F. Jack, *An introduction to the history of life assurance* (London, 1912), p. 216.

treating the valuation of life annuities. Textually, the report demonstrated the application of probabilities in a game of chance to the probabilities of life expectancies.[83]

At about the time Pascal and Fermat were exchanging their letters Laurent Tonti, an Italian, persuaded Mazarin to issue the first "tontine" in France. This was an annuity granted by the government in exchange for a loan. It rested on the " principle of association and took some account of the probable duration of life." The idea did not originate with Tonti, but he was the first to put it to practical use on such a large scale and its influence was widespread. Similar systems were adopted in other countries: in Holland, as noted, in 1671, in England (1692), and in Brandenburg (1698).[84] The first tontine of 1653 and the second of 1656 were not successful, probably because of the current distrust of the credit of the government. Tonti died, a debtor, in the Bastile, during the administration of Colbert, the state having cut off his pension in 1661. His scheme was revived, however, in 1689, this time with greater success.[85] Referring to this re-establishment, one intendant wrote the *contrôleur général:* " I can scarcely tell you how enthusiastically it is received in this province . . . each presuming that he will live longer than the rest and

[83] De Wit was an adept mathematician and at 23 published a book, the *Elementa curvarum linearum.* He was probably familiar with Pascal's theory of probability as well as with the published work of Huygens. The pamphlet mentioned in the text, entitled *Waardye van Lyf-renten naer proportie van Lasrenten,* was inexplicably lost for two centuries. C. Walford, *The insurance cyclopaedia* (6 vols., [incomplete], London, 1873), II, 184-187. Excerpts from the report are reprinted in I, 100-103; Jack, pp. 216-217; Levasseur, I, 53, II, 292.

[84] Jack, pp. 176, 211-215. An idea of the operation of the French Tontine can be gotten from articles in the tontine decree of 1689 quoted in Isambert, XX, 87-96: The depositors were divided into fourteen classes. The first class included ages 1 to 5 and classes continued by steps of 5 to the fourteenth class of ages 65 to 70. After registration and proof of age the subscriber paid 300 *livres* and was paid interest on a basis " proportional to age." Thus, those of the 1st and 2nd classes, that is 1 to 10, who, " in the course of nature " ought to enjoy the interest longer, were paid on the basis of 5%. The 13th and 14th classes found the returns increased to 12½% and other classes enjoyed proportional returns. As the number in each class decreased, because of death, the survivors' incomes increased until the last survivor in each class received the total interest income for the class. If there was any residue after the last survivor of a class the state received it. Pp. 88-91.

[85] Depping, *Correspondance,* III, xxii-xxvi, see also letters to Colbert, *ibid.*. pp. 17-22.

hoping thus to arrive to a great fortune. . . ." [86] Adam Smith, using a French statistical source, estimated that, by 1764, approximately one eighth of the public debt of France, or 300,000,000 *livres,* consisted of annuity capital from which 30,000,000 was paid each year to subscribers.[87]

Apart from the use of the idea of probability to support the finances of a state, the experience with the tontine is of interest because of its contribution to the building up of later mortality statistics.   Halley's *Estimate of the degrees of the mortality of mankind, drawn from the curious tables of the births and funerals of the city of Breslaw with an attempt to ascertain the prices of annuities upon lives,* which has been called (by Levasseur) the " first work of mathematical statistics which merits the name," was written in 1693 at the request of the government of William III which wished to contract loans on the basis of annuities.[88] The first scientific tables of mortality in France were those of Deparcieux in his *Essai sur les probalités de la durée de la vie humaine* (1746).   His material was furnished by the 9,320 deaths which took place in the two tontines of 1689 and 1696.   This part of Deparcieux's work was considered by Levasseur to be still useful near the end of the nineteenth century.[89]

The most significant action in the matter of demographic statistics in the seventeenth century can be traced to the initiative of Colbert.   Beginning with the year 1670 he had published monthly, for the city of Paris, the number of *actes de l'état-civil* (baptisms, marriages, burials).   The curés of all the parishes of the kingdom had been required to register

[86] M. de Séraucourt, Intendent of Berry, to the Contrôleur-Général, December 17, 1689, A. de Boislisle, *Correspondance des contrôleurs-généraux,* I, 211.

[87] Smith, *The wealth of nations* (London, 1929), pp. 733-734.

[88] Levasseur, I, 53, II, 291 and note. " This was the real beginning of a theory of annuities, for the tables which had been previously published had not been scientifically constructed." (Walker, *History of statistical method,* p. 36.) " The first work to throw any real light on the regularity of social phenomena was Captain John Graunt's *Observations on the London Bills of Mortality* (1662)." (*Ibid.*) For this work and those of Sir William Petty on political arithmetic, plus an excellent " introduction " see C. H. Hull, ed., *The economic writings of Sir William Petty, together with observations upon the bills of mortality, more probably by Captain John Graunt* (2 vols., Cambridge, England, 1899).

[89] Levasseur, I, 56 and note; Faure, " The development of statistics in France," p. 265.

these acts since the edicts of Villers-Cotterets (1539) and Blois
(1579). The publication of this series was interrupted from
1684 to 1709, but from the later date it has been a continuous
practice. These figures, derived from all the generalities,
provided the source for the very important demographical
studies conducted by the intendants near the end of the *ancien
régime*.[90]

Today perhaps the first idea that comes to mind with reference to governmental statistics is that of a population census.
It does not seem likely that any general or official census of
the population of the kingdom, as a whole, was conducted
during the years of Colbert's ministry. This does not mean,
however, that this matter was of no concern to Colbert or the
King. Population was an expression of the wealth of the
state and, as such, could not be ignored, nor was it. Then why
was no general census conducted? The answer seems to be
that the need was not sufficiently felt. The years 1661 to
1683 were, generally speaking, years of prosperity and apparently of increasing population.[91] The King and his Minister
seem to have taken this idea more or less for granted. When
in 1671, all intendants were required to investigate the populations in their generalities it was in order to discover the
extent to which it had *increased* over the past several years
and hence to provide information for judging the increase of
the King's power therefrom.[92] The primary interest in the
number of the people was centered in its relationship to taxation and, particularly, to the *taille*. Here Colbert relied, in
the main, on a system already long established—the tax rolls.
The efforts in this direction were mostly applied to eliminating
the abuses practiced by the tax collectors, by checking and

[90] *Ibid.,* pp. 248-249, 261-265; Levasseur, I, 248-256.
[91] *Ibid.,* p. 196.
[92] " The king desiring to be informed if the number of his subjects has increased since several years, H.M. has ordered the *commissaires départis dans
les provinces des pais d'election*—intendants—to make a comparison of the number of *cottes*—tax assessments on tax rolls—of the parishes of this year with
that of five or six years past; and although in Provence this verification cannot be made in this way, I am persuaded, nevertheless, that you can easily
give him this information and satisfy thus the curiosity of H.M. which does
not consist only in being informed of the increase in the number of his
subjects by this means, but also in having a true knowledge of his power by
this increase." Colbert to d'Oppède, President of the Parlement of Aix, June
1671, Depping, *Correspondance*, III, 215-216.

supervising the lists to discover those who had been unjustly exempted, and to re-apportion the burden with more attention to ability to pay.[93]   The *taille* was distributed among the generalities by *brevet;* in the elections the *taille* was distributed by *commission* and in the parishes by *department.*   After the intendants had reduced the older officials connected with this distribution to almost complete impotence, the *commission* and *department* became almost exclusively the work of the intendants and abuses were vastly reduced.   But in the roll, great disproportions continued to exist.[94]   The solution which Colbert would have liked to apply was to eliminate the *taille personelle,* based on an arbitrary estimate of the sum capacity of the payor, and to substitute throughout the kingdom the *taille réelle,* based directly on his property.   As the latter was assessed on property and the former on the person, it was less subject to capricious multiplicity of privileges.   Moreover, property lists, already existing, usually made the assessment easier and more uniform.   In line with this aspiration, Colbert desired to draw up a vast land census for the whole realm on the basis of which the *taille* would be equitably divided and the income of the state better regulated.   The project failed, however, due to the hostility of vested interests, the physical difficulty of carrying out the task, and the fear of disrupting a tax system already functioning.[95]

Though a general census was not conducted during the

[93] Cole, *Colbert,* I, 304; Clamageran, II, 606, 617-630; Clement, "Introduction," Colbert, *Lettres,* II, part I, lxv-lxxxiii, letters *passim.*

[94] Marion, *Histoire Financiere de la France,* I, 3-4. The rolls were, Marion says: "the work, in the countries subject to the personal tailles, of collectors chosen by turn among the taillables, charged with dividing at will following a vague and arbitrary estimation of the property of each payor, and ordinarily guided by their sentiment of favoritism, or antipathy, or fear, or vengeance, or, more frequently, by the provision of the difficulty more or less great that they would find in collecting each quota." The appearance of poverty and the fear of wealth were consequently traits ". . . deeply ingrained in the popular mind."

[95] Cole, *Colbert,* I, 304; Lavisse, *Louis XIV,* VII, part i, 190. Clamageran, II, 628-629; Colbert, *Lettres,* II, part i, lxxxii-lxxxiii; Marion, I, 9-10.   This scheme anticipates the projects of Vauban who desired to have the state draw up a great statistical cadastre of population, geography, land holdings, live stock, and wealth for all the kingdom. See his "Description geographique de l'election de Vézelay" (1696) and the *Projet d'une dixme royale, suivi de deux écrits financiers par Vauban* (1707), edited by E. Coornaert (Paris, 1933) in Collection des principaux economistes.

period of Colbert's ministry it is well to note that information on the local trends in regard to population was frequently required and, as seen in the examples cited above, this type of inquiry might even be applied to the kingdom as a unit. Further, it must be noted that the statistical function of the intendant which was, in a real sense, the creation of Colbert, equipped the administration with officials trained to carry out such a task in case of need.

Before the end of the century the pressure of the financial demands of the wars, the apparent uneasiness of Louis XIV as to the success of his government, the question of the effect of Huguenot migration on wealth and population, and the desire to instruct the heir-apparent in the condition of the kingdom he was scheduled to rule, brought about the first nation-wide enumeration in France.[96]   In 1694-1695 the *contrôleur-général*, Pontchartrain, requested total enumerations to facilitate the levying of a capitation tax.   Inadequate preparation and too great haste, among other things, seem to have prevented the scheme from being successful.[97]   In 1697, the Duke of Beauvillier, possibly at the instigation of Fenelon and Vauban, submitted questionnaires to all the intendants on which they were to draw up memoirs for the instruction of the Duke of Burgundy.   These questions, without the addition of those on the effect of the Huguenot migrations and on total population, were almost the same as those submitted by Colbert to the intendants in 1663.[98]   The resulting memoirs of 1700 were extremely variable in quality, but taken together, as we have previously commented, they comprise the most complete document we possess on the France of Louis XIV and they give the " only general account of French population before 1780 which has an official character." [99]

[96] Faure, " The development of statistics in France," p. 251; Levasseur, I, 201-202.

[97] A. de Boislisle, *Mémoire sur la généralite de Paris*, I, xxiv, 551-553.

[98] See Chapter IV; compare with A. de Boislisle, *Mémoire sur la généralite de Paris*, I, 2-3, Boulainville in his *État de France* (1727), I, who reproduces the Colbert instructions as being those used by Beauvillier.

[99] This seems to be the general conclusion of modern historians of French statistical development. Levasseur, I, 201-202; Faure, " The development of statistics in France," p. 250; H. Sée, " The intendants' memoires of 1698 and their value for economic history," *The Economic History Review*, I (1928), pp. 308-312. The most harsh critic of the memoirs was Boulainvilliers in his

In the colony of Canada an actual census of population by name was taken at least as early as 1666.[100] The one-hundred-and-fifty-four-page manuscript containing these returns is deposited in the archives at Paris and a transcript is preserved in the archives at Ottawa.[101] The population of the country continued to be a matter of interest to Colbert and the King. Instructions to an intendant sent out in 1668 carried the order to " make a roll or census of all the inhabitants of the country and mark their sex, age, and state, if they are married or not and how many children they have." He was also to inform himself, quarterly, on the number of births, deaths, and marriages, and the census was to be renewed yearly in order to determine whether the colony grew.[102] It is possible that these figures were padded by the representatives of the Compagnie des Occidentales. For after that venture was dissolved, discrepancies turned up in the new figures when compared to the older ones. In 1674 Colbert wrote the Count of Frontenac:

His Majesty has been surprised to see, by the tables which you have sent me, that there are only 6,705 men, women and children in all the compass of Canada; on which he is convinced that whoever made these tables by your order is considerably mistaken . . . there being more inhabitants some years before. . . . For coming years, His Majesty wishes that you apply yourself to have these tables made more accurately, so that he may be better informed of the number of the inhabitants of this colony.[103]

État de France. See A. de Boislisle's critical introduction to the Mémoire sur la généralite de Paris, I, for a thorough discussion of this criticism in relation to the memoir on the generality of Paris. There were two main methods of conducting enumerations in the seventeenth and eighteenth centuries in France. By the counting of hearths—the division of the tailles was usually based on the number of hearths in a parish—and by the use of figures on the actes de l'état-civil (baptism, marriages and burial). Seventeenth- and early eighteenth-century enumerations were ordinarily conducted by the first method while the latter was the basis of those surveys conducted by the intendants in the middle and late eighteenth. See A. de Boislisle, Mémoire sur la généralite de Paris, I, xix-xxxi. Direct enumeration by head was tried by Pontchartrain and even by some of the intendants framing the memoirs of 1697-1700, but it was generally abandoned as too difficult. Ibid., Faure, pp. 257-265; Levasseur, pp. 248-256; Depping, III, p. viii; Jonnès, État économique et social, pp. 260-262.

[100] See Chapter V, above.

[101] Godfrey, " History and development of statistics in Canada," Koren, ed., The history of statistics, p. 179.

[102] Instruction to M. de Bouteroue, April 5, 1668, Colbert Lettres, III, part ii, 402. A similar instruction was given to the sieur Gaudais, May 1, 1669, ibid., p. 445.

[103] Ibid., p. 577 and note.

In a letter to an intendant, in 1676, Colbert still expressed the King's perplexity over the small figure of the latest census, giving the number as 7,832 and noted that " he expects that the new census which has been made this year will be much more ample." [104]   The next census indicated a population of 8,515.   The King was still pained but was convinced of the verity of the number, and the intendant was ordered to bend his efforts to increase the number and the general wealth.[105]

Thus, although no general census of the French population was taken in the years 1661 to 1683, spot enumerations and data on population trends were regularly required.   Such statistics were useful in the evaluation of wealth and particularly, from the point of view of the state, as it applied to taxation.   Stress was also placed on registers of government personnel.   In a limited area we have seen the utility of such lists concerning the members of sovereign courts.[106]   On a broader plane, the drawing up, maintenance, and checking of military registers and lists emphasized the care of an economy-minded government to arrive at an expenditure more justly proportioned to services received.   Secondly a supply of man-power for the war machine was made more certain through large-scale conscriptions and registrations.

When Louis XIV had commenced his personal reign he had had to deal at once with the problem of relating the sums granted to commanders for the pay and subsistence of their troops to the number of troops actually under their command. At the second meeting of the *conseil de trois,* March 10, 1661, the King asked for statements on the true number making up the garrisons of the fortresses in order to confound the governors who traditionally presented exorbitant demands for their subsistence at the end of each year.[107]   Louis, in later years, related to his son how he had combatted the confusion and dishonesty which had marked the army in this respect.   " But in order to provide against this confusion a more efficient precaution and to assure that my troops always remained complete, I ordered that each month I be sent the muster rolls

[104] Colbert to M. Duchesneau, April 15, 1676, *ibid.,* p. 606.
[105] Colbert to M. Duchesneau, April 28, 1677, *ibid.,* p. 615.
[106] See Chapter V, above.
[107] J. de Boislisle, *Conseil de 1661,* I, 13, 148.

of all the corps that I paid, however distant they might be. . . ." This alone would not be sufficient safeguard, however, so that, in addition, " in order to know if I was faithfully served in this I expressly sent gentlemen to all parts, in order to surprise and see the troops unexpectedly. This kept the captains and *commissaires* in continuous need of fulfilling their duty." [108]

The most spectacular measure of the government of Louis XIV and Colbert along these lines was the initiation of the *inscription maritime*. The desertion of French shipping by French sailors for service abroad was among the more notorious complaints of the government and writers on commerce during the better part of the seventeenth century. If the navy required personnel the customary manner of acquiring them was by closing the ports and impressing all suitable men who could not escape or who lacked influential friends or relatives. To his cousin the Duke of Beaufort, Admiral of France, the King decried the impossibility of maintaining great armaments " if I do not discover means of changing the . . . nearly insurmountable aversion which seamen have to engaging themselves to serve aboard my ships." [109] At the time he was writing, steps had already been taken to change these conditions.

As early as 1661 the King in his council, at the inspiration of Colbert, ordered the drawing up of a register of all naval officers.[110] It is clear that no adequate documents of such nature existed, for, a short time later, an agent wrote Colbert that he would send him a list of all naval captains " whom we know at present " with whatever information he had on their life and merits.[111] A general enrollment of sailors commenced in 1665 with the closing of the ports of Poitou, Xaintonge, Aunix, Brouage, and la Rochelle and the denial of permission to all ships in these ports to depart without lists of their crews being made and submitted to the admiralty

---

[108] Longnon, *Louis XIV, mémoires*, pp. 216-217.

[109] In the specific instance Louis XIV was disturbed over the harshness of the discipline maintained by certain officers and directed the Duke to search out and punish the officers who mistreated their crews. Louis XIV to the Duke of Beaufort, April 19, 1669, Colbert, *Lettres*, III, part i, 120; see La Roncière, *Histoire de la marine française*, V, 365.

[110] J. de Boislisle, *Conseil de 1661*, II, 132, 135, 300.

[111] Colbert de Terron to Colbert, September 14, 1661, *ibid.*, p. 312.

authority.[112]   September 22, 1668, saw the beginning of a series of ordinances calling for the enrollment of seamen in the maritime provinces.[113]   The tenor of these decrees may be derived from the following quotations extracted from the *Édit pour l'enrolement des matelots en Provence* (1670):

> Louis, *etc.* The care which we have for some years past given to the re-establishment and increase of our naval forces having directed to our attention several abuses and great difficulties in securing and forming crews for the great number of war ships which we have built, we have deemed it necessary, in order to avoid falling into the necessity of closing all the ports of our kingdom, and disturbing and disrupting thereby the commerce of our subjects, each time that we desire a few ships to put to sea, as has been done in the past, to have a general enrollment made of all the naval officers and sailors of our realm and to divide them in three classes, in order to have one alternately and continually in our service. . . .
>
> . . . all the said officers, mariners and seamen included in these rolls will enter our service forthwith, alternating one year out of three, according to the divisions made by the said rolls.
>
> While actively serving aboard our ships, they will be paid their full salary . . . and, when ashore, they will be paid one half of their wages.
>
> The province will be divided into four departments in each of which there will be a *commissaire de marine*,[114] bearing the roll of the department, and officers to undertake the execution of the rolls and to advise all seamen of each class when they will be called to board our ships.[115]

If discharged on the west coast the men should receive a month's additional pay for travel expenses home.   The call to service of any class was to be announced in parish churches ten days prior to the date set for reporting.   For failure to comply within that time they could be punished as deserters.

---

[112] G. Daniel, *Histoire de la milice françoise* (2 vols., Paris, 1721), II, 680-681. While the Montmorencys directed the navy, two general enrollments were ordered, in 1608 and 1624, but what success they met is not indicated by La Roncière who mentions them. See his *Histoire de la marine française*, V, 366 note. The later order was reproduced in the Code Michaud of 1629 with the direction that the lists be submitted to Richelieu. See Isambert, XVI, 332-333.

[113] La Roncière, V, 366; J. de Crisenoy, *Les ordonnances de Colbert et l'inscription maritime* (Paris, 1862), pp. 8-9; Isambert, XVIII, 198; Daniel, II, 681.

[114] See Chapter V, above.

[115] "Édit pour l'enrôlement des matelots en Provence," Tournay, May, 1670, in "Appendice," Colbert, *Lettres*, III, part ii, 663-665; See also Crisenoy, pp. 9, 20. See extract from similar edict for Brittany, in Colbert, *Lettres*, III, part ii, 663 note; see Isambert, XVIII, 612, 367, 370.

During their year of service, the seamen were not to engage
in any other branch of the marine, and private shipowners or
captains who hired such men were subject to fine. Copies or
extracts of the rolls were to be sent to the seats of the admiralty
in the province and to the record offices of the communities
where the seamen resided. The rolls were to be renewed and
verified in March of every year. Seamen would be given free
certificates containing their name, age, years of service, and
signal number (?) for identification and protection during
their off years. This would give them the right to ship independently. In order to encourage service, during the year of
duty, enrollees were to enjoy exemption from quartering of
troops, city watches, collectorship of *tailles,* law suits and con-
straint of person for debt and other privileges.

The carrying out of the *inscription maritime* met with varying fortunes. Letters of Colbert to the *commissaires de marine*
and intendants disclose him successively congratulating and
reprimanding these officials on the rate of their progress.[116]
When the intendant at Bordeaux reported difficulty among
the Basques and desired to escape the difficulty by substituting
an arbitrary levy, Colbert refused, and reminded him that in
most maritime provinces sailors reported for enrollment of
their own accord. At any rate, if the intendant continued to
lag, " His Majesty will know how to make himself obeyed." [117]
Riots, mass flights and impressment marked the efforts in
Navarre, Rochefort, Havre, Dieppe, and Marseille but the
Bretons, attracted by the prospect of half pay when out of
service, enrolled in droves. Whereas a census of 1667, in
Brittany, had disclosed only a little more than 5,000 sailors the
inscription maritime revealed 20,000.[118] In case seamen did

[116] Congratulating, see Colbert to the sieur Brodart, *commissaire général de
marine* at Toulon, February 28, 1670; censoring, see Colbert to M. de Seuil,
intendant de marine at Brest, February 28, 1670, *Lettres,* III, part i, 219-220.
The commissioners were instructed to send directly to Colbert exact and attested
lists of all the officers, sailors and soldiers enrolled giving their names, ages,
residence, stature, physical markings, and wages promised them at enlistment.
Haste was emphasized so that he, Colbert, might exactly ascertain the amounts
he would have to provide from the treasury. See above, also general instruction
to commissioners, p. 193.

[117] Colbert to M. Daguesseau, intendant at Bordeaux, August 16, 1670, *ibid.,*
pp. 261-262.

[118] La Roncière, V, 367-368.

not voluntarily enlist the hearth-lists of the maritime parishes were checked and rolls made therefrom.[119] The benefits which the enlisted men enjoyed such as half pay in the reserve status [120] and the privileged position in the community were added to from time to time. Wages were paid to their families during campaigns; free instruction was given to their children by the village *curés*; payments were made at the home to avoid the ruinous expenditures of newly landed sailors; and 2 per cent of their wages were retained to provide hospitalization or pensions amounting to three years of wages for injury.[121] The *inscription maritime,* buttressed by such positive aids, was at least a partial success and, generally speaking, ended the necessity of arbitrary impressment although the navy had vastly expanded.[122] The system, once it began to function, added to the service of the state navy about 60,000 sailors or around 15,000 men a year, not counting officers, specialized classes of workmen, and galley slaves.[123] The *inscription maritime* had at least one admirer abroad. At one place in his *Naval Minutes* Samuel Pepys listed the points in which the " well-governing " of the French navy surpassed his own. Among these were:

The King of France's well-payment of his seamen and provision against the diverting of the moneys appointed thereto.
The enrolling of his seamen, with all the circumstances thereto.
Provision for sick and wounded and the widows of the dead.
Support of their families when they are at sea.[124]

The gradual increase in the statistical emphasis which marked the regime of Louis XIV and Colbert was evidenced by such things as the attention given to estimating population trends,

[119] " Instruction aux lieutenans généraux pour le Roy dans la province et duché de Bretagne," September 4, 1669, Colbert, *Lettres,* III, part i, 159.
[120] Financial difficulties of the state curtailed this benefit within a few years.
[121] La Roncière, V, 369-370.
[122] Daniel, II, 681. During the war with Holland, it became temporarily necessary to call up reserves and resort to impressment. La Roncière, V, 368-369. Clement in his " introduction " to Colbert, *Lettres,* III, part i, xx-xxx, gives a much less optimistic account and sees the class system as almost abandoned after 1684.
[123] Clement, " Introduction," Colbert, *Lettres,* III, part i, xxv. Daniel noted that 60,000 were enrolled in the maritime provinces by 1681, *Histoire de la milice françoise,* II, 681-682; Spanheim spoke of 40,000 being raised from Bayonne to Dunkerque and 12,000 from Languedoc and Provence, *Relation de la cour de France,* p. 304.
[124] Samuel Pepys, *Naval minutes,* ed. by J. R. Tanner (London, 1926) (Publications of the Navy Records Society, vol. LX), pp. 361-362.

to checking, revising and supervising tax lists, to the drawing up of a general cadastre of the realm, to the publication of the *actes de l'état-civil,* to the census of colonial inhabitants, or in the creation of extensive lists of government personnel either in the administration or the military. Bodin and Mont-chrétien had indicated the value of enumerations in judging the strength and wealth of the nation through population, in facilitating and assuring the collection of taxes, in improving the just distribution of tax burdens, in regulating defense and warfare, providing against the extortion of officials, and in administering colonies. The policies praised by the theorists were thus clearly understood by the practical administrators of Louis XIV and during the period from 1661 to 1683 great strides were made in applying such theories to the active conduct of the state.

In judging and controlling the wealth of the nation, population figures were perhaps of less apparent importance than economic statistics. We have commented on the demands for foreign trade figures which were intersticed in the correspondence of Colbert with consuls and other representatives of France abroad. For example, the wine production and trade of the Rhine drew his close attention because of the competition with the sale of French wines in Holland. Envoys in Germany were instructed to submit memoirs listing all the toll stations along the river, the amount of tolls anually collected converted into equivalents in French terms, as to money and weights, and the ratio to the vaue of the merchandise taxed. All must be so clearly formulated that the King could easily judge the status of the trade from the reports. Year by year checks, comparisons, and reports were required and received.[125] The Ambassador to the Netherlands was instructed to learn, by fair means or by bribery, of the number of Dutch ships, the quantity of French wine and other merchandise annually imported, consumed locally and re-exported.[126] In like manner,

[125] See Chapter V, above; also letters Colbert to the Abbé de Gravel, May 17, 1669; October 26, 1669; September 19, 1670; to M. Dupré at Cologne, October 16, 1679, Colbert *Lettres,* II, part ii, 468-469 and notes; 494-495 and notes; 550; 707. M. Dupré was instructed to attend the fairs and check the balance in the competition of French and German commodities, " type by type " and determine thereby whether the French were the losers or gainers.

[126] Colbert to de Pomponne, March 21, 1669. In this much quoted letter, Colbert sets forth his philosophy of trade. *Ibid.,* pp. 461-464.

the attempt to discover the amount of French manufactures and wines consumed in England was a matter of continuous interest.[127]

Within France itself, customs data and market figures were frequently consulted by Colbert in an effort to evaluate the level of business activity. A letter to M. de Souzy, intendant at Lille, provides an example of the scientific attitude of Colbert towards the selection of this type of administrative information. Like a true modern he shows his distrust of the "interests" and his reverence for the verity of numbers. It is a lesson to one of his subordinates in the efficacy of applying the Political Arithmetic of statistics to government:

I have received the letter which you have taken the trouble to write me, the 15th of this month, on the subject of the complaints of the merchants of Lille relative to the decrease in their commerce, on which you are drawing up a memoir which you promise to send me. I will say to you on this point that this matter is very difficult to understand, all the more as all the information which you will receive through the merchants will be confounded with their petty individual interests which are conducive neither to the general good of commerce, not to that of the State. However, when, independently of their memoirs and complaints, one knows how to seek and unravel the truth, it is sometimes easy enough to find it.

For this purpose, without stopping with all that which these merchants will tell you, it is necessary that you investigate personally, unbeknownst to them, if there are duties to pay on all the merchandise, or if the bales which come into and go out of this paritcular city are stamped. It may also happen that there are there public packers who collect taxes for the packing. By these general means, you can have a certain knowledge of the number of bales which enter or leave, or on which duties are paid, or which have been stamped, or which have been packed during the three, four, five or six last months; and, by comparing this quantity with that of years past, you can judge absolutely whether there has been a decrease in the commerce or not, this being the only and true means of knowing it.

I well know that a great application to detail is needed for these types of investigations, but the advantages which one derives from them are also very considerable. In order to enlighten you, by a very great example, of the methods which I pursue here, I will tell you that, when I inform myself through all the merchants of the kingdom of the state of commerce, they unanimously maintain that it is entirely ruined; but when I turn to consider that the King has diminished by

[127] For instance, see Colbert to Colbert de Croissy, Ambassador to England, March 20, 1669, *ibid.*, pp. 460-461.

a third the customs of the kingdom, that he has augmented the farms of these customs by a third and more, and that the farmers, not only do not request any diminution, but even remain in agreement that they gain, I take therefrom a demonstrative proof, and one which cannot be contradicted, that the commerce augments considerably in France, notwithstanding all that which the merchants can say to the contrary. You see well that if, without hindrance, you examine this matter following these principles, it is impossible that you can be mistaken.[128]

Tables of prices appeared with increasing frequency in letters of the intendants to the *contrôleur général*. Elaborate figures have been found describing month by month trade on the Canal de Languedoc and compilations have been discovered derived from registers of customs bureaus of grains entering and leaving the Five Great Farms.[129]   Along with the increasingly technical nature of the information which Colbert demanded from his agents, the centralization of this activity in the office of *contrôleur général* pointed the way for the creation of statistical bureaus of government.   The regular correspondence required of the intendants with the *contrôleur général* assured a continuous stream of general and statistical reports on the economic conditions of the kingdom which, when consulted, as one historian observes, " affords an insight into the conditions of the time rivalled only by the elaborate governmental publications which began in the principal European countries in the latter half of the nineteenth century." [130]

The effect of the system of inquiry on the conduct of the state in a specialized field is suggested in Colbert's regulation of the grain trade.   In the sixteenth century, the kings had shown an evident desire to regulate the grain trade with reference to local conditions and had even established a bureau to collect pertinent information.   The king could then regulate the trade through his council.   However, the information supplied was scanty and the central officials found little but vague rumors on which to act.   As a consequence this work was practically limited to the Seine Basin.   " Lack of information," concludes A. P. Usher, " was thus the principal cause for the

---

[128] Colbert to M. de Souzy, January 24, 1670, *ibid.*, pp. 514-515.
[129] Usher, *History of the grain trade in France*, p. 271.
[130] *Ibid.*, pp. 271-272.

failure of the royal efforts to control the grain trade in the sixteenth and early seventeenth centuries." [131]

Colbert exhibited a most complex and apparently contradictory policy towards the grain trade. The right to export was frequently denied and restored and he often seemed to discriminate in this regard between province and province.[132] Permission to carry the trade outside a province or across the frontiers was seldom granted for periods of more than a few months.[133]   Pierre Clement attributes this policy to the need which the ministry felt of provisioning the armies at reasonable prices and to the continuing fear of Colbert that France might again experience a famine as in the years 1661 and 1662.[134] The complexity of the program, however, arose directly from the sensitivity of the *contrôleur général* to the condition of grain supply in the provinces as a whole. Circular letters to the intendants show the minister constantly inquiring as to the size of harvests or harvest prospects. Typical is a circular letter of 1663. Unusual weather conditions were causing him some fear as to the effect on crops, therefore the intendants were to " inform me in detail of the present state of crops in your generality, and if, by all appearances, the harvest will be good; indicating to me, please, those places which have been afflicted by hail or other accidents, and those which have suffered no hurt, so that I may give account to the King." At another time the intendants were to send similar information, including local grain prices, " so that His Majesty can make the decision which he will see as most advantageous to the good of his service and for the commerce of his subjects. . . .[135] When late reports indicated a change in the position of the harvest in his generality, the intendant at Bordeaux was ordered, at the last minute, to desist from publishing a decree

---

[131] *Ibid.*, p. 268. See the market reports for Paris and similar reports following reproduced in A. de Boislisle, *Mémoire dur la généralite de Paris,* I, 659-674.

[132] Clement calculates that in a period of 14 years (1669-1683) export was prohibited during 56 months. Colbert, *Lettres,* IV, xlv; on the grain trade and Colbert see pp. xl-xlvii.

[133] *Ibid.,* p. xlv.

[134] *Ibid.,* pp. xl-xlvii.

[135] Circular letters to the intendants: July 15, 1663; August 22, 1670, *ibid.,* pp. 216; 233.

previously sent to prohibit the export of grain.[136] In short, Colbert's grain policy was determined by the information received on general crop conditions, and on the basis of these reports he formulated adjustments. " The apparent complexity of the grain trade policy is wholly due to its intimate connection with current conditions." [137]

Another field may be cited in which the conduct of state-supervised surveys produced marked change in administration, a remarkable increase in the income of the crown and, incidentally, an extensive collection of statistical records. In 1661 Louis XIV and Colbert initiated an inquest into the condition of the royal forests of the kingdom. This process ultimately resulted in the great forestry regulations of 1669 [138] but perhaps the most happy consequence, from the standpoint of the King, was an increase in royal revenues from the forests from a negligible sum in 1661 to 1,411,313 *livres* in 1683.[139] After the deduction of 304,550 *livres* in charges there was a net receipt into the treasury of 1,106,763 *livres*.[140]

The reform in the administration of the royal forests was part of the general reorganization of the domain which was mainly directed towards reassertion of the King's rights which had been alienated over a long period of years.[141] The forestry survey was conducted also as a means of giving the government an exact account of the extent and wealth of its forestry assets and to assure the execution of a conservation program in an area so important to the supply of domestic and, particularly, naval needs for timber and timber products.

From the standpoint of statistics the most interesting result of the survey was the production of a huge collection of memoirs, reports, and statistical tables giving a detailed picture

[136] Colbert to M. De Ris, intendant at Bordeaux, July 24, 1881, *ibid.,* II, part i, p. 162.

[137] Usher, p. 294.

[138] Clement, " Introduction," Colbert, *Lettres,* IV, li-lxvii.

[139] Mallet, *Comptes rendus,* pp. 280-284; Cole, *Colbert,* I, 311 gives the figures 168,788 (1661) to 1,028,766 (1683). No source is cited but they are probably taken from the table in Colbert, *Lettres,* IV, 607-608, source cited *Archives des finances.*

[140] Mallet, pp. 313, 341. The royal forests in 1682 were 1,287 in number with an area of 434,611 hectares. Clement " Introduction," Colbert, *Lettres,* IV, lvxi.

[141] The royal domain was constitutionally inalienable under the *ancien régime.*

of the number, extent, produce, income, location, administrative, personnel, value and rights connected with royal forests. These records were the answer to the questions issued by Colbert to a small army of agents between 1661 and 1669. Unfortunately, the series of the memoirs from these agents, comprising seventy-six volumes, was destroyed with the burning of the ministry of finance in 1871.[142] However, charts, memoranda, extracts and manuscripts based on or taken from these are still to be found in sufficient quantity to give a good idea of their thoroughness and quality. Most of the information on waters and forests in the memoirs of the intendants of 1697-1700 was apparently derived from this source.[143] The British museum possesses a manuscript giving an itemized description, in tabular form, duly attested by clerks, of all the royal forests accompanied with an atlas of ninety-four sheets. On a particular sheet, in separate columns, will be found the names of the royal agents conducting the reform, the name of the administrative district, the name of the forests therein, their areas in *arpents,* the location and the quality of the terrain, the nature and age of the wood, authorized cuttings, the officers of each administrative unit, their wages, their cutting rights, the money value of these cuttings, the names of authorized users of the forest, their cutting rights, the value thereof, authorized pasturage, pannage, and faggotry. The numerical expressions of the areas, quantity and value of the cuttings are totalled at the foot of each column with notations of the registration of the contained information at the offices of the local administration.[144]

The direction taken in the evolution of the institution of the intendants, the canalizing of the reporting function into the office of the *contrôleur général,* and the development of archival deposits during the years of 1661-1683 created a pattern for a government of scientifically oriented inquiry. An increasing emphasis on the use of statistical data during the period indicated the trend which the administration was taking towards the realization of such a government. Within a decade

---

[142] A. de Boislisle, "Introduction," *Mémoire sur la généralite de Paris,* I, lxi-lxii and notes.
[143] *Ibid.,* p. 1.
[144] A sheet is copied in *ibid.,* pp. 586-587.

after the death of Colbert the *contrôleur général* was working to draw up systematic tables of statistics applicable to the whole realm on exports, imports, population and other economic data. Very early in the eighteenth century the first department of the French public service which devoted itself specifically to the collection of statistics was created. Colbert may never have had the idea or desire to carry his program so far, but his labors, and those of his master, to create a regime of orderliness laid the necessary groundwork for all future efforts under the *ancien régime* to apply the aid of statistical method to government.

CHAPTER VII

THE MECHANICS OF THE REGIME OF ORDER

ECONOMIC ADMINISTRATION

Mercantilist doctrine is as clearly related to the scientific and rationalistic spirit as is laissez faire. The preoccupation of its critics or students with its more patent errors and inconsistencies, with its contrasts in detail to the rational system of Smith, its connection with aspects of nationalism, state power, economic and political unity, protectionism, bullionism or social welfare and organization has produced a general tendency to disregard this relationship. Yet the mercantilist, equally with the laissez-faire economist, presumed a natural order of things and propounded economic laws which he believed rationally derived from the study of this order. The economic world of Petty or Colbert presumed, consciously and unconsciously, the mechanical world of the new philosophy. If the apologists for the system were frequently guilty, in the light of present understanding, of faulty calculations, misinterpretation or confused thinking, it must be remembered that contemporary science was likewise confused. In any case, the ensemble of mercantilist thought in the seventeenth century represented the most advanced expression, up to its time, of a rational approach to state administration. In it, the political economy of the state was subjected to restrictions and policies of guidance suggested by a mathematical concept of welfare. The whole state was conceived as a delicatedly balanced instrument that should be regulated by inviolable principles; and provinces within states, or states in their relations with each other, were believed bound together by inflexible laws of mutual necessity and interaction. Like the scientist, the politician ignored, in theory, the easy providence of teleological philosophy. True, society, economic or political, was thought of as being mechanically contrived but this did not mean it was by necessity mechanically efficient. Like the scientists discovering and applying principles derived from the study of nature, the statesman or political economist discovered and applied formulae for the more efficient attainment of ends. This belief in natural mechanics and in the inflexible validity of mechanical law, common to most scientists and statesmen of the period, throws much light on the development of the concept of a-moral sovereign power, on the widespread disdain for the little people, on the impatience with obstruction, on the political optimism, on the relentless ferocity of the law, and on numerous other political and social characteristics of the seventeenth century which the historian has delighted to preserve for our instruction or interest. These same presumptions cannot be ignored if one is to have a full understanding of the economic administration of Colbert and Louis XIV.

I

These presumptions on the part of Colbert, as they related to his economic policy, are generally implicitly revealed throughout his published correspondence. This shows that Colbert was not, strictly speaking, a theorist. That is to say, he rarely seemed to think it necessary to fortify his policy by a general analysis of the principles involved. He stated them, and frequently, but he rarely attempted to prove them. He apparently accepted these principles as self-evident truths which needed but to be stated to be believed. In short, one would search almost in vain to discover any innovation in economic thought attributable to Colbert. Colbert's importance, from the standpoint of economic theory in general, and mercantilism in particular, lies in his amplification, definition and application of contemporary mercantilist doctrines. His practical work, in this regard, is most obvious in his economic administration and has been the subject of many studies.[1]

---

[1] A discussion of the complex economic administration of Colbert in the brief space which proportion permits in this study is a reckless undertaking. The need of giving completeness to the design of this work requires such a discussion however. Up to the present, it is this aspect of Colbert's administration which has received the lion's share of historical attention. Consequently the literature is voluminous and often of high calibre. The oldest comprehensive work on the economic policy of Colbert is Felix Joubleau's *Étude sur Colbert, ou exposition de système d'économie politique suivi en France de 1661 à 1683*, (2 vols., Paris, 1856). It is poorly organized and written without the benefit of Clement's publications on the archival material. It has been entirely superseded. The collections of official correspondence and memoranda of Clement and Depping,

As we have said, Colbert was not a theorist. His longest economic work (it can hardly be dignified as a treatise), is a slender finance memoir devoted primarily to villification of Fouquet. However there were times when he more or less extended himself in pointing out the connection between policy

frequently cited already, are the most convenient sources for the study of Colbert's economic administration. Clement's biography of Colbert and his introductory essays to each of his volumes of Colbert letters still remain, collectively, among the best secondary treatments. But the "definitive" secondary accounts of the economic administration of Colbert are the several works of P. Boissonade and C. W. Cole. It would be difficult to judge the comparative value of their works. If Cole's volumes are better organized and more complete, Boissonade's are more imaginative, mature, and better written. Boissonade's general study on the economic administration of Colbert should not lead to the neglect of his illuminating regional study on *L'organisation due travail en Poitou depuis le XIe siècle jusqu'à la Revolution* (2 vols., Paris, 1900) or his study, in collaboration with P. Charliat on *Colbert et la compagnie du commerce du nord, 1661-1689* (Paris, 1930). For the study of Colbert's economic policy no other secondary works are of a value comparable to those of Cole and Boissonade, but several general histories of trade, commerce and industry may be useful. Henri Hauser's *Travailleurs et marchands dans l'ancienne France* (Paris, 1920) is a collection of very thoughtful essays on a wide variety of economic subjects. Recommended also are: Eli Heckscher's *Mercantilism,* trans. by M. Shapiro (2 vols., London, 1932); E. Levasseur, *Histoire du commerce de France* (2 vols., Paris, 1911); H. Pigeonneau, *Histoire de commerce de la France* (2 vols., Paris, 1897). Inferior to Levasseur, it extends only through the regime of Richelieu. Henri Sée, *Histoire économique de la France* (2 vols., Paris, 1939-1942) is much the best of the general works for France. Several specialized studies should be mentioned: On industry: Ch. Ballot, *L'introduction du machinisme dans l'industrie Française* (Paris, 1923); A. Des Cilleuls, *Histoire de régime de la grande industrie en France aux XVIIe et XVIIIe siècles* (Paris, 1898). Very broad and undefined it is rendered of little use by Germain Martin's much superior *La grande industrie sous le règne de Louis XIV* (Paris, 1898). On crafts, corporations and general organization of work: Boissonade's work on Poitou cited above; relatively inferior is G. Fagniez, *Corporations et syndicats* (Paris, 1905); excellent is H. Hauser's "Les pouvoirs publics et l'organisation du travail dans l'ancienne France" in his *Travailleurs et marchands* cited above; the most complete study is that of E. Martin Saint-Leon, *Histoire des corporations de métiers depuis leurs origines jusqu'à leurs suppression en 1791* (4th ed., Paris, 1941); a useful source collection of ordinances for the regulation of crafts is that of R. De Lespinasse, ed., *Les metiers et corporations de la ville de Paris* (3 vols., Paris, 1886-1897). On commerce and colonies: Boissonade, Cole and Charliat, cited above; Levasseur, cited above; S. L. Mims, *Colbert's West Indies policy* (New Haven, Conn., 1912) is outstanding; Pigeonneau, cited above; and as a contemporary commentary, Jacques Savary, *Le parfait négociant* (2 vols., Paris, 1675). On tariffs: Two articles are very important. A. Callery, "Les douanes avant Colbert et l'ordonnance de 1664," *Revue historique,* XVIII (1882); S. Elzinga, "Le tarif de Colbert de 1664 et celui de 1667 et leur signification," *Economisch-historisch Jaarboek,* XV (1929).

and principle. This was especially true in the memoirs which he addressed to the King; memoirs intended both to inform and to arouse the sympathy of his master concerning his projects and his accomplishments. Perhaps the most revealing of these notes, from the standpoint of the relationship of the current scientific assumptions to practical administration, is a " Mémoire au Roi sur les finances " of 1670.[2] Too long to quote, it justifies extensive analysis because of its exposition of the role of mechanical law in the economic activity of the state. The year 1670 was for Colbert and Louis XIV a year for reckoning. They had now, for almost a decade, imposed on the people a new government which was aimed at the revitalizing of the state from top to bottom. Louis was elated, as his memoirs show, by the review of his accomplishments.[3]

As for Colbert, he began his report with a declaration of his intention to enlighten the King and an assertion that his own nine years of successful administration and certain " arithmetical and demonstrable truths which cannot be contradicted " had served as a basis for what he was now to reveal. As he pointed out, these years had witnessed a tremendous increase in royal revenues (23 to 70 millions). He was disturbed, however, by a new phenomenon which had recently introduced itself. The abundance characteristic of these years seemed to have levelled off. Instead of plenty, he now found the current expenditures of 75 million *livres* to exceed the revenues by 5 millions. For the first time in nine years the demand for revenue was apparently overweighing the tax supply. What were the causes of this new situation and what the solution?

The most obvious answer was that expenditures were too heavy, but, besides admitting this, he preferred to add, as another factor, an exploratory discourse on the mathematical disproportion which existed between the tax burden and the tax-paying capacity of the people. Like Richelieu before him, Colbert believed, in theory at least, that there normally existed an exact mathematical relationship, natural and inviolable in a healthy state, between these two aspects of finance.[4] All

[2] Colbert, *Lettres*, VII, 233-256.
[3] See Chapter IV, above.
[4] Richelieu was very explicit on this point as we have seen. A curious corollary, likewise shared by Richelieu and Colbert, was the doctrine that a tax

income of the people, he wrote, should be considered as divided into three "natural" and "legitimate" portions: that part reserved for profit, investment and subsistence, that part for rents and seigneurial dues, and that part due to the king. Though he did not specify the percentage proportions, it is clear that he believed that there is a just and natural proportion between the divisions, and he looked on these relationships as fundamental to the consideration of state revenue. A disequilibrium would make unavoidable the return to the old Fouquet policy of expediency and the eventual ruin of state finances.

By this reasoning state finance was reduced to a problem of mechanics in which whatever gain was made in revenues, if the economy was in a condition of equilibrium, must arise from a proportionate gain in what he designated as " circulating wealth." The problem might be mathematically expressed thus: Assuming a relatively static circulation of 150 million *livres,* one would always find a " proportion between these 150 millions and the money received by Your Majesty in revenues, in such a way, that, if on this basis of 150 millions the revenues amount to 50 millions for example, it should follow certainly that if one could attract into the kingdom 200 millions the revenues of Your Majesty would increase proportionately, as, on the contrary, if the 150 millions were diminished, the revenues would decrease proportionately." Using this same method of analysis, he discovered that similar relationships were applicable to the provinces of the kingdom as distinct from, but complementary to, this total picture.

At the present time, though he knew there was actually more money in France than formerly, there was, for various reasons, less money in circulation.[5] Complicating the picture

burden, properly applied, was a spur to industry. In a letter to M. de Marillac, intendant at Poitiers, October 9, 1674, Colbert expressed this principle. Commenting on the backwardness of that city, he wrote: " But remember that the only thing which makes the city of Poitiers beggarly and miserable, as it is, is the laziness of its inhabitants who, not being spurred by some reasonable tax, which gives them a little trouble to supply it and which pushes them, by this means to labor, fall noticeably into the misery where they are now." It is of course necessary to note that on this occasion the state was at war with Holland and was sorely in need of extraordinary revenue. Colbert, *Lettres,* II, part i, 356.

[5] The reform of the financial administration had deprived the bourgeoisie of

further was the increasing prestige of the royal power which, by its very weight, had been able to extract greater and greater sums from a people who were, because of the progressive contraction in circulating wealth, less and less able to bear the burden. The consequence was a fateful disequilibrium in the natural portions of the income of the people; the King might be paid, but only at the expense of the landlord and the savings of the peasant. This condition could not continue. The normal proportion of money in circulation to royal revenues, 150 millions to 45 or 50 millions, had been violently changed to the present disproportionate pattern of 120 millions in circulation against 70 millions in revenue.

Only two solutions presented themselves to this problem. First, a reduction in taxation. On a number of counts this was not an adequate solution. Secondly, an increase in the amount of money in circulation. This was the more feasible, and it could be accomplished in three ways. One, by attracting money into the kingdom; two, by preventing its export; three, by permitting the means to the individual for obtaining a profit.

Therefore, as we now see, the equation of national welfare was inextricably bound up, in Colbert's mind, with another important concept of his: a belief that the supply of wealth circulating in Europe as a whole was fairly static. The disequilibrium of the economic equation in France could be corrected internally by the reduction of taxes, a difficult solution and we surmise derogatory to the glory of the King, or, as an alternative or aid, by a process of subtracting or transposition of the economic assets of neighboring or distant states. In other words, the restoration of equilibrium to the French equation entailed a disequilibrium in another area. From this point of view, the French economy was but an integer in an equation of international proportions, a mathematical expression of the old dictum of Bacon: ". . . whatsoever is

several avenues of profitable speculation. The uncertainty of many fortunes due to the prolonged investigations of the *chambre de justice,* established to ferret out the speculative chicaneries and thefts of the financiers and farmers during the period of Fouquet, had driven capital into hiding. The encouragement of industry, and other great enterprises sponsored by the government had, as yet, failed to compensate for these restrictions.

somewhere gotten, is somewhere lost." This is clearly seen in Colbert's elaboration on these three points:

As in these three points consist the grandeur and the power of the State and the magnificence of the King, by all the expenditures which the great revenues support, which is all the higher as it simultaneously abases all the neighboring States, seeing that there is only a static quantity of money circulating in all Europe, which is increased from time to time by that introduced from the West Indies, it is certain and demonstrable that if there is only 150 million *livres* of money in circulation, one cannot succeed in adding to it by 20, 30 or 50 millions without, at the same time, taking away the same quantity from neighboring States; this explains that double elevation which we have seen so obviously increase for the past few years: on the one hand raising the power and grandeur of Your Majesty, on the other throwing down that of your enemies. . . ."[6]

Now Colbert came down to the crux of his memoir, a plea for his industrial and commercial program. "Only commerce and all that which depends on it" could have produced this great effect and could solve the present problem for the future. The work had been well begun by means of discriminatory tariffs and taxes on foreign cargoes, by means of lowering or abolishing customs barriers to internal commerce, by rendering rivers navigable, by regulating the tariffs of the "five big farms" along mercantilist principles, by encouraging home manufactures, by encouraging new industries both in agriculture and commerce, by excluding the Dutch from much of their former overseas trade through great companies, by restoring port facilities and constructing canals. But this program was, he said, still in its infancy and would necessitate in the future, as in the past, considerable expenditures of revenue.[7] These

---

[6] In a memoir of the year before Colbert had said: "This State not only is flourishing of itself, but also by the necessity which it creates in all neighboring States. Extreme misery appears everywhere. Only Holland still resists. Yet its power in money noticeably diminishes." Colbert, *Lettres,* VII, 230.

[7] It is interesting to note that Colbert had contemplated such an economic program long before he was in any position to effectuate it. In a memoir to Mazarin of 1653 he wrote: "It is necessary to re-establish or create all the industries, even of luxury; to establish the protectionist system through the customs; to organize the producers and merchants into corporations; to lighten the fiscal burdens harmful to the people; to restore to France the transport of its commodities; to develop the colonies and attach them commercially to France; to suppress all the intermediaries between France and the Indies; to develop the navy to protect the merchant marine." Quoted in E. Levasseur, *Histoire du commerce,* I, 294.

expenditures would produce, however, four or five hundred percent interest by retaining 8 or 10 millions annually in the kingdom. Therefore, to conclude, he believed that these great projects must be encouraged at all cost. To do this the budget should be balanced and expenditures should be administered in such a way as to " keep money in the kingdom " and to be " spread through the provinces with the necessary proportion and equality." [8]

Aside from the mechanical notions, implicit and explicit in this memoir, several points justify special attention. In the first place, it should never be forgotten that every economic policy of Colbert was subordinate to the fiscal needs of the state. His whole industrial and economic program was so bound up with these considerations that it is difficult, and from his point of view it would be fictitious, to deal with them apart from finance problems. One can assume, almost without exaggeration, that Colbert never thought of any factor of the economy, large or small, whether relating to the personal characteristics of entrepreneurs and merchants or to the grand work of naval armament, without converting these factors into debit or credit units in a general inventory of national wealth. Secondly, it must be noted that the end of all this calculation was to ascertain the power and prestige of the King or the state, and to procure the means of adding to it. In addition, this calculation rested on the belief that money was the prime essential to power. For as he put it: " it is only the abundance of money in a State which determines the difference of its grandeur and its power." [9] Therefore, in dealing with the economy as a

[8] The whole process was further dramatized to the King by comparing it to a warrior's occupation: " I beg permission to inform Your Majesty that it seems to me that since he has taken over the administration of his finances, he has maintained a war of money against all the States of Europe. He has already vanquished Spain, Italy, Germany, England, and several others whom he has reduced to very great misery and necessity and enriched himself from their spoils which has given him the means of doing so many of the great things which he has done and continues to do daily. Only Holland remains which struggles still with great force." The view of commerce as a form of warfare was common to most mercantilist thinkers, but it is perhaps an exaggeration to believe, as one competent authority seems to, that commercial war was generally considered as but a preparation for armed conflict. E. Silberner, *La guerre dans la pensée économique du XVIe au XVIIIe siècle* (Paris, 1939), pp. 12-122, *passim*.

[9] Quoted in Des Cilleuls, *Histoire de la grande industrie*, p. 22; In a letter

whole or in parts Colbert was perpetually applying one criterion: " Would it attract money? "

This being the paramount consideration of Colbert's economic policy and adding to it his acceptance of a mechanical concept of the relatively static wealth of Europe, it followed that his economic administration was always conducted with one eye on the treasury and the other on the relative prosperity or wealth of foreign powers. In speaking of this wealth he ordinarily used the term *" argent "* but, as all versed modern authorities now admit, this expression of the mercantilists must not to be taken too literally to signify a confusion between money and real wealth. In drawing up an international balance sheet Colbert habitually thought in terms of those commodities and agencies for which money is but an abstract equivalent. The idea of static wealth and the interaction of state economies was allied in an important fashion with another concept which is frequently overlooked. Colbert, and most other mercantilist thinkers of his time, had an unprecised theory of natural share and comparative advantage. They did not push it to the extreme of some eighteenth-century theorists, but, like them, they deduced it from a supposed natural order. Several quotations from Colbert will show the relevance of these ideas to his general economic program. In a well known letter to de Pomponne, Ambassador to Holland, he propounds his idea of natural share:

All the world's maritime trade is carried on with twenty thousand ships or there about. In the natural order of things, each nation ought to have its share in proportion to its power, to the number of its people, and to its sea coasts. The Dutch have, of this number, fifteen or sixteen thousand and the French perhaps five or six hundred at the most. The King employs every means he believes useful to attain a little closer to the natural number which his subjects should have. If the Dutch employ the same means, there is room for hope that they will produce the same effect that His Majesty aspires to, namely, that they will approach also to the natural number which they should have and, in so doing, give much aid to the design of His Majesty. The particular proof of this general truth would be too long to deduce for

---

to M. Rouillé, intendant at Aix, March 29, 1679, Colbert objected to the free export of gold and silver from Marseille, a practice which was " contrary and prejudicial to the universal and fundamental law of all States which, under the penalty of death, prohibits the export of gold and silver." Colbert, *Lettres*, II, part ii, 696-697.

you; but you will understand if easily in the course of all the affairs of this nature which will pass through your hands.[10]

This letter, while it reveals Colbert's faith in the natural order of things and his belief in the inflexible workings of natural laws, significantly emphasizes the contingencies. The existence of the natural right to a share does not, as he makes clear, necessarily produce that share. It was one thing to recognize a general law and quite another to apply it to attain a desired goal. Though a goal was justified by a decreed natural order, it could be reached only by the rational utilization of the absolute advantage which this order implied and by the active assistance of the state. This reasoning he makes further apparent in letters and memoirs relating to France's commerce with Spain.

Colbert was particularly sensitive to the status of the trade with Spain. Spain was the mine from which France extracted, by this lever of trade, an important portion of the gold and silver supply on which the royal power so much depended. He was keenly apprehensive concerning the competition of Dutch and English merchantmen with the French at the port of Cadiz and was continually complaining through the Ambassador at Madrid that French trade was discriminated against. This was unusually irritating because it affected an area in which he believed that France enjoyed an advantage.

The French have such a great advantage over all the other nations, from the fertility of her soil, the great quantity of hemp and flax which it brings forth, and from her industry which produces the best and most beautiful manufactures that, provided they are assisted and protected and that they are either better treated than foreigners, or at least as well treated, there is no doubt that they will attract the greater part of these riches into the kingdom.[11]

---

[10] Colbert to de Pomponne, March 21, 1669, *ibid.*, p. 464. Twenty years before Jean Eon in his *Le commerce honorable,* gave a very similar analysis, p. 21.

[11] Quoted in Cole, *Colbert,* I, 408, see also pp. 404-410; Colbert memoir to Louis XIV, 1669, Colbert *Lettres*, VII, 230-232; "Instruction to the marquis of Villars, Ambassador to Madrid," May 15, 1679, *ibid.,* II, part ii, 699-705. Colbert's belief in absolute advantage and natural production was shown in minor details as well as in general policy. Thus, when the Chevalier De Terlon, Ambassador to Denmark, informed him that one Desbordes, attracted by privileges, had settled in Denmark to initiate the manufacture of salt and asked for instructions, Colbert advised him not to worry for "it is impossible that the climate of that kingdom can permit it. You know that in Normandy,

As we have seen, the economic premises of Colbert, on the higher level, were deduced from an underlying concept of a mechanically ordered and integrated economy embracing not only, as he saw it, his own country but Europe and the world as a whole. Commerce, agriculture, industry and individuals, cities, nations and systems were inextricably interdependent and, together, formed a cohesive entity in which any economic action on one part was automatically reciprocated on another. When France prospered he automatically assumed the decay of Holland, England or Spain. If his basic conceptions were relatively simple, he was, nevertheless, quite aware of the progressive complexity of relating all elements as one descended to the level of practical action. However, he seldom denied himself the compliment of thinking he understood these relationships, even in the smallest details, and he was persuaded that the great mass of the people were incapable of comprehending them. Only princes and statesmen, men elevated to a sufficient height to survey horizons beyond the petty interests of individuals, could do so, if they would.

Further elaboration of Colbert's economic thought is perhaps best presented by treating of his activities in regard to specific branches of his economic program. By this convenient, if somewhat artificial, device his program will be considered under the headings of industrial regulation and supervision, the encouragement of enterprise, the tariff and, finally, the colonial policy. Before proceeding it may be wise at this point to request the reader to keep in mind that which Colbert himself seems seldom, if ever, to have forgotten, which is, that all the mechanical details and procedures of his economic policy were subordinate and complementary to the broad principles and ends which we have already described. Indeed, it was this ability of Colbert's to constantly connect small matters to great ones that is probably responsible for whatever title to genius history has accorded him. It was this faculty which gave his program such remarkable consistency, made his name a synonym for a system and assured him the reputation of one of the

Picardy, Holland and England they have never been able to do it because the heat of the sun is not sufficiently great, not having in France than the coasts of Poitou, Aunis and that of the south of Brittany where they make it." Therefore, he concluded, Desbordes' project was "visionary." Colbert to De Terron, November 4, 1672, *ibid.*, pp. 666-667.

greatest of its administrators by a nation which has long cherished the virtue of " order."

II

A discussion of Colbert's program for the regulation of industry should begin with some notice, however brief, of the progress of industry in France up to his time. In addition the writer will take the opportunity of introducing at this point a few comments on three elements in Colbert's economic thought which, while not directly a part of any scientific or rational presuppositions on his part, were nevertheless too constant in importance to bear neglect. These were his moral concept of diligence, his scorn of individual business men, and a certain ignorance of history.

During the first half of the sixteenth century France witnessed a gradual introduction of new industries. Skilled workers and new techniques were imported, especially from Italy, and France began to manufacture its famous luxury products. But even before this time there had existed a substantial woolen industry. In the last half of the century, however, the religious wars had produced a general industrial decline. The administration of Henry IV, Sully, and Laffemas marked a period of revival and was notable for its encouragement of luxury production and the great attention given to silk. From the death of Henry to the coming of Colbert contemporary writers in France were in signal agreement that commerce and industry were suffering a continuous decay.[12] As we have noted in previous chapters, however, the same period was significantly productive of men with advanced economic notions. These notions were to be those of Colbert himself, and so we might almost believe it was Colbert who complained that this industrial and commercial ruin arose from " notre nonchalance " and " la vigilance des Étrangers." [13]

Like all other mercantilists, Colbert thought of work as a divine source of the welfare of the state and, correlatively, of laziness as its greatest scourge. Hence he shared also with

---

[12] Martin, pp. 19-24; Pigeonneau, II, 350-463; H. Sée, *Histoire économique de la France*, I, 114-124; P. Boissonade, *L'organisation du travail en Poitou*, I, 23-29.

[13] Jean Eon, *Le commerce honorable*, p. 44.

them the dismay over the common disinclination of Frenchmen of wealth and rank to associate themselves with commerce. The growing realization of the importance of commerce to the state and a recognition of its bellicose characteristics, on the international level, had already led many men to deny that its pursuit, on certain levels, constituted a derogation of *noblesse.* This was proportionately true as it related to the various branches of commerce, and the laws had been tending, more and more, to acknowledge the latitude of "honorable" enterprise.[14] Nonetheless, it was still customary in Colbert's day, as it was to be throughout the period of the *ancien régime,* to retire from business, when successful, and invest in lands, titles, offices and government securities. The effect, to impede the development of business and industry, was widely deplored, and Colbert disliked, on principle, the *rentiers, bourgeois-oisifs, gens de justice,* and the more than a million functionaries, of whom he was one, who in total constituted a nearly ruinous drain on the finances of the state.[15]

In addition to his hatred of "*fainéantise,*" Colbert possessed a perfect disdain for the ability of ordinary merchants and entrepreneurs to pierce the complexities of their personal situation and to see the general plans and laws which worked for the betterment of the kingdom as a whole. In a particular case he wrote to the intendant at Rouen:

I have seen the memoirs of the merchants of Rouen which you have sent me, and I have truthfully told you that these sorts of merchants

---

[14] Jacques Savary, who can be considered to accurately reflect Colbert's ideas, makes clear this hierarchical view. "Everyone agrees that wholesale commerce is more honorable the more detached it is from retail trade." Why? Because (1) It transcends that "city wall." (2) It is detached from "all sorts of persons" having only to contact manufacturers and retailers. (3) In most kingdoms and states it is legally recognized as non-derogatory to nobility. But wholesale commerce in itself was felt to be stratified: at the lowest level, dealing with trade in the provinces; above this, between neighboring states; and, finally, between distant lands. This last was the most honorable because of the risk involved, frequently calling for the courage of soldiers, because of the great capital requirements, and because these people were the most important agents for exporting national surpluses and supplying national deficiencies. *Le parfait négociant,* II, 1-2.

[15] See Boissonade, *Colbert,* pp. 4-5; Eon, pp. 44-50. Colbert himself amassed a huge fortune in the service of the King which he invested, for the most part, in lands, titles for himself and family, offices, rents and a great collection of foreign luxuries and manufactures. See the inventory of his estate in Colbert, *Lettres,* VII, 379-396.

are incapable of thinking of anything except their petty relief; but I add to that, that at a time less authorized than this, I don't know but what I would not punish these people who, without order, without any commission, take it upon themselves to draw up these memoirs . . . you may be certain that, in all they suggest, there is nothing at all which tends to the general good of the commerce of the kingdom, but only to their particular trade.[16]

A personal horror of sloth, a recognition of the addiction of Frenchmen to it, of the necessity of commerce and industry to support the national glory, and of the blindness and selfishness of individuals, made Colbert the sponsor of a thorough-going intervention of the state into the conduct of the economy. Without it, the interests of individuals would obstruct his rational program at every turn. For instance, his conviction that French industry could capture the foreign market only by the maintenance of high quality [17] could not be an implemented policy without vigorous supervision. He complained, in this regard, that " all merchants generally want complete freedom of their trade, and especially in manufactured goods the length, width and quality of which they always desire to change and reduce for considerations of a small profit they make." This would tend to the complete ruin of the cloth industry in which one should maintain the principle of conformity, and, therefore, it was necessary to override " the motives of small private interests which do not deserve consideration among the general motives for the good of the state." [18]

Another factor encouraged Colbert's policy of governmental intervention in industry and commerce. This arose from an error in his historical knowledge. He was convinced that before " the year 1600, and even up to 1620 and beyond, there were no manufactures of cloth in England or Holland." At that time, he thought, " all the wools of Spain and England were carried to France to be spun and woven and were used then not only for internal consumption but also . . . were useful to the Marseillois, who carried on alone the trade with

[16] Colbert to M. Le Blanc, intendant at Rouen, January, 1679, *ibid.*, II, part ii, 694.
[17] A holdover from medieval craft tradition.
[18] Colbert to M. Daguesseau, intendant at Toulouse, January 28, 1682, Colbert, *Lettres,* II, part ii, 728.

the Levant, to exchange for the precious merchandise of the Indies, which . . . having brought them back to France, they distributed through all of Germany." These manufactures, he believed, employed an "infinite number" of people and kept money at home.[19] This accounts for Colbert's constant reference to the "renewal" of industry and, when he looked at the laws, to the "renewal" of *règlements*.[20] Like many a bad historian, Colbert had accepted literally the evidence of the ordinances.

For many reasons, therefore, he saw that France was in need of a calculated program, administered and enforced by the state, to restore her industries: "the fertile sources of the prosperity of the kingdom." The latter day inapplication in commerce, disorder in manufactures, tolerance of foreign interlopers, decline in quality of goods and dyes, and easy export of money, called for a renewal of industrial regulation pertaining to quality, dimensions and good dyes, and for state aid to the Levant trade, assistance and protection for manufactures, for state encouragement of home consumption by restrictions and the fashion of the court, for stimulation of production by research and experimentation in chemistry, and mechanics and by surveys of mineral resources, and for the creation of commercial companies and the introduction of new industries.[21]

Colbert was not the first to have some kind of a program of this nature, but no one previously had so clearly defined the ends and means. As Boissonade has perhaps justly, if effusively, described it:

> The *système etatiste* is formulated by him with a rigour, a logic, a clarity without equal. With him thought is at the service of the action. Before acting he desires that his reason discern clearly the causes of his action. He studies, consults, composes *portefeuilles* or dossiers; he relates the facts to principles and maxims, as did Richelieu. The grandiose work which he has accomplished has been long meditated and matured; nothing is undertaken without having discerned clearly the reasons for undertaking them.[22]

[19] Colbert, "Discours sur les manufactures du Royaume" (1663), *ibid.*, II, part i, cclvii; cclvii-cclxii.

[20] Des Cilleuls, pp. 26-28.

[21] Colbert, "Discours sur les manufactures du Royaume" (1663), *Lettres*, II, part i, cclviii-cclxii.

[22] Boissonade, *Colbert*, p. 2, 6-8.

In his industrial program the aspect of *règlementation* was to Colbert, as to his contemporaries, the most essential part.[23] Properly enforced, general regulations would assure that perfection of production which would make inevitable the capture by French industrials of the foreign markets. Moreover, it would benefit the entrepreneur and workers alike by the gift of greater order and efficiency. By its indirect stimulus to production it would assure the employment of idle women and children. To the innumerable cries of distress which answered the enforcement of his new industrial ordinances, Colbert opposed an attitude of paternal severity:

> I have always found the manufacturers obstinate to remain in their errors and in the abuses which they permit in their manufacturers. But when one has employed authority to force them to execute the new *règlements* . . . they have seen their manufactures noticeably increase and foreigners come to buy in the kingdom . . . so that it is necessary to use firmness and authority to vanquish the obstinancy of the manufacturers.[24]

The industrial regulations revived or created by Colbert varied in nature from broad directives aimed at business as a whole to specific instructions for the control and guidance of individual manufacturers. A general purpose, however, is evidently common to all. They were aimed at creating a uniformity and order of operation and production which would not only assure high quality but transform industry and commerce into calculable units in the sphere of law and public finance.

Though not ordinarily classified among the industrial regulations, the great commercial code of 1673 is significantly illustrative of this motive and historically is a most useful example, because it provided the stimulus, through Colbert's patronage, for the writing of Jacques Savary's *Le parfait négociant* (1675). This book was immediately accepted as an authoritative guide to business law and efficient business procedure. It was translated into several languages and, through a series of revisions and amplifications by son and grandson, retained

[23] For the story of Colbert's regulations in general, see *ibid.*, pp. 209-216; Cole, *Colbert*, II, 363-457.

[24] Colbert to M. De Bezons, intendant at Toulouse, March 13, 1671, *Lettres*, II, part ii, 614-615.

much of its prestige until the nineteenth century. The first edition was not, as later ones, a dictionary but a commentary on the code. It instructed business men in the mechanics of complying with the new laws. Savary, one of the authors of the code, explained that it had been formulated at the behest of Louis XIV in recognition of the need for and benefit of commerce to the state. Louis had fostered the development of business by his personal attention, his authority, his finances and by grants of privileges, and now he had decreed a great *réglement* which would establish good faith and order in enterprise.[25]

This order, wrote Savary, " is the soul of commerce, without which it cannot survive, for by good order one has a perfect knowledge of all one's affairs; thus succeeding more easily than when one lives in confusion." [26]   In the past, neglect to maintain this order had been the prime contribution to business failures. Particularly, he cited the fact that a widespread lack of understanding or practice of proper bookkeeping techniques brought about among the masters a perpetual state of confusion which made failure almost inevitable. The keeping of proper books induced the necessary order, and because of its benefit to the merchant, to the courts, and for the realm, the King had been led to require the keeping of books in his ordinance.[27] The manner of keeping them was carefully specified to insure against peculation. Furthermore, legal incentive to comply with the law was given by the provision in the ordinance, for the first time in general French law, of a clear distinction between simple failure and fraudulent bankruptcy. In defining this distinction, it was noted that " wholesale " or " retail " " *negocians* " or " *marchands* " and " *banquiers* " who had failed to answer their creditor demands and who could not present registers and journals in good order, as prescribed by this law, could be judged " fraudulent bankrupts "

---

[25] Savary, *Le parfait négociant,* I, 1-2.

[26] *Ibid.,* p. 249.

[27] *Ibid.,* pp. 251-253, 33-35, 37. Title 3, Article (8) of the ordinance states: " Merchants will also be required to draw up, with the same delay of six months, an inventory, under their signature, of all their movable or immovable effects, and of the active and passive debts, which will be re-examined and renewed every two years." (*Ibid.,* p. 320; Isambert, XIX, 96.) For similar provisions relating to the keeping of registers and journals, see Title 3, Articles (1-6), *ibid.,* pp. 95-96.

and were subject to the "punishment of death." [28] Savary's book commented that these provisions would protect the honest but unfortunate merchant against his creditors and, at the same time, by forcing the maintenance of good order and good faith, would elevate French commerce. [29]

Further consideration of Colbert's regulations for industry and commerce will be broken down under two headings: the nature of the *règlements*; the machinery of enforcement.

The regulations elaborated under the direction of Colbert presented the basic character they were to retain until near the end of the *ancien régime*. Boissonade has classified them in three categories: those governing the techniques of production, those affecting the police, and those touching administration and jurisdiction. [30] That is to say, the regulations pertained to the preparation of raw materials, to processes of manufacture, to the general police work and to the judicial sanctions destined to assure the execution of the rules. In spite of the number of such statutes under his administration, Colbert showed himself to be relatively restrained when compared to the administrators of the next century. [31] He limited himself to drawing up regulations which were comparatively simple and easy to follow, which were, on the whole, " less specific, less meticulous, and less severe, than the older guild regulations. They represented an attempt on the part of

[28] *Ibid.,* Title XI, pp. 104-105; Savary, I, 253; II, 255-300.

[29] *Ibid.,* p. 320; An interesting illustration of this legal meaning is contained in a letter of Colbert to M. Tubeuf, intendant at Tours, January 4, 1679. Colbert took up the case of one sieur Brillon, merchant of Paris, who was being so pressed by his creditors, to the tune of 183,000 *livres* at Paris and 580,000 at Tours, that he was near bankruptcy. But the King had had his books examined and found them in " good order " and revealing " good faith." Therefore, Colbert instructed the intendant to assemble the creditors of Tours, as had been done at Paris, and to inform them of the King's findings and that the sieur Brillon's misfortunes arose from disorders abroad over which he had no control. He recommended that the creditors of Tours, as those at Paris had already agreed to do, agree to a new contract—apparently involving an *arrest de surseance.* This he felt would be to the interest of all creditors since the procedures of justice would not only ruin Brillon but further jeopardize the debts. Colbert, *Lettres,* II, part ii, 693.

[30] Boissonade, *Colbert,* pp. 209-210.

[31] Between 1683 and 1753 Boissonade counted no less than a thousand regulations issued by the central government.

Colbert to generalize in broad terms what seemed to him the most desirable features of existing local regulatory systems, and to put behind such regulations the authority of the government." [32]   Because of his view of the economics of trade these regulations applied above all to the great exporting industries such as woolen cloth, silk, linen, stockings, and paper.   Thus approximately two thirds were related to woolens and four fifths to textiles.[33]

The most important industrial regulation was the general regulation of 1669 on: " The length, width and quality of cloths, serges and other stuffs of wool and linen."   Like all such regulations it was the ′product of a long process of research and surveys on the part of Colbert, the intendants, and a host of other officials and agents.   Like most other industrial regulations too, it was not entirely new, resembling in fact an edict of 1571.   Its declared purpose was to render uniform all cloths " of the same type, name and quality in whatever place they may be made, both to increase their sale inside and outside our kingdom, and to prevent the public from being cheated."   To accomplish this it went into the details of manufacture and specified the dimensions, the process for weaving, dyeing, fulling, selvaging, calendering etc. so that no excuse might permit the production of bad quality material.   Though relatively minute we are assured by the two most competent authorities on Colbert that it appeared liberal when compared to the *règlements* of his successors.[34]   This regulation, though designating the cloths in over a hundred places, was not all inclusive and between 1665 and 1681 particular regulations were drawn up for a number of other centers of woolen manufacture.[35]

Supplementary to the textile *règlements* appeared in 1669 two great regulations on dyeing which were followed in 1671 by a technical instruction vulgarizing the best methods of growing plants and preparing and using the coloring products.   The regulations, and particularly the instructions, were the fruit of

---

[32] Cole, *Colbert,* II, 394; Boissonade, *Colbert,* pp. 210-211.
[33] *Ibid.;* Cole, *Colbert,* II, 415.
[34] *Ibid.,* pp. 382-393. The ordinance is quoted in full in Cole, pp. 383-393; see Boissonade, *Colbert,* 211-213, 207-208.
[35] *Ibid.,* p. 211.

extensive research, mostly empirical but some scientific, in which individual dyers, government officials, and the *Académie des Sciences* had collaborated.   The instructions were published over the opposition of certain corps of dyers who bewailed the release of trade secrets.[36]   These instructions, along with the *Parfait négociant,* illustrate the unusual degree of Colbert's practical minded and rational approach to the implementation of his policies.

In spite of such aids and in spite of threats, severe punishments, the fortification of the law, and a grinding persistency of the administration, the regulations did not meet with universal compliance.   Pleas were frequently addressed to the Minister requesting a total or partial relaxation of the regulations as they concerned particular manufacturers.   Ordinarily these pleas were rejected.[37]   Or, more significantly, manufacturers and merchants sometimes complained that they could not obey the prescriptions of the *règlements* without ruin to themselves because of the unfair competition of stuffs manufactured elsewhere in the kingdom which ignored the rules. A usual answer was to demand the observation of the regulations, while, at the same time, intendants or their subordinates in the offending provinces were ordered to enforce the rules more vigorously.[38]

Before treating of the machinery employed by the King and Colbert to apply their regulations, it is pertinent to examine briefly the legal aspect of the generation of the power of the state, or king, to assert the "dictatorship of work."   It is necessary to remember in this regard, cautions Henri Hauser, that in the France of the *ancien régime* or the Middle Ages the right to work was not a natural and free right of man but was, rather, a concession of the public power as a dependence of the seigneurial domain.   The extension of the royal power over work is, therefore, the familiar story of the triumph of this power over the competence of lords and commune.   However extensive, legally, theoretically or actually, the competence

---

[36] *Ibid.,* pp. 217-218; Cole, *Colbert,* II, 404-413.

[37] See for instance, Colbert to M. Barillon, intendant at Amiens, March 7, 1670, relative to complaints of the *maire* and *échevins* of Amiens, Colbert, *Lettres,* II, part ii, 520-521 and note 521.

[38] See for instance, Colbert to M. Le Blanc, intendant at Rouen, December 26, 1681, *ibid.,* p. 724.

of communes or seigneurs over work—and there was the greatest variability throughout the *ancien régime*—this competence was always imperfect and precarious. Even before the royal power was so elevated as to efficiently intervene, the local authority of the communes and seigneurs had customarily appended to their charter grants to corporations the significant reserving clause: "*à la charge par eux de se pourvoir devers S. M. pour obtenir ses lettres-patents de confirmation.*" First as suzerain then as sovereign the royal authority vindicated its right to edict, modify or override the local power. Initiative asserted, it was expressed in two fashions: by general *ordonnances* or by the grant of particular privileges by which a particular subject or corporation was exempted from the restrictions of milieu. Ordinarily, it must be pointed out, these privileges were solicited by the subjects rather than initiated by the sovereign. By such acts the King was not suppressing seigneurial or communal rights; he was in legal feudal fashion intervening to assert his higher rights. He did not, strictly speaking, destroy, check or limit local rights, he "contented himself with ignoring them temporarily because his right is superior to all particular right." [39]

Whatever the legal authority, the administration of regulatory ordinances for industry by the Valois or early Bourbons had produced little durable effect. This arose from their failure to develop an efficient machinery of enforcement.[40] Colbert's agencies for that purpose had existed for the most part before his time, but he was the first to coordinate these agencies within a manageable instrument of state policy. At the top of the organization was Colbert himself who, as the servant of the King in his various offices, particularly that of *contrôleur général*, enjoyed a legally dictatorial competence over the economy of the nation. To his privileges he added his indefatigable energy and work and his methodical approach which introduced clarity, logic, and continuity into a system formerly incoherent and obscure. Finally, to an almost unbelievable extent, he measured every economic issue by the common denominator of state welfare as he saw it. As we have

[39] On all this legal aspect see the essay of H. Hauser, "Les pouvoirs publics et l'organisation du travail dans l'anciennce France," pp. 130-216.
[40] Boissonade, *Colbert*, pp. 11-12.

previously seen, Colbert and the King created a special *conseil de commerce* the membership of which was largely recruited from among the leading business men of the realm. This *conseil* was never anything but a body to provide expert advice and, as we have also indicated, it was soon absorbed into Colbert's bureaucracy.[41]

Of much greater importance in his organization was the role played by the intendants. The power of royal control of industry being an application of "police power," the intendants as "*hommes du roi*" and administrators of "police" in the provinces had as one of their principal functions the surveillance of industry. Theirs was the duty of general supervision, of seeing that agents sent by the central authority to apply the *règlements* did so. These agents were directly responsible to them. The intendants were held largely answerable for the prosperity of their generalities. They acted as liaison between the entrepreneurs and merchants and the King. *Maires, échevins* and other local officials having jurisdiction over manufactures were supported and supervised by the intendants to make more certain the enforcement of the *règlements*. All contests between factories and inspectors of manufacturers or between these inspectors and wardens or judges were subject to their jurisdiction. They could intervene to summon industrial cases involving manufacturers or workers from the competence of ordinary courts and parlements and subject them to their own review and decision. Their power of interpreting *règlements*, to facilitate execution, amounted, in some cases, to actual legislation.[42] Their *subdélégués* could also personally inspect factories and report to them. The intendants were, in short, the primary support of Colbert in establishing manufactures in the provinces and in supervising their regulations.[43]

The multiple duties of the intendants and the dignity of their office placed them in a situation of "high surveillance" and they, therefore, had little direct relationship with most entrepreneurs. It was the inspectors of manufactures, an

[41] *Ibid.*, pp. 15-16, 23-24; G. Martin, pp. 103-106.
[42] Which to their chagrin frequently aroused the ire of Colbert or the King when it was believed they had interpreted with too great latitude.
[43] Martin, pp. 111-115; Boissonade, *Colbert*, pp. 16-18.

office created by *règlement* in 1669, who applied themselves
to the more personal enforcement of the regulations. When
assigned by the *contrôleur général* to particular provinces they
reported immediately to the intendants for instructions. After
instruction they presented themselves at the nearest manufacturing city and summoned the *maires* and *échevins* to inform
them of the King's *règlements* and to command their cooperation in applying them. They also called meetings of masters
and *jurés* to explain to them the *règlements* and distribute
texts thereon. Further, as their title suggests, they made personal inspections to see that the regulations were executed.
They conducted surveys, consulted and advised with city bodies
on the state of manufactures, and sent a report every two
weeks to the central administration. They had no legal
authority over cases involving the manufacturers but they could
sit in on such cases and report on the process to intendants.[44]

Beneath these strictly " royal " officials was another group
traditionally associated with corporations and city governments.
By a series of decrees several of these were brought into closer
coordination with the royal organization as " *juges des manufactures* " in the lower echelon.[45] More important were the
gardes and *jurés*. These officials, elected annually by the
masters of corporations until 1691, when the general fiscal
policy of the crown subjected the office to sale, had existed
for centuries, but it was Colbert who, in a decree of 1669,
precised their role as regulatory agents of his administration.
They were required to make visits and inspections following
a carefully prescribed procedure. Their principal duty was
to prevent fraudulent manufacture and to inspect everything
connected with the manufacture, preservation, and stowage of
goods and raw materials. They did not set fines but reported
defections. Their most exacting duty was to inspect, pass
and affix the royal stamps on finished products, an activity
which was centralized in certain conveniently located *chambres
de commerce* where all goods must be brought for stamping and
inspection before sale. Multiple stamping, reinspections, and
the surveillance of inspectors of manufactures or *subdélégués*
and heavy fines for laxity made this an onerous task. In

[44] *Ibid.*, pp. 18-22; Martin, pp. 116-124.
[45] *Ibid.*, pp. 125-129.

general, however, they exerted themselves to seeing to the execution of the orders of the central authority and were fairly effectively controlled by the inspectors.[46]

A thoroughgoing control and direction of French industries required more than a series of *règlements* and a coordinated hierarchy of officials to enforce them; it was also necessary to introduce the weight of the royal power into the very organization of production. This could be best done by the control of the old corporations, guilds, or as they were frequently called, *jurandes*.

Colbert was by no means the first to attempt a move in that direction. As early as 1270 St. Louis had commissioned his prevot of Paris, Estienne Boileau, to draw up the famous *Livre des metiers*. Undoubtedly, before this time, customs had already imposed on artisans of crafts obedience to certain professional rules. The *Livre* of Boileau codified these customs and defined an organization of work which, in its essentials, persisted until the suppression of corporations in the late eighteenth century.[47] In general, from the thirteenth century to the sixteenth, the kings played a passive role and contented themselves with confirming the acts of local communities, authorizing new corporations and revising or extending, through their prevot, the provisions of Boileau's *Livre*. The initiative remained on the side of the communities.[48] Nevertheless this initiative was significantly exercised under the supervision and by the grace of the king's prevot.

Henry III was the first king to issue a general *règlement* for the organization of corporations and to make the corporative regime obligatory for the whole kingdom. The purpose of his ordinance of 1581 was ostensibly to alleviate the condition of artisans by removing many of the artificial impediments to mastership. Actually the purpose was almost entirely fiscal, to obtain new revenues by the sale of confirmations of mastership and corporation charters.[49] Following this precedent,

---

[46] *Ibid.*, pp. 130-153.

[47] Martin Saint-Leon, *Histoire des corporations de metiers*, pp. 71-74; Martin, pp. 155-156.

[48] Martin Saint-Leon, pp. 71-262, 264; Lespinasse, *Les metiers et corporations*, I, i.

[49] Martin Saint-Leon, pp. 263-267. See the text of the edict in Lespinasse, I, 84-94, see also p. ii.

Henry IV, in 1597, issued a similar ordinance. The reasons he gave were the same, but he added that the fees of confirmation were especially desirable " to satisfy the very just debts which we owe the colonels and captains of the Swiss, who with their lives and fortunes " aided in the conservation of the state.[50] In any case, the ordinances of Henry III and Henry IV, either as revenue measures, as aids to journeymen, or as instruments of unification, if such a motive was seriously entertained, were failures. They did set, however, a convenient fiscal pattern which the early Bourbons did not fail to copy, and they left behind important traditions to be revived and applied by Colbert. They marked an official point of departure for a new era of government intervention into corporative communities. This policy tended to deprive the corporations of their independence by changing them into state institutions. The corporations retained their election rights, but even these were gradually contracted as more and more offices were granted for money considerations.[51]

Colbert's ordinance of 1673 reiterated those of 1581 and 1597 and, as with them, the fiscal motive loomed large.[52] France was in the midst of her Dutch war and extraordinary revenue was essential. But Colbert was also well aware of the utility of the measure in effectuating his industrial program, and he exerted himself with characteristic vigor to obtain full compliance. His transfer of jurisdiction in cases affecting industrial production from royal courts to the competence of the *maires, échevins,* and other city officials, plus his emphasis on the universalization of the corporative system, has led some to speak of his " municipalization " of industry, and, in the light of the customary view of the growth of royal authority, this requires some explanation.

The *jurande* was only a means to an end for Colbert. It offered to him an ideal method of introducing uniformity into the productive organization and of subjecting it to rational direction of the state. Despoiled of their ancient autonomy,

[50] *Ibid.,* pp. 96-101.

[51] Martin Saint-Léon, pp. 267-269; Boissonade, *L'organisation du travail en Poitou,* II, 400-421; Fagniez, *Corporations et syndicates,* pp. 46-47; H. Sée, *Histoire économique de la France,* I, 259-260.

[52] See text, Lespinasse, *Les metiers et corporations,* I, 117-119.

the corporations could be used to assure discipline and the perfection so desirable to encourage export.[53] From the standpoint of discipline alone, the *corporation jurée* offered many advantages against the relatively uncontrolled and irrational liberty of free industry.[54] Colbert also saw in his policy a relief for entrepreneurs and workers from the interminable and costly processes to which they were subjected in presidial courts and an expedition of justice which would increase production. Further, he wished to interest the cities in his industrial program, to spur them to the creation and supervision of manufactures at their own cost, and to rid the central administration of the burden of many details.[55]

As a whole, Colbert's policy concerning the corporations both strengthened and weakened that system. The number of guilds in France, particularly during the administration of Colbert, increased in the seventeenth century.[56] There seems to be general agreement that royal intervention, in spite of pious declarations to a contrary intention, favored the entrepreneur against the worker and that the lot of the journeyman worsened in the course of the century.[57] Too, it appears that in spite of the vigor of the central administration the corporative regime, outside the cities, was still the exceptional form

---

[53] Boissonade, *Colbert*, pp. 243-244; Cole, *Colbert*, II, 442-446; H. Hauser, *Travailleurs et marchands*, pp. 188-190.

[54] For instance, consider the contrasting situation between free and corporate production in the matter of apprentice, journeyman and mastership. In free industry, the apprentice was engaged with his free consent under conditions varying according to the bargaining agreement of master and apprentice. There were no regulations of the duration of apprenticeship or of the number of apprentices. In the *corporations jurée* the conditions of apprenticeship were set by statutes and contract clauses were rigidly controlled. The time of apprenticeship, the number and obligations were all regulated. In free industry journeymen were not bound except by the obligations made by virtue of private agreement or by customs and loose general regulations. In corporate industry, in contrast, the statutes regulated in advance the discipline, obligations, and practices of journeymanship. In free industry, no masterpiece, extraordinary costs, fees, taxes and only simple formalities were required to pass from journeyman to master. In corporative communities numerous proofs, great fees and many other restrictions discouraged the journeyman attaining his monopoly position. Boissonade, *L'organisation du travail en Poitou*, II, 37, 53-54, 76-77.

[55] Hauser, *Travailleurs et marchands*, pp. 189-190.

[56] Cole, *Colbert*, II, 441,447. Boissonade asserts that under Colbert the regime was extended to 157 towns or villages in Poitou alone. *L'organisation du travail en Poitou*, II, 4-5, 438-448.

[57] *Ibid.*, pp. 255-273, 273-282; Martin Saint-Leon, pp. 450-453.

of industrial organization.[58]   Martin Saint-Léon points up in
a thoughtful fashion some of the anomalies in the conduct
of the state with reference to the corporations.   On one hand
it desired to strengthen the corporate form of industrial organization by forcing its extension throughout the realm.   At the
same time it was actually contributing to the weakness of
corporate organization by subjecting it to additional tax burdens, by interfering in elections, by royal official supervision
of its work, and by the oppressive weight of *réglementation*.
Initiative was transferred from the industrial organization to
the government, and this was to remain a characteristic of
French industry throughout the *ancien régime* and well into
the nineteenth century.[59]   Already in 1614 the *cahiers* of the
Third Estate had dramatized the conflict between the bourgeois, who wished to see the corporations autonomous, and
the kings who desired to see them as wheels of the state.
Actually, believes Martin Saint-Léon, the corporation was
incapable of maintaining itself in a period of industrial flux.
It was opposed to the "assimilation of progress," and its
statutes were too inelastic to absorb large changes.   "It had
indeed a kind of confused awareness of its immobility in the
midst of universal change, but it could not arise to the occasion
by either action or prohibition."   Instead, it inveighed against
the privileges.   For the royal government combatted this
immobility of the corps by importing foreign workers and
entrepreneurs, who could introduce new crafts or methods,
and endowed them with privileges.   The same impairment of
the corporate monopoly was extended to inventive natives.
Thus, on one hand, the government was trying to strengthen
the corporations while at the same time creating an elite industry outside of its control, thus placing the older corporations
in the position of routine departments of government.[60]

However true all this may be, it only illustrates the intellectual limitations to the reasoning of men like Colbert, but
it is well to recall that Colbert was interested in the corporations for one reason in particular: as an instrument to extend
and enforce his program of *règlementation* to assure perfection

[58] Boissonade, *Colbert*, pp. 252-254.
[59] On this point see Ballot, *L'introduction du machinisme dans l'industrie*.
[60] Martin Saint-Léon, pp. 336-338, 335-465, *passim*.

in production.   In realizing this purpose, he undoubtedly enjoyed considerable success.   Looked at from another view, Colbert's emphasis on the regulation and supervision of industry represented an effort to reduce the complex of industrial production to controllable figures in the grand mathematical equation of French economic welfare or power.

III

It is difficult at the present day to think of the regulation of industry, in the general view, in any sense except as an industrial obstacle however necessary it may be considered in certain instances.   To Colbert and his contemporaries, on the contrary, it would appear perfectly logical to speak of the " encouragement " of industry by "*réglementation*."   Therefore, it is almost with apologies to Colbert that we turn from the topic of regulation to that of the encouragement of enterprise.   As we have commented at the beginning of this discussion, Colbert looked on the encouragement and re-establishment of industry as a prime function in the equation of French prosperity and power.

Industry in the vocabulary of this Minister was often a generic term which implied the total productive structure of the nation, including agriculture.   Yet the physiocrats were partly, though not entirely, correct in attacking Colbert for his neglect of agriculture.   Actually, he considered agricultural produce as one of the mines of French strength and encouraged it in some directions, for instance horse breeding and silk culture.   But a combination of factors seems to have led him to give it secondary attention.   Except for wines and their derivatives, and a few other products, the export of agricultural produce would be discouraged in the interest of self-sufficiency. True, France normally exported grain, but Colbert was always anxious over the prospect of famine and was willing to prohibit export at the least indication of dearth.   The idea of exporting wool, hides, and almost all minerals or other raw material essential to industry, was, of course, contrary to all mercantilist maxims.   Now as we have seen, in Colbert's view of the economy the establishment of a favorable trade balance was the crucial and overbearing point.   Except for wine, and sometimes grain, the French agricultural produce did not directly contribute much to this favorable balance. It was manufactured goods which was considered the magnet for gold and silver.

Another factor appears to have contributed to Colbert's relative indifference to agriculture. Agriculture was less manageable, less subject to that rational calculation which he loved to apply to his industrial plans. For a person of his character, a man permeated with a passion for " l'ordre," who was habitually " surprised " or " astonished " or " dismayed " when a rational formula failed to produce a calculated result, this wild factor must have substantially dampened his interest. Some of these mathematical and psychological motives are conveniently revealed in an address of the Intendant D'Aguesseau, in the name of Colbert, to the Estates of Languedoc. He deplored the decline of certain privileged manufactures at Clermont and urged the Estates to go to their rescue. Answering any objection that these manufactures were unnecessary, he admitted that the agriculture of Languedoc produced some important crops, but he argued that it was manufactures which would bring money into the province to supply the needs of the state; and concerning agriculture:

. . . everyone knows that the products of the soil are uncertain and are exposed to a thousand accidents before arriving at maturity, that abundance and dearth are equally to be feared, and that the market depends on a thousand strange causes, but that this is not the case with manufactures, that they are subject neither to the changes of the seasons nor the inconstancy of the elements, that they depend on the art, industry and application of men; that if we survey the foreign countries we shall find that those which have laid their foundations on manufactures are much richer than those which have only agricultural products.[61]

Aside from the issuance of *règlements* and the creation of an organization to supervise and enforce their observation, perhaps Colbert's most important method of encouraging industry was by privileges. Industries which were so fortunate as to receive this attention may be classified, as they were by his administration, into two groups: the *manufactures royales*

[61] " Deliberations des Etats de Languedoc en faveur des manufactures de draps du Levant (Mercredi, 3 Xber 1681)," quoted in Boissonade, *Colbert,* pp. 333-334.

and *manufactures privilegiées.* To the first group belonged those in which the workers produced primarily for the state and were paid by the state. These manufactures were created to supply the needs of the king and court and to encourage national industry. Such manufactures were the Gobelins and Savonnerie. Also in this group belonged those industries which had been granted by *lettres patent* numerous privileges including the right to affix the royal arms above the door of their atelier and the right to issue goods under the royal stamp and title of *" manufacture royale de. . . ."* In the second group belonged certain manufactures which, while unable to use the name *" royale,"* secured privileges as, for instance, the monopoly of a certain manufacture in a particular region.[62] The value of the privileges was as variable as the industries to which they were granted. That they could be extremely valuable is shown by the example of the fabulous grants of money, as loan or gift, of exemptions and privileges to the famous cloth establishment of the Dutch Van Robais family at Abbeville.[63]

That these privileges and immunities heaped by Colbert on the new industries and their entrepreneurs did not always produce the desired result is curiously and eloquently demonstrated by the case of Elias Hal. Colbert related the story to the French Ambassador at Stockholm:

Seven or eight years ago the King brought from Sweden, in order to establish the manufacture of tar in France, a certain Elias Hal. This man, after having worked towards this establishment for three or four years, having informed me of his desire to settle down in France, His Majesty ordered me to take the trouble of arranging a marriage for him and gave him, at the same time, 2,000 *écus* for his use at his marriage and disposed 2,000 *livres* of appointments for him annually, which has always been well paid. I, at the same time, discovered a girl at Bordeaux who brought him a very honorable marriage. But, at the beginning of the last year, by an unparalleled perfidy, he took all the tar of the peasants of Médoc, carried it to the King's warehouses, received 22,000 *livres* of His Majesty's money, abandoned his wife and children, boarded a ship, and no one has heard tell of him since.[64]

---

[62] Martin, pp. 8-16.

[63] Cole, *Colbert,* II, 142-147; for similar examples see *ibid.,* pp. 147-361, *passim.*

[64] Colbert to M. de Feugières, Ambassador at Stockholm, May 19, 1673, Colbert, *Lettres,* VII, 292-293.

Colbert's program of privileges was extended to many kinds of industry, but it was naturally the woolen cloth industry, traditionally the greatest manufacture of France, which was the chief beneficiary.   On the whole, in spite of many failures, Colbert was able to introduce an impressive number of new textile industries into France.[65]   The silk industry, though not supported as vigorously as woolens, advanced superlatively under Colbert's regime.   He aided the older works of Paris, Lyon, and Tours and also established new ones at Reims, Rouen, Toulouse, and Nimes.   It was in this period that France began to assert her primacy in the world silk market.[66] The silk-stocking industry, utilizing the stocking frame, was practically created for France by Colbert, and by 1673 silk stockings were being manufactured on frames in eighteen French cities.   England, which had enjoyed a near monopoly of this manufacture, soon found France a serious rival.[67]   Wool stocking production was also aided and also prospered despite attempts, urged by the wool stocking-makers' guilds, to prevent the use of stocking frames.[68]   A huge lace monopoly, including all France, was created to oust the Venetian product.   Although at the industry's height it employed thousands of workers and the King and court set the style for " *point de France*," it was a venture of doubtful worth.[69]   The prestige given to French manufactures in general by the luxurious, artistic commodities manufactured by the great state and royal factories as the Gobelins, Savonnerie, Beauvais, and Aubusson was sufficient justification, in the mind of Colbert, for the expense of their privileges.[70]   The mining industry and industries for the manufacture of mirrors, glass, and earthenware, anchors, cannon, and other munitions, iron and steel, bronze, tin and soap, leather and sugar, were all, in varying degrees, encouraged by privileges and other aids.[71]

[65] Cole, *Colbert*, II, 141-187.
[66] *Ibid.*, pp. 187-206; Martin, 166-169; Boissonade, *Colbert*, pp. 175-179.
[67] *Ibid.*; Cole, *Colbert*, II, 207-216; Martin, pp. 169-174.
[68] Cole, *Colbert*, II, 217-237.
[69] *Ibid.*, pp. 238-286; Martin, pp. 188-190.
[70] Cole, *Colbert*, II, 287-302.
[71] "Mining," Boissonade, *Colbert*, pp. 130-150; Des Cilleuls, *Histoire de la industrie*, p. 23. "Mirrors, glass, grande earthenware," Cole, *Colbert*, II, 304-320; Martin, pp. 195-197. "Anchors, cannon and other munitions," Cole, *Col-*

As noted, privileges were frequently accompanied by money grants or loans. Ordinarily, however, the pecuniary aid was less direct, made in the form of tax exemptions, tariff differentials, the arbitrary raising of prices, and by assuring state purchases at high prices. Boissonade has attempted to make some evaluation of this aid and, while he admits his inability to give totals, he presents some imposing figures. For the period 1664-1683, for instance, the accounts of the bureau of buildings [72] showed direct money grants of about 2,000,000 *livres*. To this must be added subventions to state manufactures, foundries, naval yards, and arsenals adding up to " some tens of millions." On the side of indirect aids he cites the approximately 16,000,000 *livres* expended in twenty years by the King and royal family for luxurious presents. In addition, too, vast sums were expended by the King and court on buildings, furniture, and clothing in order to astonish the world. Finally, notice should be taken of the solid sums squeezed out of the provincial estates by the persistent nagging of Colbert.[73]

Industry was encouraged further by less obvious means. For instance, consider the large number of technological treatises the writing of which were inspired by Colbert, or subsidized, or ordered by him or state institutions. In this category belonged the work of Desargues on perspective and stone cutting; Bruant on surveying and his *Architecture practique;* architectural works by Perrault, Blondel, and Mignard; Savary's *Le parfait négociant;* Barreme's *Compte faites* and his *Grand commerce des changes.* Isnard, at his instigation, produced a treatise on silk spinning, Albo on the preparation of pastel, Albo and Perrot on dyeing. We have already commented on the instruction on dyes which accompanied the *réglement* on dyeing. Colbert's friend Denis de Sallo founded the first scientific journal, the *Journal des savants* (1665), one

bert, II, 335-349; Boissonade, *Colbert*, pp. 93-103. " Iron and steel, tin, bronze," Boissonade, *Colbert*, pp. 150-154; Cole, *Colbert*, II, 320-333. " Soap," *ibid.,* pp. 349-355; Martin, p. 193. " Leather," *ibid.,* pp. 191-192; Cole, *Colbert,* II, 355-358. " Sugar," *ibid.,* pp. 359-361; Martin, pp. 192-193.

[72] See Colbert's accounts as *surintendant des bâtiments* published by Guiffrey, *Comptes des bâtiments due roi.*

[73] Boissonade, *Colbert*, pp. 49-53.

of the main purposes of which was to advertise new processes useful to industry.[74]

The state was likewise a promoter of inventions and mechanical research. In this activity, as we shall see later, the *Académie des sciences* was the main collaborator.[75] All this activity, however, as far as the technological progress of industry was concerned, produced mediocre results. The outstanding exception was in the silk industry, in which by the end of the seventeenth century, something resembling modern mechanization was underway. Colbert attempted to introduce the complicated silk spinning machines, already in use in Piedmont, into France, but great advances in this direction were not made until the middle of the next century.[76] The story of the silk stocking frame is more happy. It is one of the most ingenious of textile machines, also a very old one. Its invention is usually traced to William Lee, an Englishman, in the year 1598. Introduced into France in the reign of Henry IV, it met great opposition at that time by the guild of stocking knitters; its introduction was discouraged elsewhere in Europe, and its use soon ceased, as far as is known. In 1656 Jean-Claude Hindret obtained the privilege of setting up a factory at the Chateau de Madrid, but his project saw little success until Colbert came to the rescue with substantial privileges. As we have seen, by 1673 silk stocking manufacture on these frames was a flourishing enterprise.[77] The introduction of another machine, the multiple ribbon loom, invented in Holland (*ca.* 1660) was also blocked, abroad as well as in France, by the pressure of the ribbon guilds and was not successfully reintroduced until 1735.[78]

A casual acquaintance with the industrial program of Colbert is likely to leave one with the impression, as it did his successors apparently, that he was an ardent champion of governmental intervention in industry, of *règlementation* and of privileges and monopolies. Nevertheless, as the sounder students of his regime have uniformly remarked, this was far

[74] *Ibid.,* pp. 31-33
[75] *Ibid.,* pp. 33-36.
[76] Ballot, *L'introduction du machinisme dans l'industrie,* pp. 300-303, 316-327.
[77] *Ibid.,* pp. 263-268.
[78] *Ibid.,* p. 255.

from the truth.[79] Colbert himself might have chided his misguided followers of the late seventeenth and early eighteenth century with his observation: " My sentiments never go to extremes." [80]

Colbert did believe that the intervention and aid of the state was essential to the establishment and success of " *grande industrie.*" He also thought that private individuals did not possess sufficient capital and that their initiative and foresight was inferior to the task of beginning great enterprises or relating their activities to the broad pattern of public welfare. However he recognized the abuses which could arise from too much aid or too much intervention. His regulations, for any particular craft, were, on the whole, less numerous, more precise, and more adaptable to the general interest, and more impartial than the multiple regulations of the corporations which they replaced or complemented. Regulations were indeed necessary to establish method in industry, to facilitate work, increase production, and raise the quality of French manufactures in order to invade foreign markets and produce a favorable trade balance. But he looked on regulations as a method of rationally generalizing production techniques and the minute elaboration of the program, the real abuses, belong more to his successors, who considered regulation as a panacea, than to Colbert.[81]

As to privileges and other aids to industry, Colbert was entirely clear. His policy was simple. He desired to guard and foster promising industry, particularly new industry. He was very much opposed to monopolies, on principle, because they created an artificial restriction on what he called " free commerce." This was an entirely logical attitude, of course, in a man who believed in a natural economy. The economic policy of Colbert can possibly be explained as an attempt to instruct, encourage, or, if necessary, to force French industry into a position of exploiting its natural or absolute advantage. To accomplish this end, privileges and aids were frequently

[79] Martin Saint-Leon, pp. 354-355; Martin, pp. 16, 94-102; Boissonade, *Colbert,* pp. 41-44; Levasseur, *Histoire du commerce de la France,* I, 296-297; Cole, *Colbert,* I, 346-350.
[80] Quoted in *ibid.,* p. 294.
[81] Boissonade, *Colbert,* pp. 206-207, 229.

necessary, but it must be remembered, if one is inclined to accuse him of being over lavish, that Colbert, in effect, was stimulating the industry of a nation which by its own blindness, as he believed, had permitted itself to fall to the lowest depths of industrial lassitude. He granted magnificent monopolies and privileges, but not as permanent grants and almost never to any but new industries or to some promising industry which had fallen into decay and required heavy expenditures to revive. C. W. Cole has concisely, and the writer thinks justly, summarized Colbert's meaning of " free commerce." " It meant not commerce free of tariff, restrictions or unhampered by government regulation, but rather, commerce in which no *unnecessary* monopolies were created, on which *unnecessarily* hampering restrictions were not placed, and on which no *unnecessary* taxes were levied." [82]

One incident drawn from the many to be found buried in the mass of published correspondence will further elucidate some of the aspects involved in his general attitude on this point. When the magistrates and corporations of Auxerre complained of the impairment of their monopoly position by Colbert's introduction into their city of new crafts, he ignored them because, as he explained:

The multiplicity of the establishments distresses them and causes them to say that they will ruin each other; but [et] there is nothing more advantageous for a city because everyone has not the same interests. . . . Add to this that these different manufactures will oblige the masters to give, perhaps, something further to the workers, and that they will produce, at least, this advantage: that the masters of a single industry cannot make themselves the masters of the workers so that they would be inclined to give them only what would seem good for them.[83]

The large number of privileges granted by Colbert appears to have raised up the hope of many entrepreneurs that the government provided an easy source of aid and, consequently, they thought they would be able to succeed in a business in which they, personally, expended little self help, initiative or money. At least, this was a grievance expressed by Colbert

---

[82] Cole, *Colbert,* I, 346; see Boissonade, *Colbert,* pp. 41-44; Martin, pp. 94-95.
[83] Colbert to M. Bouchu, intendant at Dijon, October 17, 1674, Colbert *Lettres,* II, part ii, 688.

himself.[84] But when these merchants or entrepreneurs requested privileges they were extremely likely to receive a rebuff. " Concerning the privileges these merchants request, I can assure you that the King will not grant it, because the privileges of the manufactures established in the kingdom always impedes commerce and public liberty." [85]

IV

The gifts of regulations, of rational direction and supervision, of privileges and financial support for industries did not complete Colbert's economic program. Also essential to this program, he believed, was the solution of the problem of tariffs. His tariff policy admits a division into three more or less distinguishable, if interrelated, parts. He believed that in order to facilitate interior commerce the number of interior tariff barriers should be reduced as much as possible and this should be accompanied by a reduction in the duties. The tariff system should be reorganized to create an orderly structure contributing to better administration and simplifying the calculations necessary to long-range commerce. Finally, the tariff emphasis should be transferred to the boundaries of the kingdom where the tariffs should be levied in such a rational manner as to encourage home manufactures and be conducive to a favorable balance of trade.

In justice it cannot be said that these ideas, in any aspect, were original with Colbert. It is to his great credit, however, that he was able sufficiently to subordinate the immediate fiscal needs of the government to a long-range calculation of fiscal dividends as to bring himself to apply his ideas. His qualified success contributes another example of the limitations of Louis XIV's absolutism.

For at least a century before the ministry of Colbert the kings had aspired to the unification of customs but had been defeated by the opposition of the provinces. Henry IV had succeeded, in 1598, in unifying the region of the so called

---

[84] Colbert to M. de Bezons, intendant at Montpellier, October 2, 1671, *ibid.,* p. 633.
[85] Colbert to M. D'Aguesseau, intendant at Toulouse, December 16, 1680, *ibid.,* pp. 715-716.

"five big farms."[86]   Therefore, in 1661, when Louis XIV
began his personal rule, *within* the border of roughly the
northern half of France, trade could be carried on without
passing through customs barriers. The border of this area,
however, was broken into unequal segments—five for export
and four for import—and, depending on the point of crossing,
the merchant had to pay one of five sets of export duties or
of four of import. There were for the entire region nineteen
distinct duties. This meant that, depending on the place of
crossing, there was a considerable variation in the amount of
duties applied to the exports and imports of the five big farms.
In 1664, for instance, export duties were set for Champagne
at about 12.87 per cent, 11.2 for Burgundy and 8.93 for
Picardy, Normandy, Berry, and Poitou.[87]

This was the simplest part of France's custom situation.
Outside of the area of the five big farms were two groups of
provinces in which no unity of customs existed. Their customs relationship with the area of the five big farms is suggested by their titles: *Provinces réputées étrangères*[88] and
Provinces d'étranger effectif. In the latter group belonged
certain free ports and recently acquired provinces and cities.
These provinces or cities were effectively treated as foreign
countries and could, if they desired, trade freely with foreigners
but had to pay customers in their trade with other provinces
of the realm.[89]   Colbert and Louis XIV would have liked to

[86] Elizinga, "Le tarif de Colbert de 1664 et 1667," pp. 231-235. As early as
1484 at a diet at Tours voices had been heard calling for the abolition of interior
customs barriers and for their levy at the frontiers of the kingdom. In 1614 the
third estate had the same request. These were feeble voices against the partic-
ularist forces, but they show that the king had allies. *Ibid.*, 235-236.

[87] *Ibid.*, pp. 236-237; Callery, "Les douanes avant Colbert," pp. 51-52, 53, 59-
61. Callery maintains that in spite of the multiplicity of the tariffs they were
well advertised and that the ordinary merchant would not be burdened by any
surprise levy (pp. 69-74). The provinces of the "five big farms" were: Normandy, Picardy, Boulonnais, the Ile de France, Champagne, Burgundy, Bresse,
Bugey, Dombes, Beaujolais, Berry, Bourbonnais, Poitou, Aunis, Anjou, Maine,
Orleanais, Perche, Nivernais, Touraine, Thouars, and the Chatellenie of Chan-
toceaux.

[88] Most of the southern half of France belonged to this group: Lyonnais, Forez,
Dauphiné, Province, Languedoc, Auvergne, the Comté de Foix, Navarre, Rous-
sillon, Guyenne, La Marche, Limousin, Saintogne, the Iles de Ré and Oleron,
Flanders, Hainault, Artois, Cambrésis, Brittany.

[89] Clermontois, the Trois-Évéches, Lorraine, Alsace, Sedan, the Pays de Gex,
Franche-Comté, and the free ports of Marseille, Dunkerque, Bayonne, Lorient.

abolish all interior customs barriers so that freedom of commerce which existed in the five big farms might be extended to the whole kingdom.[90]

The most important action of Louis XIV and Colbert in freeing interior commerce of unnecessary burdens was the tariff reforms embodied in the tariff act of 1664. This act was notable for its introduction of order and simplicity into the tariff system, but only for the five big farms. For fiscal reasons, the provinces outside of this area declined to adhere to the reforms. With certain specified exceptions, the act of 1664 reduced the multitude of export and import levies for the five big farms to two sets: one for import, another for export. In doing so Colbert was achieving, at least in part, two ends of his general tariff policy. He was insuring the better administration of the system and lessening the calculating problem of long-distance traders. As he himself put it, the tariff of 1664 " contributed greatly to the relief of the subjects of His Majesty by reducing the great multiplicity of duties to a single one." Secondly, he encouraged interior commerce by a mean reduction, though a small one, in the duties.[91] The tariff, in addition, applied another criterion of sound customs policy as interpreted by Colbert. It was moderately protectionist. Indeed so moderate by nineteenth—or twentieth—century standards that the present-day student has

[90] Cole, *Colbert*, I, 423; Elzinga, " Le tarif de Colbert de 1664 et 1667," p. 238.

[91] Quotation from Cole, *Colbert*, I, 426. The preamble of the act precised these purposes in exaggerated language. After describing the dismaying complexity of the tariffs formerly levied in the area, Louis XIV says: " And after having heard this report we have clearly recognized that it was absolutely necessary in order to attain to the re-establishment of commerce within and outside and to that end which we have set ourselves of *reducing all these duties to a single one for imports and another for export* and even to diminish them considerably in order to encourage, by this means, all our subjects of the maritime provinces to undertake distant voyages and those of other provinces to take interest therein, to establish at the same time the old manufactures, to form companies for introducing new ones, to stimulate the industry of our subjects and to procure them the means of employing usefully the advantages which they have received from nature, to banish sloth and to divert by honest occupation the inclination, common to most of our subjects, for a life of idleness and *rempante* (?) under the title of divers sinecures or under false appearances of a mediocre attachment to belle lettres or to politics, which through their ignorance or malice usually degenerates into a dangerous chicane which infects and ruins the most part of our provinces." Elzinga, " Le tarif de Colbert de 1664 et 1667," pp. 259-260. The entire act is reprinted here, pp. 249-265.

been inclined sometimes to deny this feature.[92]   On the whole, duties were increased on manufactured goods in import and lowered on their export, while it lowered the duties on raw material in import and raised them on raw material export. An excerpt from the correspondence of Colbert shows quite clearly his mercantilist and rational approach to the tariff question and explains also his moderation in 1664. Formerly, he told the King, the tax farmers of the area had tended to regulate the level of the duties in their own interests without regard to any over-all rational concept or theory.

. . . having always heavily taxed the farm produce, merchandise and manufactures of the kingdom which they saw leaving in abundance, and lightened the entry duty on foreign merchandise and manufactures in order to encourage the entry of a greater quantity, without worrying over whether money left the kingdom by this means. This was indifferent to them provided that their farms produced some gain during the time of their enjoyment of it.

Finally, after having well studied this matter, Your Majesty decreed the tariff of 1664, the duties in which are regulated on an entirely contrary maxim. That is to say, all the merchandise and manufactures of the kingdom were notably relieved, duties lowered and the foreign ones burdened; however, with moderation, in as much as there being no manufactures established in the kingdom, this increase in duty, if it were excessive, would have been an extraordinary burden on the people bcause of their need for the aforementioned foreign merchandise and manufactures. But this change commenced to provide some means of establishing the same manufactures in this kingdom. . . .[93]

In summary, we may assert that the tariff of 1664 reveals Colbert as the intelligent servant of the state, adapting his program to circumstances rather than succumbing to that dogmatism frequently associated with his name by the physiocrats.   Was the moderation of his tariff act attributable, as he claimed, to the consideration of the welfare of the entire people?   Was it due to his inability to ignore the " interests "?   Or was it a rationally conceived preparatory step in a calculated

[92] For instance, Elzinga is reluctant to admit this point (*ibid.,* pp. 244-245); Cole recognizes in it elements of protectionism (*Colbert,* I, 426-428); Callery, calls it slightly protective, pp. 90-91. Levasseur calls it protectionist, *Histoire du commerce,* I, 354-355.

[93] Colbert, " Mèmoire au Roi," 1670, Colbert, *Lettres,* VII, 241-242.

long-range program? His writings and his actions give support to all these assumptions.

At any rate, the tariff of 1664, from the protectionist point of view, was only introductory. In 1667 was issued the second great tariff act of his administration. Though the discriminatory rates were still moderate in most cases, as compared with a modern protective tariff, it was not so considered in his day, and it was an important step in the direction of the war of 1672 with Holland. Proposed as a modifying act to the tariff of 1664, it was actually so different as to be considered a new act entirely. Aimed primarily at Holland, its revisions sent import customs soaring upwards on about fifty-seven articles which, for the most part, were produced by French infant industries. Thus the tariff on wool stockings was raised 366 per cent, silk stockings 183 per cent, and cotton 100 per cent.[94] England obtained a re-establishment of the tariff rates of 1664 at the commencement of the Dutch war, and Holland, to Colbert's chagrin, obtained the same by the treaty of Nimwegen (1679).[95]

Another significant distinction between the tariff of 1667 and that of 1664 was the fact that it was not limited to the area of the five big farms. The new rates were levied at the frontiers of the kingdom. Taken together, the acts of 1664 and 1667 represented a very broad step in the direction of a national, unified and orderly customs system. Many anomalies continued to exist in that system, and it would take the French Revolution to accomplish most of the ends of Colbert's program. Moreover, even in his own day, inertia, custom or political fortunes set at naught much of his effort. Vauban, long after the death of Colbert, remarked that " the peasant and proprietor prefer to allow their commodities to rot at home rather than transport them with so much risk and so little profit." [96] The effect these particular tariffs had on the industrial program, of which they were a part, is impossible

---

[94] Elzinga, " Le tarif de Colbert de 1664," pp. 247-248; Cole, *Colbert*, I, 428-429; Levasseur, *Histoire du commerce*, I, 356-359. A comparison between the duties of 1667 and 1876 showed that the latter were much higher, and the tariffs of 1892 and 1910 were higher still.

[95] *Ibid.*, pp. 359, 362-363.

[96] Quoted in Sée, *Histoire économique de la France*, I, 224.

to assess. Colbert, obviously, believed them a great boon. Certainly the tariffs of France had never been so successfully or rationally subordinated to the general economic interests of the state.

V

Any rounded consideration of Colbert's economic administration, however brief, could not neglect the subject of colonies and distant trading areas and the great chartered companies which were created to exploit colonial resources for the benefit of France. In the arithmetic of national welfare this aspect of Colbert's program was an integral factor. Not only would colonies supply raw materials for the maintenance of new French manufactures, thus in a sense extending the area of her natural advantage, but they would provide a market for national manufactures which could not be disposed of elsewhere. Also, in Colbert's concept of a relatively static world wealth, the revival or extension of French trade with the colonies or distant markets meant a subtraction from the sum of trade to be shared by Holland and England. In other terms, the King could be told that " it would considerably augment the money within his kingdom and it would diminish notably the power in money of the two states of England and Holland which are the only two which can balance, in a fashion, that of His Majesty." [97]

Finally, by its direct and indirect effect on industry, productivity and employment in the realm, a revival of foreign commerce would increase the circulating wealth so necessary, as we have seen, to balancing the national economic equation. Such motives are implicitly revealed in even the official declarations of the King concerning commerce. Take, for instance, a declaration of 1664:

And as we clearly recognize that the welfare of the people consists not only in the considerable diminution of the taxes which we have granted them for the last two or three years, but much more in the revival of the commerce of our realm, by which means alone abundance can be attracted within it and support not just the luxury and prodigality of a minority, as was formerly the

[97] Colbert to Louis XIV, 1681, quoted in Levasseur, *Histoire du Commerce,* I, 367.

case arising from the dissipation of our finances, but be spread among the people generally by means of manufactures, by the consumption of commodities and by the employment of an infinite number of persons of nearly all ages and sexes which commerce produces; all of which makes for a very happy conciliation between an abundance of temporal and spiritual goods; seeing that by assiduous work people are withdrawn from all occasions of mischief, inseparable from idleness.[98]

Whatever the theoretical utility of colonies and the trade necessary to put them to account, it was up to Colbert to translate theory to practical advantage. When he came to the ministry the prospect was extremely discouraging. In spite of the activities of Henry IV and Richelieu who, together, had authorized twenty-two overseas companies in forty-three years, in spite of rich colonies in Canada and the Caribbean isles of Martinique, Guadeloupe, and St. Christophe, and in spite of earlier ventures made in South America and East Africa, the maritime commerce of France was in a state of utter atrophy.[99]

To establish or reassert France's prestige in the field of distant or colonial commerce Colbert believed that the intervention of the state was essential. Savary was undoubtedly expressing his views in the *Parfait négociant* when it was noted that long-distant commerce was too ambitious an undertaking for individuals and required great companies. Certainly, he wrote, " the English and Dutch would not have preserved their commerce in all the places where they are today if they had not established great companies to that end. . . . "[100]

In quick succession Colbert founded the East India Company, the West Indies Company, the Company of the North, and the Levant Company, and several smaller ones.[101] Technically, with the exception of the first, all were signal failures and, during Colbert's lifetime, it too seemed to offer small promise. These companies were created to *exploit* the colonies already in the

[98] " Declaration du Roy portent establissement d'une campagnie pour le commerce de Indes Orientales " (1664), Colbert, *Lettres*, II, part ii, 785.

[99] Levasseur, *Histoire du commerce*, I, 278-289, 364-368. In the same period the great Dutch East India Company aroused the admiration and envy of the world. Between 1602 and 1661 it earned an average dividend of more than 25 per cent. *Ibid.*, p. 366.

[100] Savary, *Le parfait négociant*, I, 112.

[101] The best discussion of the companies, as a whole, is Cole, *Colbert*, I, 475-532; II, 1-131. Unless otherwise indicated, this section is based on these pages.

French possession,[102] to aid in adding to possessions, and to encroach on the trade of other maritime powers in distant markets.

The history of one of these companies, the West Indies Company, has been well told by S. L. Mims and, using his work as the main source, it will serve as an appropriate illustration of Colbert's activities and attitudes concerning overseas trade and colonies.[103] As in the case of other great companies, the finances of that of the West Indies were contributed largely by the King, and the King and Colbert together secured the rest of the needed money from those who were most sensitive to their influence. " Thus of the grand total of 5,522,345 *livres* 8 *s.* 6 *d.,* the King furnished no less than 3,026,545 *livres* 8 *s.* 6 *d.* Almost all the remainder was furnished by revenue-farmers, tax-collectors and officials, acting in the great majority of cases under the orders of Colbert. Only very insignificant sums were furnished by merchants or others capable of directing such an important enterprise." [104] The letters-patent of 1664 creating the Company granted it monopoly privileges in trade for forty years and suzerainty over all the colonies already established, or to be conquered by it, on the mainland of South America

[102] The colonies were considered as tributary to the economy of France. An anonymous memorandum on measures proper to the administration of the island of Madagascar, carrying in the margins comments of Colbert or possibly Louis XIV, illustrates this point very clearly. Such typically mercantilist propositions are advanced as prohibiting the growth of vines, olives, flax or hemp, or, " Let no one establish there any considerable manufacture of things which are made or can be made in France," for if this were allowed, it would ruin the investment of the East India Company and " oblige the Company to transport from France gold and silver, a thing to be avoided as much as possible for numerous reasons." Quoted in Cole, *Colbert,* II, 571.

[103] Mims, *Colbert's West Indies policy.* The recent book of N. M. Crouse, *The French struggle for the West Indies, 1665-1713* (New York, 1943) is an interesting complementary work for Mims. It presents the political and military struggle of the French against the Dutch, Spanish and, particularly, the British to establish themselves securely in these islands.

[104] Mims, pp. 81-82; the procedure followed in the case of the East India Company was, if anything, even more exaggerated and tyrannous. See Cole, *Colbert,* I, 483-501. F. C. Lane, " Colbert et le commerce de Bordeaux," *Revue historique de Bordeaux* . . . , (July-October, 1924) on the bordelais merchants, comments, relative to the West India Company: ". . . n'eurent, semble-t-il, aucune part à la souscription." (p. 177.) By an extraordinary combination of pressure and patience, the King and Colbert, working mainly through the intendant, were able to pry some money from these merchants to help finance the East India Co. *Ibid.,* pp. 173-177.

from the Amazon to the Orinoco, together with the island of Cayenne, all the French West Indies, Canada, Acadia, Newfoundland, and other islands and the mainland of North America from Northern Canada to Virginia and Florida. It was privileged to govern these regions and its interests were promised the protection of the King's arms and ships.[105]

It was the misfortune of the Company that so great a proportion of its capital had been provided by persons who by training and inclinition were mostly indifferent to and some, perhaps, hostile to trade. There may have been those who were fashionably enthusiastic at first, but the fact that the investment, aside from the King's, was generally obtained by threats and every form of mild extortion makes the presumption unlikely. To be sure, once they had invested, the stockholders were anxious to see the Company prosper, but only a small number of them possessed the training, initiative, skill and business acumen to carry out the plan successfully. The merchants, of course, were the ones who supposedly had this skill. Committees or chambers of commerce, after the Dutch models, were created in which the policies of the company were supposedly determined by the merchants in consultation with Colbert or his agents. Actually, as we have noted, Colbert had little respect for the opinions of " selfish " merchants, and the real government of the Company resided in Colbert himself. He controlled it with all the thoroughness with which he controlled royally sponsored industries. *Règlements,* colonial policy, offices, ships, schedules, cargoes, rewards: all were provided or passed upon by the Minister. The Company was almost a department of the central government.[106]

After 1668 Colbert gradually relaxed the monopoly position of the Company and permitted the competition of private French traders. Whereas in 1662 only three or four ships of French traders had visited the French West Indies, the number mounted rapidly until, in 1670, there were sixty, and in 1672, eighty-nine annually visiting the isles. In December 1674 the privileges of the Company were revoked and the trade thrown open to all private French traders. In its liquidation the accounts showed a completely bankrupt corporation which had been

[105] Mims, pp. 69-70.
[106] *Ibid.,* pp. 71-82, *passim;* Cole, *Colbert,* II, 6, 7-55 *passim.*

sustained only by the generosity of the crown. All so-called
" voluntary " subscribers were, however, fully reimbursed for
their investment, but the King suffered a loss of about 3,500,000
livres. Technically, the West Indies Company was a failure.[107]

But another side was presented by Jacques Savary, speaking,
one suspects, for Colbert. The King and Colbert, through the
Company, had succeeded in driving out the trade of the Dutch
in the French West Indies and had, reciprocally, created a
French trade involving a hundred ships annually and several
millions in merchandise. Thirty refineries, he claimed, had been
ruined in Amsterdam alone. The Company had made additions
to the royal domain. All the people of the kingdom now received sugar, tobacco, ginger, and other commodities at half
the former price paid to the Dutch intermediary. Thus refined
sugar, formerly 22 to 24 *sols.* was now 12 to 13 *sols.* per pound
and " other merchandise proportionately." This difference
amounts, he added, " to some very considerable sums which
are turned to the profit of the subjects of His Majesty." [108]

All this might appear to be a kind of special pleading, as it
undoubtedly was, but the facts of the case seem to lend support
to him. Savary also throws a light on Colbert's limited endorsement of monopolies. When Savary defended the glory of the
King in excusing the dissolution of the West Indies Company,
he pointed out that its purpose, namely, of expelling the Dutch
from a lucrative trade, had been accomplished and that, therefore, restrictions were no longer necessary or desirable.

. . . if the Company of the West no longer survives, it is not
through failure, but because it is no longer needed; having been
formed only as a means of wresting the commerce of these islands
from the hands of the Dutch who monopolized it for sixty years
past. Consequently, His Majesty having attained the goal, set forth
for himself when he created this Company, has considered it proper
to dissolve it and leave the commerce of the West free so that a
greater number of his Subjects can participate in the profit to be
found therein.[109]

The excuses of Savary have received a favorable audience
among the modern historians.

[107] *Ibid.,* pp. 12-25; Mims, pp. 150-179.
[108] Savary, *Le parfait négociant,* II, 132-134.
[109] *Ibid.,* p. 130. See Mims, pp. 179-181; Cole, *Colbert,* II, 26-27.

VI

Looking at Colbert's economic program as a whole, it is difficult to avoid the question: "Was it a success or failure?" In a world where an academic division in opinion over the feasibility of a controlled or free economy tends to force a political choice between one of two hostile power spheres, this question becomes extremely significant. Therefore, an answer to the question might have the greatest political or social importance. No competent historian has had the temerity, to the writer's knowledge, to make the conclusive assessment. The answer, as we have insisted from the beginning of this study, would be irrelevant to our inquiry. Nevertheless the student would be incomprehensibly incurious who ignored such a question.

To look at such a question a second time is to annihilate its meaning. The word " success " alone is freighted with prejudices. To give it pertinence the inquiry must be associated with any number of qualifications. Thus: " Did Colbert's economic program increase the wealth of the state? " " Did Colbert by his economic program succeed in increasing the power of the state? " "Did he introduce order into the economy? " " Did he improve the general welfare? " It is immediately apparent that any such direction of the question arouses a multitude of other qualifications. Does the particular question permit a long over a short-range view? Does it refer to Colbert's specific purposes or to desirability by present standards? Then, to be sure, there is always the inevitable " if " factor. What would have been the result under different circumstances or following different procedures? Without further belaboring the obvious, it is clear that any answer to the general question must arise from a sum of answers to smaller questions. It is clear, also, that any such answer could conceivably be rationally satisfactory only when framed with reference to some particular set of assumptions and definitions. To all the logical difficulties, conceivably surmountable, must be added the insurmountable obstacles to understanding which arise from the imperfection of historical evidence. Let us work backwards through this chapter to suggest some of the possible evaluations and, at the same time, observe the pitfalls which may discourage their acceptance in any specific situation. The success of Colbert's chartered trade companies and his colonial policy is typically difficult to judge. From the standpoint of bookkeeping, his companies may be deemed complete failures. Yet, even in the short run, that is, during Colbert's lifetime, Savary saw the West Indies Company as a successful and glorious enterprise. As for the long run, it has been argued that Colbert's colonial ventures laid the foundations for great commercial prosperity in the eighteenth century.[110] It is possible to think, as one writer has suggested, of the financial drain which Colbert levied on the kingdom to support his colonial enterprises as a high " protection cost." This cost, so great in the period of Colbert as to render his companies bookkeeping failures, had, nevertheless, the result of forcing up the " protection cost " of competitors, particularly the Dutch, in certain areas of the colonial trade. In the next century, perhaps largely as a result of Colbert's aggressive expenditures of men, material, and money, the French colonial traders within these certain areas reaped a dividend. This was their " protection rent," a profitable income which was equivalent to the difference between their " protection cost " and that of the marginal competitors.[111]

Colbert's tariff program also admits of several evaluations, some favorable, some unfavorable. Elzinga, for instance, finds the tariff of 1664 highly praiseworthy but condemns the tariff of 1667 as conducive to retaliatory measures abroad and eventually to the war of 1672.[112] But see what Colbert himself had to say of the effect of discriminatory tariffs against foreign sugars:

I must tell you that when I made the tariff, we had two ills in this business which were considerable: one, that all the sugar of the isles went to Holland to be refined, and secondly, that we had no refined sugar except by way of Holland, England, and Portugal.

I was convinced that . . . it was sufficient to establish customs in such a way that the subjects of the King were persuaded to build refineries, and, by giving them some diminution of tariffs on our raw sugar, to exclude easily that of the foreigners.[113]

---

[110] *Ibid.,* p. 131.

[111] Frederic C. Lane, " The economic meaning of war and protection," *Journal of social philosophy and jurisprudence,* VII (April, 1942), 254-270.

[112] Elzinga, " Le tarif de Colbert de 1664 et 1667," p. 248.

[113] Colbert to Colbert de Terron, intendant at Rochefort, July 12, 1669, Colbert, *Lettres,* II, part ii, 476-477.

What relative value Colbert's sugar tariff had for the development of the sugar industry in France and how much this development owed to his colonial policy and the West India Company, it is impossible to know. Between 1674 and 1682, however, it has been estimated that sugar production in the West Indies increased 50 per cent. In 1664 the Dutch furnished nearly all the refined sugar consumed in France. By 1683 there were twenty-nine refineries in France and five in the isles, refining annually about 20,700,000 pounds. By 1670 Colbert claimed that France was exporting refined sugar. By the end of his ministry France was on the road to her supremacy over England as the supplier of sugar to Europe.[114]

No phase of Colbert's administration has elicited more praise and greater censure than his methods of encouraging industry. Even among his admirers there have been those like Germain Martin who, undoubtedly influenced by their " liberal " economic outlook, felt that the system of privileges was a reprehensible part of his program. Admitting that he was parsimonious in this regard, Martin still felt that Colbert erred by ignoring innumerable small crafts which were to reveal great vitality in the next century.[115] This judgment, whether just or not, belongs to the realm of the incalculables.

The criticism does call attention to one aspect of Colbert's industrial planning which may be marked down as a failure. It must be immediately remarked, however, that it was a failure only from the standpoint of requiring perfection. Colbert did not succeed in subjecting all French production to the corporative regime. He extended that regime as never before, and in the cities the small crafts were almost uniformly subjected to the supervision of wardens and visitors. In the countryside, the most important productive area of industry, production still continued to be small scale, individual or family and unorganized; in a word: free.[116]

---

[114] Mims, pp. 260-280.

[115] Martin, *La grande industrie sous Louis XIV,* pp. 100-102, 354, As an illustration of this vitality Martin cites the following figures. In Languedoc, between 1702 and 1713, small crafts produced 17,710 pieces of cloth against 32,735 for " grande industrie." In a later period, 1713-1723, when privileges were less important, the small crafts produced 51,506 pieces against 27,680 for the royal manufacturers.

[116] *Ibid.,* pp. 17-18; Sée, *Histoire economique de la France,* I, 276.

The evaluation of Colbert's industrial program cannot be made from the negative assertion of what he failed to do. Such considerations must be balanced with what he did do. Unfortunately, this is primarily a statistical problem and the available statistics are sadly inadequate. As we have previously noted such figures were usually administrative secrets and the destruction or dispersal of records in the French Revolution and since has complemented the vigilance of the ancient bureaucracy. C. W. Cole has analyzed the famous report on the manufactures of France (1692-1693) and has presented some interesting ideas suggested by his study. However, as Mr. Cole would be quick to point out, the report is substantially reliable only for a specific time and, in the absence of records of equal validity and breadth for the previous and later times, it is of limited value in making a comparative estimate. The report is illuminating, nevertheless, because it concerns the state of industry at a time when the effects of Colbert's plans should have been maturing and, apparently, before the wars and the Protestant troubles had produced a marked setback.

It revealed, for instance, a notable tendency towards a capitalistic type of industrial organization in the cloth and hat industries. It indicated an annual production of about one million pieces of goods, or between 30 and 40 million square yards. In all phases, it presented a picture of a various and vigorous industrial scene which seems distant from the gloomy tableau which Colbert described for the France of 1661. It gives, concludes Cole, the " definite impression that France had, by 1692, outstripped all her industrial competitors in Europe." [117]

To be more explicit, by 1680 Colbert could boast that French mirrors were depriving the Venetians of 1,000,000 *livres* per annum. At his death, the French could offer small mirrors at a higher price and large mirrors at a cheaper price than Venice. In 1680 the Minister believed that the French cloth manufactures were subtracting 4,000,000 *livres* annually from the Dutch wealth, and he laid it down as a policy to avoid any further privilege grants to cloth industry. At the expense of the Italian cities, Lyon grew to be the leading silk manufacturing center of the world, and, by 1685, the silk industry in the generality of Lyon had in operation 18,000 looms and employed 120,000

[117] Cole, *Colbert*, II, 573-588.

families. A growth in the iron, arms, and munitions industries enabled Colbert and Louvois to create the greatest war machine of Europe while at the same time freeing it from its former dependence on imports.[118]

If it is granted that by the end of Colbert's administration France had become the greatest industrial nation of the world, which appears to be so, it does not necessarily follow that the program of Colbert was responsible for that accomplishment. It may be more significant that the most pronounced industrial progress of the seventeenth century in France occurred in the two periods of comparative peace during the reign of Henry IV and the ministry of Colbert. It might be argued that the condition of peace was the greatest spur to French industrial advancement and that without the presence of Colbert's burdensome program of patronage industry would have prospered even more than it did. Such an argument would be based on the assumption that a condition of peace is naturally conducive to economic progress. The assumption is a rational laissez-faire position deduced from certain premises but it has never been conclusively proved and at best is only partly true. It was undoubtedly true that the condition of peace was useful to Colbert, as it was to Sully and Laffemas, in carrying forward part of his program. However, it should be noted that, aside from this condition of peace, both periods were dominated by what in seventeenth-century France might be termed " progressive " ministries. Too, it should be remembered that in both periods much of the impulse to economic activity may be considered as derived from an anticipation of and a desire to prepare for war.

If we assume that his program was beneficial, and not restrictive, it can be said that, from Colbert's point of view, his program was an almost complete success. His purpose, it will be recalled, was to revive the establishments that had supposedly flourished in the time of Henry IV and to add new industries. On both counts, he had succeeded admirably.

The dolorous fortune of French industry in the last decade of the seventeenth century and in the first part of the next cannot be laid exclusively at Colbert's door. If industries were

[118] *Ibid.*, pp. 314, 155-156; Boissonade. *Colbert*, pp. 176-177, 95-97, 103, 152-154.

over-regulated, it was probably the successors of Colbert who were responsible. It should not be forgotten, when this frequently mentioned point is made, that regulation was an old guild characteristic which Colbert possibly relaxed. Other factors to be considered are the effect of the revocation of the Edict of Nantes,[119] the strict adherence by administrators without Colbert's suppleness to the outlines of a program which they did not understand, the ruinous effects of the wars, particularly that of the Spanish Succession, the increasing pressure of royal fiscality, and the apparent inability of the new administrators to recognize, as Colbert usually did, that his program was a means and not an end.

The criticism, sometimes advanced, that Colbert overstressed luxury production is made with an eye to England's industrial triumph on the basis of production for the commonalty.[120] It should be recalled that the most important commerce, certainly at the international level, was still in the seventeenth century a luxury commerce. Colbert can hardly be blamed for his failure to anticipate the industrial revolution. Moreover, as J. U. Nef has made clear, England's choice of cheaper production was dictated as much by nature as wisdom.[121] Finally, it may be added that Colbert had a significant role in making France the luxury capital of the world, a position which she has continued to maintain until recent times.

In conclusion it should be remarked that Colbert's administration of the economy was guided by principles with which the majority of the intellectuals of his day would have agreed. His system was not tyranically imposed so much as ardently solicited. Since the days of Bodin one economic writer after another had called for the intervention of the state to impose order on a chaotic community of entrepreneurs and workers. The scientist and philosopher had created the vision of a mechanical universe in which all natural phenomena were related by mathematical laws. The universe of the scientist had an analogous expression in the economic mechanism which, to

[119] Ch. Weiss, *Histoire des refugies Protestants de France* (2 vols., Paris, 1853), I, 104-122.
[120] On this point see Heckscher's *Mercantilism*, I, 189-203; 221-223.
[121] J. U. Nef, *The rise of the British coal industry* (2 vols., London, 1932), I, 224-261, *passim*.

Colbert, was the world of trade, commerce and power. It was the mission of the state to restore order in the economy. As the administrator chosen for this task, Colbert reasonably could no more ignore the economic laws which governed economic relationships than the true philosopher the laws which governed nature. In the past the failure to discipline production by law had, he believed, left industry and commerce subject to the anarchical guidance of egotistical and selfish individuals. Whatever the estimate of Colbert's relative success, it must be granted that his economic convictions left him little honest choice but his adopted program.

CHAPTER VIII

THE MECHANICS OF THE REGIME OF ORDER

THE MILITARY, THE LAW, TECHNOLOGICAL EDUCATION, AND THE ACADEMY OF SCIENCES

In the seventeenth century the desire for a system of order was evident in the most diverse activities. We have seen the effect of such an ideal on the development of political philosophy. It was explicit in the creation of a system of inquiry in the government of Louis XIV, in the development of administrative archives, in the attempt to reform the finances of the state, in the increasing reliance on statistics, and in the economic administration of Colbert. Even the area of letters was dominated by the influence of the formula of order. Malherbe carried forward a revolution in the French language in applying regulations and principles to it to attain purity. Those qualities which he admired above others were clarity, exactitude, and simplicity. They were the same attributes which gave to mathematics its status in the method of Descartes. Malherbe, writes Brunot, in his *Histoire de la langue française*, initiated " the reign of grammar, a reign which has been in France, more tyrannical and longer than in any other country." [1] Defending

----

[1] F. Brunot, *Histoire de la langue française des origines à 1900* (10 vols., Paris, 1905-1943), III, part i, 2-8. Boileau in his " L'Art Poetique " expressed a similar sentiment concerning Malherbe:

> Prenz mieux votre ton. Soyez simple avec art,
>   Sublime sans orgueil, agreable sans fard.
> N'offrez rein au lecteur que ce qui puet lui plaire.
>   Ayez pour la cadence une oreille sévère:
> Que toujours dans vos vers le sens coupant les mots
>   Suspende l'hémistiche, en marque le repos.
> . . . .
> Enfin Malherbe vint; et, le premier en France
> Fit sentir dans les vers une juste cadence;
> D'un mot mis en sa place enseigna le pouvoir,
>   Et reduisit la muse aux règles du devoir.

B. Willey in his *The seventeenth century background* gives an extensive and thoughtful treatment of the Cartesian influence on seventeenth-century literature in England, pp. 86-92, 205-295.

the French against the Latin language, La Laboureur, in 1669, cited its cleanness, clarity, and penetration which enabled the user to express his concepts promptly and exactly. Synonyms he considered as marks of poverty rather than richness in a language as they only led to confusion and useless duplication.[2] Even a defender of the Greek and Latin, one Michel Belot, justified the superiority of the older tongues on the grounds that "they express better the secrets of the sciences than French."[3]

Colbert, though himself no stylist, was extremely conscious of the benefits of a mathematical language. For instance, a subordinate was drafting a *règlement de police*. Colbert underlined the need of precision in its wording, " as this is a work of very great consequence, I believe we cannot revise it too much in order to render it as perfect as can be." He submitted a number of corrections to be applied. Thus the term *chòse* which was much repeated should be erased throughout as too indefinite and "above all it is important that you apply yourself to diction, to make it correct, intelligible, to weigh all words, in order to eliminate entirely the useless ones, and to suppress all superfluities and repetitions."[4] The Minister frequently reprimanded his son Seignelay for grammatical errors.[5] In a note Colbert received from him in which he had used the phrase *"pour faire scavoir les ordres de Sa Majesté"* he wrote on the margins: *" Cela ne se dit point en français. On dit: ' donner des ordres et faire scavoir les intentions.' "*[6] An intendant of fortifications was ordered to instruct himself in how to form the style of his letters in such a way as to render an

[2] La Laboureur, *Avantages de la langue française sur la langue latine* (Paris, 1669), pp. 116-125.

[3] M. Belot, *Apologie de la langue latine contre le preface de monsieur de La Chambre, en son livre des nouvelles conjectures de la digestion* (Paris, 1637), p. 5. It was a central position of de La Chambre that the contrary was the case.

[4] Colbert to Colbert de Terron, Intendant at Rochefort, March 4, 1671, Colbert, *Lettres*, III, part i, p. 345. Louis XIV, in his *conseil de trois*, July 15, 1661, complained of the prolixity of the reports of his diplomatic agent in Holland, M. de Thou. De Brienne, the secretary of the *conseil*, was ordered to inform him as a " friend " to keep his letters free of " little affairs or useless circumstances which do not deserve to occupy H. M. an instant." J. de Boislisle, *Conseil de 1661*, II, 181; 187 note.

[5] For instance, Colbert to Seignelay, April 17, 1672, Colbert, *Lettres*, III, part ii, 80.

[6] *Ibid.*, note.

account " so neat and clear " that even those who had no knowledge of his work could understand it.[7] While he was pushing the project of creating a usable theory of ship construction Colbert urged those working on it to collect naval terms carefully inasmuch as a uniformity of language would facilitate the formulation of the theory.[8]

The effort to reorganize the incoherent fabric of the state along more rational lines may be further illustrated by a glance at the changes introduced into the operation of the army and navy and even into the operation of law. In these fields too, science, or the rational spirit of science, directly or indirectly worked to effect profound alterations.

During the years of Colbert's ministry the department of the army was directed, in the main, by the combined talents of the King, Michel Le Tellier, and his son Louvois. But, even in this field, the role of the ubiquitous finance minister was not inconsiderable. The supervision of fortifications, for instance, was mostly divided between Louvois and Colbert while the necessity of providing funds made the latter a frequently unhappy partner in councils of grand strategy.

The army of Louis XIV has been called the first " great national army of Europe."[9] It was notable not only for its numerical strength, far exceeding in this regard any previous armies of France or of any other European country since the days of Rome, but also for its organization, discipline, and equipment.[10]

[7] Colbert to M. De Linières, Intendant of Fortification, June 16, 1674, *ibid.*, V, 113.

[8] Memoir to Seignelay (1673), *ibid.*, III, part ii, 140.

[9] H. Guerlac, " Vauban; the impact of science on war," in *Makers of Modern strategy, military thought from Machiavelli to Hitler,* edited by E. M. Earle (Princeton, 1943), pp. 26-48: As the title indicates, this essay deals specifically with the scientific aspects of the development of Louis' army. The main emphasis is directed towards showing the more direct effect of science upon military affairs with the work of Vauban and the developments in the science of fortifications, their defense and methods of attack, as the prime illustrations. I have relied heavily on Guerlac's essay in this section and also on the following works: C. Rousset, *Histoire de Louvois et de son administration politique et militaire* (4 vols., Paris, 1862-1864) ; Daniel's *Historie de la milice françoise*; A. M. Mallet, *Les travaux de Mars ou l'art de la guerre* (3 vols., Paris, 1691 ed.) ; E. Boutaric, *Institutions militaires de la France avant les armées permanents* (3 vols., Paris, 1863).

[10] This expansion was a reflection, primarily, of the growing importance of the infantry due, in turn, to the increase in the efficiency of firearms and the emphasis

The French army under Louis had its organization definitively fixed, and any other modifications up to the end of the *ancien régime* were on details and to provide for minor administrative improvements which did not alter its general structure.[11] Those who were the chief movers in the program of army reform were significantly the civilian, bourgeois administrators Michel Le Tellier and Louvois.[12] Even during the lifetime of Mazarin, Le Tellier had commenced his program of reorganization which was, in general, carried to completion before the death of Louvois in 1691. It was characterized by a sustained effort to apply the prescriptions of order and system to the management of the war machine.[13]

Almost from the moment the King assumed the personal direction of his government the subject of army reform was the point of a series of resolutions and *règlements* which issued from his *conseil de trois*. A number of ordinances between 1650 and 1660, doubtlessly inspired by Le Tellier, had attempted to regulate the precedence and attributes of rank in the armies, but the question was still strongly agitated in the early period of Louis' personal rule. Thus in the council meeting of June 1, 1661, the King was called upon to order a certain lieutenant of a Piedmont regiment to recognize the superiority of the captains of the regiment of La Ferté-Sonneterre although the latter regiment was junior. A few days later a similar situation between a lieutenant-colonel and captains of a senior regiment was decided in the same way; rank had its privilege and its superior authority.[14] An ordinance of the twenty-eighth of July 1661, clearly defining the hierarchy of all officers from lieutenant-colonel to ensign, markedly curtailed the anarchic conflicts which had been so common among the officers of differing

on seige warfare. In the Army of Charles VIII, infantry outnumbered the cavalry two to one. By the end of the seventeenth century the ratio was about five to one. Richelieu's military establishment attained to around 100,000 in 1635, twice as large as that of the late Valois kings. Louvois raised this to 400,000 for Louis XIV. Guerlac, " Vauban," pp. 26-27.

[11] Boutaric, *Institutions militaires*, III, 416-417.

[12] This is an important point made by Geurlac. To this bourgeois participation he attributes much of the technical and administrative improvements introduced into the army.

[13] See for a general account, Rousset, *Louvois*, I, 164-255.

[14] J. de Boislisle, *Conseil de 1661*, I, lxxxi; II, 4, 14, 42. Similarly the fifth of July, pp. 149-150, 154.

regiments or those endowed with differing degrees of nobility.[15]
This decree was occasioned partly by the death of the last Duke
of Epernon to whose family had belonged, since Henry III,
the office of *colonel général de l'infanterie,* a powerful position
which gave them extensive control over the infantry. The ordinance suppressed the office.[16] A strict hierarchy of command
gradually replaced the system of loose discipline which had
characterized the royal forces made up of semi-independent
companies led by their recruiting captains. A temporary rank
of *maréchal général des armées,* first held by Turenne, in 1660,
unified the command at the top and placed it directly under the
King. The highest permanent rank was set at marshal and in
set steps descended to the ensign.[17] The authority to command
obedience was definitely fixed by rank and, within the same
rank, by seniority. In the time of Richelieu, and even in the
early days of Louis' reign, marshals in the same army had
rotated in their command, but seniority soon became the established criteria.[18] The alteration which these reforms produced
in the position which the higher nobility had traditionally enjoyed in the armies was at the bottom of Saint-Simon's bitter-
ness towards the regime of the " roturier " Louvois.[19]

Other innovations were made in the interest of system and
order. The wearing of uniforms, although not universally required, was stressed and uniforms were widely adopted. The
purpose was to create an *ésprit de corps,* to aid in the identification of divisions, and to help prevent desertions.[20] Standardiza-

[15] *Ibid.,* I, lxxxii-lxxxiii; Daniel, *Histoire de la milice,* II, 3-88. This was but
the first of a series.

[16] J. de Boislisle *Conseil de 1661,* II, 244-246, 251-252.

[17] Thus, in order: Marshal (in command of an army), lieutenant-general (in
command of a division), *maréchal de Camp* (junior to the lt.-genrl. but in
command of a division; in a battle he might command the left wing of the army
while the lt.-genrl. commanded the right wing), brigadier (in command of a
brigade), *mestre* (of infantry or dragoons), lieutenant-colonel (command of a
batallion), captains (company), lieutenant (2nd in the company), sous-lieuten-
ant (3rd), cornette (3rd or 4th in company of cavalry), ensign (3rd or 4th in
company of infantry). Daniel, *Histoire de la milice,* II, 3-66; see also A. M.
Mallet, *Travaux de Mars,* III, 8-21 for various petty officers.

[18] A notable exception was the voluntary service of the senior Marshal de
Boufflers under Marshal de Villars at Malplaquet. Daniel, II, 17, 21.

[19] This change can easily be exaggerated. The nobility were still considered
the only really fit officer material.

[20] Rousset, I, 185-188.

tion was applied in the matter of arms and rigorously maintained. The length of swords and pikes and the calibre of muskets and cannon were standardized.[21] During much of the last half of the century there was a struggle between those favoring the musket and those advocating the adoption of the flint-lock. The latter weapon finally replaced the former, and after Vauban invented the first satisfactory bayonet, permitting the gun to be fired with the blade attached, the pike likewise soon disappeared.[22]

Wages for rates and ranks were for the first time made invariable.[23] A system of permanent arsenals, warehouses, and foundries distributed through the kingdom assured a better and more readily supplied army than Europe had yet seen. Barracks were especially constructed, particularly in frontier regions, to limit the quartering of soldiers on the population. Hospitals, including the magnificent Hôtel des Invalides at Paris, ambulance service, and a pension system were provided for the care of wounded and diseased.[24] The constitution of the engineer corps as a separate body was a goal which Vauban continuously strived to reach. Apparently he met with only a qualified success although the engineers were increasingly recognized as specialists.[25]

Such reforms in the armies under the guidance of Louvois were carried out and enforced primarily by civilian agents. *Intendants d'armée* and their subordinates, the *commissaires,* already existed. Their duties were to see to the payment of troops and in general to supervise logistics. Like Colbert in his relation with the intendants of the provinces, Louvois bound these officials to him by the most jealous supervision and the requirement of a regularized and prodigious correspondence. They were rigidly confined in their activities to the business aspect of the army, and the least attempt on their part to interfere in the purely military details invariably drew a sharp rebuke

[21] *Ibid.,* pp. 188-194, A. M. Mallet, III, 32, 38; Cole, *Colbert,* II, 336-341; Daniel, I, 462.

[22] Guerlac, " Vauban," p. 38; Rousset, I, 194; Daniel, I, 436, 466-467 see illustrations; Boutaric, *Institutions militaires,* III, 422.

[23] Rousset, I, 195-196.

[24] *Ibid.,* pp. 249-255; Boutaric, III, 425, 388-390; Guerlac, " Vauban," pp. 38-39.

[25] *Ibid.,* p. 38; Rousset, I, 241-247; Daniel, II, 89-91.

from the War Minister. " Around the person of the minister,"
writes H. Guerlac, " grew up a genuine departmentalized government office complete with archives. By 1680 five separate
bureaus had been created, each headed by a *chef de bureau*
provided with numerous assistants. It was to these bureaus
that the intendants, the commissioners, even commanding officers, sent their reports and their requests. From them em-
anated the orders of the ministers of war. . . . " [26]

The best remembered agents of the central administration
were the inspectors-general. Instituted in 1668 by Louvois these
were highly placed military officers chosen to carry out inspections, at least once a month, in the regiments of infantry,
cavalry, and artillery. They reviewed troops, inspected equipment and personnel, recommended changes, enforced discipline
and reported on the merit of officers for promotion purposes.
They were the direct agents of the Minister of War and were
responsible for correcting many abuses and restricting the
powers of the colonels. Because of their great authority they
were often transferred. Their effectiveness and the weight of
their disciplinary authority has been perpetuated in popular
memory by the term " Martinet " the name of the colonel of a
crack regiment who was the first inspector for the infantry.[27]

Louvois did not completely transform the French army into
a modern war machine but by the time of his death it was well
on the road to becoming one. A new order and system was
expressed in the improvements of discipline, logistics, housing,
materiel and administration. The army was no longer a disorganized military force dominated by its captains and *mestres
de camp* but a defined group governed by a hierarchy of officers
with defined powers and responsibilities. The emphasis on
siege warfare which characterized so much of the military conduct during the reigns of Louis XIV and his eighteenth-
century successors has been cited as a further reflection of the
application of the economy of the rational spirit to military
action. The essence of the theories of Vauban, the foremost
exponent of this type of warfare, lies in attaining the desired
goal by the shortest route or by the most reasonable and least
bloody manner. Aside from the technical aspect, relating to
the principles of mathematics and engineering involved in the

[26] Guerlac, " Vauban," p. 28; Rousset, I, 66-71; Boutaric, III, 424.
[27] *Ibid.*, p. 418; Rousset, I, 205-210; Daniel, II, 85-88.

construction of fortresses and of the systems of attack, siege warfare, as envisaged by Vauban and his disciples, depended for success on the most careful and long-range calculations. Such planning extended in delineated steps from the initial strategical designs, formulated in the King's council, to the ultimate tactical achievement of victory. No detail of the problems of logistics, personnel or hazard could be overlooked. Ideally, all exigencies should be anticipated and provided against. Writing specifically of the eighteenth century, but citing Vauban as the prime exponent, H. Nickerson in his book, *The Armed Horde,* notes the suitability of this discipline to the mind of the time. This mind, "nourished upon mathematics and in love with precision, was delighted with the regularity of its method of siege work, by which the resistance of a fortress or even of each unit of one could be calculated in advance to a day." [28]

In 1690 the envoy from Brandenburg, Spanheim, described the advantages of the French army which arose from the reforms of Louvois. Among others he counted the *règlements* and customs introduced into the training of officers and men and the efficiency of troops which was derived " from the great and good order there is in France for the maintenance and subsistence of the troops, by the regularity of payments . . . by the erection of storehouses, by the provision of victuals, as of regulation bread, by provision for the sick and wounded, or finally by the distribution of forage. . . . " He emphasized the rôle of the intendants and commissioners and other civilian administrators on whom Louvois so much depended and towards whom he was so severe in expectations. Louvois himself was pictured as being " particularly aided by the great order which he applies in the review and expedition of the affairs of his department." This "order," " regularity," and " exactitude " were utilized by the Minister to give himself the time to neglect nothing. The purpose of his organization was to see that nothing escaped attention, nothing was neglected and that all might be executed with proper secrecy and efficiency.[29]

[28] H. Nickerson, *The armed horde, 1793-1939* (New York, 1940), pp. 43-45. Vauban did not set forth his principles in writing until near the end of his life. The most convenient expression of them appeared in his treatises: *De l'attaque et da la defense des places (ca.* 1703-1707).

[29] Spanheim, *Relation de la cour de France,* pp. 314, 192-194. Richelieu

Turning to an appraisal of the French naval arm, Spanheim found it administered with similar " application," " vigilance " and " good order." [30] This navy which Spanheim admired in 1690 had scarcely existed when Louis XIV took over the control of the state in 1661. It was largely the creation of Colbert. When the latter had come to power it had comprised only eighteen warships. All except one of these would have been classified by him as third or fourth rank. In 1677, the fleet numbered one hundred and sixteen warships exclusive of twenty-eight light frigates making a total of one hundred and forty-four.[31] The annual state expenditures on the navy increased from about three hundred thousand *livres*,[32] near the end of Mazarin's regime, to around thirteen and a half million *livres* in 1670; with an average annual of nearly ten million *livres* for the period of Colbert's ministry.[33] Richelieu had initiated a program of navy construction with the idea of building a fleet of forty good ships, well-manned and gunned, for the Atlantic, and thirty galleys, to balance the power of Spain, in the Mediterranean. Although he made a strong beginning towards realizing the goal, his death and the distractions of the Fronde terminated the project.[34]

The department of the navy was the special pride of Colbert and to its management he carried all the force of his ability. He was certainly more free to exercise his personal wishes in this direction than were the Le Telliers in the army, for the King never evidenced any strong predilection for the governance of marine affairs. On the contrary, all the efforts which Colbert made to inveigle Louis into visiting the shipyards, and these efforts were very considerable, were without avail until

considered the prompt payment of soldiers a necessity but " absolutely impossible in wars which require extraordinary efforts," *Testament politique*, II, 104.

[30] Spanheim, p. 304.

[31] Colbert, *Lettres*, III, part ii, 699, 682-692. These figures do not include 4 cargo ships and 8 fire ships in the fleet of 1661 or the 24 cargo ships, 17 fire ships and 14 long barks in the fleet of 1677.

[32] The last year for which I can find figures on the expenditures under Mazarin is 1656. See Mallet, *Comptes rendus*, p. 247.

[33] *Ibid.*, pp. 352-357; to supplement this statistical picture see La Ronciere, *Histoire de la marine*, V, 306-440 *passim*; Daniel, II, 679-689; Clement's " Introduction " to Colbert, *Lettres*, III, part i, pp. i-lxviii.

[34] Richelieu, *Testament politique*, II, 116, 117-118; Colbert, *Lettres*, II, part i, p. iii; La Ronciere, V, 325.

1680.[35] Even this inspection by the King arose from his accidental presence at the port of Dunkerque.[36]

One of the more interesting experiments conducted by Colbert in the administration of the navy was that connected with the improvement in the art of shipbuilding. Not only does it illustrate the growing importance of rational methods over the empirical methods of the past, as applied to this particular area of the government, but it reveals the naïve faith placed in a formula by many men of seventeenth-century France. In 1671 councils of construction were established in the arsenal ports of the kingdom, the purpose of which was to serve as colleges of experts to collect, test, and systematize all the information that could be gathered dealing with the construction of ships, foreign or French.[37] Meeting frequently at specified times, membership in the councils was automatically granted to the highest officers of the naval hierarchy, extending from the admiral to the captains of the ports.[38] Avoiding confusing numbers, it was permissible to summon to its conferences, for expert advice, captains and *commissaires de marine*. In their sessions they studied the measurements, proportions and moulds of Dutch, English, and French ships and were empowered to visit and examine all ships in the ports. From the officers aboard they inquired of all the good or bad points that might

[35] Louis XIV, while he did not have an active aversion to the navy and naval warfare, was nevertheless little impressed with its utility and it seems to have required a constant struggle on the part of Colbert to keep the King sufficiently interested to support his naval program. The memoirs of the glory-loving Louis may suggest the cause of this indifference. He notes that many nobles interceded with him for the privilege of proving their valor in the armies but not in war at sea. He attributed this to the notion that individual prowess in land warfare is displayed " more advantagesously than in maritime war in which the most valiant have practically no opportunity to distinguish themselves from the most feeble." Longnon, *Mémoires de Louis XIV*, p. 123.

[36] La Ronciere, pp. 329-336. In a letter to Colbert on this occasion Louis described his inspection and voiced his admiration. " The works of the navy are surprising and I did not imagine things as they are; in short, I am very satisfied." Gaxotte, *Lettres de Louis XIV*, pp. 73-74.

[37] Or more precisely, as Colbert explained the project to one Intendant, to: " make his [the King's] ships better than those of the English and Dutch, if possible." Colbert to Colbert de Terron, Intendant at Rochefort, March 5, 1671, *Lettres*, III, part i, 346.

[38] These officers were the admiral, vice-admirals, lieutenant-generals, intendants of the Navy, commissioners-general, squadron chiefs, port captains, and the *contrôleur* of the port, as secretary.

aid them to judge good or bad construction. These judgments were registered. "On these facts and on the experience of officers" they drew up "in concert" estimates of measurements and proportions proper for ships avoiding faults found in those previously built. Each year, when the King's orders for ship construction were received at the yards, master carpenters drew up plans and submitted them to the councils. There they would be criticized, corrected, and signed and a copy of the findings was given to the master carpenter to execute. After ships were constructed a "good" carpenter was placed aboard to record and report deficiencies to the council. The captains of these ships likewise submitted reports on their operation. Thus the councils were continually correcting.[39]

Scarcely had the councils of construction been decreed before Colbert was writing one intendant that: "His Majesty is astonished that . . . captains alter whatever seems proper to them in their ships . . . since . . . that is absolutely prohibited." It was to remedy this "disorder" that the councils had been created. All changes must be made only on the authorization of the councils and if at any future time any captains chose to disregard these prohibitions the King would "punish him in such fashion that no other will repeat it."[40]

Colbert's intention was to enable his technicians and specialists, by disciplined cooperation, to formulate workable theories of ships' construction which would have practical applicability in rendering the French fleet superior to all others. The disorderly mass of carpenter's mysteries was to be translated into a workable science. Such an idea was not without precedence. In the sixteenth century the humanist mathematician Vettor

---

[39] Only the notation of the registration of the "Règlement sur la tenu du conseil de construction," March 22, 1671, is given in Isambert, XVIII, 432; however, a description of their operation is given in a "Mémoire sur le project d'etablissement d'un conseil des constructions" written by Colbert but undated. This is printed in the "Appendice" of Colbert, *Lettres*, III, part ii, 674-675; see also Daniel, II, 682. The work of the councils of construction and the *règlements* on constructions resulting therefrom were matters of concern to the British admiralty who assumed that the French had discovered the building secrets of the English and Dutch and who desired to check their own practices against the French to avail themselves of any improvements made. See Samuel Pepys, *Naval minutes*, p. 353.

[40] Colbert to M. Matharel, intendant of marine at Toulon, June 11, 1671, Colbert, *Lettres*, V, 312. The prohibition did not apply to changes essential to navigation.

Fausto had won fame in Venice by his attempt to link science to the mechanical art of the shipwright, but his influence was limited.[41] In England around 1600, the lines of ships had begun to vary according to the use proposed. Formerly, for instance, there had been no distinction made between merchantmen and men-of-war except that the latter were possibly strengthened.[42] As early as 1604 a certain captain George Waymouth reprimanded the contemporary shipbuilders " because they trust rather to their judgment than their art, and to their eyes rather than to their scale and compass." [43] But there was by no means any agreement in the England of the seventeenth century that the craft of the shipwright could be elevated to the status of a science. Samuel Pepys, for example, was apparently quite undecided on this point.[44] Conversations with the two leading English shipbuilders of his day, Sir Anthony Deane and Sir Phineas Pett, seemed to confirm the notion that there could be no certain rules applied to the business.[45] Colbert was not unaware of the difficulties but he, nevertheless, believed that positive formulae for construction

[41] F. C. Lane, *Venetian ships and shipbuilders of the Renaissance* (Baltimore, 1934), pp. 54, 64-71.

[42] A paper of William Borough, comptroller of the navy, set forth three orders:

(1) Shortest, broadest, deepest order for merchant ships, most profitable	Keel = 2 x beam amidships Draft in hold = 1/2 beam
(2) Mean best proportion for merchandise, also serviceable for all purposes	Keel = 2 or 2-1/4 x beam Draft in hold = 11/24 of beam
(3) Largest order for galleons or ships of war made for advantageous sailing.	Keel = 3 x beam Draft in hold = 2/5 beam

M. Oppenheim, *A history of the administration of the royal navy and of merchant shipping in relation to the navy* (New York, 1896), I, 126.

[43] Quotation from the Jewell of the arts (1604) in *ibid.*, p. 186.

[44] In his *Naval minutes* is met the following query: " Is there anything in the whole art of building or guiding of ships that was ever found out by much learning, but all by the plainest and most unlearned builders and boatswains? And therefore should anybody think of there being any great mystery therein, or anything required but trial and experience common to all nations, even the most barbarous, viz. not as to what does relate to the science of Astronomy, but purely to the structure of a ship and contrivance of its sails, masts, yards, rudders, anchors, boats, oars, sounding-lead and line, etc.," p. 158.

[45] Thus: " Sir A[nthony] D[eane] says that no one shape of a ship can be in general said to be the best; for every distinct use requires a different shape, and the skill lies only in building best for the particular use designed "; Sir Phineas Pett declared that " they are under no more certain rules at this day touching the length of their masts than the place of settling them "; also that no ship could be truly built according to plans. *Ibid.*, pp. 9-10, 14, 16.

17

could be devised which would enable the French to build ships which were very near to perfection. He appears to have worked constantly towards this goal after 1671. In 1673 a *règlement* was issued which established precise dimensions for the ships of the five rates in the French navy.[46] This, however, he did not consider at all final. By September of 1678 he felt he had had sufficient experience to define his thoughts on the matter and to initiate the steps necessary for the preparation of a master theory. He explained his ideas to the *intendant de marine* at Toulon:

My intention is then to work towards making a theory on the subject of ship construction, that is to say, to establish such exact measures and proportions of all the members, and parts of a ship of each of the five rates . . . that . . . in building a ship following these measures and proportions, which would have been determined, this ship would be . . . as perfect as could possibly be made, and would excel . . . all foreign ships. . . .

I know that this is not a very easy thing to do, and even that it is necessary that so many different things agree and be of an exact quality that it can often happen that two ships built on the same proportions and with all possible care, one is found to be light and the other heavy; which is caused by the quality of the wood, of their seasoning, of their different weight . . . and from an infinity of other circumstances . . . but I know well also that, while all these things may be very difficult, they are not always impossible, and that, provided you wish it well and that you give to it all the needful application, it is nearly impossible that one should not arrive at a solution, if not at the last perfection, at least closely approaching it. . . .

The councils of construction were to convene and study ships of each of the five rates to the smallest detail to effect the realization of the plan.[47] Standardized large-scale models were

---

[46] Isambert, XIX, 118; Pepys *Naval minutes,* 353. The ship list of 1677 gives the following information:

1st rate,	12 ships,	2400 to 1400 tons,	120 to 80 guns.
2d rate,	26 ships,	1500 to 1000 tons,	78 to 60 guns.
3d rate,	30 ships,	1000 to 700 tons,	60 to 48 guns.
4th rate,⎱ 5th rate,⎰	48 ships,	750 to 250 tons,	48 to 22 guns.

Besides these there were:

Light frigates,	28 ships,	350 to 20 tons,	28 to 2 guns.
Fire ships,	17 ships,	300 to 90 tons,	24 to 4 guns.
Auxiliaries,	24 ships,	600 to 60 tons,	20 to 2 guns.
Long barks,	13 ships,	50 to 20 tons,	6 to 2 guns.

" Appendice," Colbert, *Lettres,* II, part ii, 682-692; see Daniel, II, 720-721.

[47] Colbert to M. Arnoul Fils, *intendant de marine* at Toulon, September 12,

made of ships of each rate and a fleet of these was floated in the canal at Versailles for the instruction of the King.[48] Replicas were transported to the various ports for the education and guidance of the shipwrights and other naval personnel.[49] An *ordonnance* of 1683 made it mandatory to construct and turn over to the port *contrôleur* scale models of all ships built.[50]

This period was marked by the beginning of the publication in France of a series of what are possibly the first formal works of modern times which attempted to link science to ship construction.[51] The Jesuit father Pardies in his treatise *La statique ou la science des forces mouvantes* (1673) proclaimed the utility of the theories of mechanics in architecture and other arts. The empirical skill of the worker would be necessarily fortified by a knowledge of mechanical laws. As an example he cited the advantages of studying the laws governing the motions of a ship's hull through water. From these considerations one might solve such structural problems as the proper rake of masts or the best shape of the hull.[52] Samuel Pepys

1678, Colbert, *Lettres*, III, part i (addition), 125-126. At the same time Colbert wrote Du Quesne, as the most able naval authority in France, to send him memoirs on the subject. Colbert to Du Quesne, September 13, 1678, *ibid.*, p. 127.

[48] These models were very large so that it was necessary to transport them disassembled to Versailles and on especially designed trucks. Thus September 1680 Colbert wrote the Chevalier De Tourville, later to become famous as the victor of Beachy Head and tactician at La Hogue, to send a certain new model to the palace which the Chevalier was to accompany. With the King and other officers he would then witness and explain its construction and all would advise on its merits in order to regulate " once for all, the proportions of all the members of each ship." The Chevalier was reminded that it would also provide a favorable opportunity for making his court to the King. *Ibid.*, p. 198; see also Colbert to the sieur Brodart, *intendant des galères* at Marseille, May 15, 1681, *ibid.*, p. 208; La Roncière, V, 332-334.

[49] *Ibid.* In the Tourville letter referred to above, Colbert informed him that the King approved his plan of having large-scale models of ships of all rates built and sent to the ports, " But, concerning the design of the ship of the second class which you have sent, His Majesty cannot agree to having it sent to Brest, until you have examined with the officers and carpenters of the port of Rochefort the objections made to its proportions by the sieur de Sueil, the memoir on which you will find attached."

[50] Isambert, XIX, 434. The same requirement began to be applied in the English yards in this period.

[51] See J. Fincham's " Dissertation on the application of mathematical science to the art of naval construction," in *A history of naval architecture* (London, 1851), pp. ix-lxxxiv, particularly pp. x-xii. See also F. L. Robertson, *The evolution of naval armament* (London, 1921), pp. 34-40.

[52] I. G. Pardies, *La statique ou la science des forces mouvantes* (first ed. 1673),

deplored the backwardness of England where, in contrast to the French, no one had produced, as they, a theory of structure for ships like a "philosopher" or "mathematician."[53] The book to which he specifically referred was the work of a protegé of Colbert, Bernard Renau's *La théories de la manoeuvre des vaisseaux* (1689). Renau's book, partly influenced by Pardies, caused some controversy among scientists, among them Huygens and Bernoulli, the latter of whom published a *Nouvelle théorie* in 1714.[54]

In 1697 the Jesuit Pierre Hotte, professor of mathematics in the royal seminary at Toulon, published his *Théorie de la construction des vaisseaux*. This influential work took notice of the efforts that had been made by the French to bring the art of shipbuilding to "perfection." Nevertheless he considered the art still the most "undetermined and most imperfect of all arts." "Chance has frequently so great a share in the construction, that we see ships built with the greatest exactness and application often prove the worst; and those which are built without any strict regard to rules answer the purpose much better." In short the attempt to find a theory he considered a failure. His solution was to push the study of the theory of bodies in motion through a medium by the aid of geometry and physics. As far as he was concerned the French industry was still too empirical, still guided by chance rather than by necessary principles.[55]

in *Oeuvres de mathématiques* (5th ed., Amsterdam, 1725), pp. 238-247. In 1677 appeared the *L'architecture navale, contenant la manière des construire les navires, galères et chaloupes et la definition de plusiers autres espécs de vaisseaux* (Paris). The author, the sieur Dassié, depicted his work as the first formal treatment of naval architecture. It was a general guide to the construction of ships of the several classes making up the French fleet and gave detailed proportions for each major section with the keel lengths as the basic unit. Although he opens with an exposition on geometry, there is actually little, if any, distinguishable attempt to apply the science to shipbuilding. However he admits the need for mathematical savants and members of the Royal Academy of Sciences to seek the means of elevating the art to perfection. Pp. 3-7 and *passim*. See also Fincham, *A history of naval architecture,* p. xi.

[53] Samuel Pepys, *Naval minutes,* p. 390.

[54] Fincham, pp. xiii-xv; see B. Renau d'Elicagaray, *De le théorie de la manoeuvre des vaisseaux* (Paris, 1689), pp. iv-v.

[55] P. Hoste (sometime Hoche or Hotte), *Naval evolutions or a system of sea-discipline; extracted from the celebrated treatise of P. L'Hoste . . . to which are added an abstract of the theory of ship-building . . . ,* translated by C. O'Bryen (London, 1762), pp. 55-62; see also Fincham, pp. xv-xix. Fincham

Colbert's efforts to improve ship construction illustrate the practical meeting of two approaches applied by seventeenth-century scientists to the solution of difficulties.   One was the inductive process, most commonly associated with the academies, and, the other, the deductive or mathematical approach. The first was the guiding method in his councils of construction. There the empirical wisdom of diverse master-carpenters, seamen and soldiers was, by planned cooperation, collected together, sifted, experimented upon, and judged, and general laws were induced to replace the individual practices in the arsenals.   On the other hand, the sponsorship of Renau and others, incidentally in cooperation with the *Académie des Sciences,* expressed the desire to deduce general rules from physical or mechanical principles assumed.   It is unnecessary within the scope of this inquiry to estimate, if such were possible, the effect of Colbert's attempt to govern ship construction by theory or rules of science.   However it is fair to observe that the French ship of the line began to enjoy about this time its tremendous prestige abroad.   French ships of war were conceded to be superior for their sailing qualities by most English builders in the late seventeenth and throughout the eighteenth centuries.[56]

Shipbuilding was but one aspect of naval activity which Colbert strove to readjust and improve by the application of the symmetry of order.   Another example, on a much smaller scale, is provided by his attempt to regulate the quality and quantity of victuals.   In 1669 he wrote to the *intendant de marine* at Toulon requesting to be sent a report on the exact quantity of victuals furnished daily to sailors, soldiers, and

speaks of this work as the first in which an attempt was made to bring ship construction under the " ruling power of mathematical science," an ambiguous phrase which possibly is contradictory since he also describes the previous works of Pardies and Renau.

[56] Fincham, pp. 62, 73, 120. See for instance Pepy's numerous references to the excellence of their construction and to the past disdain of their qualities, *Naval minutes, passim,* but particularly pp. 241-245. Even the naval policy of the United States was influenced by the reputation of the French for sound construction methods employed in their naval department. In November 1814 the Secretary of the Navy, William Jones, in a most important report to Congress which formed a basis for subsequent legislation for the reorganization of the Navy Department, suggested that: " Of the French Naval system, the department of construction is universally admitted to be the most perfect in existence, and is worthy of imitation." *American state papers, Naval affairs,* I, 321.

officers aboard a royal ship so that he could draw up a general treatise thereon if time permitted.[57] When the term of a contract with the general commissary of provision drew near a close in 1678 experiments were projected to determine the weight losses occasioned in the cooking of the various kinds of meat and to discover if the meat stipulated in the operating contract was sufficient for the subsistence of crews. The experiments were made and the tabulated results showed, at least to the satisfaction of Colbert, that sailors received a half as much again as they required and that galley slaves were overfed by a third. He was "astonished" that these surveys had revealed conditions and an area for economy which the intendants had failed to report.[58]

The increased discipline which Louvois obtained in the army by the regulation of rank and seniority in command was supplied in the navy by parallel measures which were rigorously enforced.[59] Not only was it necessary to define and order the proper relationships and prerogatives of officers but to supply similar definitions to guide the conduct of officers with men and of all personnel with reference to their obligations and rights in the general organization of the navy. Previous kings of France had done practically nothing in the way of providing naval regulations. By the time of the death of Colbert a large body of articles for the government of the navy had been created in the interest of order and uniformity.[60]

---

[57] Colbert to M. D'Infreville, *intendant de marine* at Toulon, Colbert, *Lettres*, III, part i, 100; see carefully itemized memoir touching this subject, pp. 486-488.

[58] Colbert to M. Arnoul Fils, *intendant de marine* at Toulon, September 7, 1678; to the sieur Brodart, *intendant de galeres* at Marseille, October 24, 1678, *ibid.* (addition), pp. 124-125; 136. Complaints over the inadequacy of provisions for the galley slaves led Colbert, four years later, to initiate investigations directed towards finding the means of improving their victuals without adding to the expense. Colbert to the sieur Brodart, October 21, 1682, *ibid.*, p. 244; in the " Appendice " of the *Lettres*, III, part ii, pp. 676-679, is printed a three year contract with a chandler, the daily amount and quality of foods of all kinds, for each classification of the crew membership, is meticulously specified. The contract is signed "Louis" and below "Colbert."

[59] Louis XIV in a letter to the Duke of Beaufort, December 8, 1665, emphasized the need of maintaining the authority and order of rank in the navy. He assured the Duke that he would protect superiors against subordinates even when they were in the wrong. (Grouvelle, *Oeuvres de Louis XIV*, V, 338-344). The major military ranks in the navy, in order, were: admiral of France, vice-admiral, lieutenant-general, squadron chief, captain, lieutenant, ensign. For a description of these and other offices see Daniel, II, 693-710, 710-712.

[60] These were such regulations as are familiar to any who has experience in

This was another important point in which Samuel Pepys conceded superior " well-governing " to the French as against the British navy [61] and another part of the program which Colbert set forth as the goal for the department. Among the maxims which he described to his son as expressing the desires of the King regarding the fleet he listed the wish that " all the navy be regulated by ordinances and regulations." [62]

The faith he had in the theory of orderliness was reflected in nearly everything to which he turned his hand. The building of large broad-side gunned ships by the English, Dutch, and French had resulted, in the period of Louis XIV, in a revolution in naval tactics. The traditional half-moon, head-on battle formation was supplanted by the system of opposing fleets in parallels in which the ships of the line relied on their superior endurance and fire power for victory. The supreme tactics were to double the line of the opposition and to maintain the advantage of the wind to assure maneuverability.[63] This new order seemed to Colbert to make it possible to draw up a set of regulations the study of which would make it possible for the crews to maneuver ships with the same concert and regularity of cavalry and infantry. Such a *règlement* would contain all the maneuvers proper to follow under the various conditions of combat.[64]

The administration of the navy was more than a matter of military regulation. It involved also the establishment and government of a great industrial plant for the building, repair, and maintenance of the fleet.[65] The small number of scattered

a modern navy: The police power of the commanding officer, regulations dealing with theft, insubordination, quarrels, desertion, asleep on the watch, absence from the post, blasphemy, legal testaments at sea, leave etc. See Isambert, XVIII, XIX, *passim* for notations, particularly XIX, 283-310; Daniel, II, 706-708, 715-719.

[61] " The body of all the rules and establishments of his navy printed together and delivered to the officers," Pepys, *Naval minutes,* p. 362; also p. 85.

[62] Colbert, instructions to Seignelay, September 24, 1671, Colbert *Lettres,* III, part ii, 45.

[63] Daniel, II, 734-746, Daniel admits, however, that on the latter point there was considerable disagreement as to which position to the wind was advantageous.

[64] Colbert to Du Quesne, September 13, 1678, Colbert *Lettres,* III, part i (addition), p. 127.

[65] See Boissonade, " Creation de l'industrie d'Etat des constructions navales pour la marine de guerre, Le systeme et l'effort de Colbert," Chapter VII of *Colbert,* pp. 107-121; La Roncière, V, 394-405.

ateliers, yards, magazines, and warehouses which had existed prior to the time of Colbert were vastly enlarged and centered in a new system of arsenal ports: Rochefort, Brest, La Havre, Dunkerque, and Toulon.[66] The talents of some of the foremost engineers and architects of France were enlisted in carrying forward a huge project to dredge roadsteads, erect breakwaters, and build fortifications, slips, ways, warehouses and administrative offices.[67] These places served as administrative bureaus, military stations, arsenals, factories, barracks, hospitals, schools, yards, and anchorages. Here were collected most of the officials of the naval bureaucracy, civil or military; intendants, commissioners, contractors, shipwrights, inspectors, port captains, engineers, pilots, teachers and all the various ranks of the naval hierarchy. In short, such establishments fulfilled the functions of the modern naval operating base combined with those of the navy yard and the headquarters of the commandant of the naval district.

Colbert began seriously to push his plans for the creation of these centers about 1670.[68] In 1674 his ideas on the control, police, and the definition of functions of officials of the ports were set forth in a *règlement pour la police générale des arsenaux de marine*.[69]

Each ship of the navy was assigned a home port at which was kept the extra supplies allotted to repair and equip it in case of damage or whenever its specified time for overhaul or alterations occurred. These supplies were segregated by type and ship, and records, in regulated tabular form, were, supposedly, carefully maintained as to the amounts and the expenditure. Colbert demanded such order in the books of the warehouses that he would always be able to discover whatever had been bought and consumed.[70] Periodic inventories were sent to him from the arsenals and he warned the inten-

---

[66] Marseille for the galley fleet.
[67] Clerville, Vauban, Renier, Blondel, Le Vau.
[68] See his "Mémoire sur le règlement a faire pour le police générale des arsenaux de marine," October 1670; "Mémoire sur tout ce qui s'observer pour former les magasins des arsenaux de marine du Roy," October 8, 1670; "Mémoire sur le règlement de police des ports et arsenaux," 1670; Colbert, *Lettres,* III, part i, 285-290; 290-297; III, part ii, appendice, pp. 667-668.
[69] *Ibid.;* Isambert, XIX, 150.
[70] Colbert, "Mémoire," *Lettres,* III, part i, 286-287; 290-297.

dants that he would maintain such a check and that it would be very difficult for discrepancies to escape his attention.[71]

By the standardization of parts and the regulation of proportions and by the assemblage of workers and classified materials at central depots, Colbert hoped to assure a quicker and more efficient repair of ships and to have material in such quantities that each ship could be twice provided therefrom.[72] Experiments were frequently conducted, at his insistence, on reducing the time of construction. In 1671 he thought the yards could be made equal to the task of building a ship in ten to twelve days.[73] A frigate was assembled at Brest, in 1679, in twenty-two and a half hours; a time which Colbert considered could be shortened.[74] At Marseille, in this year, before visiting dignitaries including the Marquis of Seignelay and the Duke of Vivonne, a galley was assembled by a force of eight hundred workmen, distinctly costumed according to their craft to avoid confusion, between the hours of 6:30 A.M. and 5 P.M. at which time the Marquis and the Duke boarded the completed ship and traveled to the Chateau d'If.[75] These displays of production efficiency were designed partly as pure spectacles which Colbert constantly hoped the King would condescend to witness. They were also advertisements of the new and superior efficiency which arose from the application of rational principles of administration to the navy.

[71] In a letter to M. Arnoul, *intendant de marine* at Toulon, September 3, 1674, he complains that he has discovered large discrepancies between the intendant's reports and his own records. (*Ibid.,* pp. 525-526). To the same, September 25, on the same subject: "I vow I do not know on what you can base this calculation . . ." (pp. 528-529). See the undated inventory of the stock of the warehouses of the arsenals in "Appendice," *ibid.,* III, part ii, 694-695. Among the 115 items specified are 420,197 pounds of service powder, 812,989 bullets *(ronds)*, 23,842 muskets, 4,469 cannons, 11,622 ells of cloth called "toiles assemblees," 1,504 barrels of liquid tar, 641 masts of 16 to 20 *palmes.*

[72] Speaking of the arsenals, "it is necessary that this equipment be in such abundance that there is enough to twice arm all galleys, to serve as a precaution against any accidents which may occur." Colbert to M. Arnoul, *intendant des galères* at Marseille, October 17, 1670, *ibid.,* III, part i, 298.

[73] Colbert to M. Matharel, *intendant de marine* at Toulon, January 2, 1671, *ibid.,* pp. 327-328.

[74] Colbert to the sieur Levasseur, *contrôleur de marine* at Brest, July 17, 1679, *ibid.* (addition), pp. 162-163.

[75] Described in the *Gazette de France* of October 28, 1679, No. 101, p. 596.

II

A more subtle evidence of the impact of the spirit of the new rationalism on government is to be found in the movement to reorganize the law. In almost every field of its operation the regime of Louis XIV, after 1661, opposed itself explicitly to the unreasoning disorder which it found, or presumed to find, in the conduct of state affairs in the past. In this sense the government was expressing the mood of the mathematical rationalism which was dominant in the philosophy of Descartes. The concept of the state as an orderly machine, so popular in seventeenth-century political theory, was but one reflection of these mechanical notions. Such ideas permeated the maxims of order and efficiency which were proposed by administrators as fundamental guides to policy. In no area was the disorder so apparently real as in that of law. To be sure, the political implications of Louis' law reform should not be minimized. Undoubtedly many of the changes expressed the royal defiance to the role of the parlements in the Fronde and were directed towards lessening the prestige of these courts. This purpose was clear in the codes themselves but explicit also was the desire to remodel the law by the means of orderly system; by the subjection of the traditional law to selection and formulation. It was, generally speaking, not the law but the method of its execution which interested Colbert and Louis XIV. It was to the question of mechanics, not morals, that they primarily directed their attention.

Along these lines, it is significant that the reforms produced in the laws were, first of all, a civilian enterprise. Colbert and his uncle, the councillor of state Pussort, were the initiators of the *Code Louis*, and only necessity directed them to associate true legists with the project. Broadly viewed, the lawyers were held in great suspicion, and the law they administered, at least in the way it was administered, was considered gothic, confused and inefficient.

The codification of the law of France is often credited to the Consulate and the Empire, and the debt which the nation owes to the reign of Louis XIV in this respect is thereby ignored. The code of civil law of the consulate did give unity and simplicity to a great body of previous customary law, and to Roman law observed in certain sections of France, as they regarded civil law. With this exception, however, the first true codes of French law date from the times of Louis. Other codes formulated at the beginning of the nineteenth century derive from that source. Thus the procedural code for civil law is but an improved edition of the *Ordonnance* of 1667. The code of commerce often reasserts articles of the *Ordonnance* of 1673 and, it has been said, mutilates some of the best provisions of the *Ordonnance* of 1681. The *Ordonnance* of 1670 also had its effect in the drawing up of the modern code on criminal procedure.[76]

During most of the reign of Louis XIII and the minority of Louis XIV legal development was relatively at a standstill. The greater part of the credit for the work done under Louis XIV to reform the laws belongs to Colbert and to his uncle. Almost from the beginning of the personal reign of the King the hand of the still silent partner was revealed in a decree of April 1661 setting in motion a project for the improvement of commerce. It was the seed of the *règlements* on commerce of 1673 and 1681.[77] A letter of Pussort to Colbert written, in September 1661, gives the definite impression that the idea of a broad legal reform was being seriously contemplated by the pair at that early date.[78] As we have seen, when the *maîtres de requêtes* were sent into the provinces in 1663 a most important part of their investigations was to be carried out in relation to the administration of justice.[79] The first significant document setting forth the needs of a general revision and reorganization of the law appears to be an undated memoir of Colbert. The Secretary of State drew up a table of the

[76] E. D. Glasson, *Histoire du droit et des institutions de la France* (8 vols., Paris, 1887-1903); VIII, 175-177; Esmein, *Cours élémentaire d'histoire du droit française*, pp. 741-742.

[77] J. de Boislisle, *Conseil de 1661*, I, 8-10, 133, 153, 162-164, xcv-xcvi; Glasson, VIII, 175.

[78] Pussort to Colbert, September 6, 1661, Colbert, *Lettres,* VI, 368.

[79] The scandalous conditions revealed in Auvergne led to the *Grands jours de Auvergne* which disciplined a territory in which the criminal activities of the nobility combined with the connivance of the legal authorities had subjected the people to a reign of terror. This affair is described in Valentin-Esprit Fléchier's *Mémoires sur les grands jours tenus à Clermont en 1665*. This has been translated under the title *The Clermont assizes of 1665, a merry account of a grim court*, W.W. Comfort (Philadelphia, 1937).

ordinances of justice published since the thirteenth century. " By all these tables, it appears clearly," he concluded, " that since Charlemagne . . . and his son . . . no king has worked . . . to incorporate into a body all the ordinances of the realm." He observed that Henry IV had had the notion of such a work as had had later Michel de Marillac but in neither case was anything accomplished. " So it is that this great work has been reserved in its entirety to Louis XIV; but it is necessary, in order to make it worthy of his application and proportioned to the splendid character of his spirit and to the magnificent deeds which he has already executed since the beginning of his reign, to render this work infinitely more excellent and perfect than all that has been conceived of and done up to the present by any of the kings, his predecessors." [80]

The framers of the codes, as pointed out above, felt that the purpose of the reforms was not to change the laws. France they considered the land in Europe best provided with sensible laws but also the land in which they were the worst executed. The need, therefore, was for codes which would assure their execution. The stress was to be on method and system rather than content.[81] The procedure generally adopted for the formulation was to send *maîtres de requêtes* throughout the realm to investigate reports, participate in the sessions of the courts, hold hearings and consult with local officials. The information and suggestions they sent back were then submitted to the discussion and study of an especially constituted *conseil de justice* and its subcommittees. Membership in these bodies was drawn, in the main, from among the King's councillors of state.[82] Perhaps the greater part of the credit for the codifications belongs to Colbert but the details of the program were carried out, primarily, by Pussort. From the beginning it was the policy to exclude the members of the parlements as much

[80] Colbert, *Lettres,* VI, 362-367; Glasson, *Histoire du droit,* VIII, 178-179; Esmein, *Histoire de la procédure criminelle en France et specialement de la procédure inquisitoire depuis le XIIIe siècle jusqu'à nos jours* (Paris, 1882), p. 178.

[81] They particularly admired the Code Michaud (1629) of Michel de Marillac, *ibid.,* pp. 181-182; see the minutes of the early conferences of the council on the reform in " Appendice," Colbert, *Lettres,* VI, 369-377.

[82] Esmein, *Histoire de la procédure criminelle,* pp. 192-194; Colbert, " Mémoire sur la réformation de la justice," May 15, 1665, *Lettres,* VI, 6-9.

as possible from the work of the reform. Pussort was particularly prejudiced against the participation of the legists but
the rest of the men working on the ordinances seemed agreed
to the need of calling on the magistrature for advice.[83] At
any rate they were unable to prevent, the representation of
parlements in the *conseil.* Guillaume de Lamoignon, the President of the Parlement of Paris, played an important, if
secondary, role in the preparation of the ordinances of 1667
and 1670. As such he gave frequent opposition to the ideas
of Pussort. In general he represented the traditional and legal
point of view as opposed to the civilian, extra-legal, and coldly
rational attitude of Pussort. The friction between the two
became most pronounced during the drawing up of the code
on criminal procedure. Here Pussort was interested in pro-
ducing efficiency, however ruthless the means. Lamoignon,
on the other hand, appears as the advocate of more lenient
methods.[84] But it was the councillors of state, the civilian,
bourgeois element of the regime, led by Pussort and Colbert,
who dominated the conferences and determined the character
of the codes. These men had the explicit ends of reforming
the magistrature, establishing a uniform and certain procedure
for the kingdom, setting forth general maxims of justice and
creating a unified body of useful laws. Order should replace
confusion.[85]

The actual work on the reform by the *conseil de justice* and
its committees began in September 1665, and the first code, the
ordinance on civil procedure, was registered in the Parlement
of Paris on April 20, 1667, in the presence of the King without
the formality of a bed of justice.[86] It was a code of civil law
procedure set forth under thirty-five headings with several

[83] Esmein, *Histoire de la procédure criminelle,* pp. 178-180, 186-187; Glasson, *Histoire du droit,* VIII, 177-178, 181-183; the animus of Colbert for the
" so called sovereign courts " is implicit in his "Mémoire sur la réformation de
la justice" of May 15, 1665, Colbert, *Lettres,* VI, 5-12.
[84] Glasson, *Histoire du droit,* VIII, 181-186, 192-195; Esmein, *Histoire du
droit,* pp. 742-743; Clement, " Introduction," Colbert, *Lettres,* VI, xiv-xv;
Esmein, *Histoire de la procédure criminelle,* pp. 188-189, 203-209.
[85] *Ibid.,* pp. 185, 188-189; " Proces-verbal des conférences tenues devant
Louis XIV pour la réformation de la justice," September 25, 1665-October 25,
1665, in " Appendice," Colbert, *Lettres,* VI, 369-391, *passim.*
[86] Glasson, VIII, 186-187; see " Ordonnance civile touchant la réformation de
la justice," April, 1667, Isambert, XVIII, 103-180.

hundred articles. The purpose, declared in the preamble, was to simplify, expedite, regulate, define, and unify civil procedure by a single ordinance which would establish a uniform style in all courts.[87]   Matters relating to judicial organization and competence were put aside and the law concerned itself almost exclusively with procedure.   This it organized from the first step in opening a civil case until the close of the process.   It suppressed local variations and established a delineated conduct for the kingdom.   " This was the first time," wrote a nineteenth-century French commentator on the law, " that the rules of procedure were collected in a methodical fashion and distinguished from matters foreign to the administration of justice.   The ordinances of Villers-Cotterets, of Orleans and of Moulins; the edicts of Cremieu, Rousillon and Amboise,[88] presented neither this clarity, this method, nor this unity of views; some pronounced only on certain parts of procedure, others dealt with justice as with an accessory matter.   The ordinance of 1667 was the first step made along the path of our modern codification; this was the first time that we saw a law trace for all courts the course of procedure from the introduction of the case to the executions of the judgements." [89]

The implicit attack which the ordinance of 1667 made against the courts caused it to be unpopular among the legists but the intendants were effectively used to see that it was applied and enforced generally.   Its universal acceptance was reflected in the appearance of a number of commentaries in the eighteenth century [90] and it served as a model for the procedural code of 1808.[91]

Though not the next code in chronological order, the ordinance of 1670, on criminal procedure, was part of the same project and represented the accomplishments of the commission which had produced that of 1667.   The finished work was an extensive code under twenty-eight headings the harsh-

[87] *Ibid.,* pp. 103-105.

[88] Sixteenth century *ordonnances* and edicts of a general reform nature.

[89] Quoted from M. Raymond Bordeaux, *Philosophie de la procédure civile* (1853) in the " Introduction " to Colbert, *Lettres,* VI, xvii; the same view is expressed by Glasson, VIII, 187-191; Esmein, *Histoire du droit,* pp. 741-743.

[90] See the bibliography in Glasson, VIII, 190-191 notes, or in Isambert, XVIII, 104 note.

[91] Esmein, *Histoire du droit,* pp. 742-743.

ness of which was suggested in the introductory statement that the purpose was to " assure public security . . . by the fear of punishments." [92]   As observed, President Lamoignon led the opposition, in the formulating conferences, to the rigorous designs of Pussort which sharply limited the means of defense which the accused could employ, but Pussort's view prevailed in the completed code.[93]   Adhémar Esmein, in his *Histoire de le procédure criminelle en France,* concludes his treatment of it with the opinion that Dante's inscription over the gates of Hell gave an adequate notion of the lot of the defendant in the French court of justice.[94]

However the law was not without its redeeming points, for like the code of 1667 it gave additional unity to the French legal procedure. While it contained no innovations in the content of the law, it applied system and order to the conduct of it.   For the first time " all the formalities of criminal instruction were minutely regulated."   The spirit of the law was rational and the interest was to produce efficiency without regard to the human equation.   It was widely attacked by the new humanitarians and publicists of the eighteenth century but at the time of its framing such objection would have found little response except, perhaps, among a few magistrates like Lamoignon.[95]   Freed of its more cruel and obdurate exactions it served, as did that of 1667, as the pattern for a Napoleonic code.[96]   Like its elder sister, it also was the subject of a number of commentaries during the seventeenth and eighteenth centuries.

The two codes of 1667 and 1670 were the only ones in the formulation of which members of Parlement had any significant share.   The second code to distinguish the reign of Louis XIV, the forestry code of 1669, arose from an investigation which we have already mentioned in connection with the history of statistical development.   Carefully selected *maîtres de requêtes*

---

[92] " Ordonnance criminelle," August, 1670, Isambert, XVIII, 372, 371-423; a most extensive historical treatment of this ordinance is given by Esmein in his *Histoire de la procédure criminelle,* pp. 177-283.

[93] *Ibid.,* pp. 208-209, 212-253; Glasson, VIII, 192-195.

[94] Esmein, *Histoire de la procédure criminelle,* pp. 283, 212-253.

[95] *Ibid.,* pp. 177-283, *passim*; Glasson, VIII, 192-195.

[96] Esmein, *Histoire du droit,* pp. 743-744; for bibliographies of commentaries, see Isambert, XVIII, 372 note or Glasson, VIII, 194 note.

were sent into the provinces in 1661 where they conducted for eight years a thoroughgoing research concerning the boundaries, rights, alienations, and wastes pertaining to the royal domain, particularly in relation to forests and waters.[97] The consequent restitutions and reclamations resulted in a several fold increase in the income to the crown from the royal domain. Of perhaps less immediate but of much greater long-range significance was the institution of a program of conservation. The maintenance of an adequate supply of national forestry resources was an extremely important requirement for the success of Colbert's mercantilistic program of industrialization and shipbuilding. The ordinance of 1669 summarized and clarified a mass of sometimes contradictory edicts of the past.[98] It thus gave a new point of departure for the administration of the forests. Among other things, it dealt with the jurisdiction of functionaries, administrative definitions, rights of communities, fees, customs, hunting, fishing, pannage and cutting privileges as they affected the royal forests and waters. This great ordinance, the most considerable conservation measure of the *ancien régime,* remained in force in a large number of its provisions until the publication of the new code of 1827.[99]

The code of 1673 on the conduct of land commerce, sometimes termed the *code marchand* and at others *code Savary* because of the predominance of Jacques Savary, the author of the *Parfait négociant,* in the conferences leading up to its creation, was remarkable from several points of view. In the first place, it gave legal definition, to an extent never realized by any previous law or laws in France, to the reciprocal relationships of the state and enterprise in a mercantilist society. In a prologue notable for its succinctness and clarity it

[97] See Clement's description of this process in the "Introduction" to Colbert, *Lettres,* IV, li-lxvii.

[98] "Edit partant réglement général pour les eaux et forêts," August 1669, Isambert, XVIII, 219-311. The prologue declared that over a period of eight years the King had collected "all the ordinances, either old or new, which concerned the matter, so that having collated them with the information which we have been sent from the provinces by the *commissaires départis* for the reformation of waters and forests, we could form on the total a body of clear, precise and certain laws, which would dissipate all the obscurity of preceeding ones and leave no longer any pretext or excuse to those who may fall in error."

[99] *Ibid.,* p. 219; see also the bibliographical note on commentaries; Glasson, VIII, 191-192; Esmein, *Histoire du droit,* p. 745; Cole, *Colbert,* pp. 542-543.

circumscribed the necessary role of government in commerce: commerce as the source of public wealth must be protected by the state; the recognition of this fundamental tenet had led to such ventures as overseas companies to displace the foreign intermediary. This explained the program of ship construction and the creation and maintenance of armies and the navy. Having succeeded in these directions, the state was now obliged to intervene to regulate and protect the conduct of business men for the preservation of whatever capital or liquid surplus they might have acquired.[100]

Therefore it specified limitations and rights connected with apprenticeship, regular business and wholesale and retail merchandising. It dealt with banking practice and described a required system of bookkeeping to be applied by all business men and merchants, either wholesale or retail. It dealt further with the mechanics of enterprise setting down prescriptions pertaining to bills of exchange, inventories, bankruptcy, interest, corporations, consular jurisdiction and other details of business conduct.[101]

This code did not create commercial legislation but it, like the previous codes of 1667, 1669, and 1670 gave order and simplicity to a mass of regulations which had varied between province and province and city and city. In certain sections, as in those articles dealing with bookkeeping, it represented a notable advance over any previous French ordinances known, and it advocated technical advances in the art of accounting. At the time of its publication it enjoyed a very broad popularity but the changing methods of enterprise made it generally *passé* in the eighteenth century although a large number of commentaries appeared on it.[102]

The last of the great ordinances of Louis XIV was perhaps the most important and most successful. This was the *Ordonnance de la marine* of August 1681. Much more extensive than that of 1673, it was, however, a complementary code applying to the regulation of sea rather than land commerce.

Private maritime law, in general, before the issuance of the

---

[100] " Ordonnance du commerce," March 1673, Isambert, XIX, 92-93, 92-107.
[101] *Ibid.*
[102] Glasson, VIII, 195-199; Esmein, *Histoire du droit,* p. 744; see also F. L. Nussbaum's comments on the code Savary in *A history of the economic institutions of modern Europe* (New York, 1933), pp. 159, 161.

ordinance of 1681, had been based, in France, on a customary usage which frequently varied from place to place. In 1670 Colbert, in a memoir on maritime laws, commented on the failure of previous kings to legislate in the field and of the consequent reliance which the French had to have, in many cases, on the inadequate judgments of Oleron, the ordinance of Wisby, or those of the Hanseatic league.[103] In order to give the French a national and uniform code, *maîtres de requêtes* were sent to all the ports of the kingdom to examine, criticize and report on " all which concerns this justice," and the familiar process which had produced the other codes was repeated.[104]

Its purposes were declared in the preamble:

. . . since our ordinances, those of our predecessors, and the Roman law contain but very few provisions for the solution of differences which arise between traders and seamen, we have thought that, in order to leave nothing desirable undone for the good of navigation and commerce, it was important to fix the jurisprudence of maritime contracts, until now uncertain, to regulate the jurisdiction of admiralty officers, and the principal duties of seamen and to establish a good police in all the ports, coasts and roadsteads under our dominion.

A few of the phases governed by the law were the duties of consuls abroad, ship and cargo reports, seizure and distribution of prizes, duties of pilots, naval regulations, maritime contracts, marine insurance, testaments at sea, letters of mark and reprisal, police, and fishing rights.[105] The law won almost immediate admiration at home and abroad. Samuel Pepys wrote that the French were the nation best provided with sea laws [106] and most of the maritime nations of Western Europe were affected by the code in drawing up their own. In France for the first

---

[103] Colbert, "Mémoire sur les ordonnances de marine," December 1670, *Lettres,* III, part i, 320-321; see also "Instruction pour mon fils," 1671, *ibid.,* III, Part ii, 53. The judgments or *Rôle d'Oleron* were, by traditional history, drawn up on the orders of Eleanor of Acquitaine after the return from a trip to the Holy Land. See the " Preface " to the commentary of P. Biarnoy de Merville, *Ordonnance de la marine du mois d'Aout 1681* (Paris, 1715). The volumes of J. M. Pardessus. *Collection des lois maritimes antérieurs au XVIIIe siècle* (6 vols., Paris, 1824-1845), gives ample testimony of a large body of previous maritime law both in Europe and the Levant.

[104] Colbert, " Mémoire sur les ordonnances de marine," *Lettres,* III, part i, 320-321.

[105] " Ordonnance de la marine," August 1681, Isambert, XIX, 282-366, *passim.*

[106] Samuel Pepys, *Naval minutes,* p. 85.

time, the body of maritime law, whether public or private, was reduced to a methodical plan and assimilated into a complete and useful code. A number of its provisions remain in force today and, with the ordinance of 1673, it served as the model of the code of commerce of 1807.[107]

The great ordinances of Louis XIV, that on civil procedure (1667), forestry (1669), criminal procedure (1670), land commerce (1673), and maritime law (1681), presented an entirely different character from the general ordinances of the fifteenth and sixteenth centuries. Those periods had been distinguished by a series of comprehensive laws dealing with varied aspects of justice, finances, and other branches of the government. Generally, they derived from the meetings of the Estates-General, or other such assemblies, and were drawn up by the chancellor of France from the lists of suggestions or grievances which were submitted by these meetings. As such they were customarily reform laws directed in a horizontal fashion towards erasing abuses detected in the structure of the state, and in consequence displayed a sweeping aspect and treated most elements only partially or in the particular regard that called for reform. They were not " codifications," writes Esmein, but " partial revisions." [108]

In contrast, the ordinances of 1667-1681 were vertical structures, true codes, edited by their practical-minded framers for practical purposes. The salient emphasis was on unity and uniformity in the application of the laws for the realm. The King, wrote Colbert, was desirous of reducing " into a single body of ordinances all that which is necessary to establish a fixed and certain jurisprudence." [109] To realize this purpose they sought to delete all they believed obsolescent from the law of tradition and to systematize and simplify the useful remainder. The dominating interest in method was reflected in the codes of 1667 and 1670 where, with few exceptions, private law was not considered. The subject matter was public law: constitutional, administrative, and procedural. The com-

[107] Glasson, VIII, 199-206, 204; Esmein, *Histoire du droit*, p. 744.

[108] *Ibid.*, pp. 738-739; see also Chapter III. My own fairly extensive reading of the ordinances in the volumes of Isambert covering the period from Charles VII to Louis XIV has confirmed Esmein's conclusion.

[109] Colbert, " Mémoire sur la reformation de la justice," May 15, 1665, *Lettres*, VI, 6.

mercial and maritime codes of 1673 and 1681 were, however, a mixture of private and public laws, a fact which acknowledged the integral relationship, from a mercantilistic point of view, of enterprise to the administration of the state. In this sense, contracts, trade conduct, and rule of admiralty were public affairs which could not be neglected. On the whole, the codes of Louis XIV and Colbert were drawn up as efficient instruments to facilitate the rational direction of the government. They were formulae for use in the new system of order. The constructive and rational orderliness which had been applied to the foundation of the speculative systems of the philosophers or to introduce greater certainty into natural science was transferred to the social and legal field. The state, as an instrument of reason, was applying rational controls on irrational individual conduct by systematic laws which supplied fixity and method.

III

The Brandenburger, Spanheim, and the Englishman, Pepys, attributed part of the success of the French naval program of their day to the technological schooling provided by the state for naval personnel.[110] Spanheim praised similarly the educational work done in the army for the training of young officers.[111] These were but two among a number of projects for technological education which were fostered by Colbert, Louvois, or Seignelay in the early years of Louis' personal reign.

We have already noted the emphasis on this point given in the works of men like More, Campanella, Bacon, Harrington, Montchrétien, Mayerne-Turquet, and Bossuet. To these might be added a long list of names including philosophers, professional teachers, politicians or economists who advocated the introduction of manual and technological instruction into general courses of learning. Among the theorists such practices were generally urged as conducive to a better understanding, as the impression of the senses was viewed as basic to education. Representative of such theorists were Descartes and

---

[110] Spanheim, *Relation de la cour de France*, p. 304; Pepys, *Naval minutes*, pp. 361-362.
[111] Spanheim, p. 313.

Comenius.   There was a notable progress in mathematical instruction during the century.   Stemming especially from the teachings of Peter Ramus, and further influenced by the support of Descartes, a number of schools, such as those of the Oratoriens and Jansenists, emphasized mechanical, mathematical, and the objective methods.   The use by the teaching orders and the literate public of scientific or technical manuals greatly increased over that of the sixteenth century.   These manuals borrowed from the works of Aristotle and Euclid to Galileo, Descartes, Pascal, and later, Newton and Leibnitz and treated of optics, probability, calculus, machines, clocks, gravitation and other technical subjects.   Economists and statesmen, usually more practical than the professional educators or theorists, were inclined to stress mechanical instruction for the poor, the establishment of ateliers and the utility of mechanical museums for the guidance of artisans.   Jacques Savary, in the *Parfait négociant* (1675), decried the ill effect of the traditional college education on those training to be business men in France, and even Richelieu had observed that schools of commerce would be of greater value to the kingdom than schools of liberal arts.[112]   Colbert understood clearly the need for extending and improving technical instruction as a means of bettering the operation of the state.   When he had an occasion to address a delegation of the University of Paris he expressed his opinion that instruction in the colleges left much to be desired.   If the student learned a little Latin they ignored " geography, history and most of the sciences which are useful to the commerce of life." [113]

While warfare was not the only field in which the state applied itself in the provision of technical instruction, it was

[112]. The most complete account of the development of the practice and theory of technological education in France during the seventeenth century is the article of F. B. Artz, " Les débuts de l'éducation technique en France (1500-1700)," *Revue d'histoire moderne,* XII (1937), 469-519. The article of Artz is the basis of this section. Other works which are informative are J. E. de Crisenoy " " Les écoles navales et les officiers de vaisseaux depuis Richelieu," *Revue maritime et coloniale,* X (1864), 759-791; Boissonade, " Colbert et l'etat promotion de l'enseignement industriel de l'éducation technique, du machinisme et des inventions industrielles," Chapter III, in *Colbert,* pp. 25-36; see Richelieu, " Des lettres," *Testament politique,* I, 168-177; also J. Savary, *Le parfait négociant,* pp. 40-42 and *passim.*

[113] Clement, " Introduction " to Colbert, *Lettres,* V. lxxxvi.

perhaps the area in which its participation was most direct. The explanation of such programs is not difficult to find. Probably the most important factor was the need of maintaining the numerical strength of a vastly increased military organization. State military training was often a slightly disguised recruiting measure. But there were other reasons. For instance, much of the military or naval art that had been formerly based on experience was becoming more or less theoretical and technical and, hence, required a more organized study. Pursuing lines initially indicated by the Italians, in the sixteenth century, fortification and bombardment were increasingly less empirical and more closely tied in with engineering or physics; with elements of geometry or with the laws of falling bodies. The ideas of Colbert and others on the theory of ship construction made necessary the instruction of naval personnel in mechanics and geometry. Long-range commerce and naval operations added new and complicating problems of navigation to old arts of piloting and dead-reckoning.

In the late sixteenth century Francois de la Noue in his widely read *Discours militaires* proposed the creation of a series of military academies for the training of young noblemen in the technical aspects of warfare. A considerable quantity of small academies for such young gentlemen, often aided by the royal or local government, were founded from the late sixteenth up to the middle of the seventeenth century. Richelieu attended one of these academies, the Pluvinel Academy at Paris. In 1606 Henry IV founded the military college at La Flèche and endowed it with a number of scholarships to enable the attendance of scions of the lesser nobility. The curriculum of such academies ideally included mathematics, history, geography, law, mechanics, and principles of fortification along with riding, dancing, and fencing. Richelieu, Louis XIII, and Mazarin did little to advance this movement, and the tendency was for the academies to degenerate into riding and dancing schools. Nevertheless, they were the most important source for trained army officers until the establishment of the *École Militaire* of 1761.

In 1682, Louvois, in order to provide a permanent corps of officer material created the *compagnies de cadets-gentils-hommes*. The members of these groups, mostly drawn from the *petite noblesse*, were clothed and paid by the state. It was planned as an extensive program to supply future officers with technical army training. Vauban, however, expressed great scorn for the program which attempted to instruct men who, in the main, were too ignorant to profit from the experience, and, after the death of Louvois, it was neglected and was finally dissolved in 1696.[114]

No distinct school of military engineering was established in France before the eighteenth century, but the new style of fortification, imported from Italy, became a highly developed art in the hands of Vauban. In 1676 a corps of engineers, which became famous throughout Europe, was detached from the infantry to work under his special direction. Training came from experience and the reading of treatises. A kind of descriptive geometry had been introduced into academies which passed for the study of fortification though it was generally too theoretical for practical use.[115] An artillery school was founded at Douai in 1679 which was later moved to Metz and thence to Strasbourg. Although it functioned with considerable success for a time, the interruptions of wars prevented continuous instruction.[116] As far as organized technological instruction for the army was concerned, the seventeenth century was a period of initiation and plans and most frequently of failure, but it also helped in creating the best trained military organization known up to its time in France.

In the navy the need for technological and professional instruction was a maxim with Colbert.[117] Besides answering the problems posed by expansion and the new sciences of fortification and ballistics, problems which it shared with the army, it had to meet the additional demands created by new construction theories, new methods of navigation, and new techniques of maneuver.

Colbert gave the most attention to navigation, gunnery, and construction. The code Michaud of 1629 had contained articles which would have provided, at royal expense, for the allocation of experienced navigators to certain maritime cities to give

---

[114] Artz, " Les débuts." pp. 502-508.

[115] *Ibid.*, pp. 509-510.

[116] *Ibid.*

[117] Colbert, " Mémoire " to Seignelay, September 24, 1671, *Lettres*, III, part ii, 44.

free and public instruction in their art. Other maritime cities were ordered to imitate the royal example.[118] From the standpoint of the state, the ordinance was without marked effect but private instruction became widespread and a center of navigational schooling developed at Dieppe.[119] Under Colbert's direction the state began earnestly to foster the development as a part of its general maritime program. It was the Minister's desire to have schools of pilots established in all ports. Pilots and naval officers should not only have practical experience but a theoretical background.[120] In the schools created, the government furnished maps, compasses, and other instruments. The course, ordinarily directed by a professor and two assisting pilots, included drafting, mathematics, charting and the determination of time, longitude and latitude. A new public school on navigation and pilotage was established at Dieppe in 1665 with classes conducted mornings and afternoons by one sieur Denis.[121] New schools of hydrography and cannoneering were also created at Havre, Bordeaux, St. Malo, and Marseille.[122] The government encroached upon the

---

[118] " Code Michaud," articles (433) (434) (436), Isambert, XVI, 330-331.

[119] Artz, " Les débuts," pp. 510-511.

[120] *Ibid.*, p. 513; the marine code of 1681, under Title VIII, contained articles on these establishments:

    Art.: (1) The principal maritime cities should be provided with professors of hydrography to give public instruction in navigation.

    Art.: (2) Mapping and charting were to be among their primary courses and acts.

    Art.: (3) Four days, minimum, weekly of schooling, the schools to be provided with " charts, sailing directions, globes, spheres, compasses, arballestes, astrolabies and other instruments and books necessary to their art."

    Art.: (4) Directors of hospitals to annually send 2 or 3 children and furnish their maintenance in order that they might learn navigation.

    Art.: (5) The professors of hydrography were to examine carefully the navigational journals in the admiralty clerk's office and correct, with the aid of pilots, any errors found.

    Art.: (6) (7) (8) The professors to perform the above duty without charge, to enjoy certain privileges and not to absent themselves without leave of the authorities. (Isambert, XIX, 293).

[121] *Maire* and *échevins* of Dieppe to Colbert, October 1, 1665, Depping, *Correspondance*, IV, 557-558; Letters from Denis to Colbert reveal that, aside from his classes, he was working on a book for Colbert which was to facilitate navigation to the East Indies. *Ibid., pp.* 558-559.

[122] Clement, " Introduction " to Colbert, *Lettres*, III, part i, xvi. The school at

schools of the teaching orders to carry forward the program.
Thus, in a letter of 1673, the Governor of Brittany, the Duke
of Chaulnes, tells of founding a class of "mathematics, hydrography and marine science" in the college of the Jesuits at
Rennes.[123] A number of such "hydrographic" schools, as they
were called, lasted until the French revolution but they appear
never to have realized the expectation of Colbert.[124]

Other important projects for technological education in
the navy were the corps of *Gardes du marine*, created in 1670,
and the schools established at the arsenal ports of Brest,
Toulon, and Rochefort for their instruction.[125] Like the *Compagnie de cadets-gentilshommes* in the army, this corps served
the dual purpose of education and recruitment. Between 1670
and 1683 the schools received 830 cadets and graduated 334
ensigns. A corps of new *Gardes* was created by Seignelay in
1683 which much strengthened the program and absorbed the
old corps altogether in 1686.[126] At one time their number is
said to have risen to a thousand.[127] At first only young noblemen were admitted but later this was relaxed to include young
men of honorable condition "living nobly." [128] They were
usually nominated, without examination, at the pleasure of
the King.[129] As instructors they not only had the best pilots
and professors of navigation but a corps of skilled master
carpenters recruited by Colbert from France, England, Holland,
and Italy.[130]

St. Malo was called the "College de marine" and was to instruct naval officers
and sailors in hydrography, cannoneering, and ship maneuvering. See letter of
Louis XIV to the *Maire* and *échevins* of St. Malo, September 10, 1669, *ibid.*,
p. 163.

[123] Duke of Chaulnes to Colbert, December 13, 1673, Depping, *Correspondance*, IV, 558 note.

[124] Artz, "Les débuts," p. 513, The *intendant en mission*, M. D'Herbigny, was
instructed by Colbert, August 26, 1672, to investigate the complaint of the sieur
Denis at Dieppe that sailors without "any theory or practice of hydrography"
were being accepted as pilots by the lieutenant of the admiralty to the hurt of,
or danger to, the ships they were to pilot. Colbert, *Lettres*, III, part i, 464.

[125] The galley fleet also had its school at Marseille.

[126] Artz, "Les débuts," p. 514; Daniel, II, 713. It seems that a considerable
proportion of the cadets were killed before their commissioning. See Crisenoy,
"Les ecoles navales," pp. 763-765.

[127] Daniel, II, 715. Artz says there were 700 in 1696, "Les débuts," p. 514.

[128] Daniel, II, 713.

[129] Crisenoy, "Les écoles navales," p. 766.

[130] Boissonade, *Colbert*, pp. 115-116.

A typical work-day routine for the cadets began in the arsenal in the morning with the hearing of mass. Afterwards they applied themselves to writing, drawing, mathematics, fortification, hydrography, dancing, and fencing. In the afternoon came musket and cannon drills and military evolutions. Finally they went into the construction yards and were instructed by the master carpenter and the most able officers on the rules, proportions, and techniques involved in ship construction. Time remaining after school might be spent in assisting at the works of the arsenal and learning the qualities of ship equipment. Not only the cadets but lieutenants and ensigns were subjected to such courses until they had qualified for exemption by examinations and conferences held twice monthly in the ports. Even ships' captains were under injunction to keep abreast of the progress in construction theory.[131]

Colbert writes of his visit to the school at Rochefort in 1680. He was well pleased but found room for improvement. The school for cannonry, for instance, needed to be enlivened by awarding prizes.[132] A master carpenter teaching at the arsenal for the galley fleet at Marseille, one Chabert, proved uncooperative because of his jealousy of trade secrets. However, the threat of imprisonment in the citadel of Marseille exacted compliance. But Colbert was not yet satisfied and wrote the intendant to supervise him:

His Majesty had been pleased to learn that the young Chabert has resumed conducting the school of construction; it is not sufficient simply that he has desisted from his obstinancy, it is necessary that he apply himself to teaching well; and, in order to know certainly if he executes his orders as he should, he [the King] desires to be sent a memoir on the manner in which he teaches the said construction . . . and if a model galley has been made which disassembles for the instruction of the said officers, that being necessary in order to allow them to learn by sight whatever will be explained by the aforesaid Chabert.[133]

---

[131] The above is paraphrased from Crisenoy, " Les écoles navales," p. 766. The description given by Daniel, II, 713-715, 682, is similar. Education aboard ship was coordinated with the education in the port. A pilot was embarked to carry on the instruction in navigation and piloting. On the return, progress reports were submitted on each cadet by the pilot and the captain.

[132] Colbert, *Lettres,* III, part i (addition), 192.

[133] Colbert to the sieur Brodart, intendant of galleys at Marseille, May 19, 1682; on the same subject see letters April 18, 1682, August 10, 1682, *ibid.,* pp. 223-224 notes. Colbert required periodic lists to be sent him to keep a check on the officers attending the courses on construction.

The educational program in the navy was not exclusively for officers and cadets. Selected sailors were chosen by the officers commanding them to be detached from their units and especially instructed in cannoneering and bombardment. A school of bombardment was set up at Toulon, in the winter of 1682, to prepare for the attack on Algiers and assure its "entire ruin." [134] The program of technological education introduced by Colbert into the navy and merchant marine had a lasting effect which won admiration at home and abroad. With some exceptions, licenses for pilots and naval officers, by the end of the seventeenth century, were issued only on the authority of professors of navigation attached to the ports. [135]

The organized study and teaching of oriental languages was another project of Colbert. The demands of merchants in the Mediterranean trade and, perhaps, the collection of many oriental manuscripts for the royal library [136] emphasized the need for more students of oriental languages. At Colbert's instigation schools were established by the Capuchins in Constantinople and Smyrna, and the city of Marseille was charged with the duty of sending six students every three years to these schools to learn the native tongues. [137] A certain Sieur de la Croix was sent to the Capuchins at Ispahan in 1673 to learn Persian. [138] There were numerous other ventures in technological or commercial education encouraged by Colbert for the improvement of enterprise. Under his leadership the state

[134] Daniel, II, 715; Louis XIV to Du Quesne, October 2, 1682, Colbert, Lettres, III, part i (addition), 241-243. See also letters and notes pp. 246-247 and 251 note. It was at these bombardments that the bomb-ketches of Bernard Renau d'Elicagaray were first employed.

[135] Artz, "Les débuts," pp. 516-517. In England about the nearest approach to the French navigational and mathematical schools was the Christ Hospital School founded by Charles II for poor boys, called "Blue Coat Boys." It was founded to instruct them in arithmetic and the "rule of three," a competent knowledge in Latin and to fit them for duty at sea. Pepys was of the opinion that the English had borrowed the idea from the French who, in turn, he thought had got it from the Spaniards. Naval minutes, p. 360 and passim.

[136] Colbert staffed the royal library with translators of the chief languages not commonly understood by the erudite: Hebrew, Arabic, German, English. See H. Brown, Scientific organizations in seventeenth century France, p. 203.

[137] Colbert to the échevins and députés de commerce at Marseille, February 1670, Colbert, Lettres, II, 518; also V, lxxvii, lxxxv, 304; Depping, Correspondance, IV, xxx.

[138] Colbert to father Raphael, superior of the Capuchins at Ispahan, October 28, 1673, Colbert, Lettres, V, 360.

took clear account of its role as the promoter of industrial progress. The ateliers at the Louvre and Tuileries instructed apprentices in various industrial arts. The Royal Academy of Painting was enlarged and, under the presidency of Lebrun, assumed a most important role in the luxury industry. Under his superior administration an attempt was also made to found academies of painting and sculpture in the principal cities of the realm. Some success was experienced at Lyons, Reims, and Bordeaux and it represents the first effort carried out by the state to create general instruction of beaux-arts applicable to industry. In 1666, Colbert founded the Academy of France at Rome where twelve students were maintained, at state expense, for three-year terms to study painting, sculpture, architecture, arithmetic, geometry, perspective, and anatomy.[139] In 1676, this Academy passed also under the regime of Lebrun's Academy. These were not simply excursions into the fine arts, they served a very practical purpose. The relationship of the arts and technical progress seemed clear and important in Colbert's brand of mercantilist philosophy with its emphasis on luxury production. Young men from the academies were employed in the Gobelins, Savonnerie, the mints, the *Imprimerie Royale*, and *Manufactures Royale* of the Louvre. Masters created in the academies became instructors in the state manufactures. Industrial arts were taught in two divisions at the Seminary des Gobelins; for two years sixty selected apprentices worked under the direction of Lebrun and a corps of instructors, and at the end of this time were sent for four years of specialized training at various ateliers. The Savonnerie, Beauvais, and Aubusson works contained schools for tapestry. The effective interest of Colbert in such technological advancement of industry was undoubtedly a major factor in making France the luxury capital of the world.[140]

[139] This Academy was under the direction of Charles Errard. Colbert was much interested in their work and maintained frequent correspondence very paternal in character, with Errard. For example: " Do not fail to write me fully every month of the status of the Academy, and send me carefully the memoirs of all the works to which you employ the academicians, and remark on the different degrees of application, of aptitude and study of the academicians." Part of the work of the Academy was to collect or copy Italian arts. Colbert built up the collection of the Louvre from around 200 paintings to 2,500. See Depping, *Correspondance,* IV, lxxxi-lxxxiii, letters, pp. 573-578.
[140] Artz, " Les débuts," pp. 492-497; Boissonade, *Colbert,* pp. 25-30; Cole, *Colbert,* I, 315-318; Colbert, *Lettres,* V, lxviii and letters *passim.*

One might mention, finally, the Academy of Architecture founded by Colbert in 1671 and placed under Blondel. This became the foremost technological school in France. There the leading architects and engineers of the kingdom met, studied and taught applied mechanics, hydraulics, stone cutting, and civil and military engineering. It also served as a consultative board for Colbert for the erection of government buildings, canals, bridges, and fortresses.[141]

Technological education has always been primarily obtained through individual experience in particular crafts, industries, or organizations. This was certainly much more the case in the seventeenth century than today but, in the political economy of the mercantilistic France of Louis XIV, the state participated broadly in a program of providing organized instruction for workers and technicians both in industry and in the military. In one respect it illustrates a further attempt by the government, as an instrument of reason, to discipline and regulate the empirical by the formulae of order and science.

IV

As in so many other matters relating to the scientific activity of the government, the establishment of a Royal Academy of Sciences by Louis XIV was anticipated in Italy. The most famous pioneer of the seventeenth-century academy movement was the *Accademia dei Lincei* in Rome (1600-1630). Founded by the Duke Federigo Cesi, on its device it depicted a lynx tearing the Cerberus with its claws; thus symbolizing the struggle of scientific truth with ignorance. Its best known members were Francesco Stelluti, Peiresc, and Galileo. There the latter carried out a number of his astronomical studies. The *Accademia* disappeared after the death of its patron.[142]

---

[141] Artz, " Les débuts," pp. 494-496. Other members: Le Vau, Bruand, Gittard, Mignard, Perrault, Mansart. In 1672, Colbert offered a reward of 1,000 *écus* for a French order of architecture. The practical utility of the Academy is illustrated by the project carried out by them, at Colbert's request, from July 1678 to April 1679. They visited all the churches and old buildings of Paris, and the environs, to see the quality of the stones; whether damaged by " air, humidity, the moon or the sun," and determined from whence they were quarried and inspected these quarries, if discovered and still existent, to ascertain the quantity and quality of the stone remaining. See " Proces-verbal of the Academy " in Colbert, *Lettres,* V, 384-385 and notes.

[142] M. Ornstein, *The role of scientific societies in the seventeenth century,* pp.

Closely associated with Galileo also was the *Accademia del cimento* (1657-1667) founded by his pupils the Grand-Duke of Tuscany, Ferdinand II, and his brother Leopold. Although Galileo was dead at the time of its founding, a large part of its activity was devoted to giving experimental proof to problems for which Galileo, or his pupil Torricelli, had given theoretical demonstrations. There a small group of scientists, Viviani, Leopold, and Borelli being the best known, worked cooperatively. Various members were assigned specific tasks but the society as a whole worked on the same topics and the results of their labors were published as an anonymous unit.[143]

England likewise anticipated the French in founding their Royal Academy. Charles II granted the charter on July 15, 1662, to the group of scholars and amateurs which had spontaneously gathered and had been meeting fairly regularly at Gresham College since 1660. In the grant, the King acknowledged the company as " benefactors of mankind; and that they have already made a considerable progress by divers useful and remarkable discoveries, inventions, and experiments in the improvement of mathematics, mechanics, astronomy, navigation, physics and chemistry." [144] The English Royal Society was not, therefore, a child of princely initiative, as had been the *Cimento* of the Medici, but rather the legal recognition of an association of a somewhat heterogeneous group

74-76. Miss Ornstein's book, first published in 1913, is the best general work I know of on the subject it treats and has been extensively utilized in the writing of this section. Other useful works are: Brown, *Scientific organizations in seventeenth century France*. More specialized than Miss Ornstein's, it deals particularly with the role of the small societies and individuals in the seventeenth century science of France; J. L. F. Bertrand, *L'Académie des Sciences et les académiciens de 1666 à 1793* (Paris, 1869), the most comprehensive modern work on the French society; C. Wolf, *Histoire de l'observatoire de Paris de sa fondation à 1793* (Paris, 1902). Poorly organized and hence difficult to use but indispensable to anyone doing research on the Royal Academy of Sciences in France are the volumes edited by Fontenelle on the *Histoire de l'Académie Royale des Sciences depuis son établissement en 1666 jusqu'à 1699* (11 vols., Paris, 1729-1734). Only the first two volumes are entitled " Histoire," the remainder "Memoires"; also useful is Gallon, ed., *Machines et inventions approuvées par l'Académie des Sciences* (7 vols., Paris, 1735-1777).

[143] The Academy disbanded when Duke Leopold entered the Cardinalate in 1667. Ornstein, *Scientific societies*, pp. 76-90.

[144] C. Weld, *A history of the Royal Society with memoirs of the presidents compiled from authentic documents* (2 vols., London, 1848), I, 121; Ornstein, pp. 103-105.

united by an interest in experimental knowledge. The Society had existed informally since about 1645.[145]

The Academy of Louis XIV and Colbert had its own antecedents. In its background was a long record of private or semi-official associations of scientists or amateurs of science. The beginning of academies in France has been attributed to the Academy of the Palace in which, during the reign of Henry III, poets and scholars discussed philosophical questions.[146] A link with the Italian academies existed through Nicolas-Claude Fabri de Peiresc (1580-1637), one of the most famous amateurs of all time. He was the close friend of Galileo, a member of the *Accademia dei Lincei* and a learned patron and advisor to the erudite of many nations. From his residence in Provence he maintained a prodigious correspondence with many of the most renowned scholars and scientists of Western Europe. Pierre Gassendi, for one, was won to the study of Galileo and Kepler through his influence.[147] A kind of public forum of science and philosophy was conducted in Paris by Theophraste Renaudot between the years of 1633 and 1642. These meetings, called *Conférences du bureau d'adresse,* were popularized through the publication of accounts of them. These accounts, in book form, had an enormous and lasting vogue and were even translated into English. The death of Richelieu and Louis XIII removed the protectors of Renaudot against the Paris faculty of medicine and the *conférences* were discontinued.[148] Nevertheless, Paris became the scientific and intellectual center of Europe during the middle third of the seventeenth century. Its literary pre-eminence was dramatized by the salons of the Marquise of Rambouillet and Mlle Scudery and the creation of the *Académie Française.* A clearing house for much of the scientific and philosophical activity of France, Germany, the Netherlands, Italy, and England existed in the conferences and correspondence centering in the personality and rooms of the priest Marin Mersenne (1588-1648). News of the advancement of sciences in all parts of Europe, from Galileo, Torri-

[145] *Ibid.,* pp. 91-100.
[146] Brown, pp. 6-7. Some of the members were Ronsard, du Perron, Desportes, Dorat, Jodelle and, perhaps, Agrippa d'Aubigné. The organization disappeared about 1584.
[147] *Ibid.,* pp. 3-5; Ornstein, pp. 56, 142, 198-199.
[148] Brown, pp. 18-25.

celli, Huygens, Peiresc or Comenius filtered into the convent
"*des péres Minimes, proche la Place Royale*" to be redis-
tributed by the letters of the father or by conferences with
mathematicians and physicists as Gassendi, Desargues, Roberval, Descartes, Fermat, Pascal, and visitors as Hobbes, William
Petty, and Oldenburg. These conferences appear to have been
held frequently and continuouly from about 1635 until Mer-
sennes' death.[149] It has been said that Richelieu, while on his
death bed, was contemplating the foundation of a great Pan-
sophic College at Paris. The idea, derived from Johann Amos
Comenius (1592-1670), was to create a university which would
combine research in natural science with the formulation of an
encyclopaedia of all knowledge and the teaching of mathematical and physical sciences.[150]

The conferences of Mersenne were perpetuated by his friend
the abbé Picot and others, and a regular academy, that of Louis
Habert de Montmor, was created complete with constitution in
December of 1657. This academy held much the same position during the years 1657 to 1664 that Mersenne's group had
held before, and it is usually assumed to be the direct parent
of the Royal Academy in France, but the fact that few of its
members were admitted to Colbert's Academy has been cited
to belie this assumption.[151]

"After the Peace of the Pyrennes had been concluded,"
writes Fontenelle in his *Histoire de l'Académie Royale des
Sciences*, "the King judged that his Kingdom fortified by the
conquests which had just been assured by him, had no other
need than to be embellished by the Arts, and by the Sciences,
and he ordered M. Colbert to work towards their advancement."[152] This work of Colbert, in consultation with leading
savants as Perrault, Chapelain, and Christian Huygens, led to
the establishment of the *Académie Royale des Sciences* in 1666.
The first full assembly of the chosen academicians met in the

[149] *Ibid.*, pp. 31-62; Ornstein, pp. 139-142. A number of the letters of Mere-
senne to and from such men as Descartes, Campanella, Gassendi, Pieresc, Rivet,
and Beeckman have been edited and published by Mme P. Tannery, *Correspondance du P. Martin Mersenne, Religieux Minime* (2 vols., Paris, 1932-1936).

[150] Brown, pp. 62-63.

[151] *Ibid.*, pp. 74-117.

[152] Fontenelle, *Histoire de l'Académie*, I, 6-7.

library of the King at the Louvre on December 22 of that year.[153]

From the beginning, the French company was much more deserving of its title "Royal" than its English predecessor. In the first place, it was much more closely supervised by the central authority, and its problems were frequently dictated by the practical needs of the state. It assumed at times, therefore, the pattern of a governmental department of research. Secondly, it received much greater support from the crown. In spite of the encomiums for Charles II which fill Thomas Sprat's *History of the Royal Society in London* (1667)[154] it seems that about the only benefit that society received in the new arrangement was a coat-of-arms and the prestige of the King's name. In 1662 Charles assigned for its support some Irish land from which it failed to receive the revenue.[155] Weld, the nineteenth-century historian of the society, could find no good reason to suppose that the King ever visited it. Though he expressed strongly the desirability of more accurate observations and cataloguing of stars, Charles left the observatory without instruments for fifteen years.[156]

In contrast, the French Academy, through the graces of Colbert, that "*Maecenas des lettres et des savants*," [157] was loaded with privileges and benefits. The full members [158] became royal *pensionnaires* with an allotted 1,500 *livres* annual income

[153] *Ibid.*, pp. 14-16, 6-7.

[154] T. Sprat, *History of the Royal Society of London* (London, 1667). See particularly pp. 133, 149-150.

[155] Weld, *History of the Royal Society*, I, 130-135. Sir William Petty, answering queries on the amount of land said: ". . . it will amount unto a great matter, but I know not what." *Ibid.*, p. 135.

[156] The King did send rarities to the Society and, in October 1662, granted it the privilege of passing all patents on philosophical or mechanical inventions. The Society was also privileged to receive the bodies of criminals executed at Tyburn. *Ibid.*, pp. 137, 172-173, 255.

[157] Spanheim, p. 167.

[158] The following list of the members of the French Academy is extracted from Ornstein, pp. 145-147 notes.

"Auzout, prominent astronomer, and inventor of the telescopic micrometer. Bourdelin, chemist.

Buot, engineer and instructor of pages. Least significant member. He had been a workman and knew no word of Latin.

Carcavi, geometer; had held position as conseiller of the Parlement de Toulouse, in which post he was successor of Pierre Fermat and his scientific

from the King, but some were even better rewarded. Huygens received lodgings at the Louvre and a pension of 6,000 *livres,* and Giovanni Dominico Cassini, called from Italy to enter the Academy as an astronomer, received a house by the observatory,

executor; in 1666 held the position of librarian of the King's library, was distinctly a non-professional person, and responsible for meetings.

Couplet, junior member; professor of mathematics at the Collège de France and student of mechanics.

Cureau de la Chambre, physician to Louis XIV, also member of the Académie Française.

Delavaye Mignor, junior member, geometer.

Dominique Du Clos, chemist, physician of Colbert; he was an alchemist, but seeing his folly before his death burnt his writings; one of the most active members.

Duhamel, anatomist; secretary, on account of his good Latinity.

Frenicle de Bessy, geometrician; a magistrate and author of work on magic squares and theory of numbers.

Gayant, anatomist; helper of Perrault.

Abbé Gallois (1632-1707), later professor of Greek and mathematics at the Collège de France, friend of Colbert; successor of Denis de Sallo in editing the *Journal des Sçavans* (1665-74); intimate with Colbert, telling him of doings of Academy. . . .

Christian Huygens (1629-95), the only foreign member among first appointees. He was Dutch, but had made his home for some time in France; mathematician, astronomer, physicist, designer and maker of instruments (air pump and telescope), not connected with any University, but typically amateur and non-professional, he is one of the most characteristic figures of seventeenth-century science. When Colbert appointed him in 1666, he was very prominent in science, had improved the telescope, had discovered two new moons of Saturn, had enunciated the theory of the rings of Saturn, and had done great work in mathematics. He had been elected Fellow of the London Royal Society. It is evident that Colbert applied to him for advice . . . about the work to be done by the Academy. . . . That he was most closely affiliated with the Academy is evident from the fact that for twelve years of his sojourn in Paris he lived in the building where its meetings were held. . . .

Marchand, botanist; head of the royal garden.

Mariotte, physicist; overshadowed by the genius of Huygens; he was one of the famous scientists among this body.

Niquet, junior member; geometer.

Pecquet, anatomist; discoverer of the thoracic duct and of the circulation of blood in foetus; a man of highest prominence in the history of physiology. . . .

Picard, astronomer; also one of the best workers; friend of Gassendi; professor of astronomy in Collège de France.

Perrault, the most active member; notable as an architect, builder of one colonnade of the Louvre. He took up successively many sciences—anatomy, zoology, physics, mechanics; conservative in his views, but an indefatigable worker. It was he who interested Colbert in science.

Pivert, junior member; astronomer.

Richer, junior member; astronomer.

Roberval, the mathematician of the Mersenne Academy."

Later there were added to the first appointees: Blondel and Cassini (1669);

and a set pension of 9,000 *livres* which was occasionally in-creased.[159] Fontenelle, the secretary of the Academy from 1699 to 1739, asserted that even the wars had never forced the dis-continuance of these pensions.[160]

The royal aid extended to the Academy was also very exten-sive in the way of material provisions. Besides rooms and labo-ratories in the Louvre, 12,000 *livres* was allotted for ordinary expenses.[161] The Frenchman, Henry Justel, corresponding with Oldenburg, the secretary of the English Academy, noted that " the King refuses nothing to the Academy. If it does nothing, it will not be for lack of aid," and at another time: " Besides the Academy will do something in time, at least it should, and if it does not it will not be the fault of M. Colbert who takes great care of it, and who gives everything that could be de-sired." [162] The most significant gift to the Academy was the observatory. Constructed on the plans of Perrault, this monu-mental [163] building, with its subsidiary buildings, was begun

---

Roemer (1672); Dodart (1673); Borel (1674); G. J. DuVerney (1674); Leibniz (1675) (?); P. de la Hire (1678); Sedileau (1681); Tschirnhausen (1682); Polheuse (1682); Lefevre (1682); De Bessé (1683); Mery (1684); Thevenot, Rolle, Cusset (1685); Varignon (1688); Tournefort (1691); Hom-berg (1691); Charas (1692); De la Coudray (1693); Morin (1693); Cassini, P. de la Hire, Boulduc, Maraldi, De Chazelles (1694); Fautel de Lajai (1696); Sauveur, Cuglielmini (1696); Fontenelle, Carbé, Tauvry (1697); Langlade (1698); Lémery (1699).

[159] No other savants received such awards. The Historian Mezeray, until he lost favor, received 4,000; the Archivist, Godefroy ordinarily received 3,600 and the Critic Chapelain 3,000. Molière usually received 1,000. Huygens was dropped from the list after 1681, presumably because a protestant. See the list of " Gratifications faites per Louis XIV aux savants et hommes de lettres Fran-cais et étrangers " (1664-1683) in " Appendice," Colbert, *Lettres,* V, 466-498; Clement, in examining the archives, discovered the recorded amounts given to savants between 1664 and 1690 to be 1,707,148 *livres*; this figure not including secret gifts and other notable pensions. *Ibid.,* p. xciv.

[160] Fontenelle, *Historie de l'Académie,* I, 13. However, the tables in Clement, mentioned in the previous note, indicate a sharp reduction in the amounts in the years of the Dutch War (1672-1678).

[161] Ornstein, p. 148; Brown, pp. 156-158.

[162] Letters of Henry Justel to Oldenburg, July 14, 1668; July 28, 1668, quoted in *ibid.,* pp. 156-157.

[163] This was a point of great dissatisfaction with some of the astronomers who felt that design had outweighed the functional element. This was particularly apparent later as the observatory was building at the very time that astronomical techniques were undergoing great changes. The same objections applied to the Greenwich observatory designed by Wren a few years later. C. Wolf, *Histoire de l'observatoire,* has written the definitive work on the subject. On the above see pp. 19-27.

in 1667 and completed around 1683, at a cost exceeding 700,000 *livres*.[164] It was equipped with the best and latest instruments, and a tremendous telescope was erected on the grounds. Aside from its observatory rooms, there were a number of laboratories for experiments in the physical sciences, chemistry, botany, etc. and an elaborate system of caves to provide a special environment for certain experiments. There was a well for experiments on pendulums, falling bodies and astronomical observations, and gardens for botanical work.[165]

In 1681 and 1682, respectively, the Academy at the Louvre and its observatory received the royal accolade by the visits of Louis XIV accompanied by the Dauphin, the Duke of Orleans, the Prince of Condé and the court. They witnessed experiments, received published works and had the construction and use of instruments explained by the leading academicians.[166]

The true founder of the Academy was not the King but Colbert. This was clearly recognized by the academicians and is apparent in the official correspondence of the Minister. Fontenelle tells of the visit of the Dauphin, Bossuet, and the Prince of Conti to the Academy in 1677 and notes that they were received by Colbert " followed by all the academicians, *famille spirituelle* of which he was the father." [167] His happy influence, sympathy, and encouragement were further evidenced by the sharp decline in the fortunes and productivity of the Academy after his death until its reconstitution in 1699.[168] There can be little doubt that Colbert was personally enthusiastic for the advancement of science and the arts.[169] He corresponded frequently with individual academicians and urged them to further efforts or complimented them on accomplish-

[164] *Ibid.*, pp. 14-16.

[165] *Ibid.*, pp. 53-112, see plates and explanations pp. 372 to end of book.

[166] *Ibid.*, pp. 116-119; Fontenelle, I, 320-321, 348.

[167] *Ibid.*, p. 241.

[168] Bertrand, pp. 39-46; Ornstein, p. 145; Louvois who succeeded Colbert as patron of the Academy had little of his interest in science.

[169] As Clement states it: " His encouragements to the Academy Française in the subject of the Dictionary, his incessant solicitude for the advancement of sciences, the paternal cares which he never ceased to exercise in regard to the Academy of Rome, show sufficiently that he was motivated by pleasure as much as by duty; duty alone could not have sustained his vigilance at the same level for twenty-three years." See " Introduction," Colbert, *Lettres*, V, lxxv-lxxvi.

ments. When the Abbé Picard was injured during his conduct of a field survey, Colbert showed great perturbation and wrote an intendant to personally see that he be provided with all necessaries. Once when Huygens fell ill, he showed similar solicitude and wrote urging him to keep him fully posted on the state of his health.[170] At another time his zeal for the work of the Academy led him to overstep his authority. He granted the members the right to examine, for their instruction, the incurables housed at the Hôtel-Dieu in Paris but the religious refused entrance to them and they returned, as reported by the academician Pecquet, "*sans avoir rien fait.*"[171]

A correspondent with the secretary of the British Academy, in a letter of 1669, commented on the distinctions between it and the French Society. The *Académie des sciences* was not "as ours" a great assembly of gentlemen but rather an exclusive organization of a small number of eminent persons selected for their particular aptitude. He commented on their pensions and upon the fact that their conferences were secret and open to outsiders only on special invitation. Finally, the "King will not only have a Titular but an effectual influence upon this royal academy."[172] This "effectual" influence, expressed through the agency of Colbert, was often directed towards utilizing the talents of the Academy to further the practical programs of the state. The point is usually made, by the historians of the Academy, that Louvois, as the successor to Colbert, discouraged the efficiency of the group by his unremitting demands that they set themselves to the almost exclusive pursuit of useful projects.[173] The distinction made between the

[170] Colbert to Picard, September 21, 1679; Colbert to Intendant of Marine at Brest, October 14, 1679; Colbert to Huygens, December 5, 1670, *Lettres,* V, 403, 407, 304-305.

[171] Bertrand, pp. 14-15. Leibniz bemoaned the absence of academical scientific associations in Germany; which he attributed not to the paucity of German genius but to the parsimony of their Princes who failed to emulate the examples of the French and English. Ornstein, pp. 185-186.

[172] Francis Vernon to Oldenburg, May 11, 1669, quoted in Brown, pp. 158-159.

[173] When Louvois first addressed the assembled group, after the death of Colbert, he expressed the hope that ". . . l'académie s'appliquât principalment à des travaux d'une utilité sensible, et prompte, et qui contribussent à la Gloire du Roi: d'était aussi le veritable but de la compagnie, qui depuis son établissement avoit toujours eu ce dessein en vûe, et qui avoit souvent préferé pour l'objet de ses recherches, les choses qui paroissoient être d'une utilité immediate à celles qui étoient plus spécieuses et peut-être plus difficiles ou plus scavantes,

adminstration of the two is perhaps justly made, for it is clear
that Colbert himself had an interest in science as pure science
or, at least, as an enterprise separated from immediate utility.
A note exists from Huygens to Colbert concerning certain
experiments on vacuum, force of powders, steam, wind and the
force of the percussion or communication of motion due to the
collision of bodies. The scientist believed that he could formulate general laws on these. Further he suggested an assembly
of physicists to draw up a natural history, " very nearly along
the lines of Verulam [Francis Bacon]. This history consists in
experiments and remarks, and is the only means of arriving
at the knowledge of causes of nature." Along the margins Colbert noted successively the words "bon." [174] A series of letters,
written in the fall of 1679, show the Minister as following
with close attention the activities of the academicians De La
Hire and du Verney in their research into the anatomy of fish
in Brittany and Normandy in connection with other dissections
of fish being made at the Academy at Paris. They were told
to continue these efforts with great diligence, making weekly
reports thereon, and to charge all necessary expenses to him.[175]
The letters of Colbert will produce a large number of such
instances wherein he displays the amateur scientific interest
typical to the times. The Huygens letter suggests the influence
of the so-called Baconian experimentalism on the Academy in
France, an influence which was explicit in the creation of the
Royal Society in England.[176]

While it would be an error to construe such interest of Col-

mais d'une untilté constamment moindre." as reported in Fontenelle, *Histoire de
l'Académie*, I, 386.

[174] The note seems to date around 1670, see " Appendice," Colbert, *Lettres,*
V, 523-524.

[175] Colbert to Picard, September 21, 1679; to De la Hire, November 10, 1679,
November 17, December 7, 1679; *ibid.,* pp. 403-404, 407-408, 408 notes.

[176] Thomas Sprat began his *History of the Royal Society* (1667) with the
following poesy:

> In Desarts but of small extent
> Bacon, like Moses, led us forth at last,
>   The barren Wilderness he past,
>   Did on the very Border stand
>   Of the blest promis'd Land,
> And from the Mountains top of his Exalted Wit,
>   Saw it himself, and shewd us it.

bert as only an adventitious luxury, the real purpose of the Academy was to glorify the Majesty of the King and to serve the state. The royal funds granted as pensions and for material equipment not only reflected the magnificence of Louis but the regimentation and control of the body by the government. Membership in the Academy was not a sinecure but a position in the civil service. Organized science, in effect, was enlisted in the aid of government.

Differing from the procedure of the Royal Society in England, whose members experimented independently and carried successful efforts to their Academy for demonstration before the others, the *Académie des sciences* conducted their experiments, observations, and discussions as joint ventures. At each session at least one experiment was projected and sessions might occur on the questions arising therefrom for several weeks or even years and necessitate extensive field work and expenditures.[177]

From the very beginning, the Academy resolved the question of the relationship of mathematical and physical scientists. It was decided that geometrical exactness would be a necessary buttress to the work of non-mathematical scientists and that, therefore, mathematical and physical problems should be considered together.[178] The opinions which Fontenelle popularized in his " Preface " on the utility of mathematics had been recognized and acted upon by the Academy long before. If some mathematical calculations were not in themselves useful they could lead to useful application. For example, the study of the problems of cycloids led to the study of the nature of cycloidal motion and the perfection of mechanism of clocks.[179] To this example Fontenelle could add many others relating to improvements in astronomy, cartography, navigation, anatomy, botany, engineering, and ballistics.[180] As he was to say in his

[177] Ornstein, pp. 139-164.

[178] *Ibid.*, p. 147.

[179] Fontenelle, " Préface sur l'utilité des mathématiques et de la physique, et sur les travaux de l'académie des sciences," in *Oeuvres de Fontenelle*, edited by J. B. J. Champagnac (5 vols., Paris, 1825), I, 51-52; see De La Hire's " Traité des epicycloids et de leur usage dans les mechaniques" in Fontenelle, ed. *Mémoires de l'Académie*, IX, 341-447.

[180] Fontenelle, " Préface sur l'utilité des mathématiques," *Oeuvres*, pp. 47-51.

" Éloge " on one academician, mathematics had been " called from the heavens . . . to appy them to the needs of men." [181]

The advancement of industrial arts and crafts was a major duty imposed on the Academy by Colbert. On his order, in 1675, it undertook the task of instructing industrial workers. The academicians Couplet and Auzout were sent on tours to investigate factories and collect information on the machinery and methods of production then current in the kingdom. A general collection of tools, machines, and instruments was initiated. New inventions and improvements were submitted to it for inspection and approval and added to the collection when approved. Cooperative effort produced a *Treatise on mechanics* and a catalogue of the machines and inventions approved. Roberval, Mariotte, Roemer, and Blondel gave much attention to mechanics, and the latter read weekly to the company a description of a different machine.[182]

Astronomy, at least during Colbert's administration, was clearly the salient occupation of the Academy, and, from the standpoint of the state, the most practical activity to which it could apply itself. No element was more important to national power, in the mercantilist theory, than foreign trade and most frequently this meant maritime trade. As long as commerce was restricted to the Mediterranean, or the coastlines, portolan charts and the skill of piloting were adequate for navigation, but long sea voyages posed new problems.[183] The ability to

[181] Fontenelle, " Eloge du Marechal du Vauban," *Oeuvres*, p. 159.

[182] Boissonade, *Colbert*, pp. 30-33; Ornstein, pp. 151; 155; See " Traité de mechanique " in Fontenelle, ed. *Mémoires de l'Académie*, IX, 1-340. The catalogue referred to was first published as Gallons' *Machines et inventions* (7 vols., Paris, 1735-1777), the first volume contains the description of about 50 inventions approved before the close of the seventeenth century. R. G. Merton comments on the practical emphasis in the experiments of the Royal Society in England. Practical considerations directed 30 to 60 per cent of the investigations, pure science 40 to 70 per cent. Of the practical problems, those of marine transportation were most important with military considerations next. R. G. Merton, *Science, technology and society in seventeenth century England* (" Osiris," IV, part 2, Bruges, 1938) pp. 522-536, 537-554, 543-557, 562-565. Samuel Pepys, Sir Anthony Deane, Christopher Wren and Sir William Petty, among other academicians of the society conducted frequent experiments on the best shape for ship hulls; Petty inventing a double bottom ship. See Pepys, *Naval minutes*, *passim*.

[183] F. Marquet in his *Histoire générale de la Navigation* (Paris, 1931), writes that it was customary in the Mediterranean even to the end of the seventeenth century to voyage cape to cape keeping the land in sight. P. 15.

determine latitude with some degree of accuracy had been acquired, but a certain method to find the longitude at sea defied all attempts at solution, and its discovery would be considered by the Academy "*la chose du monde la plus utile au public.*" [184] Great rewards were offered to anyone making such a discovery. At one time a German was negotiating with the King, for a prodigious recompense, to release the secret of longitudes. The King agreed but contingent upon tests being made by Colbert and Du Quesne and Huygens, Carcavy, Roberval, Picard, and Auzout of the Academy. His method turned out to be an invention which roughly corresponding to the modern marine log had made no allowances for current, drift, winds, etc. The judges were not impressed.[185] The following year Colbert sent an astronomer with similar claims. He, likewise, failed to convince although in some respects he made a favorable impression.[186]

Dead-reckoning, time, and the relative position of celestial bodies are the essential elements in determining position on the high seas. Therefore astronomy is of prime concern to navigation and especially cataloguing the movements of the stars. As Fontenelle expressed it: "The end of Astronomy is to have the exact tables of the celestial movements."[187] For this purpose the Academy conducted a continuous program of charting the heavens. The improvement in quality of instruments was likewise a constant and necessary theme in this regard.[188] Giovanni Dominico Cassini in 1668, the year before he joined the company of the Academy, had published his first tables of the movements of the satellites of Jupiter. Much of the work of the academicians, in the early years, was directed towards amplifying and correcting these tables.[189]

Under the auspices of the Academy, Huygens published his

---

[184] Fontenelle, *Histoire de l'Académie*, I, 67, 40-44.

[185] This was in the year 1668. *Ibid.*, pp. 67-69.

[186] *Ibid.*, pp. 111-114.

[187] *Ibid.*, p. 46.

[188] Perrault, Buot, Roemer, and Cassini are among the academicians whose improved astronomical instruments are described and illustrated in Gallon's *Machines et inventions*, I, 35-38 and plates No. 8; 67-69, No. 17; 81-83, No. 22; 85-88, No. 23; 89-91, No. 24; 93-94, No. 25; 133-142, No. 44. The use of the telescope to measure terrestrial angles was first noted in the writings of the academicians.

[189] Marquet, p. 127.

Horologium containing the description of the pendulum clock. After the telescope this was the most important aid to astronomy in the century.[190] The pendulum of Huygens permitted much greater accuracy in setting the time of observations. In 1675, the King granted the Dutchman a privilege for the invention of a portable clock of marked accuracy and particularly suited " to find the longitudes both on land and sea." [191] This was a spiral spring watch, forerunner of the chronometer, which occasioned the quarrel between Huygens and Hooke on the priority of invention. Extensive tests of the pendulum clock were made at sea by the navy.[192] Unfortunately efforts of the Academy, although resulting in an epochal progress in the methods of determining longitudes on land, were unable to resolve the same problem on the seas. The variable conditions of sailing, the lack of steady platforms, and the size of instruments required made the methods which were successful ashore of limited use aboard ship. However an incalculable service to navigation was provided by the advancement by the Academy of the science of cartography.[193]

The financial grants of the King enabled the Academy to indulge in the luxury of research far afield. The Abbé Picard was sent, in 1671-1672, to check on Tycho Brahe's observations at Uranibourg in Denmark. There he made a series of observations and discovered errors in the figures of Brahe and, most notably, returned with a new academician, Roemer.[194] The

---

[190] Ornstein, p. 154.

[191] Colbert, *Lettres,* V, 305 note.

[192] A naval officer at Toulon writes Colbert, April 23, 1669, that at Colbert's orders experiments have been conducted for the past year on pendulum clocks at sea. He asks for further aid, speaks of corrections, correspondence with Huygens, and notes a new clock is being made by the order of the Duke of Beaufort. The Cardinal D'Estrees at Rome wrote Colbert, July 13, 1672, describing a new clock of one " Compani " by which he " contends ability to arrive at the knowledge of the meridians." Depping, *Correspondance,* IV, 567-568; 583-584.

[193] Marquet, pp. 127-131.

[194] Fontenelle, *Histoire de l'Académie,* I, 146-150; Bertrand, pp. 27-29. The French Ambassador at Denmark was directed by Colbert to extend Picard all possible assistance. Colbert to the Chevalier de Terlon, July 17, 1671, Depping, *Correspondance,* IV, 579. In a letter to Picard while there Colbert expressed pleasure over his progress, requested more frequent news and urged him to remain until he had fully carried out his charge. October 30, 1671; January 15, 1672, Colbert, *Lettres,* V, 318, 319-320. See the relation of the voyage by Picard with notation of his observations in Fontenelle, ed., *Mémoires de l'Académie,* VII, part i, 193-230.

latter won immortality for his calculations of the velocity of light based on observations of the satellites of Jupiter. In 1670-1671 the sieur Jean Richer, another academician, was sent successively to carry out observations in the East Indies and at Cayenne " in order to make there several astronomical observations . . . and to test the clocks and pendulums which have been constructed in order to discover the longitudes at sea." [195] His discovery of the difference in the periodicity of the swing of the pendulum at Cayenne and at Paris led to Huygen's deduction on the oblate shape of the earth.[196]

Immediately related to the problem of astronomy and navigation was the problem of cartography. The state had many uses for charts [197] and under Louis XIV it began an intensive program calling for the collaboration of professional map-makers, engineers, intendants and the Academy of Science, to revise the maps of France and the globe. Maps were needed for such purposes as judging the need of public works, particularly

[195] Colbert to Colbert de Terron, Intendant at Rochefort, March 10, 1670, *Lettres,* V, 294 and note; Colbert to the directors of the West Indies Co., Depping, *Correspondance,* IV, 579.

[196] Bertrand, *Académie des sciences,* pp. 33-37; see Richer's relation of his voyage to Cayenne in Fontenelle, ed., *Mémoires de l'Academie,* VII, part i, 233-326. Another astronomer, the sieur De Glos, professor of mathematics and corresponding member of the Academy made latitude and longitude observations at Garée, Cape Verde, Guadeloupe, Martinique and Saint Thomas. See Colbert to D'Oppède, Ambassador at Lisbon, *Lettres,* V, 421-422, 421 note.

[197] Charting was a cornerstone of Colbert's naval program. " The King desires an exact description made of all the coasts of his kingdom, and that the work be carried out continuously in his ports to draw up marine charts. . . ." (Colbert to Seignelay, September 24, 1671, *Lettres,* III, part ii, 46.) The instruction to the sieur Pene, February 5, 1678, Geographical Engineer delegated to draw up charts of the coasts of Normandy, gives insight into the methods and purposes. The King requires very exact charts of cities, fortresses, villages, chateaux. His Majesty's intention " being to have, from La Hogue up to Tréport, very exact maps of all sinuosities of the coast, all the entrances of the rivers, with exact notes and taken on the spot without reliance on the reports of anyone, of all the anchorages, highs and lows of tides, dunes, cliffs, creeks and inlets, together with all the places where enemies could land if they were sufficiently strong to make descents; with particular plans of each place where they could make them, and some plans and estimates of all the works which could be made in each of these places, either to break up entirely the said landings, or in order to fortify them in such a way that they may be easily defended." Similar instructions were sent to other engineers and officials for work on the coasts of Biscay and Guyenne, Cherbourg to the loire, neighboring isles, Dordogne, La Gironde, Saintonge, Pays d'Aunis and others. *(Ibid.,* part i [addition], 77-78 and notes.)

roads; [198] for determining the efficient operation of mines; [199] for regulating the forests; [200] administering the elections and generalities and distinguishing tax districts;[201] for directing military activities, strategically and tactically; [202] and in defin-

[198] See letters of Colbert to M. de Herbigny, intendant at Grenoble, April 5, 1679; to the same, April 22; to the sieur Dieulamant, October 2, 1679; to sieur Braund, engineer, September 4, 1682 on charting all rocks to be removed from the river Doubs; similarly on the Loire to the sieur Mathieu, engineer, October 30, 1682; Colbert, *Lettres*, IV, 479 and note; 481; 491; 545; 551. On the feasibility of constructing the Canal du languedoc, Colbert to Clerville, May 8, 1669, *ibid.*, p. 319.

[199] Colbert studied a map of Languedoc, especially prepared by his engineer, de Clerville, to show "the relation of our mines to each other" to confirm a growing resolution to abandon some in favor of others. Letter to Clerville, September 27, 1669, *ibid.*, p. 433.

[200] Maps of the forests were among the requirements of the great forestry survey. See for example Colbert's letters to M. de Froidour, commissioner for the reform of the forests of Languedoc, September 29, 1670, June 26, 1671, *ibid.*, pp. 235-242.

[201] The intendants and other officials, map-makers and engineers, were employed to prepare charts or improve what old ones existed, the main end being to redistribute the tax districts for the convenience of the tax payers and also to give the intendants and their subordinates a true picture of the areas of their generalities, this picture at the beginning of Louis' personal reign being still confused, and, finally, to inform the central government. (See Colbert to M. de Seraucourt, intendant at Bourges, August 14, 1683; to Charles Colbert, commissioner to the Estates of Brittany, September 22, 1663, *ibid.*, II, part i, 224-225, 242.) The intendant, De Menars of Paris complained of the inadequacy of old charts of his generality, particularly errors in distance, which hampered him in setting up tax districts. New charts were apparently made but, perhaps, with some faults for Colbert wrote later: "It seems to me that you would have done well to take with you him who made the maps of the generality, because you would have verified if these charts are well made or not." Colbert to De Menars, June 18, 1681, *ibid.*, p. 159; Colbert to De Menars, October 23, 1681 in J. de Boislisle, *Mémoire sur la géneralite de Paris*, I, xi and note; The N. Sanson, H. Jaillot, *Atlas nouveau contenant toutes les parties du monde* (1689-1690) contains detailed interior maps of France, excellently made, North-South axis, showing generalities, elections and governments, which could well be put to administrative use. The maps are, incidentally, the finest published land maps made up to the time.

[202] See note 197. Daniel, in his *Histoire de la milice* (1721), I, 342-343, describes a march of Marshal Luxembourg in 1694 in which he performed in six days a movement twice the distance travelled by the enemy. Such maneuvers had not been possible before, says Daniel, because, among other things, of the lack of exact topographical charts. These had not been made before the reign of Louis XIV, Sir H. G. Fordham writes of a manuscript map which he discovered in the Ministry of War at Paris, undated but apparently of the period of Colbert, 8 feet 4½ inches by 7 feet 3 inches, in bright colors, showing roads and rivers in France and probably drawn up by the intendants of the several generalities. *(Some notable surveyors and map-makers of the sixteenth and eighteenth centuries and their work* [Cambridge University Press, 1929], p. 28.)

ing anchorages, roadsteads and harbors for the benefit of general commerce and the navy.[203]

The scientific and accurate cartography of France can be traced to the seventeenth century. In 1630 a first step had been taken by Richelieu who called a congress to establish a working meridian. By a decree of 1634, based on the work of the congress, the prime meridian was arbitrarily set at the Isle de Fer, the most westerly of the Canaries, and Paris was assumed to be 20 degrees E.[204] But doubt of this longitude later led the Academy of Sciences to work on the presumption of a zero meridian at the observatory.[205] The second step was the fixing of a sufficient number of points by astonomical observations to determine, once for all, the general definition of the topographical distribution of the kingdom and its relation to the earth's surface.[206] The final stage was to work by the process of triangulation to fill in the map from these set points.[207] The astronomers of the Academy were the men who, in the main, carried foward the last two steps of the program. The triangulation of France, it is true, is usually associated with the Cassinis in the eighteenth century, but they simply carried to completion a project already begun by their ancestor Giovanni Cassini and his colleagues.

It has been said of the date of the publication of Cassini's table of the motions of the satellites of Jupiter that " it is

Topographical maps, of the modern type, designed for military use, showed an embryonic form under Louis XIII. The first systematic efforts by the state to draw them up dates from the period of Colbert, but methods were not agreed upon and great variation as to quality existed until the middle of the eighteenth century. Col. Berthaut, *Les ingénieurs géographies militaires, 1624-1831* (Paris, 1902), pp. 2-14.

[203] In a letter to Seignelay, March 9, 1678, Colbert mentions fifty charts he has had made of the entrances to Brest and that he is sending 20 of each type to Brest. (Colbert, *Lettres,* III, part ii, 214.) In a letter to Colbert de Terron, intendant at Rochefort, August 18, 1670, the Minister notes the necessity of collating information collected from all voyages for use in drawing up marine charts. *(Ibid.,* part i, 264.) In instructions to one La Favollière, February 14, 1674, chosen to make maritime charts, he is ordered to be most exact because of the utility of his work for the King's service and the welfare of commerce. *(Ibid.,* p. 311, note.)

[204] Fordham, *Map-makers of the sixteenth and seventeenth centuries,* p. 41.

[205] The observatory was determined to be 20 degrees 1 minute 45 seconds E in 1724, a special expedition having been sent to the Isle de Fer. *Ibid.*

[206] *Ibid.,* pp. 41-42.

[207] *Ibid.,* pp. 42-48.

necessary to inscribe it in gold letters in the history of geography." [208] Starting with these tables, and the amplified and corrected versions which they drew upon them, Cassini and the astronomers of the Academy had devised a more certain and simple method than any formerly known for determining longitudes.[209] The academicians simultaneously observed eclipses of the satellites of Jupiter at various places over the world using the pendulums of Huygens for accuracy in time checks. Since formerly only the eclipses of the moon usually had been so observed and these occured infrequently and gave inaccurate results, and since the eclipses of the satellites of Jupiter occurred at least once a day and the results obtained were quite accurate, an ambitious program of establishing points could be carried forward.[210] Richer's voyage to Cayenne and Picard's to Uranibourg were a part of this program. Cassini, Roemer, De La Hire, Picard, and others travelled to all parts of the kingdom working on this project carried on over many years. Picard's work is especially notable. He measured accurately, for the first time, a degree of a great circle of the earth. He also surveyed a scientifically established meridian on which all the future surveys of the Academy were to be based. The measure of the degree of an arc of a great circle permitted the first scientifically accurate deduction of the dimensions of the earth. An interesting story exists connecting this work with the *Principia* of Newton. When Newton, in 1666, had wished to verify certain of his ideas on planetary motion his failure to apply the correct length to a degree of a great circle had led to a negative result in his calculations and had forced him to abandon the hypotheses. When, several years later, he learned of Picard's measure he resumed his work and received exact verification.[211] In 1672 Cassini writes Colbert that in observing

[208] M. Vivien de Saint-Martin, *Histoire de la géographie et des découvertes géographiques depuis les temps le plus reculés jusqu'à nos jours* (Paris, 1873), p. 416.

[209] Marquet, p. 127.

[210] MM. Varin, des Hayes and de Glos, "Voyages au cape Verd en Afrique et aux Isles de l'Amerique," in Fontenelle, *Mémoires de l'Académie*, VII, part ii, 431. See E. Raisz, *General cartography* (New York, 1938), p. 46; Wolf, *Histoire de l'Observatoire*, pp. 62-63.

[211] Vivien de Saint-Martin, *Histoire de la géographie*, pp. 417-420. See also L. A. Brown, *J. D. Cassini and his world map\of 1696* (Ann Arbor, 1941), pp. 23-26.

the height of the pole at Toulon he has discovered it a " degree more northerly" than on the geographical maps.[212] In the same year he visits Fontainebleau, Brion, Cosne sur Loire, Charité sur Loire, Tarare, Lyon, Athein in Dauphine, Avignon, Bausset, Lesques, Nice, and Notre-Dame de La Garde.[213] In 1677 MM. Picard or De La Hire are at Brest and Nantes; in 1680 at Bayonne, Bordeaux and Royan; in 1681 at Saint Malo, Mont Saint Michel, Cherbourg, Caen, Dunkerque, and Calais; and in 1682 in Provence, and always they send back their new findings to the Academy.[214] The result was a revolutionary new outline map of the world laid down by Cassini on the floor of the observatory at Paris in 1682.[215] The corrections carried by this map, and other maps drawn up by the academicians, to even the best work of former cartographers were most considerable. For example, if the new map of France was imposed, in the same scale, on the most accurate map of the kingdom drawn up to that time—the Sanson map presented to the Dauphin in 1679—the contraction in the dimensions of the realm was startling. Louis XIV is said to have remarked to Cassini that all his conquests could not compensate for the losses in his territory occasioned by the success of the Academy.[216] However, the Academy had but set the dimensions; the work of filling in was still to be done. A beginning was made in such work as that of the academician Picard who, in his *Measure de la terre* (1669-1670), described the use of new and more accurate surveying instruments such as the telescopic theodolite, and the use of the pendulum in carrying out triangulations. Systematic

---

[212] Cassini to Colbert, November 15, 1672, Depping, *Correspondance*, IV, 591.

[213] " Observations astronomiques faits en divers endroits du royaume pendant l'année de 1672 par Monsieur Cassini," in Fontenelle, *Mémoires de l'Académie*, VII, part i, 349-375.

[214] " Observations . . .," *ibid.*, pp. 377-428. See Vol. VII, parts i and ii for a large number of observations of like nature reported from all over the world by academicians and corresponding members. See also Vol. I, 304-305, 311-312, 336-340, 351-356.

[215] C. Wolf, *Histoire de l'observatoire*, pp. 63-64; Raisz, p. 46. The history of this map is interestingly related by Brown, pp. 39-62.

[216] See the maps so superimposed and the explanation, " Pour la carte de France corrigée sur les observations de MM. Picard et De La Hire," in Fontenelle, ed., *Mémoires de l'Académie*, VII, part i, 429-430 and the frontispiece; C. Wolf, *Histoire de l'observatoire*, p. 64; Raisz, pp. 46-47; The Sanson-Jaillot *Atlas nouveau*, contains a reproduction of the map presented to the Dauphin, plate 22.

programs of triangulation, particularly along the coast lines, were initiated in the period of Colbert.[217]

Professional map-makers in France continued to publish atlases but, as they admitted in their prefaces and introductions, the new accuracy of their work arose from the collaboration of the scientists subsidized by the government.[218] Maps appearing in the finest of the published atlases of the century, the famous *Neptune française* of 1693, though very excellent for the times, appear to have been generally much inferior, and less detailed, than official maps from which they were in many cases copied.[219] Samuel Pepys in an interesting passage in his *Naval Minutes* praised the *Neptune* and at the same time, with the battle of La Hogue as the main example, suggested the military advantage which a navy might derive from such accurate maritime guides.

It seems worthy considering that instead of the mighty business heretofore made of an imaginary discovering of our coasts to the French, they have in the year 1691,[220] when they were in an actual war at sea

---

[217] Picard, "Measure de la terre," in Fontenelle, *Mémoires de l'Académie,* VIII, part i, 133-192. Picard's triangulations were conducted in Picardy.

[218] The *La Neptune française ou atlas nouveau des cartes marines* (1693) was issued under privilege of the King by a group including professional map-makers and scientists. I have not seen this atlas but have used the *De fransche neptunus* published in two volumes at Amsterdam in 1693-1700 by Pierre Mortier. This atlas was based on the French *Neptune.* The introduction is in Dutch but is a translation of the introduction of the French edition. This, in turn, is reproduced in the 1792 edition of the *Neptune* in France. The introduction declares the *Neptune* to be the product of the collective efforts of the Academy of Sciences and several engineers and pilots. The perfection of its charts are derived from the work fostered by Louis XIV "His Majesty has not only established an Academy composed of the most savant Mathematicians and Astronomers, who have determined by their observations the latitudes and longitudes of the principal places of the earth, but he has at the same time employed several able Engineers and Pilots to survey the coasts, both of his Kingdom and in foreign lands, and to amass from all sections the maps and memoirs which might serve this design. On these determinations of latitude and longitude, and on these Maps and Memoirs, we have drawn up this collection, which His Majesty has graciously desired be given to the Public," *Le neptune francais ou recueil des cartes maritimes* (3 vols., Paris, 1792-1803), III, 2. Also p. 2 of the 1693 *Fransche neptunus.*

[219] For instance see the comment on Plate XXVI in the *Neptune française* (1792-1803), p. 9. Moreover, the publishers of Atlases, because of the expense of making new plates, frequently used old ones. The Mortier, *Neptunus* of 1693, is certainly no exception and the plates based on the French *Neptune* are said to be inferior to those in the original, *Neptune française* (1792-1803), p. 8.

[220] The *Neptunes* I have seen, and the secondary works speak of 1693 as the

with the Dutch and us in conjunction, published their *Neptune Francois,* containing that most august set of sea-charts, and particularly that most accurate one of their own coasts, made by special survey and incomparably beyond anything before extant. Notwithstanding which, Mr. Russel [221] could not follow with any of our ships those greater ones of theirs that fled before them into St. Malo's. And as to 1693, when the whole Navy of France were abroad under Monsieur Tourville in the ocean and D'Étree in the Mediterranean, and ourselves with the best fleet that ever England was mistress of, and the Holland's together with us at sea in the Channel and Bay of Biscay, and their coast left wholly open to us, we were not able or thoughtful enough to improve that advantage, with the aid even of this extraordinary light thereto, to make our promised descent upon any part thereof.

A little further along Pepys noted that the *Neptune* had served " to carry the French ships into St. Malo's, though we could not make it serve us to follow them by." [222]

In general the work of professional cartographers greatly improved in the seventeenth century. This was particularly true in France with the maps produced by the Sanson family and their relative Jaillot. The leadership in this type of cartography passed in the latter part of the century from Holland to France and was maintained there during the course of the eighteenth century. Color on maps for decorative purposes began to disappear, ships and fanciful animals were likewise disappearing and were altogether absent in the Sanson or Jaillot maps. As decorations were eliminated, notes providing geographical information became more common. The most important reformation in cartography in the century, however, was the longitude and latitude measurements of the French Academy. It is clear that the improvement in popular cartography in France was directly accountable to the government-sponsored collaboration of the professional map-makers, engineers, and the scientists. [223]

As far as the government of Louis XIV and Colbert is concerned, the emphasis on cartography represents not only a prac-

---

date of the first edition, yet J. R.Tanner notes that Pepy's copy No. 2999 in the Pepysian Library is dated 1691. See *Naval minutes,* p. 316 note 5.

[221] The English Admiral, Edward Russell, later Earl of Orford (1653-1727).

[222] Pepys, *Naval minutes,* pp. 316-317, 325.

[223] Raisz, pp. 41-42; 45; Fordham, p. 37. See note 218 above. Nicolas Sanson (1600-1667) held the office of royal geographer. He belonged to a family, Dutch in origin (Jansoon), which had long practised the art of cartography.

tical example of the use of science and scientists to advance the purposes of the state but a further extension of the system of organized enquiry. Maps are, in a special sense, as G. N. Clark has pointed out, closely related to statistics. The former are an "abstract statement based on measurement" while the latter are "abstract statements based on measurement, counting and calculation." [224]

Another project to which the Academy could give its attention, while conducting its astronomical and cartographical surveys for the government, was to collect information for the formulation of tide tables. Apart from the obvious advantages to commerce of such statistics Colbert saw a military one. In a letter to an intendant in 1670 he observed:

> As, in all the combats which may occur in the channel or its environs, there is perhaps nothing of greater importance than being well instructed on all the movements of the sea by the tides, near the shores, through the capes and by the different winds . . . it would perhaps be very useful and advantageous to the service of His Majesty to seek out, in all the ports of the kingdom most frequented by merchants, the most experienced captains and pilots, and to select two, three or four, and have them to draw up some exact tables by revolutions, that is to say by reference to the times at which the seas recommence their similar motions.[225]

Within a little more than a year a work of some such nature seems to have been completed for Colbert wrote the same intendant to " Send me promptly the book on the course of the tides." Again the military advantages were emphasized:

> . . . you may be sure that the action which the English and Dutch admire the most is that which was taken by Ruyter,[226] who receiving chase by the English ships and, having a perfect knowledge of all the

---

[224] Clark, *Science and social welfare in the age of Newton*, p. 126.

[225] For example he desired to know where the tides entered the channel, that is, by way of Brittany, England or the Pas de Calais, its rises on all the coastline of France and England; at what times, day or night, the rises occurred on the coast of Brittany etc. " Aside from these general observations on the regular movements, it would be necessary to note those irregular movements, to know those caused by the coasts, the capes and the different winds." Colbert to Colbert de Terron, intendant at Rochefort, November 18, 1670, *Lettres*, III, part i, 310-311.

[226] Michael Adrien Van Ruyter (1607-1676), a great Dutch admiral, defeated the English fleet in 1666 and thwarted the attempted descent of the combined English and French fleets on Holland in 1672.

tides, anchored in such a manner that his ship did not drift, and the flood of the tide carried the English some distance away so that he saved himself in this fashion.[227]

The itinerant astronomers of the Academy as Picard and De La Hire while making their astronomical and cartographical observations along the coast, likewise assimilated data on the tides which were submitted with their other reports to the Academy. Elaborate tide tables, ascribed to the Academician Sauveur and other scientists, pilots and engineers, were published in the *Neptune française* of 1693.[228]

Researches made towards improving the efficiency of the mechanical equipment of industry, in furthering astronomy, navigation, and cartography were by no means the limits of the activities of the Academy. In the years 1674, 1675, and 1678 its members were hard at work on the problems of nivellation and hydrostatics. This was done at the express order of the King who was constructing aqueducts at Versailles.[229] At another time Colbert required jars of distilled mineral waters from all the provinces of the kingdom to be sent to the Academy for testing their different components and their worth.[230]

In conclusion one might mention one other case in which the Academy was used to foster the practical needs of the state. Among the more important projects were the ballistical experiments directed in the years 1677-1678 by Francois Blondel (1618-1686) [231] with the assistance of Buot, Roemer, Cassini,

[227] Colbert to Colbert de Terron, December 14, 1671, *Lettres*, III, part i, 408.

[228] Fontenelle, *Mémoires de l'Académie*, VII, part i, 387-388, 394-395, 402, 404. The tide tables referred to cite 237 places in Denmark, Germany, Netherlands, Flanders, Scotland, England, France, Brittany, Ireland, Spain, and Portugal. There were besides tables which discovered the days of the week, days of the month known; date of the month, day of the week known, projected from 1692 to 1750; hours of high tide, 1692-1750; declination of the sun 1692-1750; mean latitude; sunrise and sunsets; to correct the apparent altitudes of sun and stars. See " Introduction " of *La neptune française* or the *Fransche neptunus*.

[229] Picard, Roemer and Mariotte were distinguished in this work. Fontenelle, *Histoire de l'Académie*, I, 206, 260-263. Of around fifty machines described in Gallon's *Machines et inventions approuvées par l'Académie* for the years 1666 to 1701, eight are pumps or machines for raising water or connected with fountains or canals.

[230] A comparative test, in 1682, of waters that might be made available to Versailles produced the judgment that the local water was equal to the others. Fontenelle, *Historie de l'Académie*, I, 367-369; Colbert to the sieur Riquet, January 11, 1670, *Lettres*, V, 291 and note 3.

[231] Councillor of State, councillor of the King in his councils, *Marechal de*

De La Hire, Mariotte, and Perrault.[232]   In the sixteenth century Tartaglia of Brescia had noted the curved line of the trajectory and had first cited the fact that the 45 degree elevation of a gun tube gives the maximum range of fire. Galileo applied the laws of falling bodies to explain the curve of the trajectory but regarded only cases of firing in which target and gun occupied the same horizontal plane. Torricelli, going further, considered targets and batteries on planes inclined to each other or on different levels.[233]

In spite of these theoretical advances the work of the artillerists had continued to be a matter of practice and chance.[234] Blondel, with the aid of the geometers of the Academy, was interested in applying physical and mathematical principles to the end of making bombs fall on a desired target. Tables were drawn up on elevation angles and weights of powder charges for standardized cannon, mortars, and bombs. The early

camp, engineer for the navy, lecturer at the royal Collège de France, member of the Academy of Sciences, First director of the Academy of Architecture, professor of mathematics to the Dauphin, diplomat, designer of the city of Rochefort.

[232] Fontenelle, *Histoire de l'Académie*, I, 235, 253-260. For a biography of Blondel see P. Mauclaire and C. Virgoureaux, *Nicolas-Francois de Blondel, ingénieur et architecte du roi* (Laon, 1938). Blondel himself describes some of the experiments conducted on ballistics in the Academy in the chapter in his work in which he attempts to resolve all the objections to his theory advanced by the traditionalists. *Arte de jeter les bombes* (Paris, ed. of 1683), pp. 357-522.

[233] Fontenelle, *Histoire de l'Académie*, I, 231-235; see also the section in Blondel on the history of ballistics, *Arte de jeter les bombes*, pp. 1-74.

[234] Blondel says that this was true even at the time of publishing his book although he and the academicians had revealed the superior methods of science several years previously. Most of the officers commanding artillery in the French army were disciples of one Maltus, an English expert, who had been called to France in the time of Louis XIII. His methods, according to Blondel, were divorced from any theoretical considerations. Several treatises on the firing of guns had been written before Blondel's, and are mentioned by him and attacked in detail. Not one of the authors, according to Blondel, had any notion of Galileo's physics of falling body and were, therefore, incapable of correctly describing a trajectory. (*Ibid.*, pp. 22-74.) William Bourne's *The arte of shooting in great ordnaunce*, first appearing in 1587 and in later editions to at least 1643, gives some confirmation to Blondel's charge. Thus as to " The manner of course the shot flyeth in the ayre " he notes: " its naturall course, so firste it is driven violently by the blast of the Pouder up into the ayre by a right lyne, and then secondlye, as the violent drifte doth decay, so it flyeth circularly, and thirdly, the force of the drifte being all decayed, it muste needes have hys naturall course, and all things that be of earthly substance muste needes returne to the earth agayne " (1587 ed.), pp. 40-41. This description is exactly repeated in the 1643 edition.

results of Blondel's work were presented to Louis XIV in a book *L'art de jeter des bombes* in 1675 but it was publicly released only in 1683 and thereafter went quickly into foreign presses.[235] The application of the new science to bombardment was said to have enabled the artilleryman to point a cannon or mortar " so accurately, that provided the target distance is known . . . one will fire on the point of a steeple." [236] The statement was obviously an exaggeration, but it seems very likely that Blondel's methods were applied in the schools of artillery to win for the French near the end of the century their fearsome reputation for accurate bombardment.[237]

With the introduction of new instruments and techniques, or improvement of the old ones, the arts of war and peace underwent, in the course of the seventeenth century, marked and progressive change and became more complex. The stocking frame, ribbon loom, pumping engines, flint-lock musket and bayonet, improved cannon, better optical lenses, clocks and astronomical instruments were all associated with modifications applied to manufactures and mining, tactics and the organization of the armies and navies, maritime commerce and navigation. Pursuing lines initially indicated by the Italians in the sixteenth century, fortification, architecture and bombardment were increasingly less empirical and more closely tied in with engineering or physics, with the calculation of stresses, with the application of the elements of geometry, and the laws of trajectory. Technological inventions rarely supplanted the less efficient mechanism as intended by the inventor. For instance, A. P. Usher cites a type of silk mill, probably invented in Italy in about the thirteenth century, which had not passed out of use there at the close of the nineteenth.[238] The stocking frame

---

[235] Blondel, *Arte de jeter les bombes, passim.* His book, says Blondel, reduces the art " to the certain rules of mathematics." The practices he advocates are explicitly declared to arise from the practical application of the principles discovered by Galileo and Torricelli. Pp. 76. See Mauclaire, *Blondel*, pp. 188-189, 284, 191.

[236] Fontenelle, *Histoire de l'Académie*, I, 235-236.

[237] Blondel was the mathematical instructor of Seignelay and accompanied him on his trip to Italy in 1671. Seignelay directed the famous bombardment of Genoa. Blondel notes that the King was so well persuaded of the utility of the new science that he set the Dauphin and his principal ministers to work studying it. *Arte de jeter les bombes*, pp. 509-510.

[238] A. P. Usher, *A history of mechanical inventions* (New York, 1929), p. 240.

was extensively applied in the France of Colbert for the manufacture of silk stockings but was forbidden in the manufacture
of woolen stockings.[239] This paradoxical tendency of science,
due to the lag of social or economic adjustment, to multiply
and complicate, as well as to simplify, the problems of society,
was undoubtedly one of the first springs in the rational and
scientific movement in the seventeenth century. The application
of rational principles seemed necessary for regulating and
simplifying the recognized multiplicity of the structure of the
visible society. In France, this reaction was best exemplified
by the attempt to create an orderly state conducted by the
règlement, a state in which all that was irrational, individual,
and conflicting might be subjected to a kind of universal arithmetic of reason. In these terms, the relation of the state to the
Academy of Sciences presents a twofold aspect. On the one
hand, it disciplined science to make it a more rational and less
unsystematized pursuit and, on the other, it represented the
prime example, in the seventeenth century, of a state enlisting
the services of science for the advancement of its own interests.

[239] Cole, *Colbert,* II, 214-217.

CHAPTER IX

CONCLUSION

Long before the opening of the seventeenth century the skepticism and the secular attitudes of man had destroyed, or seriously weakened, many old traditions, ideals, and beliefs. While he tended to free himself from the artificial restrictions imposed on him in the medieval world, he had equally exposed himself to the uncertainties of life in a new, vital, unexplored, relatively boundless, and infinitely confusing world of nature. In the seventeenth century the paramount concern of thinking man was to rediscover some order in nature or to reduce the new intellectual tendencies to certain rational and constructive principles which might explain or control the recognized complexity of nature. In answer to such a desire, he developed a constructive and scientifically oriented rationalism. The universe was explained as a function of form, space and extension, a mathematical concept and therefore accessible through the medium of the universal science of mathematics and mathematical reason. Nature, thus, as a geometric system, could be better understood and turned to greater advantage for society by geometric and systematic formulae. Order and system were the divining rods with which man discovered utility in the midst of apparent confusion.

In a parallel fashion, political theorists developed the notion of a rational state. Here economic and political patterns that were associated with feudalism, the seigneurial system, the guilds, and theocracy had disappeared or lost their force before the combined strength of a national consciousness and a nationalist politics. In a political and economic sense, therefore, the man of a new age, as a member of a political community, experienced some of the same freedom as the philosopher facing his new world of nature and subjected himself to similar perplexities. It might well be argued that this sense of indecision and ignorance of the way was largely responsible for the period of political unrest which marked the end of one order and witnessed the introduction of the new. This was the state of license from which was generated the absolute sovereign. In France, the politically irresponsible monarch who thus emerged came to represent, as in the person of Louis XIV, the embodiment of the national genius. Subject to the control of the king was the political society which, within its national boundaries, exhibited all the complexity, irrationality, and indiscipline which seemed to the ignorant man to characterize nature itself. The problem of the rational king, therefore, was to introduce the harmony of order into this society.

As far as France was concerned, until Louis XIV assumed the personal direction of his state, the rational government pictured by political theorists was primarily an expression of aspirations. With the exception of the short reign of Henry IV reform in administration remained an ideal confined largely to writings. Nevertheless, certain political and administrative developments, marking the first half of the seventeenth century in France, indicated the need and prepared the way for the work of Louis XIV and Colbert. The Duke of Sully gave, in his management of state finances, a practical illustration of the benefits to be derived from order, discipline, and application. The steady deterioration in the actual functioning of the tax and financial systems, after the death of Henry IV, underlined the desirability of introducing a more rational method of assuring accountability. Perhaps the most important political preparation for the governmental innovations of Louis XIV and Colbert lay in the solidification of the institutions of the intendancies. Finally, the collapse of the Fronde had ended any effective opposition to the will of the King in his state.

The King who took hold of the political fortunes of France in 1661 was vested with all the legal, theoretical, and political authority necessary to transform a government of confusion into a government of order. All that was required was that he have the inclination and the will to do so. Louis XIV was thoroughly imbued with an exaggerated opinion of the dignity and role of kings. To him a king was the symbol of the reason of the state, and he was determined to translate the symbol into a reality. Like Descartes he thought of reason as the ability to select from a body of evidence a right opinion; therefore, a machinery of inquiry was an essential preliminary to the formulation of state policy. He also exhibited in his character a sense of skepticism, a suspicion of tradition, a diligence, a practicality, a passion for knowledge and for exactitude, a love of order, and a faith in the effectiveness of system and method which made him the natural director of a program of rational reform in administration. These attributes were shared and magnified in the personality of Colbert.

Through his own efforts, and with the cooperation of Colbert and other ministers, Louis attempted to create a rational and mechanical state which operated according to set principles and in which the presiding intelligence of sovereign reason could be made to control individual instincts. This reason was to supply security, certainty, and efficiency in the conduct of private life and subordinate this conduct to the interests of the state. As in natural science, this security, certainty and efficiency were to be obtained by the application of rational formulae. Their political expression was in the laws and *règlements*.

In a brilliant period of accomplishment, between 1661 and 1683, Louis XIV and Colbert effected a veritable revolution in the techniques of government in France. Before the death of the great Minister, that government had already assumed many technical attributes suggesting the influence of the scientific spirit and commonly associated with the administration of modern states. Thus statistical and social surveys became a recognized and inseparable part of government. The functions of the intendancy were significantly extended into the field of statistics, and the canalization of these functions into the office of the *contrôleur général* pointed the way to the establishment of regular statistical bureaus. In a development analogous to the urge of contemporary scientists to give utility to the facts of nature by tabulation, arrangement, and classification, administrative archives were created for the collation, classification, and preservation of useful data. Along similar lines, the emphasis in seventeenth-century science and rationalism on the veracity of mathematics, its importance as a guide to reason and as a certain measure in quantitative calculation, was reflected in this new government by the vigorous application of accounting methods in reforming the financial structure.

The economy of the nation was coordinated as never before under the direction of a rational and superior authority. Colbert, as the heir and executor of a system of regulation of industry, commerce and labor, saw the *règlement* as the essential means of assuring the success of the French in industrial competition with other nations. Though regulations had existed formerly, Colbert condensed, clarified, related and enforced them with such vigor and imagination that the economic system of which they were a reflection has since borne his name. Here again we detect a familiar pattern of seventeenth-century thought; review, selection, simplification, and the promotion of formulae. Production was disciplined by the reason of the state through *règlements*. The economy was interpreted in the light of a presumed equation of wealth and administered according to laws deduced from a concept of a mechanical order of nature and society.

The new spirit of the regime was further indicated by the alterations made by Louis, Le Tellier, Louvois, and Vauban in the operation of the army. An undisciplined, disorganized military was transformed into a disciplined, defined force governed by *règlements* and by a regular and exact administration. New instruments were introduced and strategy and tactics became more formal and scientific, more dependent on calculation and long-range planning. In the navy, Colbert carried forward a program based on rational principles and utilizing the advantages of science.

In like fashion, much of the traditional and confused law of the realm was collected, collated, and criticized, much was deleted and the remainder systematized in order to convert it into a simple, unified and efficient instrument for the control of individual conduct within the state. The great codes of 1667-1681 were rational formulae designed to introduce certainty and predictability into naturally uncertain society. By an intensified program of technological and technical education the state attempted to further industry and the military and to discipline and regulate the empirical by the imposition of order and the aid of science. Finally, and primarily under the leadership of Colbert, the government pursued an active policy of fostering science and scientific research. It was hoped that the state, as well as science, would acquire substantial benefits from the association of political with scientific activities and talents.

The monarchy of which Louis XIV took control in 1661 was a mystery of anachronisms and anomalies. It was certainly no longer feudal, yet there persisted in it a strong feudal flavor. It provided the government for an apparently unified and vigorous national state, but it was, a state which was strangely riven by institutions and practices inherited from an age of economic and political particularism. The king was admittedly absolute in theory and practice,, but he was, nevertheless, limited by tradition and frequently by an inert and ancient bureaucracy. It was beyond the power of even Louis XIV to dissolve all the difficulties inherent in this historic confusion. The achievement of Louis, with Colbert as his main collaborator, was to superimpose on it a new monarchy, a rational and scientific regime. By a carefully calculated strategem the older institutions were deprived of their functions or transformed into new orders with old names. Whatever was vital or useful in the old system tended to be absorbed by a host of councils, bureaus, and ubiquitous officials divorced from all traditional allegiances except to the sovereign. These were the representatives and engineers of a regime of order and science, of the modern state in France.

INDEX

Abbeville, 99, 221.

Absolute advantage, 201, 225-226.

Académie des Sciences, 211, 224, 258 n., 259, 286-308;
contrasted with the British Royal Academy, 287-293;
foundation of, 286;
organization, general functions, plant and personnel of, 287-294;
precursors of, 283-286;
work of, 294-307;
on astronomy and navigation, 294-297;
on ballistics, 305-307;
on cartography, 297-304;
on industries and crafts, 294, 294 n.;
on nivellation and hydrostatics, 305, 305 n.;
on tide tables, 304-305.

Académie Française, 285.

Academy of France at Rome, 282, 282 n.

Academy of the Palace of Henry III, 285, 285 n.

Accademia dei Lincei, 283, 285.

Accademia del Cimento, 284, 284 n.

Accounts, see Finances.

Actes de l'état-civil, 175-176, 179 n., 185.

Adam, C., ed., *Oeuvres de Descartes*, 35 n.

Admiralty offices, 183, 272.

Agriculture, 219-220.

Aides, 125 n., 133.

Aiguillon, Duchess of, 149.

Aix-La-Chapelle, Treaty of, 151.

Albo's treatise on dyes, 223.

Alchemy, 27.

Algiers, attack on, 281, 281 n.

Aligré, E. d', 118, 159, 160.

Allen, J. W., *A history of political thought in the 16th century*, 30 n., 34.

Althusius, Johannes, 50, 53;
Politica methodica digesta, 50 n.

Amazon river, 235.

American State Papers, Naval Affairs, 259 n.

Anchors, 222.

Andréossy, Sieur de, 108.

Annuities, 173-175, 175 n.

Aquinas, Thómas, 30, 30 n., 53 n.

Arabic, 281 n.

Arc-en-Ciel, damage to, 114.

Architecture, Academy of, 283, 283 n.

Archival registers, Colbert originates system of, 152.

Archives, 64, 72, 135, 147-153, 153 n., 172, 173, 179, 190, 311.

Aristotle 16, 22, 35 37, 53, 275.

Arms, standardization of, 248-249.

Army administration:
bureaus of, 250;
efficiency of, 246-251, 277;
program of technological education in, 274, 276-277;
rational reorganization of, 247-251.
See also, Arms, Arsenals, Flint-lock musket, Fortifications, Hospitals, Louvois, Pensions, Pike, Rank, Uniforms, Vauban.

Arnauld, Antoine, 26.

Arnauld, Simon, see Pomponne.

Arnoul, Pierre, 112-114, 256.

Arsenal, The, 71.

Arsenals:
Army, 249;
Naval, 143, 253, 259, 261-263, 279, 280.

Art, 39.

Artillery:
English, 306 n;
French, 307.

Artz, F. B., "Les débuts de l'education technique en France," 275 n.

Aspremont, Sieur d', 92.

Astrology, 27-28 n.

Astronomy, as aid to navigation the primate study of 17th century science, 294-297.

Aubigné, Agrippa d', 285 n.

Aubusson, the works at, 222, 282.

Austria, Anne of, Queen, 77 n., 87, 94, 94 n., 121, 122, 157.

Authority, see Tradition.

Auzout, A., 287 n., 294, 295.

Avity, P., d', 34, 39, 60, 171;
Les estats, empires et principautez du monde, 34-35 n.

315

22